W9-CXL-437

The PRAYING CHURCH IDEA BOOK

Douglas A. Kamstra

With Foreword by
Alvin J. Vander Griend

FAITH ALIVE®
Christian Resources

Grand Rapids, Michigan

Unless otherwise indicated, the Scripture quotations in this publication are from the HOLY BIBLE, NEW INTERNATIONAL VERSION, © 1973, 1978, 1984, International Bible Society. Used by permission of Zondervan Bible Publishers.

Faith Alive Christian Resources published by CRC Publications.
The Praying Church Idea Book, © 2001 by CRC Publications, 2850 Kalamazoo Ave. SE, Grand Rapids, MI 49560. All rights reserved. With the exception of brief excerpts for review purposes, no part of this book may be reproduced in any manner whatsoever without written permission from the publisher. Printed in the United States of America on recycled paper. ✪

We welcome your comments. Call us at 1-800-333-8300 or e-mail us at editors@faithaliveresources.org.

Library of Congress Cataloging-in-Publication Data
The praying church idea book / [compiled by] Douglas A. Kamstra; with foreword by Alvin J. Vander Griend.
     p.   cm.
   Includes bibliographical references.
   ISBN 1-56212-558-3
   1. Prayer. I. Kamstra, Douglas A., 1952-
BV210.2.P655 2001
248.3'2—dc21

                                                 2001023691

10 9 8 7 6 5 4 3 2 1

To those who have taught me to pray:
my father and mother,
William and Adrianna Kamstra

To those at the top of my prayer list:
my wife Marilyn,
and my children, Brian, Joel, and Eric

CONTENTS

section 1: prayer formats

section 2: the leader's prayer life

section 3: prayer ministry ideas

section 4: harvest prayer ideas

section 5: small group prayer ideas

section 6: worship ideas

section 7: prayer retreats

section 8: resources

FOREWORD

There is a mounting prayer move-ment in America today, and pastors are increasingly aware of it. Both the quantity and quality of prayer are increasing. As a result, more and more pastors are wondering how to revive prayer ministries in their churches and are looking for resources to facilitate new and fruitful prayer ministries. Doug Kamstra's *Praying Church Idea Book* meets this need and answers all kinds of questions that pastors and church leaders have about prayer formats.

Prayer is important to the church. The great leaders of the church have always been men and women of prayer. The truly effective churches throughout the centuries have been churches of prayer. It is by prayer that the power of God is directed and acti-vated in every dimension of the church's life. Without prayer churches are powerless and fruitless. But restoring prayer to the place of priority in the church will take more than correcting the church's thinking and improving its teaching about prayer. It will take improving its practice of prayer as well. That's where *The Praying Church Idea Book* comes in. It's designed to provide prac-tical helps to church leaders who want to build praying churches.

Many new books on prayer are being published today. Many of them are useful, elucidating Bible prayer themes and answer-ing questions today's Christians have about prayer. However, there is a void. Very few of these books speak to the pressing practical prayer questions the church is facing today.

That's why *The Praying Church Idea Book* is such an important contribution to the field of prayer. It deals with these practical issues thoroughly and thoughtfully.

This is not a book that anyone is going to sit down and read from beginning to end. Instead it will serve as a reference tool that pastors and other church leaders will turn to again and again. Prayer leaders will want to peruse the forty prayer methods in the "Prayer Formats" section. Pastors will be challenged and encouraged by the sec-tion on the "Leader's Personal Prayer Life." Ministry leaders will find help among the fifty-five items under the heading "Prayer Ministry Ideas." There are even sections for small group leaders, for worship leaders, and for evangelism/mission leaders. So wide is the potential use of this book within a local congregation that churches may want to own several copies.

The Praying Church Idea Book will serve in many churches as a companion to the widely used *Praying Church Sourcebook* (pub-lished by CRC Publications). It adds to the basic concepts and strategies, so well laid out in the *Sourcebook*, the kind of detail that will give confidence to those who are launching into these strategies and using prayer formats with which they are unfamiliar.

I enthusiastically recommend *The Praying Church Idea Book*. My friend Doug Kamstra has done a masterful job of re-searching and organizing prayer strategies and formats. Regular use of this book will save the average church leader many hours of time and will help prevent mistakes when launching new prayer ministries. As you use this immensely helpful tool you'll thank God for Doug Kamstra, as I do, and you'll turn to it often as you search for fruitful prayer ideas to help make your church a "house of prayer."

Alvin J. Vander Griend
National Lighthouse Facilitator

PREFACE

Prayer has been a fundamental component of the Christian's life and worship since the disciples asked Jesus, "Lord, teach us to pray." Many believers give daily thanks at meals, confess their sins and ask for forgiveness, intercede for family members, pray for the sick, ask for the protection of missionaries, raise up the needs of the world, pray for their pastor and church, and "stand in the gap" for the lost. Of all the activities to which a Christian is called, prayer is the most important (Heidelberg Catechism, Q&A 116). Yet statistics continue to indicate that many church members spend little time in prayer.

Of all the activities to which the church is called, prayer is the most important (see Isa. 56:7; Matt. 20:13; Mark 11:17; Luke 19:46). Individual churches frequently build reputations. Some are recognized for dynamic pastoral leadership, others for strong lay leadership. Some make an impression by being avant-garde; others experience growth by pursuing denomination guidelines. Some are known for their care-giving; others are characterized as "warm and friendly." Some are evangelistic; some are concerned with justice and social issues; some focus on personal spiritual growth. Some pride themselves on ministering to singles; some emphasize the family. While these churches help to meet a variety of spiritual and physical needs, many churches tend to overlook the obvious— that is, the centrality of prayer.

The early church had no large buildings, well-financed budgets, or long-range plans. While these things may all be helpful in growing the church in the twenty-first century, none of them are indispensable; prayer is. When the disciples realized they were neglecting prayer, they reminded the church of their first priority and called the church to elect deacons so they could return to praying (see Acts 6).

Today's church, especially in North America, is deeply in need of a new prayer theology. Traditionally, we have relied on theologians to build the framework for our religious practices. It is the intent of this book, however, to promote a practice of prayer that will ultimately result in a prayer theology. As long as we have so little prayer in our personal lives and our churches lack the power prayer brings, any theology of prayer will remain incomplete. Once we begin to pray, seeking the presence of God on our knees for an extended time, our theology (that is, our understanding of God) can only grow. And the best way to learn to pray is to pray.

Over the past decade, there has been a visible increase in prayer throughout the world. Prayer is moving out of the privacy of our prayer closets into businesses (small group prayer meetings and Prayer Boxes), into schools (Moms in Touch and See You at the Pole), into politics (National Day of Prayer and Pray at the Polls), and onto the streets (prayerwalking and Lighthouses of prayer). Some believe this increased interest in prayer is a reaction to the moral melt-down in many nations. Others cite increased secularism, coupled with an increase in persecution of Christians, as the force driving believers to their knees. Still others point to the growing interest world-wide in the supernatural or the recent passage from one millennium to the next. Whatever the reason, there is an increased passion among Christian leaders for revival. Many prayer initiatives have declared this century as the time to fulfill the Great Commission (unachieved in the twentieth century) so every person on earth will have heard the gospel of Jesus Christ. As a result, many prayer initiatives have an evangelis-tic, rather than a pietistic, focus. After cen-turies of evangelism and missions, Christians increasingly realize that prayer—and only prayer—will usher in the gospel to every nation.

The result must be that churches get serious about prayer. They need to proclaim a passionate call to prayer; they need to make a conscious and conscientious effort to teach believers to pray. Churches need to get out in front of the growing prayer move-ment and take the lead. Without prayer, our churches will lose their focus and influence.

But let's be clear. Prayer is not the lat-est fad, the current church-growth tech-nique, or a last-ditch effort to combat an increasingly secular society. Prayer is the expression of our hunger for divine com-panionship, of our desire for intimacy with our Creator, of our need to build a deeper relationship with our Lord. Prayer is seeking God: surrendering ourselves to God's will, receiving God's gifts and blessings, welcom-ing God's presence in our lives, expressing our gratitude to God, and interceding on behalf of others in need. Unfortunately, too many Christians view prayer as a dreary obligation, a shopping list of needs, or a meaningless religious ritual. As the disciples realized, we need to be taught to pray. We need to pray.

This book is not a theology of prayer, a study of the effectiveness and power of prayer, or a statement of the struggles and pain of prayer. Rather it is designed solely to challenge, encourage, and direct the local church to become a "house of prayer." The goal is not to add programs or simply to add prayer services, but to build a praying church. Prayer is not a means to an end. Prayer is not primarily a duty. It is the nour-ishment of a relationship—between heaven and earth, between God and people, between a Savior and sinners, between the Lord and his servants, between a Father and his children, between the head of the church and its members. God calls us into relationship. God calls us to pray.

* * * * * * * * * * * * * * * * * *

In compiling this book, every attempt has been made to seek permission and give proper credit to the appropriate source. Unfortunately, in some instances, because some of this information has been used so much, so often, and by so many people, the original source may have been lost. Upon appropriate notification, these items will be properly credited in a subsequent edition.

In order to make this book as useful as possible, consider purchasing *The Praying Church Sourcebook* by Dr. Alvin J. Vander Griend (1996, CRC Publications). It is available at your local Christian bookstore, by calling 1-800-333-8300, or on-line at www.FaithAliveResources.org.

I offer my special appreciation and deep gratitude to those who have mentored my prayer life—my father and mother; to those who have supported my passion for growing praying churches—Dirk Hart, Lori Worst, the Christian Reformed Home Missions staff, and the Calvary staff and congregation; and to those who assisted and encouraged me in the writing of this book—Dan Ackerman, Emily Brink, Jack Dik, Brad Long, Don McCrory, Betty Veldman, and John Witvliet. A special thank you to Al Vander Griend, who has been a mentor, an encourager, and an editor.

Douglas A. Kamstra

INTRODUCTION

TOWARD A PRAYING CHURCH

My house will be called a house of prayer for all nations. (Isa. 56:7)

I would love to see our churches become houses of prayer. I know you would, too. All too often, however, they are places for everything and anything except prayer. I say this with sorrow, for I believe it saddens the heart of God. True, we need to have our business meetings and our committee meetings and our Bible studies and our self-help groups and our worship services, but if the fire is not hot at the center, these things are only ashes in our hands. (Richard Foster, *Prayer*, 1992, pp. 197-198)

In Isaiah 56:7, God says that his "house" shall be known as a "house of prayer." Following his triumphal entry, Jesus entered the temple, tossed out the money changers, and reiterated his Father's imperative: "My house will be called a house of prayer" (Matt. 21:13). Being a house of prayer is more than simply believing in prayer. (Statistics say that almost all Christians and a majority of non-Christians believe in prayer.) Being a house of prayer involves more than having an interest in prayer, more than periodically praying in church, and more than having a number of active prayer ministries. Being a house of prayer means that the church's primary identifying mark is prayer. Richard Foster sadly, but accurately, underscores the fact that very few local churches are houses of

prayer and that the church as a whole has failed miserably to live up to this biblical command.

There are, however, some encouraging factors. Consider:

- City-wide prayer rallies are sweeping communities across the United States, drawing the participation of tens of thousands of Christians.

- According to George Barna, even 63 percent of those who do not attend church still pray regularly.

- In Houston, 150 high school students gather twice a week to pray for revival.

- A multilingual prayer rally in Boston's historic Park Street Church brought together 800 Christians from 75 center-city churches.

- The divorce rate among couples who profess to be Christians is 28 percent. The divorce rate among couples who pray together daily is less than one-tenth of one percent.

- Promise Keepers has brought men to pray together across denominational, ethnic, and generational lines. In 1998, more than one million men gathered on the Washington Mall in a solemn assembly to pray.

- Pastor's Prayer Summits have brought pastors together across denominational and ethnic lines in more than 100 regions in the United States and Canada and thirty other countries.

- The Assemblies of God is enlisting over one million people to regularly offer up intercessory prayer.

- John Maxwell and his VIP prayer ministry have set out to raise up one million men who will commit to pray for their pastors.

- The Denominational Prayer Leaders Network annually brings together more than thirty denominations representing more than 150,000 churches in North America to talk about prayer.

- The National Day of Prayer broadcast is viewed by tens of thousands of worshipers.

- Books on prayer and prayer ministries have multiplied. There are more than 2,500 titles in print focusing on prayer.

- *Pray!* magazine, the first periodical entirely devoted to prayer, became self-supporting after only three years.

- Churches are hiring prayer coordinators, encouraging intercessors, and training believers.

- More than three million students participate annually in See You at the Pole.

- Small multiracial prayer groups are meeting in South Africa.

- In Korea, tens of thousands of high school and university leaders gather for prayer.

- Significant prayer ministries have emerged from crusades led by Billy Graham, Luis Palau, John Guest, Ed Silvoso, and others.

- The All-Japan prayer movement is seeking the evangelization of the country's one hundred million people.

- Up to 250,000 people pray through the night in Seoul, Korea, every Friday. It is no coincidence that nine of the world's twenty largest churches are in Korea.

C. Peter Wagner summarizes what is happening around the world when he says, "Prayer is out of control. Not since Pentecost itself, has history recorded a level of prayer on six continents comparable to what is happening today" (*Confronting the Powers*, 1996, p. 11).

the call to pray

But what, really, is so important about being a house of prayer? Why should this particular command stand above any other?

Prayer is, first of all, about spending time with God. Simply being together is a necessary part of any growing relationship. Our relationship with God will become stronger as we share our dreams and joys, our burdens and our pain, our frustrations and our celebrations. Our dependence on God will become a reality as we express that continuing dependence in prayer.

Second, it is through prayer in concert with our study of Scripture that God makes his will known to us. God is at work in the world and invites us to join him in that work. Because we discover God's will through prayer, prayer is the primary, or initial, work of believers. The power of prayer is that the Holy Spirit enables us to do the work of God when we, through prayer, discover God's will and join him in that work.

As if these reasons alone were not sufficient, God gives us additional reasons to pray:

- **God commands us to pray.**

    Be faithful in prayer (Rom. 12:12).
    Pray continually (1 Thess. 5:17).

- **Jesus modeled prayer.**

    Very early in the morning, while it was still dark, Jesus got up, left the house, and went off to a solitary place, where he prayed (Mark 1:35).

Prayer characterized the ministry of Christ, who is the head of the church. He prayed when choosing his disciples (Luke 6:12), on the mountain of transfiguration (Luke 9:29), on retreat (Mark 6:46), at the Last Supper (Matt. 26:27), in the Garden of Gethsemane (Luke 22:39-46), and on the cross (Luke 23:46). Luke emphasizes that prayer was a regular part of Jesus' life (Luke 3:21; 5:16; 6:12; 9:18, 28; 11:1; 22:32, 40-45).

- **Scripture emphasizes the importance of prayer.**

I urge, first of all, that requests, prayers, intercession and thanksgiving be made for everyone (1 Tim. 2:1).

Throughout Scripture we are reminded of the importance of prayer through calls to prayer, models of praying people, and the recorded prayers of specific people. In all, the Bible contains 667 verses that deal with prayer.

- **Prayer is one of the church's most valuable resources.**

Prayer is always available to the church—no matter the church's location, the size of its membership, or its available resources. Prayer provides the church with strength, guidance, and power. When churches, pastors, church leaders, intercessors, and members pray, things happen: relationships with God deepen, community grows, and people come to salvation. W. Stanley Mooneyham said, "Let us stop complaining that we don't have enough people, enough money, enough tools. That is simply not true. There is no shortage of anything we need—except vision, prayer, and will. Prayer is the one resource immediately available to each of us."

- **Prayer works.**

Scripture is full of accounts of answered prayer. Consider Exodus 17:8-16—the account of the famous battle when Moses prayed, hands raised, while Joshua and the Israelites fought the Amalekites in the valley below. The passage clearly illustrates that the difference between victory and defeat was prayer. Other accounts involve Elijah, who called upon God and received fire from heaven (1 Kings 18:36); Daniel, who by praying defied King Darius's order (Dan. 6); Peter, who was freed from prison by the prayers of believers (Acts 12:1-18); and Paul and Silas, who offered up praise to God in prison and led the jailor and his family to Christ (Acts 16:25-34).

History also is full of examples of answered prayer. Martin Luther's prayers fanned the fire of the Reformation. Revival swept England when John Wesley prayed. European intercessors prayed, and the Berlin wall crumbled. Martin Luther King Jr. and many others led the Civil Rights Movement by their example of prayer. God answers prayer.

- **Prayer pleases Jesus.**

This [requests, prayers, intercession, and thanksgiving] is good, and pleases our Savior (1 Tim. 2:3).

- **Prayer reminds us that God is in control.**

"Ah, sovereign Lord, you have made the heavens and the earth by your great power and outstretched arm. Nothing is too hard for you" (Jer. 32:16-17).

- **Through prayer we receive God's gifts.**

Ask and it will be given to you (Matt. 7:7).

This is the confidence we have in approaching God: that if we ask anything according to his will, he hears us. And if we know that he hears us—whatever we ask—we know that we have what we asked of him (1 John 5:14-15).

- **God uses our prayers to change the normal course of events.**

  Elijah was a man just like us. He prayed earnestly that it would not rain, and it did not rain on the land for three and a half years. Again he prayed, and the heavens gave rain, and the earth produced its crops (James 5:17-18).

- **Prayer provides a foundation for sharing the gospel.**

  Devote yourselves to prayer, being watchful and thankful. And pray for us, too, that God may open a door for our message, so that we may proclaim the mystery of Christ, for which I am in chains. Pray that I may proclaim it clearly, as I should (Col. 4:2-4, 12).

- **Prayer plays a significant role in bringing people to salvation.**

  I urge, then, first of all, that requests, prayers, intercession and thanksgiving be made for everyone…. This is good, and pleases God our Savior, who wants all to be saved and to come to a knowledge of the truth (1 Tim. 2:1-4).

- **Prayer is how we receive strength to endure trials.**

  Do not be anxious about anything, but in everything, by prayer and petition, with thanksgiving, present your requests to God. And the peace of God, which transcends all understanding, will guard your hearts and your minds in Christ Jesus (Phil. 4:6-7).

- **Prayer prevents us from falling into temptation.**

  Watch and pray so that you will not fall into temptation. The spirit is willing, but the body is weak (Matt. 26:41).

- **Prayer gives power over demons.**

  He replied, "This kind can come out only by prayer" (Mark 9:29).

- **Prayer brings healing to nations.**

  If my people, who are called by my name, will humble themselves and seek my face and turn from their wicked ways, then will I hear from heaven and will forgive their sin and will heal their land (2 Chron. 7:14).

- **Prayer brings healing to people.**

  Is any one of you sick? He should call the elders of the church to pray over him and anoint him with oil in the name of the Lord. And the prayer offered in faith will make the sick person well; the Lord will raise him up. If he has sinned, he will be forgiven. Therefore confess your sins to each other and pray for each other so that you may be healed. The prayer of a righteous man is powerful and effective (James 5:13-16).

- **Prayer enhances our fellowship.**

  But you, dear friends, build yourselves up in your most holy faith and pray in the Holy Spirit (Jude 20).

the trouble with praying

If God commands it, why isn't prayer the central focus of our churches? We can cite several reasons. Some are merely excuses we offer to save ourselves the embarrassment of admitting we have been preoccupied and disobedient. Others, however, are valid, and we ought to urgently deal with them.

1. Alvin Vander Griend, Mission America's national Lighthouse facilitator, suggests that we lack a proper theology of prayer. Not that we have *no* theology; on the contrary, numerous pieces of a prayer theology are floating around. Some pieces are biblical; some are not. Some resonate experientially; some do not. Unfortunately, the pieces are all mixed together and need to be sorted out. A biblical theology of prayer would help us better understand the priority and role of prayer. However, developing a proper theology of prayer must begin with *prayer!*

2. Prayer is, by design, a silent ministry. Innumerable believers quietly—yet fervently—pray behind the scenes and in their prayer closets. In fact, prayer warriors tend to shun publicity. So while much prayer is occurring, the "model" warriors often remain hidden. Much of a parent's prayer life takes place behind closed doors—hidden from their children's eyes. Most of the prayer warriors in a church remain anonymous. These are the models. We need to coax them out of hiding to teach the rest of us to pray.

3. Prayer ministry in a local church is both a "public" (visible) and "private" (behind the scenes) ministry. But few churches have an intentional prayer ministry—one that has a stated purpose and a plan for continued growth and development. Few churches are houses of prayer. As a result, there are few models to observe, few references to check, and few people to resource.

4. While most pastors recognize the importance of a strong prayer ministry, their personal involvement in prayer is often deferred by their already overloaded schedules. So pastors often ignore or delegate the prayer ministry. Since prayer lacks priority in their own lives, it seldom becomes a priority in their ministry. John Maxwell, in his book *21 Laws of Leadership,* notes that a leader cannot lead where he or she has not been. Unfortunately, if the pastor is not visibly involved in the ministry of prayer, few others in the congregation will sense its importance.

5. Discouragement is one of Satan's most effective weapons. He tries to discourage us on many fronts: we find it too difficult to pray for three hours every morning, as Martin Luther did; we are frustrated by the feeling that we are praying alone or to no one; we waver when our prayer team shows little sign of progress. And when a congregation becomes intentional about becoming a praying church, Satan penalizes it through increased spiritual warfare. Cheryl Sacks, writing in

Bridgebuilder newsletter, notes that things will go well for a while and then— WHAM!—Satan retaliates and the warfare intensifies.

6. Impatience is a twenty-first–century vice. We are accustomed to instant pudding, ten-minute oil changes, fast food, and the resolution of major life crises in thirty-minute sitcoms. Influenced by our culture, we take our impatient nature to God in prayer only to be placed in his "waiting room." While sometimes we wait only for days, it is not uncommon to wait for years, even decades. Our impatience leads to frustration; our frustration leads to discouragement.

7. Jonathan Graf, editor of *Pray!* magazine, suggests that our lack of prayer is a reflection of an independent and self-sufficient spirit (*Pray!*, July/August 1998, p. 13). We feel prayer is unnecessary— even a waste of time. We forget we need God's help because we think we can handle things ourselves. So we have developed a lifestyle in which God is only tangentially involved.

8. In addition to our impatience and independence, there are other cultural factors that influence our prayer life. In an affluent society—when our freezers are full and our checkbook is handy—it is difficult to pray with any real passion for "our daily bread." When doctors can treat most every illness at the local hospital, it seems less imperative to "call the elders of the church to pray over [you] and anoint [you] with oil." When we have extravagant homes, extended vacations, and plans for the future, it is hard to pray, "May your kingdom come."

the marks of a house of prayer

While we might expect all Bible-believing churches to recognize the importance of prayer, many churches don't understand what it means to be a house of prayer. Jesus never said, "My house shall be called a house of preaching" or "a house of music" or even "a house of worship." Jesus said, "My house shall be called a house of prayer." Yet when people talk about churches the dynamic of prayer is seldom mentioned.

Jesus said, "The gates of Hades shall not prevail against [the church]" (Matt. 16:18). This is a call to arms—to take up and use the weapons God has given us. This call emphasizes the primary purpose of the church: not to impact political life, nor to build monumental facilities, nor even to provide safe havens for fellowship, but to be active in the spiritual battle. And one of our primary weapons is prayer. Brad Long writes:

> Jesus addressed his words about the gates of hell not to individual Christians, but to the church. He wants Christians to pray as a church. He wants to form us into an army, subdivided into cohorts who are learning to pray in one accord. The effective army is the army that learns to communicate well, to trust its leaders, to reconnaissance regularly—in short, to function together in one accord. The evil one, Luther noted, does everything he can to prevent this from happening, because he wants to keep his gates intact. (*Prayer that Shapes the Future*, p. 191)

So what exactly does it mean to be a house of prayer? The Bible doesn't say exactly. But we can fairly assume that a house of prayer is a church where

- prayer is understood as the primary work.

- prayer is the most identifiable ministry.

- prayer is at the heart of every facet of the church's mission and ministry.

Based on these assumptions, a house of prayer would normally include these factors:

1. **The pastor is committed to prayer.** In a house of prayer, the pastor and pastoral leadership are deeply committed to and passionate about prayer. Pastors realize that the primary work of the church is prayer. This is clearly visible in their personal prayer lives, in their leading of worship and prayer, and in the frequency that they teach on prayer. The "praying church" pastor believes prayer is critical, essential, and imperative.

2. **Leaders lead by prayer.** The governing board, staff, and ministry leaders are people of prayer. Praying leaders pray for the members of the congregation; they pray before, during, and after making decisions; they pray daily for the pastoral leadership in the church. When church leaders pray, not only do they model prayer but God's Spirit moves in the church.

3. **Members are serious about prayer in their personal and corporate lives.** A noted prayer leader has said, "If personal and family prayer is neglected, other attempts at prayer are like sprinkling a plant with water while leaving the roots dry." The ministry of prayer in the church is not limited to those with the spiritual gift of intercession; it is designed for all the members of the body of Christ. In a house of prayer, members

- make prayer for their pastor, leaders, other members, and community a daily priority.

- practice regular (and extended) personal and corporate prayer.

- consider prayer a major factor in making their daily decisions and in problem solving.

- prioritize their personal time with the Lord and participate in family devotions.

- are growing spiritually.

4. **Prayer is integral, intentional, and integrated into the church.** In addition to being a priority for pastors, leaders, and individual members, prayer must

be a primary factor in the ministry of the congregation. However, simply adding a prayer ministry to a church's list of ministries and programs does not make it a praying church. Prayer is not a program. It must be the lifeblood of the church—written into the DNA of the congregation. This means that prayer must be a priority (integral), a deliberate strategy (intentional), and a significant factor in every area of ministry (integrated).

In Acts 1:14, we read that the church "all joined together in constant prayer." After Pentecost, "they devoted themselves to the apostles' teaching and to fellowship, to the breaking of bread and to prayer" (Acts 2:42). In a praying church, prayer is visible throughout the life of the congregation:

- The importance of prayer is reflected in the church's core values and mission statement.

- The prayer ministry has a defined (and written) prayer strategy that includes a purpose statement, goals, and objectives.

- Prayer focuses the direction of the church, guides the ministry teams, empowers the ministries, and unites the church.

- Prayer is a priority in every meeting, a prerequisite to every decision, and a key factor in every ministry. The strength of the church is found in prayer.

- Prayer is emphasized in worship through corporate prayer times, lay participation, and regular teaching on prayer.

- Prayer is visible in the lives of its members. A praying church holds high expectations for its people in the area of prayer, and its members are held accountable to pray. A praying church recognizes the need

to offer various opportunities for prayer; scheduled opportunities are offered throughout the week, and people are encouraged to pray on their own.

- Prayer is an integral part of every worship experience.

- The church has a place specifically designated for prayer that is easily accessible and regularly used.

- The prayer ministry, like the education, worship, and evangelism ministries, is included in the church's budget.

5. **The emphasis on prayer is both internal and external.** A praying church prays for its members and for the lost with equal passion. So in addition to interceding for the church's members and ministries, a praying church regularly "stands in the gap" for its neighbors, community, nation, other nations, and the world. A praying church regularly intercedes for the "harvesters" and for a rich harvest.

> **Any church without a well-organized and systematic prayer program is simply operating on a religious treadmill.**
> **—Paul Billheimer,**
> ***Destined for the Throne***

6. **The church is visibly united in prayer with other churches in the community.** A praying church realizes that God's church is one body. Unity is both a prerequisite for and a result of effective prayer. A praying church comes together regularly with other churches—across denominational, ethnic, and cultural lines—to pray. Having broken down the walls that tend to separate fellow believers, we can more effectively break down the walls that separate people from God.

7. **There is regular training in prayer.** A praying church intentionally develops intercessors. Training in prayer comes in Sunday school classes and educa-

tional offerings, through teaching and preaching in worship, and from experiences in prayer meetings and praying together. Training is offered for children, youth, adults, and seniors. People are regularly encouraged to "raise the bar" in their prayer life.

8. **Members gather for a regular prayer meeting.** If a church is a house of prayer, then the prayer meeting is an essential hour of the week. In a praying church, the weekly prayer meeting is the furnace that keeps the church warm.

9. **A designated prayer team provides leadership.** The team has been identified through prayer, designated by the pastor and church leadership, and anointed by the Holy Spirit to provide leadership. This team is entrusted with the responsibility of keeping the prayer ministry vibrant and growing.

10. **God is answering prayers.** A praying church knows when God answers prayer because they consciously identify, record, and celebrate God's answers. Lives are transformed, people are coming to know the Lord, and the church is growing spiritually and numerically. While the church understands that God doesn't always say "yes," they know that God always answers.

getting started

Building a praying church might sound like an overwhelming task. It is. There is no way you, or an entire prayer team, or even the senior pastor and the whole leadership board can accomplish it. Only God can. Building a praying church is always the work of God.

The call to a prayer ministry must be God's call. Sometimes God places this call in the heart of an individual intercessor who begins to pray for the church, its leadership, and the community. Often, God calls more than one person in a congregation—although it may be months or even years before they discover each other. Sometimes God may call a family or a small group to begin praying. Sometimes God may call the pastor, a staff member, or a member of the leadership board. But while the leadership of the senior pastor is imperative in building a praying church, prayer is primarily a ministry of the people of God—and the call to pray is often heard first by people with the spiritual gifts of intercession, discernment, or prophecy. That is why when you sense God calling you, respond as Samuel did by saying, "Speak, for your servant is listening" (1 Sam. 3:10). Becoming a house of prayer begins in dialogue with God.

While there is no set formula (be suspicious of anyone who suggests there is), there are some basic steps for developing a praying church:

1. **Pray.** Ironically, many churches that desire to become a house of prayer skip the most important step. The initial tendency is to jump right in—start a prayer group, build a prayer chain, set up a school of prayer . . . We figure the quicker we get started, the quicker we can become a praying church. But the place to start is prayer.

The second tendency is to have our plans already set before we go to God in prayer. Then we essentially ask God to bless our own plans. Sometimes God will; frequently God doesn't. It is far better to discover God's will and join him in it. If we follow his will, his blessing is guaranteed.

The third tendency is to short-circuit the process. We call a few people together to pray and then move immediately into planning. Sometimes God answers prayers instantly; more frequently, however, our praying must go on for a season—a month, a year, or even longer. Avoid running ahead of God. Avoid the temptation to do things in your time. The timing is always the Lord's.

What should you pray for?

- Ask God for a spirit of prayer to fall upon your church.

- Ask God to raise up more people to whom he has also given the burden of building a praying church. When God does that, come together periodically to pray.

- Ask God to anoint people in your congregation with the gift of intercession.

- Ask God for wisdom and vision. What does God want your church to do? Who should be involved? What is the church ready for? (See James 1:5.)

- Ask God to use prayer to begin building a passion for reaching your community and city for Christ.

- Ask God to tell you what he wants you to do.

As you pray, listen carefully for God's answer. And don't stop praying once you have an answer. Scripture says God's word is often confirmed by two or three witnesses (Deut. 17:6) or sometimes by a special sign (Judg. 6:35-40). Frequently, the "witness" is Scripture: God points you to a passage that clearly designates his leading during your devotions, during a small group Bible study, or during a worship service. Sometimes the witnesses are other believers who have received the same answer. Other times the witnesses are the doors that God opens or closes; observe how things seem to be falling into place: Are people stepping forward? Are the necessary resources becoming available? Is God giving a sense of peace about the decision? When the work is from God, the pieces of the puzzle continue to fall into place until the picture (God's vision) is clear.

Sometimes God asks us to wait. This can mean a variety of things:

- God isn't ready. (Remember, God has perfect timing.)

- There is a sin (personal or corporate) that needs to be confessed before God will answer.

- God is waiting for us to realign our hearts with his will.

- God wants to teach us something— patience, humility, dependence, or trust—before he moves us toward being a praying church.

Sometimes, already in this initial step, opposition may arise. Opposition must be evaluated as carefully as confirmation. Its purpose may be to remind us to continue praying, to challenge us to listen more closely, to invite us to rethink the idea or the timing, or to warn us that the devil isn't happy with the idea that a church may become a house of prayer.

2. **Discover the vision.** A vision is a picture of the future that motivates you to see it happen. Businesses develop visions. They set goals for product development, productivity, sales, delivery, and profit. All too often, churches adopt the same process. The church's responsibility is not to develop a vision, but to discover the vision God has established. This is imperative, for in the future, when the ministry appears to struggle, when we get weary in our persevering, when criticism seems to build, we can take courage from the fact that God will see his vision through.

Through prayer and through the confirmation God provides, God forms his vision in our hearts and minds. Ironically, it takes prayer to "discover" God's vision for our praying. Brad Long writes:

"To cultivate a praying church, it is necessary to have received a vision from God, which will drive the leadership and eventually the congregation to prayer. A prayerless church does not receive a vision from God." (*Prayer that Shapes the Future*, 1999, p. 193)

Piece by piece, the vision becomes clear. However, in putting the puzzle together, avoid the temptation to clone an apparently "successful" prayer ministry from another congregation. God won't give your church another church's vision. While the vision God gives you may be similar in many respects to another church's, your vision is unique—reflective of your members' gifts and resources, of your church's ministry, and of your community's needs.

Normally, a vision answers the basic questions Who?, What?, When?, Where?, Why?, and How?

- Who should be involved?

- What will the prayer ministry look like?

- When should we begin?

- Where will the focus of the ministry be?

- Why do we need a prayer ministry?

- How do we proceed in building a house of prayer?

The answer to these questions constitutes the vision and ultimately sets the direction of the ministry.

When the vision is clear, write it out and use scriptural support. This will help you share it with the congregation.

Example

The prayer ministry of Community Church exists to involve all worshipers (*who*) in daily prayer (*what*) through training and encouragement (*how*) to enlarge our love for Jesus Christ, to evangelize, to equip believers for service (*where*), and to bring God glory (*why*)!

3. **Define the vision.** While having a prayer ministry is not the equivalent of being a praying church, it is a significant step toward intentionally becoming a house of prayer. There are a number of patterns that churches generally fall into:

- In many churches, prayer is assumed. The church confesses to believe in prayer—during worship, at meetings, and as appropriate in the various ministries of the church. Prayer is often seen as a personal responsibility—between the believer and God. Periodically, the sermon may deal specifically or tangentially with prayer. Unfortunately, in many of these churches, more prayer is assumed to be happening than actually is.

- In a few churches, prayer is the sole (primary) focus. Prayer is the ministry of the church. This is a church marked by prayer meetings, prayer groups, and a heavy emphasis on prayer in worship. They nurture their relationship with God and pray for the lost. And extensive prayer results in intensive fellowship. While these churches are "birthed" with the vision of being a church focusing only on prayer, as they "grow up" (either in size or age) they often add programs that dilute their emphasis on prayer. These churches tend to become introverted, focus on personal piety, and remain fairly small. It also appears to be very difficult to transition an established church into this model.

- In some churches, the pastor recognizes the importance of prayer, takes on the responsibility of leading the prayer ministry, and makes deliberate efforts to build prayer into the life of the church. The pastor may preach a four- to six-week series on prayer, participate in a national prayer initiative, or organize a thirty-hour prayer vigil. This model can work well. But most pastors are overworked and responsible for many other ministries, so frequently the prayer ministry gives way to other pressures.

- In some churches, the emphasis on prayer is left to the respective ministry leaders. So, if the pastor is sold on prayer, worship and messages may emphasize prayer. If the youth pastor believes prayer is essential to effective ministry, a number of prayer ministries may be incorporated into the youth program. On the other hand, the evangelism or education ministries may not have consistent prayer support. This model provides an inconsistent emphasis on prayer within the church because prayer is dependant on the commitment of each ministry's leader.

• In a few churches, prayer is a distinct ministry in the congregation. That is, in addition to ministries like evangelism, education, worship, counseling, and fellowship, there is a stand-alone prayer ministry. The prayer ministry sets its own goals, recruits and trains its leaders, develops its own programs, and has its own budget. Part of its responsibility is to support and encourage prayer "for" and "in" all the other ministries. This distinct prayer ministry

— gives a clear signal to the congregation that prayer is important.

— doesn't get lost among the other programs of the church.

— can organize and provide a holistic emphasis on prayer.

— encourages more members to become involved in prayer.

— holds someone accountable for recruiting, training, and supporting pray-ers.

— makes it possible to develop and organize other prayer ministries within the church.

— assists in identifying those with the gift of intercession.

— is integral in providing a foundation for the other ministries of the church.

Implementing this patttern—a distinct prayer ministry—is a critical step in building a house of prayer.

4. **Disseminate the vision.** Once the vision has been discovered and defined, it must be shared. There appears to be a proper order for building consensus and sharing the challenge:

• **Get the senior pastor(s) on board.** The pastor must be willing to enter into the discipline of prayer. This is the first priority. In order for the program to be effective, the senior pastor must be an enthusiastic participant and model.

• **Get the leaders on board.** Leaders should be aware of and supportive of the church's prayer ministry. Ask them to pray about it. Get the endorsement of the leadership board; share the vision with ministry leaders. Work closely with the leadership, responding to their input and keeping them well informed.

Encourage the leaders to promote the vision by participating in it. Leaders in the church must embody the vision for prayer by being people of prayer and by actively participating in the prayer ministry of the church.

• **Share the vision with the congregation.** In sharing the vision with the congregation, explain why a prayer ministry is necessary—many people assume they are already spending a lot of time in prayer. And continue to share the prayer vision on a regular basis—at least monthly—in a variety of ways.

5. **Develop a team.** If you decide to have a distinct prayer ministry, a prayer coordinator is essential. A prayer team is even more effective. Ask God to raise up a prayer coordinator or potential members of a prayer team. When introducing new prayer ministries, ask God to identify an additional prayer-team member to lead the ministry. The pastor and church leadership group should approve and encourage the prayer coordinator and prayer team.

> Dee Duke, pastor of Jefferson (Oregon) Baptist Church, once shared a memory of his father with me: He was around ten years old, and his father took him to the nearby ship yards. They came to a large ship floating next to the dock on slack ropes, and his father walked over to the ship and began pushing on it with all his might. He continued to do so for about twenty minutes, all the while Dee thinking his father must be crazy trying to move the huge ship. Then suddenly the ship began to move backwards, pulling the ropes taut. As they sat on the grass together afterwards, Dee's father said, "I don't know how it works, or what law of physics is involved, but my energy gets stored up in that ship until there is enough to move it. There are two lessons to be learned here. The first is, if I had quit, if I had stopped at nineteen minutes, it never would have moved. And second, if you had helped me, we could have done it twice as fast."

Prayer leaders should have a passion for prayer and the spiritual gifts of organization, compassion, and encouragement. A prayer leader with the gift of intercession is a blessing but not a necessity. For additional information on the qualifications for prayer leaders see Prayer Coordinator (pp. 180-184).

In some situations, the Lord calls a member of the congregation to the ministry of prayer, but the possibility of that person being designated as prayer coordinator remains remote. If you are a lone prayer warrior, you should

- commit to pray regularly.

- pray for a prayer partner—someone to hold you accountable to your commitment to pray.

- ask your prayer partner to pray with you on a weekly basis. Invite others to join your prayer time. Pray for your pastor. Pray that God will begin to make your church a house of prayer.

- learn more about prayer. Take advantage of prayer resources (books, seminars, and so on) and opportunities to pray.

- begin to publicly model prayer: in home, in your neighborhood, in church ministries, in worship.

- become a Lighthouse in your community.

- wait on the Lord. Listen for God's direction to proceed.

6. **Plan the work.** The primary purpose of this book is to assist committed individuals, leaders, and ministry teams to accomplish this sixth step. In preparing to make a church a house of prayer, careful planning is necessary. Prayer must play an integral part in every facet of ministry:

- **Leadership.** The pastor must become a person of prayer. A survey of pastors at a conference in Dallas indicated that more than 95 percent of pastors pray less than five minutes a day. The pastor should be able to set aside a significant amount of time (one-half to a full day per week) for prayer (see Acts 6:3-4). Only a praying pastor can lead a praying church.

The leadership board should also spend time together in prayer. This should be a top priority.

In churches with three or more staff members, bring the staff together weekly for extended (one to three hours) prayer. In churches with one or two staff members, have the staff join with other key leaders for extended prayer.

At the same time the leaders are praying for the church, the church must be praying for the leaders. Begin a Prayer Shield ministry (see pp. 214-217). When a church begins to earnestly seek God's will, the spiritual attacks will intensify. While the church is the target for these spiritual attacks, the pastor and his or her family are the "bull's-eye." Pastors and leaders need to be protected. Recruit people who are willing to pray every day for the pastor and for other leaders.

See The Leader's Prayer Life section of this book for additional assistance in this area.

- **Education.** Develop opportunities for people to learn how to pray. This might include developing a resource library of books, videos, and tapes on prayer; offering educational courses on prayer; holding regular prayer retreats; or sponsoring an annual prayer emphasis week with opportunities for people to be trained in prayer.

Ministries such as Children's Prayer Ministry, Prayer Library, and School of Prayer, described in the Prayer Ministry Ideas section of this book, are designed to assist in this area.

- **Pastoral Care.** Intercede for church members. This ministry should offer support and encouragement to all church members. A prayer chain is helpful for those in crisis. A prayer team can visit those in the hospital or those confined to their homes. A team of intercessors can pray through the directory each week. Prayer calendars can encourage people to pray for specific groups of people (marrieds, singles, parents, children, elderly people, and so on) and specific church ministries. Share with the congregation the answers God is providing and celebrate them together.

The Prayer Ministry Ideas section of this book describes ministries such as Elder Care Ministry, Prayer for Healing, and Prayer Support Group that offer assistance in this area.

- **Small groups.** In many churches, the small group ministry provides caregiving, spiritual nurture, and discipleship training. It is an ideal place for people to learn to pray for each other. This book's section on small group prayer is designed to encourage praying in small groups.

- **Evangelism and missions.** Effective evangelism and missions involve intentional and active prayer for people in your local community (evangelism) and around the world (missions). The term *Harvest Prayer* describes both special mission prayer initiatives and the integration of evangelistic prayer in the life of the church.

Locally, consider becoming a Lighthouse church, or join with other churches in praying for your city. In considering world missions, pray for the 10/40 or 40/70 Window or participate in the Adopt-a-People program. The Harvest Prayer Ideas section of this book provides guidance in this area.

- **Worship.** Prayer must be a meaningful part of worship. This can include corporate prayer, opportunities for people to receive prayer, and regular preaching on prayer.

In addition, worship services must receive significant prayer. Pray before, during, and after worship for spiritual protection, the Spirit's presence, anointed preaching, receptive hearts, enhanced fellowship, visitors, and so on. Consider using a special prayer group, rotating through your church's small groups, or asking people to pray while they are worshiping in order to implement this ministry.

The section on worship ideas offers options to use in this area.

In addition to preparing an overall prayer ministry, consider some additional details:

- Each prayer ministry should submit its budget needs to the prayer ministry team. The prayer ministry team should submit the needs of the entire prayer ministry to the church's leadership at the appropriate time.

- Prepare job descriptions for key positions. Sample job descriptions for a prayer coordinator and prayer team members are found in the Prayer Ministry Ideas section.

- Provide a balanced program with some variety to involve a wide group of people with differing preferences.

7. **Work the plan.**

- **Start slowly.** Avoid the temptation of doing too much too quickly. Begin with a couple of ministries. Get them up and going before introducing new ministries. Be sensitive to ministries currently going on.

- **Explore resources.** Look for appropriate resources: books, tapes, people, and training opportunities. What people are available for consulting? What are nearby churches doing? Which people have the gift of intercession? What seminars on organizing a prayer ministry are available?

- **Recruit participants.** When you introduce a new prayer ministry, people who have been praying for such an opportunity will immediately become involved. But recruiting pray-ers is an ongoing responsibility in prayer ministry. Many churches hold annual, or even quarterly pledge campaigns asking people to pledge to pray for a specific need for a specific period of time. Other churches rotate the recruiting throughout the year by highlighting one prayer ministry each month. A few churches continue to recruit throughout the year for every ministry.

When recruiting, promote the prayer opportunity in a variety of ways—bulletin announcements, encouragement from the pulpit, testimonies of the ministry's impact, word of mouth, and personal invitations to join. Always ask people to commit for a specific period of time (the first request should not exceed one year).

Build in opportunities to appreciate people who fulfill their commitment and then encourage them to sign up again.

- **Provide training.** Train people through preaching in worship services, through teaching in Sunday school, and by developing skills in adult education opportunities. Hold special seminars and workshops and provide "on-the-job" training. Give people an opportunity to practice prayer at retreats, at prayer vigils, in their personal devotions, and even during worship services. People need to hear messages on prayer, to be taught about prayer, and to have opportunities to practice prayer.

Teach multiple formats for prayer. Some formats will appeal to some people; other formats will appeal to others. Keep the praying fresh. Keep it focused on God.

- **Maintain flexibility.** Involve the entire church—children, youth, singles, couples, families, the elderly, and so on. Continue to pray and look for new ways God might be leading you. Schedule events at different times and for different purposes.

- **Continue to expand your ministry.** Develop new prayer ministries in the context of current ministries. For example, if you have an effective small group ministry, bring the small group leaders together. Challenge them to incorporate prayer into their small groups (see Small Group Prayer, p. 242), or ask a small group to adopt a prayer ministry as their ministry. If you have a prayer chain that operates during the day, consider expanding it to involve more people, span more time, or deal with more prayers than just emergencies.

As the Lord blesses your current prayer ministry and as the needs continue to surface, add additional ministries. As you develop a variety of prayer ministries to meet diverse interests, additional people will become involved.

- **Persevere.** Building a prayer ministry requires a long-term commitment. Initially, progress is often slow. Comparisons to large, successful ministries that have been growing for decades foster discouragement. Be persistent and keep praying.

  Remember, the devil considers prayer an act of aggression. Spiritual warfare and counter-attacks are common. When you begin to resist the enemy's darkness and take ground for Christ's kingdom, you will encounter spiritual opposition. Expect Satan to do what he can to stop you.

  God will draw people into his movement. God can use a "Gideon's band" as well as large legions. God places certain burdens on certain hearts. Yet, over time, with solid teaching, continual encouragement, and faithfulness, more and more people will discover the vision and your church will become the house of prayer God intends it to be.

8. **Evaluate.** Periodically, it is imperative to pause and honestly address the hard questions: When people describe our church, do they mention prayer? Is prayer our number one priority? Are we a praying church?

  In our world, we strive to do things with excellence and success. We set goals that stretch us. We make them quantifiable. We assume that if we meet our goals, we are successful. We figure if we are successful, we must be doing things right.

  Unfortunately, this often results in discouragement (our numbers are down from last year), frustration (a couple of old ministries dried up when we added the new ones), and feelings of failure (a neighboring church's prayer ministries seem to be going much better than ours).

  Thankfully, God isn't interested in the world's definition of success. Scripture instead talks about ministry in terms of service, sacrifice, and suffering. Scripture's model of success is Jesus—who humbled himself in birth, suffered persecution throughout his ministry, and willingly offered his life on a cross.

  It is important to regularly evaluate the prayer ministry using the proper criteria, such as "faithfulness," "authenticity," "spiritual growth," "obedience," "intimacy with God," and "bearing fruit." While goals and numbers can be helpful in evaluating the ministry, we must be careful that they do not define it. Some questions to ask:

- Is prayer a part of the church's stated mission and core values?

- Is the pastor given time to pray? Is it part of the pastor's job description?

- Is prayer an extended part of each leadership meeting?

- Is prayer a regular part of every worship service?

- Are members of the congregation willing to participate in public prayer?

- Does the pastor regularly preach on prayer?

- Is there regular teaching on prayer in the education ministry?

- Are there opportunities for people to be involved in prayer throughout the week?

- Are intercessors regularly appreciated?

- Are answers to prayer publicly noted and celebrated?

- Does the staff pray together on a weekly basis?

- Is there intentional prayer for the lost throughout the week?

- Is the prayer ministry included in the annual budget?

- Have those with the gift of intercession been identified in your congregation?

The answers to the following questions should include personal experiences as well as numerical statistics:

- What answers to prayers have been received over the past year?

- What growth has been experienced in the prayer ministry over the last year?

- What growth is evidenced in the personal lives of church members?

- What growth has our church experienced through conversions?

- Has the percentage of people involved in a prayer ministry increased over the past year?

Whether you have a "Gideon's band" or a "legion of intercessors," the essence of a successful prayer ministry is perseverance and faithfulness. Our finite eyes seldom see the full impact of prayer, a praying people, and a praying church. Our finite minds seldom comprehend how God uses our prayers to move mountains. The primary question to ask in evaluating your prayer ministry is simply, "Have we been faithful?" If you answer in the affirmative, God is using your prayers to build his kingdom. God will bless your congregation.

9. **Celebrate.** Seeing God's answers to prayer reinforces our sense of God's faithfulness. Seeing God's faithfulness encourages us to pray more. Praying more brings more answers to prayer. Share God's answers with as much regularity and passion as you share the needs. And when God answers prayers, celebrate! Celebrate God! Here are some ideas:

- Hang a banner in the church declaring "God answers prayer" and inviting people to write answers to prayer on the banner.

- Start a visual prayer chain where the petitions and intercessions are one color and the answers are another color. Every time a prayer is answered,

the "petition link" is taken down and replaced with an "answered link."

- Share answers to prayer as well as requests for prayer during worship.

- Place a "prayer answer box" next to your "prayer request box."

- Hold a special worship service periodically to celebrate "God sightings" (testimonies of people who have seen God at work in answer to prayer).

- Include periodic testimonies during worship by people who have prayed and received answers.

- When people return to church after an illness or hospitalization, welcome them back to worship and thank those who prayed for their recovery.

- Hold an annual appreciation dinner (or breakfast) for those who have been involved in the church's prayer ministries.

Section 1

PRAYER FORMATS

GROWING IN PRAYER

The key to building a praying church is to build a praying people. This section is designed to encourage people to learn to pray, to practice the disciplines of prayer, and to enjoy the privilege of spending time with God.

In one sense, there is no wrong way to pray—as long as the prayer is directed to God from a sincere and contrite heart. However, there are distinct prayer forms that can enhance our faithfulness in prayer.

The purpose of spending time alone with God is to develop an intimacy with him, to learn how he wants us to live, and to intercede for the things that are close to his heart. To achieve this purpose, we must spend time with God, find a regular place to pray, and stretch our relationship with God by varying our discipline of prayer.

time

Most of us know the familiar story of Jesus at the home of Mary and Martha (Luke 10). Martha uses her time, energy, and expertise in the kitchen to prepare a meal for Jesus while her sister, Mary, simply sits and listens to Jesus. Martha is every pastor's dream—a hard worker, a good organizer, active in ministry. However, we must remind ourselves of Jesus' response to Martha's demands that Mary help her in the kitchen: that he values the service Martha is extending, but he values the time Mary is spending with him more. Mary is sitting at the feet of Jesus—a place and posture we tend to overlook in our busy culture.

In our fast-paced culture, where there is much to do and be done, we tend to look like Martha. Time is a premium, so it seems foolish to "waste" it. But while both time with the Lord and time in his service are important to the kingdom, Jesus prioritizes the time we spend with him. In his book *Too Busy Not to Pray*, Bill Hybels writes that if we are too busy to pray, we are simply too busy.

We must make time to pray. We need to schedule it on our calendars like every other important "meeting." We must factor it into our daily routines. Spending extended, regular time in prayer will radically deepen our personal discipleship, transform our priorities, invigorate our service, and increase our awareness of God's presence.

place

Some prayer leaders recommend having one place to meet God. They call this place the "altar" and encourage people to go there on a regular, daily basis (for example, for an hour every morning). This altar can be as simple as a favorite chair.

Others emphasize that believers are to live prayerful lives and should pray throughout the day wherever and whenever the Holy Spirit moves. We should be praying while

- waiting in line (at the grocery store, bank, and so on)
- riding the bus or a taxi
- waiting for someone
- doing dishes
- driving
- watching the evening news
- browsing the local library
- eating dinner
- visiting a local retreat center
- worshiping at church
- walking
- taking a shower or a bath
- exercising

In reality, both having an altar and praying throughout the day are important pieces of a healthy prayer life. We need to be disciplined enough to have a regular, daily prayer time; and it is the disciplined routine that gives rise to the spontaneous opportunities.

variety

There are nearly as many different ways to pray as there are pray-ers. Some people write out their prayers; others prefer more spontaneous praying. Some people pray silently; others pray aloud. Some people prefer praying alone; others like to pray in a small-group context or lead prayer in worship. Some people are comfortable with shorter periods of prayer; others prefer to pray for extended periods.

> In talking to pastors and other leaders over the years, I've always tried to stress that everyone is led by God to pray in a little different way. In fact, it often seems one person's approach may even contradict another person's approach.
> —Warren Wiersbe

While there is considerable variety among pray-ers; there appears to be less variety in an individual's prayer life. It is not uncommon for us to learn a form of prayer (for example, seated, with head bowed, hands folded, and listening as the leader prays) and use that prayer form exclusively. We tend to resist "stretching" our prayer formats—yet it is this "stretching" that promotes growth. Using a variety of prayer formats

- allows us to grow spiritually and to build intimacy with Jesus.

- helps us avoid the overuse of a single format that produces a mechanical prayer life.

- prevents boredom and keeps our prayer lives fresh and vibrant.

- continues to make prayer relevant by allowing us to adapt as our needs change over time.

In order to grow, we need to be challenged—perhaps prodded and pushed—to step out in faith, to take a risk, to try something new that jars our comfort zone. Perhaps this means praying aloud when we have prayed only silently before; perhaps it means leading in prayer when previously we have only participated; perhaps it means spending an hour in prayer when we normally spend only minutes; perhaps it means praying the Names of God when we are used to the A.C.T.S. format.

While most new prayer formats may feel uncomfortable at first, they can do much to enhance our relationship with God. And because different prayer formats will be helpful to different people, refusing to try new ways to pray may mean we never discover a prayer format that brings us more fully into God's presence.

how to use the formats

This section includes many formats for prayer. Some emphasize seeking God's presence; some seek his power; some request God to act; some encourage simply spending time with God. But whatever the nature of the formats, they are offered for one purpose: to help bring you into the presence of God.

These formats come with no guarantees: no format is helpful if it goes unused, and no one format is a prescription for intimacy. Modify, adapt, and change the prayer formats to meet your personality, style, and specific needs. While being comfortable with a certain prayer may be an indicator from the Holy Spirit that this is a good fit, it may also signal that there isn't enough "stretch" in the format to bring growth. While it may take some time and experimentation to find additional prayer formats that are helpful, don't lose patience. The benefits are worth the effort.

The explanations that follow are not intended to be exhaustive. They simply introduce the prayer format and provide sufficient information to begin using it. In many cases, additional references are offered for further study.

Each format is labeled by three indicators—setting, level, and time. The *setting* indicator acknowledges that some prayer formats fit better in one setting than another. This guide recognizes five basic *settings*:

- *individuals* (for personal quiet times)

- *families/households* (for example, around the table after dinner)

- *small groups* (three to twelve people participating in a formal or informal small group, including smaller Sunday school classes)

- *large groups* (thirteen or more people, including larger Sunday school classes)

- *congregations* (usually a larger group, particularly in a worship setting)

The *level* indicator recognizes that some prayer formats are simpler to use than others. Normally, pray-ers should begin simply. When they are comfortable with the *initial* formats, they should be challenged to step up to an *intermediate* level prayer format and ultimately to participate—at least periodically—in an *intense* prayer format. These levels do not imply that one prayer format is more effective than another or that God hears the higher level prayer first. But as pray-ers move from initial to intermediate to intense prayer formats they will notice growth in time commitment, personal vulnerability, and dynamics not commonly found in our spiritual lives (for example,

reflection, contemplation, and spiritual confrontation). The more intense the prayer format, the more the pray-er is asked to stretch.

Some prayer formats involve a greater time commitment than others. The *time* indicator suggests the average amount of time necessary to use that particular prayer format appropriately and is admittedly subjective. These time labels should never be used as limits or time constraints:

- *short* designates a prayer format that can be used effectively in less than ten minutes

- *medium* designates a prayer format that requires ten to thirty minutes

- *long* designates a period of thirty minutes to one hour

- *extended* requires one or more hours

Remember, the format is simply designed as a conduit into the presence of God. The format of prayer should never replace the function of prayer.

prayer positions

People often ask, "What is the proper physical position for prayer? Is one position more conducive to prayer? Which positions does Scripture recommend?" While Scripture does not appear to recommend a specific prayer position, it does identify at least five distinct physical positions for prayer. They are (in alphabetical order):

- **Bowing the head.**

  Then the man bowed down and worshiped the LORD, saying, "Praise be to the LORD, the God of my master Abraham . . ." (Gen. 24:26).

  Moses bowed to the ground at once and worshiped, "O Lord, if I have found favor in your eyes," he said, "then let the Lord go with us" (Ex. 34:8-9).

- **Kneeling.**

  The woman came and knelt before him. "Lord, help me!" she said (Matt. 15:25).

  [Jesus] withdrew about a stone's throw beyond them, knelt down and prayed (Luke 22:41).

- **Prostrate.**

  Going a little further, [Jesus] fell with his face to the ground and prayed . . . (Matt. 26:39; see also Mark 14:35).

- **Standing.**

  [Solomon] stood and blessed the whole assembly of Israel in a loud voice . . . (1 Kings 8:55).

  The Pharisee stood up and prayed about himself: "God, I thank you that I am not like other men. . . ." But the tax collector stood at a distance. He would not even look up to heaven, but beat his breast and said, "God, have mercy on me, a sinner" (Luke 18:11, 13).

- **Raised hands.**

  When Solomon had finished these prayers and supplications to the LORD, he rose from before the altar of the LORD, where he had been kneeling with his hands spread out toward heaven (1 Kings 8:54).

From these Scriptures and others we may draw some basic conclusions:

- Prayer can be offered to God from any meaningful position.

- The position taken in prayer often reflects the type of prayer being offered (for example, submission—prostrate; worship—standing). That is, the nonverbal (body language) ideally matches the verbal (prayer).

- The position of prayer may change during a single prayer.

- The pray-er's position can enhance the pray-er's praying.

- Prayer is an active—not a passive—activity.

A.C.T.S.

This is probably one of the most-used and best-known prayer formats. The acronym serves as an outline for structuring prayer.

a

The first part of prayer is *adoration*. We offer praise for who God is, for what God has done, and for what God has yet to do.

c

Adoration is followed by *confession*. We acknowledge our sins and our need for God's forgiveness. Our confession must be open, honest, and specific.

t

Next is *thanksgiving*. We thank God for his goodness and for his answers to our prayers.

s

Finally comes *supplication*, where we lay both the needs of others and our needs before God.

Sometimes an additional "S" is added to the acronym, representing *surrender*—

waiting on the Lord and being willing to accept his answers in obedience

Setting: individuals, families/households, small groups, large groups, congregations

Level: initial

Time: medium, long, extended

Agreeing in Prayer

Jesus calls us to agree in prayer (Matt. 18:19). He wants us to pray "in agreement" with God's Word and with other believers for a specific, desired outcome.

Scripture doesn't require that two or more pray-ers agree about everything—but that they agree about what they are praying for. So two pastors from different denominations can pray together. A husband and a wife—even after a heated argument—can come together in prayer. Church leaders, in spite of disagreeing over some policy issues, can stand side by side in prayer. Jesus calls us to pray about those things we agree on, and to agree on those things we pray about.

Praying in agreement, also known as "praying in accord," allows the Holy Spirit to introduce the themes. So this prayer format requires intensive and intuitive listening to the Holy Spirit. It requires those praying to pray through the theme(s) together until the Holy Spirit moves them to another issue. When Christians pray together, the Holy Spirit usually speaks the same thing to two or more as they pray. Likewise, the Spirit never contradicts himself.

While people praying in agreement normally are together, it is not necessary that they be in the same room—or even be praying at the same time. One of the best examples of praying "in agreement" has been the intercession focused on the 10/40 Window (see p. 277 for a description). Intercessors around the world receive information on particular people groups and then pray for these groups on their own schedule. Although these pray-ers will never be in the same place physically, they pray in agreement as they pray for the same things.

Charles Finney, in his book *Lectures on Revivals of Religion* (Fleming H. Revell, 1988), offers the following suggestions for praying in agreement:

- **Avoid long prayers.**

  The prayers should always be short. When individuals suffer themselves to pray long, they forget where they are, that they are only the mouth of the congregation, and that the congregation cannot be expected to go along and feel united in prayer if they are long and tedious, and go all around the world and pray for everything

> **Nothing tends more to cement the hearts of Christians than praying together. Never do they love one another so well as when they witness the outpouring of each other's hearts in prayer. Their spirituality begets a feeling of union and confidence, highly important to the prosperity of the church. It is doubtful whether Christians can ever be otherwise than united, if they are in the habit of praying together. And where they have had hard feelings and differences among themselves, they are all done away, by being united in prayer. The great object is gained, if you can bring them really to unite in prayer. If this can be done, the difficulties vanish.**
>
> **—Charles Finney, *Lectures on Revivals of Religion*, p. 117**

they can think of. Commonly those who pray long in meetings do it not because they have the spirit of prayer, but because they have it not.

- **Avoid lectures or sermons.**

  Some pray out a whole system of divinity. Some preach, some exhort the people, till everybody wishes they would stop. They should keep it to the point, and pray for what they came to pray for, and not pray all over the universe.

- **Focus on one thing at a time.**

  Everyone should pray for some one object. It is well for every individual to have one object for prayer. Two or more may pray for the same thing. When one leads and the others follow, but are thinking of something else, prayer is hindered. Their hearts do not unite, do not say "Amen."

- **Follow the Holy Spirit's leadings.**

  Great pains should be taken, both by the leader and others, to watch carefully the motions of the Spirit of God. Let them not pray without the Spirit, but follow the Spirit's leadings. Be sure not to quench the Spirit for the sake of praying according to the regular custom. Avoid everything calculated to divert attention away from the object.

- **Pray aloud and clearly.**

  People cannot agree with what they do not hear or what they do not understand. Avoid speaking in tongues in this setting.

- **Stay focused.**

  This prayer format requires checking our personal thoughts and prayers, focusing on what is being prayed, and agreeing with the biblical prayers of others. Avoid changing the subject unless you are convinced the Spirit is prompting you to do so and the previous subject has been exhausted.

- **Feel free to vocalize your agreement.**

  Praying in agreement can involve praying the prayer with someone, praying for similar things immediately following the initial prayer, or offering your personal "yes" or "amen" during (or at the conclusion of) the prayer.

Setting: families/households, small groups, large groups

Level: intermediate, intense

Time: medium, long

Examples

Moms in Touch; Shield a Badge; Marches for Jesus; See You at the Pole; National Day of Prayer

Resource

Brad Long and Doug McMurry, *Prayer that Shapes the Future* (Grand Rapids, MI: Zondervan, 1999).

Alphabet Prayer

The Alphabet Prayer format can be used in a couple of ways.

praying through the alphabet

The leader begins with "A," and participants say the attributes and/or names of God that begin with that letter using a single word or short phrase. This can be done by simply naming the attribute (for example, "almighty") or by saying a sentence of thanksgiving (for example, "God, I thank you for being an awesome God"). People can participate as often as they would like with each letter. When the list is exhausted, the leader announces the next letter. It is not necessary to do the entire alphabet at one sitting, nor is it necessary to go in alphabetical order. However, the most creative and heartfelt responses often come after the familiar ones have been mentioned. On one occasion, "Z" brought out, "God, you are the 'Zamboni' of my life."

praying around the circle

One person begins by thanking God for an attribute starting with "A," the second person thanks God for an attribute starting with "B," and so on. Continue to go around the circle until the entire alphabet is completed at least once. The letters "Q" and "X" may be omitted.

Here is a partial list of the attributes and/or names of God:

A—almighty, all-powerful, Adonai, Advocate, Alpha (and Omega), Ancient of Days, Anchor, Author of Life

B—Beginning, Begotten Son, beloved, Branch, Bread of Life, Bridegroom, Bright Morning Star

C—caring, Cornerstone, Counselor, Creator, Chosen

D—Deliverer, Door, Defender, Divine Physician

E—eternal, everlasting, ever-present, Eternal Life, El Shaddai (The All-Sufficient One), El Elyon (God Most High), El Roi (The God Who Sees All), End

F—faithful, Friend, Finisher of our Faith, Firstborn of Creation, Forgiving Father, Fortress

G—good, gracious, Great Shepherd, guileless, Guest, God

H—holy, helpful, Head of the Church/ Body, Hope of Glory, humble, High Priest

I—influential, Immanuel, innocent, "I Am," infinite, incomparable, inscrutable, invisible

J—jealous, just, joyful, Judge, Jesus, Jehovah (The Self-Existent One), Jehovah-Jireh (The Lord Is My Provider), Jehovah-

Mekoddish (The Lord Is My Sanctification), Jehovah-Rapha (The Lord Who Heals), Jehovah-Rohi (The Lord Is My Shepherd), Jehovah-Shalom (The Lord Is Peace), Jehovah-Tsidkenu (The Lord Is My Righteousness), Jehovah-Shammah (The Lord Is Present with Me)

K—kind, King, King of Kings

L—loving, Lord, Lord of Lords, Lamb of God, Life, Light of the World, Living Water

M—merciful, Mighty God, Morning Star, majestic, Mediator, merciful, Most High, Messiah

N—Name above All Names, God of the Nations

O—omnipresent, omniscient, omnipotent, Omega

P—powerful, perfect, Physician, Prince of Peace, Potentate, Personal God, Preserver, Prophet

Q—question-less

R—Redeemer, Ransom, Resurrection and Life, Righteous Judge, Rock, Refuge

S—Savior, Shepherd, Sinless One, spotless, Strength, Son of David, Son of God, Servant of God, Suffering Servant, Stone, Scapegoat, Sanctuary

T—Truth, Temple, Thunder, Tower, Treasure

U—Unspeakable Gift, unchangeable, unequal, unsearchable

V—Vine

W—wonderful, Way, Word, Word of Life, Wisdom

X—(e)xcellent

Y—Yahweh

Z—zealous

Setting: individuals, families/households, small groups, large groups, congregations

Level: initial, intermediate

Time: medium, long, extended

Authoritative Prayer

In Matthew 10:1 we read that Jesus gave the disciples authority to drive out evil spirits and heal those who were sick. Acts 16 tells of Paul's praying to drive an evil spirit out of a slave girl. Seventy-two people in Luke 10:17 were ecstatic when they found that "even the demons submit to us in [Jesus'] name."

Richard Foster calls this type of prayer "authoritative prayer." He writes:

> In authoritative prayer we are calling forth the will of the Father upon the earth. Here we are not so much speaking to God as speaking for God. We are not asking God to do something; rather, we are using the authority of God to command something be done. (*Prayer: Finding the Heart's True Home*, 1992, p. 229)

Foster cites Exodus 14, when Israel, trapped between the Red Sea and the advancing Egyptian army, "cried out to the Lord." God's response is most interesting. Instead of intervening with a miracle—as he had so many times in the past—God says, "Why are you crying out to me? Tell the Israelites to go forward. Raise your staff and stretch out your hand over the sea to divide the water . . ." (Ex. 14:15-16). Sometimes we need to stop petitioning and start performing. Foster says, "God was telling Moses to take control over the situation, which is precisely what he did. That is precisely what we do in authoritative prayer."

The gospels reveal Jesus' exercise of authoritative prayer. Consider, for example, Mark 4:39: Caught in a furious squall with panicked disciples, Jesus commands the forces of nature, "Quiet, be still!" In John 5:8-9, he says to the lame man, "Pick up your mat and walk." And in John 11:43, Jesus raises the dead when he commands, "Lazarus, come out."

As Richard Foster points out, not only did Jesus exercise this authority, he delegated this authority to believers when "he gave them power and authority to drive out all demons and to cure diseases, and he sent them out to proclaim the kingdom of God and to heal the sick" (Luke 9:1-2). In fact, Jesus says, "I tell you the truth, anyone who has faith in me will do what I have been doing. He will do even greater things than these, because I am going to the Father" (John 14:12).

As believers we have been given the power of Jesus' name and the presence of the Spirit to continue Jesus' work in this world. However, as a form of warfare prayer, authoritative prayer is subject to misuse and abuse and should be used carefully, in the context of community (i.e., seldom alone), and under the authority of the church (pastors and elders).

Setting: individuals, small groups

Level: intense

Time: short, medium, long

Resources

Richard Foster, *Prayer: Finding the Heart's True Home* (San Francisco: Harper, 1992).

C. Peter Wagner, *Confronting the Powers* (Ventura, CA: Regal, 1993).

Terry Teykl, *Acts 29—Fifty Days of Prayer to Invite the Holy Spirit* (Muncie, IN: Prayer Point Press, 1998).

A.W.C.I.P.A.

Lorraine Espinosa of Bonita, California, submitted this example to *Pray!* magazine (May/June 1998, p. 14). The outline works well in a variety of settings. Simply spending ten minutes in each section means an hour of prayer.

a is for adoration

"Enter his gates with thanksgiving and his courts with praise" (Ps. 100:4). Thank God for his many gifts and blessings. Be as specific as possible. Praise God for his character and qualities such as love, grace, power, and holiness.

w is for waiting

"Be still and know that [the Lord] is God" (Ps. 46:10). Be quiet and simply listen for God. God often speaks, but we need first to still the noises of our hearts and minds in order to hear him. Welcome God's words of refreshment, encouragement, and direction.

c is for confession

"Search me, O God, and know my heart. . . . See if there is any offensive way in me" (Ps. 139:23-24). "If we confess our sins, he is faithful and just to forgive us our sins and purify us from all unrighteousness" (1 John 1:9). Ask for forgiveness for specific sins as the Holy Spirit shines his spotlight into your heart. Remember God forgives and makes all things new.

i is for intercession

"I looked for a man among them who would . . . stand before me in the gap on behalf of the land so I would not have to destroy it" (Ezek. 22:30). "I urge, then, first of all, that requests, prayers, intercession and thanksgiving be made for everyone" (1 Tim. 2:1). Plead for other people—especially those who are not able to plead for themselves. "Stand in the gap" for another so you can sense God's love for this person, this person's needs, and your part in meeting those needs.

p is for petition

"By prayer and petition . . . present your requests to God" (Phil. 4:6). Tell God your personal needs. Talk with God about your relationship with him, with those close to you, and with others. Share your desires. Ask God to make his will known in your life.

a is for adoration

"Let everything that has breath praise the LORD. Praise the LORD" (Ps. 150:6). End with praise and thanksgiving to Jesus.

—Reprinted by permission of Lorraine Espinosa.

Setting: individuals, families/households, small groups, large groups, congregations

Level: initial, intermediate

Time: medium, long, extended

Bidding Prayer

Bidding prayer is a form of intercessory prayer in which the prayer leader calls for specific prayers during the course of the prayer time. For example, "Let us pray for our world" (often followed by a listing of particular concerns, hot spots, crisis areas, and so on). Or, "Let us pray for the sick" (followed by a listing of specific names).

A period of silence follows the bidding—allowing people to pray for the need that has just been mentioned. (A variation allows people to pray for a short time aloud, either taking turns or simultaneously.) This prayer format allows people to become actively involved in prayer while still receiving some guidance.

Example from *The Book of Common Prayer*

Let us pray for the Church and for the world.

Grant, Almighty God, that all who confess your name may be united in your truth, live together in your love, and reveal your glory in the world.

Silence

Lord, in your mercy

Hear our prayer.

Guide the people of this land, and of all the nations, in ways of justice and peace; that we may honor one another and serve the common good.

Silence

Lord, in your mercy

Hear our prayer.

Give us all a reverence for the earth as your own creation, that we may use its resources rightly in the service of others and to your honor and glory.

Silence

Lord, in your mercy

Hear our prayer.

Bless all whose lives are linked with ours, and grant that we may serve Christ in them, and love one another as he loves us.

Silence

Lord, in your mercy

Hear our prayer.

Comfort and heal all those who suffer in body, mind, or spirit; give them courage and hope in their troubles, and bring them the joy of your salvation.

Silence

Lord, in your mercy

Hear our prayer.

Almighty and eternal God, ruler of all things in heaven and earth, mercifully accept the prayers of your people, and strengthen us to do your will; through Jesus Christ our Lord. Amen.

Setting: families/households, small groups, large groups, congregations

Level: initial, intermediate

Time: short, medium, long

Centering Prayer

Centering prayer is an attempt to eliminate the "outside noises" (lawns being mowed, children talking in the background, breakfast being prepared in the kitchen) and the "inside noises" (thoughts about things that didn't get done, plans for tomorrow, things we said or shouldn't have said). Before we can effectively listen for God, we must put away the distractions.

Centering prayer helps us focus on where we are and who we are—what the devotional masters often call "recollection." (The Quakers know this process as "c e n t e r i n g down.") Centering prayer cultivates a receptiveness to the quiet whisperings of God. As we listen with our whole being—heart, mind, soul, and strength—we place God at the center so that our whole, undistracted being focuses on him.

Centering prayer usually involves focusing on a "sacred word" such as a name or attribute of God and repeating it over and over very slowly. After settling into a quiet place, say the word as an invitation to God's presence. Whenever distracting thoughts enter your mind, repeat the word in order to refocus your thoughts. End the prayer with two or three minutes of additional silence.

Setting: individuals

Level: intermediate, intense

Time: medium, long

Richard Foster talks about a simple focusing exercise he calls "palms down, palms up." To begin this exercise, place your palms down as a symbol of your desire to release all your concerns to God. Inwardly you may pray, "Lord, I give you my anger toward Bob. I surrender my anxiety over not having enough money to pay the bills this month. I release my frustration with my daughter this afternoon." After several moments of surrender, turn your palms up as a symbol of your desire to receive from the Lord. Pray silently, "Lord, I would like to receive your divine love for Bob, your peace about my finances, your patience with my daughter." Having "centered down," spend the remaining moments in complete silence.

Classic Prayers

As a regular routine, or as a change of pace, reading the prayers of disciplined pray-ers can be helpful. Classic prayers provide a model for continued prayers, as well as challenge us to deal with issues we tend to overlook. Reading them slowly and repeatedly will help focus your attention on God's presence.

Consider praying the prayers of Martin Luther, John Wesley, Thomas à Kempis, Brother Lawrence, and the Taizé community. Some examples follow.

Lord, make me an instrument of your peace.
where there is hatred, let me sow love;
where there is injury, pardon;
where there is doubt, faith;
where there is despair, hope;
where there is darkness, light;
and where there is sadness, joy.

O Divine Master,
grant that I may not so much seek to be consoled as to console;
to be understood as to understand;
to be loved as to love.
For it is in giving that we receive;
it is in pardoning that we are pardoned;
and it is in dying that we are born to eternal life.

—St. Francis of Assisi

O High and glorious God,
enlighten my heart.
Give me unwavering faith,
sure hope,
and perfect love.
Give me deep humility,
wisdom and knowledge, that I may keep your commandments. Amen.

—Carlo Carretto

Behold, Lord, an empty vessel that needs to be filled. My Lord, fill it.
I am weak in the faith; strengthen me.
I am cold in love; warm me and make me fervent, that my love might go out to my
neighbor.
I do not have a strong and firm faith; at times I doubt, and am unable to trust you
altogether.
O Lord, help me.

—Martin Luther

Dear Jesus,
Help me to spread your fragrance everywhere I go.
Flood my soul with your spirit and life.
Penetrate and possess my whole being so utterly that my life may only be a radiance
of yours.
Shine through me
and be so in me
that every soul I come in contact with may feel your presence in my soul.
Let them look up and see no longer me
but only Jesus.
Stay with me
and then I shall begin to shine as you shine,
so to shine as to be a light to others.
The light, O Jesus, will be all from you;
none of it will be mine.
It will be shining on others through me.
Let me thus praise you in the way you love best: by shining on those around me.
Let me preach you without preaching,
not by words, but by my example;
by the catching force—
the sympathetic influence of what I do,
the evident fullness of the love my heart bears to you.

—Mother Teresa

Anima Christi (Soul of Christ)

Anima Christi, sanctifica me.	Soul of Christ, sanctify me.
Corpus Christi, salve me.	Body of Christ, save me.
Sanguis Christi, inebria me.	Blood of Christ, inebriate me.
Aqua lateris Christi, lava me.	Water from the side of Christ, wash me.
Passio Christi, conforta me.	Passion of Christ, strengthen me.
O bone Jesu, exaudi me.	O good Jesus, hear me.
Intra tua vulnera absconde me.	Within Thy wounds, hide me.
Ne permittas me separari a te.	Don't allow me to be separated from Thee.
Ab hoste maligno defende me.	From the malignant enemy, defend me.
In hora mortis meae voca me,	At the hour of my death, call me,
Et iube me venire ad te,	And enjoin me to come to Thee,
Ut cum Sanctus tuis laudem te	So that, with Thy saints, I praise Thee
In saecula saeculorum. Amen.	Forever and ever. Amen.

—Saint Ignatius

Grant me, O Lord, to know what I ought to know,
to love what I ought to love,
to praise what delights Thee most,
to value what is precious in Thy sight,
to hate what is offensive to Thee.
Do not suffer me to judge according to the sight of my eyes,
nor to pass sentence according to the hearing of the ears of ignorant men;
but to discern with a true judgment between things visible and spiritual,
and above all, always to inquire what is the good pleasure of Thy will.

—Thomas à Kempis

O God, you are the fountain of all truth; we ask you to protect your church from all
    false teaching.
Protect the Church
    from all teaching and preaching which would destroy men's faith;
    from all that removes the old foundations without putting anything in their place;
    from all that confuses the simple, that perplexes the seeker, that bewilders the
        way-faring man.
And yet at the same time protect the Church
    from the failure to face new truth;
    from devotion to words and ideas which the passing of the years has rendered
        unintelligible;
    from all intellectual cowardice and from all mental lethargy and sloth.
O God, send to your Church teachers
    whose minds are wise with wisdom;
    whose hearts are warm with love;
    whose lips are eloquent with truth.
Send to your Church teachers
    whose desire is to build and not to destroy;
    who are adventurous with the wise and yet gentle with the simple;
    who strenuously exercise the intellect, and who yet remember that the heart has
        reasons of its own.
Give to your Church preachers and teachers who can make known the Lord Jesus
    Christ to others because they know him themselves;
and give to your Church hearers, who, being freed from prejudice, will follow truth
    as blind men long for light.
This we ask through Jesus Christ our Lord. Amen.

—William Barclay

Scriptural examples

The prayers of Jesus
Matthew 6:9-13; 11:25-26; 26:39, 42; Luke 11:2-4; 23:34; John 11:41-42; 12:27-28; 17

The apostolic prayers
Ephesians 1:15-23; 3:13-21; Colossians 1:3-8, 9-12; 1 Thessalonians 1:2-3; 3:9-13; 2 Thessalonians 1:11-12

Setting: individuals, families/households, small groups, large groups, congregations

Level: initial, intermediate, intense

Time: short, medium

Resources

John Baillie, *A Diary of Private Prayer* (New York: Charles Scribner's Sons, 1949).

Henri J.M. Nouwen, *A Cry for Mercy* (New York: Doubleday, 1981).

Kenneth G. Phifer, *A Book of UnCommon Prayer* (Nashville: Upper Room, 1981).

Mother Teresa, *Words to Love By* (Notre Dame, IN: Ave Maria Press, 1983).

Contemplative Prayer

Contemplative prayer is an advanced format that requires an extended period of time—without interruption—to spend in God's presence. Being contemplative is simply the practice of being deeply aware of God's presence; it is prayer with few or no words.

Examples of contemplative prayer include, but are not limited to:

- Art/media meditation (Icons have stirred no little controversy throughout church history, however, the Orthodox tradition has long used icons to train and focus the mind on God. The major misconception is that using icons is the equivalent of praying to images—a violation of the second commandment. Proponents argue they are praying to God through the icon—that is, the image merely serves to focus their attention away from themselves and onto God. Paintings, sculptures, stained glass, or a natural object, such as a flower, tree, mountain, or river, are some common icons.)

- Biblical imagination

- Centering prayer

- Guided or bidding prayer

- *Lectio divina*

- Music meditation

- Prayer imaging (Some contemplatives feel using the imagination distracts from contemplation.)

- Praying the Psalms

- Praying Scripture

- Silence

In pursuing contemplative prayer, consider the following steps:

retreat

Establish a regular time and place to give God your undivided attention. The place should be free from distractions like telephone, television, people, and distracting noises. Take your Bible, prayer journal, and a pen. Plan on setting aside at least an hour. While this prayer format can be used at any time, those who use this prayer format as a discipline recommend at least two to three times a week.

focus

This is the time of your day you have set aside to seek the face of God. As you begin to quiet yourself, other "noises" will seem to increase. Initially you will become more conscious of external noises—from the refrigerator hum to the birds chirping. As you work through the external noises, internal noises will sound: things you need to do, things you have forgotten to do, and so on. These are normal, but distracting. Begin in centering prayer.

listen

Listening is hard work. With the "noises" quieted, acknowledge God's presence; center your mind on him. Relax your body. Get comfortable. Assume one of the biblical prayer positions—bowing, kneeling, standing, hands raised, or prostrate—and listen in silence. Do not rush this time—for those new to this prayer format it may initially take several hours before you "hear" God.

pray

Prayer is hard kingdom work. Vary the prayer format periodically. Include the aspects of praise, thanksgiving, intercession, confession, and petition. In the midst of the battle take periodic breaks (rest) to contemplate the greatness of God, the person of Christ, and the power of his Spirit. When spending extended time in contemplative prayer, alternate prayer with listening.

journal (optional)

Journaling is a return to words. As a result, some contemplatives prefer not to journal. But while journaling may be considered optional, it is often a very helpful aspect of contemplative prayer. Note your thoughts about the time you have spent listening to God. Write out your prayers. (See also Prayer Journaling, pp. 92-93.)

The goal of contemplative prayer, as Richard Foster notes, is "to bring this stance of listening prayer into the course of everyday experience. This does not come immediately. However, over time we experience more and more an inward attentiveness to the Divine Whisper throughout all life's motions—balancing the checkbook, vacuuming the floor, visiting with neighbors or business associates" (*Prayer: Finding the Heart's True Home*, p. 163).

Setting: individuals

Level: intermediate, intense

Time: extended

Resources

Tricia McCary Rhodes, *The Soul at Rest: A Journey into Contemplative Prayer* (Minneapolis: Bethany House Publishers, 1996).

———. "God's Healing Oil: The Ministry of Contemplative Prayer," *Pray!* (July/August 1999), pp. 22-24.

Richard Foster, *Prayer: Finding the Heart's True Home* (San Francisco: Harper, 1992), pp. 155-166.

Corporate Prayer

Some would define corporate prayer as praying with other Christians. But a group of people in a room praying is no more corporate prayer than a few people sitting in a room are a small group. Corporate prayer is more than individual prayer in a group setting. Corporate prayer is a group of people who have come together to discover together what the Holy Spirit is asking them to pray together. Multiple in number, they come before the Lord as one. Corporate prayer is "praying in agreement" (see pp. 39-40) with all the people present together.

In some traditions, corporate prayer involves one person praying at a time while the others support and encourage the pray-er with their silence (praying in agreement) or simple words of support (a periodic "amen," for example). The pray-er speaks for all those who are praying. In this sense, the pastoral (or congregational) prayer is corporate prayer.

In other traditions, corporate prayer involves multiple people praying aloud at the same time. In some cases, this corporate prayer is as a large group, in other cases the large group may be broken down into small groups or triads. This is the common prayer format

We always open our services with everyone present praying together at the same time. When I hear my people praying, it sounds like the forceful roar of a mighty waterfall.
—Rev. Paul Cho, *Prayer: Key to Revival*, pp. 101-102

in Korean churches and many black American churches.

different types of corporate prayer

- Spouses

- Family

- Prayer partners

- Prayer triads

- Small groups

- Meetings (meetings with a primary agenda other than prayer—for example, a church board)

- Prayer meetings (meetings with the primary agenda of prayer)

- Prayer gatherings (for example, prayer walks, prayer journeys, concerts of prayer)

- Congregational worship

- Regional worship (multiple congregations/denominations worshiping and praying together)

- National initiatives (for example, denominational assemblies, National Day of Prayer Broadcast)

- International initiatives (for example, World Day of Prayer, Conference on Prayer and Fasting)

guidelines for corporate prayer

1. Determine the procedure you will follow (large group vs. small group; individual prayers vs. simultaneous prayers; and so on).

2. If you plan to invite people to pray individually . . .

   • Limit individual prayer time to two to three minutes.

   • If the group is large, use a microphone.

   • Do not allow participants to preach or instruct in prayer.

   • Break into small groups to enable more people to pray (aloud) more often. (This is also a good way to transition people from one format to another.)

   • Begin by requesting several people to pray for the Lord's direction. In some cases, the Holy Spirit may have already indicated the direction/ theme of prayer to the leader. If not, encourage each person present to be sensitive to the Spirit's leading by carefully listening to others. Once the direction appears set, the leader should assist keeping the intercessors "on track."

3. If you will invite people to pray aloud at the same time . . .

   • Encourage people to begin by praying for protection.

   • Provide a theme (for example, "revival" or "unity") or sufficient specifics (names and needs of people) so people can pray effectively.

4. Pray the promises/prayers of the Scripture.

5. Focus on asking/petition/intercession (avoid explaining, God already knows).

6. Don't be afraid of silence. Silence is often very appropriate. Praying quietly is as important and effective as praying aloud.

transitioning

If you are accustomed to praying individually and would like to adapt a style where people pray "in concert" (all together aloud), consider the following steps.

1. Break into small groups. Encourage people to pray aloud—one at a time—in their small group. This will assist some people in overcoming their tendency toward self-consciousness when praying aloud.

2. Break into pairs where partners take turns praying aloud. Providing prayer request cards, focus cards, and/or a specific theme or need will facilitate this level of prayer.

3. In the small groups, spend a few moments sharing your requests first. Then invite all participants to pray at once in low voices. No one hears specific words, just murmurs. The sound this makes is the beautiful sound of prayer.

4. Try praying in the small groups for a short period of time where everyone prays aloud for specific needs and/or according to a predefined theme.

5. Once steps 1 through 4 have been taught, practiced, and integrated into small groups, introduce the same steps into your prayer meeting (and/or worship).

6. Go very slowly. The transition can often take years. This prayer format may be difficult to do successfully if your group/ congregation is not accustomed to it.

Setting: families/households, small groups, large groups, congregations

Level: initial, intermediate, intense

Time: short, medium, long, extended

Resource
David Bryant, *Concerts of Prayer* (Ventura, CA: Regal Books, 1998).

Evangelistic Prayer

What would your city be like if every neighbor and neighborhood were prayed for daily? It would be a city in transformation with many people coming to Christ! That's what God wants. God's desire is for all people to be saved and for all of us to "live peaceful and quiet lives in all godliness and holiness" (1 Tim. 2:2).

What will it take? God's plan to transform personal lives and whole cities calls for prayer—believers praying for their neighbors and being available to them. A neighbor, as defined by Jesus' parable of the Good Samaritan (Luke 10), is any person who needs your help.

examples of evangelistic prayer

H.O.P.E. (Houses of Prayer Everywhere) Ministries has introduced an evangelistic prayer strategy. It calls for praying . . .

5 blessings for

5 neighbors for

5 minutes a day for

5 days a week for

5 weeks.

H.O.P.E. encourages intercessors to pray for their neighbors using the word *bless* as an acrostic:

Body—health, protection, strength

- for physical health and well-being
- for protection from injury, disease, depression
- for appropriate rest; for strength; for energy

Labor—work, income, security

- for a blessing on their business
- for a blessing on fulfillment in their job; for meaningful employment
- for a blessing on their coworkers— to make working pleasant

Emotional—joy, peace, hope

- for the strength to have victory over depression, stress, and other difficulties
- for joy and fulfillment in life
- for acceptance of God's will in life

Social—love, marriage, family, friends

- for the relationship between spouses
- for the relationships in their immediate family; for their children
- for their relationship with their parents
- for their friends

• for a desire to live according to God's Word in all relationships

Spiritual—salvation, faith, grace

• for a hunger to read, study, and understand God's Word and obey it

• for a growing and uninterrupted prayer life

• for a growing sense of awe for God; for thanksgiving for his protection, provision, and power

• for the power and perseverance to resist sin and temptation

• for a meaningful church relationship; for unity with other believers

The "Celebrate Jesus" prayer initiative of Mission America encourages people to use the following guide to pray for the unsaved:

• Ask God to open their spiritual eyes (2 Cor. 4:4).

• Ask God to set them free from spiritual captivity (2 Tim. 2:25-26).

• Ask God to give them ears to hear (Matt. 13:15), faith to believe (Acts 20:21), and the will to respond (Rom. 10:9).

• Ask God to send people into the person's life to witness to them (Matt. 9:38).

• Ask God for ways to build caring relationships (1 Cor. 9:22).

• Ask God for opportunities to witness (Col. 4:3).

• Ask God for boldness to witness (Acts 4:29).

• Ask God for an opportunity to invite them to a "harvest" event (Luke 14:23).

Setting: individuals, families/households, small groups, large groups, congregations

Level: initial, intermediate, intense

Time: short, medium, long

Resources

Alvin J. VanderGriend, *Make Your Home a Lighthouse* (Grand Rapids, MI: H.O.P.E. Ministries).

―――――. *Developing a Prayer-Care-Share Lifestyle* (Grand Rapids, MI: H.O.P.E. Ministries, 1999).

Fasting and Prayer

In Matthew 6:16-18—Jesus' instructions on fasting—Jesus uses the phrase "When you fast." Notice that he didn't say, "*If* you fast." Fasting isn't an optional activity for believers.

The word *fasting* literally means "to cover the mouth." So, in fasting, we cover the entrances or accesses to our inner being. While traditionally fasting has been limited to abstaining from eating and drinking, people are increasingly fasting from many things. Fasting—"covering the entrances" —ought to include our eyes and ears as well as our mouth. We ought to filter what is taken into our heart as well as into our stomach. As a result, people are increasingly fasting from things like television/radio, a specific habit, reading the newspaper, and sex.

Believers around the world are rediscovering the power of combining fasting with prayer. Miraculous interventions of God, revivals, and healings continually occur as the result of prayer and fasting. Yet, while the Bible refers to fasting almost a hundred times, it is almost totally absent as a practice in the lives of North American Christians.

The basic concept of fasting is simple: when the empty stomach growls or the mind wants to fill itself with a meaningless sitcom, we turn those urges into a call to pray and to spend time with God. That means that during a time of fasting, prayer is significantly increased and we are brought closer to God.

While most fasting is done on an individual basis, a growing number of denominations, churches, small groups, and pastors (as well as communities, cities, regions, even nations) are beginning to pray and fast together for God's forgiveness, for spiritual direction, and for revival.

when to fast

- When we need to hear from God more clearly. (In Ex. 34:28, Moses fasted, heard from God, and then "wrote on the tablets the words of the covenant—the Ten Commandments.")

- When there is an urgency in spiritual matters. (In 1 Kings 19:8, Elijah fasted because of the urgency of the moment.)

- When we are confronted with an unsolvable problem. (In 2 Chron. 20, King Jehoshaphat called the nation to fast when he was threatened by three armies.)

- When in need of God's protection. (In Ezra 8:21-23, Ezra called the returning Jewish exiles to fast and pray for their return to Jerusalem.)

- When we need to know the heart and feel the burden of the Lord. (In Ezra 10:6, Ezra prayed and fasted when he felt the heart of God.)

- When seeking God's direction and guidance to proceed. (In Esther 4, Queen Esther asked all Jews in Susa to fast for three days while she sought favor from King Xerxes to save her people.)

- When we need to develop a compassionate spirit. (In Isa. 58:7, fasting is enjoined in order to "share your food with the hungry and to provide the poor wanderer with shelter.")

- When we must break the yoke of bondage. (In Isa. 58:6, fasting is used to "loose the chains of injustice and untie the cords of the yoke.")

- When we need healing. (In Isa. 58:8, the prophet promised "quick healing" following fasting.)

- When we seek answers to our prayers. (In Isa. 58:9, Isaiah says, "Then [after fasting] you will call, and the LORD will answer.")

- When we desire a spiritual breakthrough. (In Dan. 10:3, Daniel got serious in prayer and fasting because he needed God to intervene.)

- When we humble ourselves before God. (In Jonah 3:5 and 10, the Ninevites, in responding to Jonah's call to repentance, believed in God, acknowledged their guilt, and called on God.)

- When we need to refocus on God (instead of on other people), on the invisible (instead of on the visible), and on heaven (instead of on the things of this earth). (In Matt. 6:16-18, Jesus reminds us that the intention of fasting is not the praise of men, but the presence of God.)

- When we are beginning a new adventure in ministry. (In Luke 4:1-2, Jesus fasted for focus at the start of his mission.)

- When we are contrite over our sins, confess, and seek God's repentance. (In Acts 9:9, Paul fasted when he realized how wrong he had been.)

- When we need to be consecrated, or set apart, for special ministry. (In Acts 13:2-3 and 14:23 the early church leaders fasted and prayed when electing and commissioning leaders.)

- When we seek to immerse ourselves in the discipline of the Christian faith. (In Rom. 13:14, Gal. 5:16, and Col. 3:5 fasting is used to deny the power of the flesh and to invite the Spirit to come in.)

> **If we want to pray with power, we should pray with fasting. This, of course, does not mean we should fast every time we pray, but there are times in emergency or special crisis when men of earnestness will withdraw themselves even from the gratification of natural appetite that they may give themselves up totally to prayer.**
> **—R. A. Torrey,**
> ***How to Pray***

types of fasts

There are three primary types of fasting:

1. The *common* (also known as "normal" or "typical") fast. This involves total abstinence from food, but includes taking liquids, such as water and fruit and vegetable juices. When participating in a common fast, drink at least twelve cups of water a day. Jesus' extended fast in the wilderness (Matt. 4:2, Luke 4:2) was a common fast. Scripture indicates Jesus "ate nothing during these days." It is assumed that he did drink.

2. The *absolute* (also known as "complete" or "total") fast. This involves abstinence from both food and water. Scripture tells us that "for three days [Saul] was blind, and did not eat or drink anything" (Acts 9:9). Also, "Moses was there with the LORD forty days and forty nights without

eating bread or drinking water" (Ex. 34:28). (This was obviously a miracle; drinking nothing for forty days is fatal.) See also Ezra 10:6 and Esther 4:16.

3. The *partial* (also known as "selective") fast. This involves restricting certain foods and drink, rather than completely abstaining from food and drink. Such a fast can be from meat, candy, chocolate, coffee, caffeine, television, and so on. "I ate no choice food; no meat or wine touched my lips; and I used no lotions at all until the three weeks were over" (Dan. 10:3).

lengths of fasts

The length of a fast is tied directly to the purpose of the fast. Some fasts are established on a regular (weekly or monthly) basis in order to promote personal spiritual growth. A longer fast of thirty to forty days may be in response to a major life crisis. Individual fasts are normally longer than corporate fasts.

The type of fast also determines its length. An absolute fast has obvious limitations. Because the body normally cannot sustain life after seven days without water, absolute fasts are commonly short. Partial fasts, where certain items are eliminated, can last for extended periods of time.

guidelines for fasting

1. Decide on your purpose. Why are you fasting?

2. Decide on the type and duration of the fast.

3. Decide if you are going to fast alone or invite others to join with you.

4. Prepare. (Planning for a corporate fast takes more time and preparation than preparing for an individual fast, but preparation is essential in every fast!)

Prepare spiritually. Begin with repentance. Ask God to bless your fast. Ask God to reveal to you what you should be doing during your fast.

Prepare physically. Get plenty of sleep. Have the appropriate juices available. Consult a doctor. (This is especially important for extended fasts and for those with health issues.) Reduce caffeine intake—tea, cola, coffee, and carbonated drinks—several days before an extended fast. (Otherwise you will experience withdrawal symptoms during your fast).

5. Participate. Adopt a schedule of worship, prayer, rest, and liquids. Always keep the focus on God. Use the time normally spent eating for prayer.

6. End the fast gradually. (Don't go to an "all-you-can-eat" buffet immediately after your fast!)

7. Wait on the Lord. He answers prayer.

Setting: individuals, families/households, small groups, large groups, congregations

Level: intense

Time: medium, long, extended

Resources

Bill Bright, *7 Basic Steps to Prayer and Fasting* (Orlando: New Life Publications).

———. *The Transforming Power of Fasting and Prayer* (Orlando: New Life Publications, 1997).

Jerry Falwell and Elmer Towns, *Fasting Can Change Your Life* (Ventura, CA: Regal Books, 1998).

Ronnie W. Floyd and Bill Bright, *The Power of Prayer and Fasting* (Nashville: Broadman and Holman, 1997).

Richard Foster, *Celebration of Discipline: Paths to Spiritual Growth* (New York: Harper and Row, 1978).

John Piper, *A Hunger for God: Desiring God Through Fasting and Prayer* (Wheaton, IL: Crossway Books, 1997).

Elmer Towns, *Fasting for Spiritual Breakthrough* (Ventura, CA: Regal Books, 1996).

Hand of Prayer

When God created us he built in one of the most effective reminders to pray—our hand. This insightful look at prayer is credited to a nurse who, when asked by a patient for some spiritual direction, gave him the following advice.

the thumb

Your thumb is nearest to you. Begin your prayers by praying for those closest to you: family members, relatives, and friends. They are the easiest to remember. To pray for your loved ones is, as C.S. Lewis once said, a "sweet duty."

the first finger

The next finger is the pointing finger. This is a reminder to thank God for those who point you to Jesus—parents, church school teachers, youth pastors and ministers. They need support and wisdom in pointing others in the right direction. Also pray for those whom you can point to Jesus.

the middle finger

The next finger is the tallest finger. It reminds you to pray for those in authority—political leaders, school teachers, police, and firemen. Pray for the president, leaders in business and industry, and administrators.

These people shape our nation and guide public opinion. They need God's guidance.

the ring finger

The fourth finger is the ring finger. Surprising to many is the fact that this is our weakest finger. It should remind you to pray for those who are weak, in trouble, in pain, or going through difficult times. They need your prayers day and night. You cannot pray too much for them.

the pinky

And finally comes your little finger, the smallest finger of all, which is where you should place yourself in relation to God and others. As the Bible says, "The least shall be the greatest among you." Your pinky finger should remind you to pray for yourself. By the time you have prayed for the other four groups, your own needs will be put into proper perspective and you will be able to pray for yourself more effectively.

—Reprinted by permission from *Prayer* 99/6 (Grand Rapids, MI: CRC Publications, 1999).

Setting: individuals, families/households, small groups, large groups, congregations

Level: initial

Time: short, medium

Hour of Prayer

Some people are overwhelmed by the concept of spending extended time in prayer. How do you go from spending five minutes at a time in prayer (a struggle for some people) to spending an entire hour in prayer? The answer is relatively simple. Divide the hour into twelve five-minute segments.

1. **Praise.** "I will praise you as long as I live, and in your name I will lift up my hands" (Ps. 63:4). All prayer should begin with a recognition of God's nature. The Lord's Prayer—the model for all praying—begins with "Our Father in heaven, hallowed be your name." Praise is that aspect of prayer that esteems God for his virtues and accomplishments.

2. **Waiting.** "Be still before the LORD and wait patiently for him" (Ps. 37:7). Time should also be given to being "quiet" in God's presence. This is not meditation or just a time for listening; it is simply taking time to let God love you.

3. **Confession.** "Search me, O God, and know my heart; test me and know my anxious thoughts. See if there is any offensive way in me, and lead me in the way everlasting" (Ps. 139:23-24). The psalmist asked God to search his heart for unconfessed sin. He knew sin was one of the greatest roadblocks to answered prayer. Early in prayer we need to make time for confession. This clears the way for powerful praying.

4. **The Word.** "The law of the LORD is perfect, reviving the soul. The statutes of the LORD are trustworthy, making wise the simple" (Ps. 19:7-8). Praise is giving back to God the words he has spoken. When we bring God's Word into our prayer, we commend God for his goodness and faithfulness and open our eyes to new possibilities from God. At this point in prayer, read God's Word.

5. **Intercession.** "Ask of me and I will make the nations your inheritance, the ends of the earth your possession" (Ps. 2:8). Our prayer now centers on intercession for a lost and dying world. Spend time praying for others who have desperate needs.

6. **Petition.** "They asked, and he brought them quail and satisfied them with the bread of heaven" (Ps. 105:40). This aspect of prayer concerns our personal needs. To petition God is to open our need to God through prayer.

7. **The Word.** "I have hidden your word in my heart. . . . Your word is a lamp to my feet and a light for my path" (Ps. 119:11, 105). Earlier you read God's Word. Now, pray God's Word. Bring actual Scripture into your prayer. We can never pray out of God's will when we pray God's Word.

8. **Thanksgiving.** "Enter his gates with thanksgiving and his courts with praise;

give thanks to him and praise his name" (Ps. 100:4). When Paul wrote to the Philippians, he instructed them to offer prayer and supplication "with thanksgiving." Thanksgiving differs from praise: praise recognizes God for who he is, and thanksgiving recognizes God for specific things he has done.

9. **Singing.** "Worship the LORD with gladness; come before him with joyful songs" (Ps. 100:2). Melody is a gift of God for the purpose of singing praises unto him. Many Christians, unfortunately, have never learned the beauty of singing a "new" song unto God during prayer. These songs may come straight from the heart with the Holy Spirit creating the melody. Paul spoke of singing "spiritual songs." To sing unto the Lord is to worship God in melody.

10. **Meditation.** "Blessed is the man who does not walk in the counsel of the wicked or stand in the way of sinners or sit in the seat of mockers. But his delight is in the law of the LORD, and on his law he meditates day and night" (Ps. 1:1-2). In meditation our mind is very active; to meditate is to ponder spiritual themes in reference to God.

11. **Listening.** "Be still, and know that I am God" (Ps. 46:10). Whether through God's written Word or by the inner "still, small voice" of the Holy Spirit, God speaks to praying Christians. But we must take time to listen.

12. **Praise.** "Praise the LORD. Praise God in his sanctuary; praise him in his mighty heavens. . . . Let everything that has breath praise the LORD. Praise the LORD" (Ps. 150:1, 6). We begin our prayer by recognizing God's nature, and we end in a similar fashion.

—From *The Hour That Changes the World* by Dick Eastman, © 1978, Baker Book House. Dick Eastman currently is the International President of Every Home for Christ, Colorado Springs, Colorado.

Setting: individuals, families/households, small groups

Level: intermediate

Time: long, extended

Intercessory Prayer

Intercession is the responsibility and privilege of every believer. It is the work of building the kingdom of God. Persistent and passionate intercession is a fundamental building block in a church becoming a house of prayer. Every believer, as a member of the priesthood of believers, must daily bring the needs of the kingdom and its citizens into the throne room of God.

While God calls every believer to intercede for others, he gives some the gift of intercession. The gift of intercession differs from the call to intercede primarily in degree. Those with the gift of intercession pray more frequently, for longer periods of time, and with more intensity. It is not uncommon for someone gifted in intercession to pray for several hours a day.

Those who are willing to make and keep a daily commitment to pray for others are, by definition, intercessors. Intercessors "stand in the gap" and pray for others—often when others cannot pray for themselves. Intercessors intentionally place themselves on the front lines of the battlefield and assume all the risks that go with it. Intercessory prayer is hard work that involves little recognition. For all these reasons, intercessors are important people in the God's kingdom.

Intercessors must live holy lives. Living with unconfessed sin blocks prayer. The psalmist writes, "If I had cherished sin in my heart, the Lord would not have listened" (Ps. 66:18). People who live with unconfessed sin also give the devil a foothold from which to wage spiritual warfare.

Moses was an intercessor. Exodus 17:8-13 describes one of his moments of intercession. While Joshua led the Israelite military into battle with the Amalekites, Moses raised his hands in prayer. As Joshua fought the physical battle, Moses fought the spiritual war. Although Moses did not receive the recognition Joshua did when the battle was won, the victory would not have happened without his prayers.

Because both the physical and spiritual sides of the Amalekite-Israel battle are recorded for us, we can see the whole picture. But since few people actually see intercessors at work, few people realize the connection between prayer and spiritual victory. Few people realize the hours of intercession behind the fall of the Berlin Wall, the rapidly growing church in China, or the powerful Promise Keeper conferences. As John Wesley said, "God moves in response to prayer."

intercessory prayer is . . .

- characterized by an overwhelming sense of urgency, expectation, even desperation. Intercessors pray about the fundamental issues of life: saving the lost, terminal illnesses, hunger relief, protection from persecution, the unity of the church, and so on. While the small or routine issues of life are also important, intercessory prayer usually deals with the eternal issues.

- simple. Having invited us as his children, God expects us to act as children—simple, dependent, and trusting. God isn't interested in flowery words or theological pronouncements. God is interested in our hearts.

- persistent. Sometimes the answer comes instantly. Sometimes God's answer takes years, decades, even centuries. But intercessors continue to pray. John Calvin once said, "We must repeat the same supplications not twice or three times only, but as often as we have need, a hundred and a thousand times. . . . We must never be weary in waiting for God's help."

- often painful. A wise person once said, "Prayer that costs little is worth little." The pain of prayer is found in waiting for God's answers, in the inconvenient times he prompts us to pray (such as waking us up in the middle of the night), and sometimes in addressing the answers he gives.

- expectant. "We have not because we ask not," Jesus said. How many prayers have not been prayed because the pray-er didn't really believe God would answer that prayer? Not only can God deal with the little issues of life, he can handle the universe. Bombard God with great requests!

- specific. Don't simply ask God to "bless all the missionaries." Instead, name them one by one. Address their specific needs. Don't just ask God to forgive all your sins; enumerate them. Don't just ask God to heal the sick; name the person, name the illness, implore God's healing.

- bold. While the primary goal of an intercessor is to discover God's will and to ask for God's assistance in conforming to it, intercessors may boldly petition God to transform his will—to save one who is lost, to heal one who is dying, to bless one who is infertile.

types of intercession

While most believers are called to be general intercessors, God calls some to specific types of intercession. *General intercessors* pray for a little of everything: their loved ones, the church and its members, their neighborhood and city, their nation and world (see 1 Sam. 7:2). *Crisis intercessors* pray for those in crisis—terminal illnesses, news headlines, the death of friends and family members, and so on (Gen. 18:20-33; 19:16-17, 29). *Personal intercessors* feel God's call to pray for specific individuals (Luke 22:31; Heb. 7:25; Rom. 8:26) such as missionaries, other Christian leaders, and so on. *Warfare (strategic) intercessors* pray against the devil's strongholds in their church and city and for the lost (Matt. 23:37-39). *Prophetic intercessors* hear God speaking to them words of encouragement, warning, and direction (2 Kings 6:12-18).

Intercession is not always exciting, but it is always hard work. It is also imperative for a church that wants to become a house of prayer. (See also Ministry of Intercession, pp. 160-161.)

Setting: individuals, families/households, small groups, large groups, congregations

Level: intermediate, intense

Time: short, medium, long, extended

Resources

Joy Dawson, *Principles for Effective Intercession* (YWAM, P.O. Box 296, Sunland, CA 91040).

Dutch Sheets, *Intercessory Prayer: How God Can Use Your Prayers to Move Heaven and Earth* (Ventura, CA: Regal Books, 1996).

Alice Smith, *Beyond the Veil* (Ventura, CA: Regal Books, 1996).

Intercessory Worship

Nothing is more important in our relationship with God than worship and prayer. Unfortunately, many believers separate them, thinking the first has to do with music and a message (Sunday mornings); the later with petition and intercession (their personal devotions). This prayer format brings worship and prayer together—like two sides of the same coin.

Both worship and prayer move us into God's presence. The Bible often describes this connection. In the Old Testament, for example, tabernacle worship appears to have been continuous (at least during the times of Israel's faithfulness to God):

> Intercessory prayer is the purifying bath into which the individual and the fellowship must enter every day.
> —Dietrich Bonhoeffer

- Those who were musicians, heads of Levite families, stayed in the rooms of the temple and were exempt from other duties because they were responsible for the work day and night (1 Chron. 9:33).

- David left Asaph and his associates before the ark of the covenant of the Lord to minister there regularly (lit. continuously) (1 Chron. 16:37; see also vv. 39-40).

- In describing the responsibilities of the Levites, David said, "Four thousand are to praise the Lord with the musical instruments . . ." (1 Chron. 23:5).

- In 1 Chronicles 25, David sets a group of people apart "for the ministry of prophesying, accompanied by harps, lyres, and cymbals . . . they numbered 288" (vv. 1, 7).

- While some believe Amos 9:11-12 (quoted in Acts 15:16-17) refers to a literal restoring of the tabernacle in Jerusalem before the end of the world, proponents of this prayer format understand that the Great Commission will be fulfilled when the symbolic "tabernacle of David" is restored—when salvation and revival are released to the nations through continuous intercessory worship.

In the New Testament, Paul calls the church to "pray continuously" (1 Thess. 5:17). In the visions given to the apostle John, the continuous worship of the Old Testament and the continuous call to prayer of the New Testament come together. In Revelation 5 we find the elders presenting God with their harps (worship, music) and their bowls of incense (prayers).

> The four living creatures and the twenty-four elders fell down before the Lamb. Each one had a harp and they were holding golden bowls full of incense, which are the prayers of the saints. And they sang a new song: "You are worthy to take the scroll and to open its seals, because you were slain, and with your blood you purchased men for God from every tribe

and language and people and nation. You have made them to be a kingdom and priests to serve our God, and they will reign on the earth." (Rev. 5:8-10)

The six petitions of the familiar Lord's Prayer illustrate the blend of worship and prayer. The first three petitions focus on God (worship), and the final three focus on human needs (intercession). More than teaching us a prayer to recite or even a pattern to use, Jesus demonstrated how worship and intercession go together. Ross Parsley, pastor of worship at New Life Church in Colorado Springs, told the participants at the First Annual Prayer Leaders Conference: "We begin thanking God and exalting him for who he is and for what he's done and then, almost seamlessly, we move into wanting to please him and live a life worthy of what he's done for us. This is our petition."

Here is a typical pattern for intercessory worship:

- An intercessor prays (usually a short prayer of one to three minutes).

- Singing (one or more singers may paraphrase the prayer in song).

- An intercessor adds to the prayer (may be the same intercessor as above).

- Singing (the same or a different singer echoes the prayer in song).

- This format repeats.

The emphasis in intercessory worship is on the apostolic prayers, the hymns of Scripture (particularly Revelation and Song of Solomon), and the singing and praying of the Psalms (the Scripture's hymnbook). As a result, most of the prayers that are used have already been written. This allows for some pre-planning of intercessory worship. At the same time, intercessory worship is open to the leading of the Spirit: intercessors and musicians must be well acquainted with the prayers of Scripture and worship music in order to allow for spontaneity and flexibility.

Mike Bickle, director of the International House of Prayer (IHOP) in Kansas City, is developing an around-the-clock intercessory worship center in Kansas City that will provide worship and prayer opportunities in eighty-four consecutive two-hour prayer meetings every week. Worship teams, musicians, and intercessors work together to lead the worship. The IHOP offers three types of prayer meetings throughout the week: *intercessory worship* that involves spiritual warfare and prayers for the city; *devotional worship* that provides opportunity to sit at the feet of Jesus; and *worship from the Word* that includes singing the Psalms, Song of Solomon, and hymns of Revelation, often in a corporate, antiphonal manner.

While an around-the-clock intercessory worship ministry is probably not feasible for most churches, this prayer format is bringing churches together in cities and regions and making an impact on their surrounding communities.

Setting: congregations

Level: intense

Time: extended

Resource

Friends of the Bridegroom
   (Mike Bickle's ministry)
P.O. Box 832
Grandview, MO 64030
www.ihopkc.com. or www.fotb.com

The Jesus Prayer

The Jesus Prayer is perhaps the simplest and yet the most profound of prayers. In its common form it is "Lord, Jesus Christ, son of God, have mercy on me, a sinner." On some occasions, however, the prayer is shortened to include only the name "Jesus."

According to Mark Galli and James Bell Jr., in *The Complete Idiot's Guide to Prayer* (Macmillan, 1999, pp. 235-237), this ancient phrase sums up the essence of the gospel and has been used throughout history to draw people closer to God. It contains the four basic aspects of prayer:

- **Adoration.** The prayer begins by recognizing that Jesus is Lord.

- **Confession.** The prayer is spoken by "a sinner." This specifically emphasizes that which is otherwise implied. The pray-er seeks God's mercy.

- **Thanksgiving.** This prayer is a recognition that Jesus has had mercy in the past, that he will heal our hearts, and that he will continue to have mercy.

- **Intercession.** This prayer contains a personal petition. By simply changing the singular "me" to "us" it becomes a prayer of intercession.

the process

- Begin by sitting still and quieting both outside and inside noises.

- Start praying. Pray the prayer slowly, softly, and quietly.

- Rest and reflect.

- Repeat the prayer slowly, softly, and quietly. As the prayer is repeated the emphasis may move from one word to the next with the pray-er reflecting afterward on that word or phrase.

- The process may continue for several minutes or hours. Continue for as long as you can.

While the Jesus Prayer is a prayer format that has been passed down through the centuries—particularly in the Eastern Orthodox church—it offers the pray-er some flexibility. Wilfrid Stinissen writes:

The Jesus Prayer can easily be fitted to liturgical times and holidays. During the Christmas season, one can, for example, pray: "Lord, Jesus Christ, who became man for me, have mercy on me." During Easter, "Lord, Jesus Christ, who arose for me, have mercy on me." At the feast of Transfiguration: "Lord, Jesus Christ, who became glorified on the mountain . . ." With variations, the prayer becomes an extension of the liturgy, it becomes a little liturgy which is in harmony with the Church's great liturgy. (*Praying in the Name of Jesus: The Ancient Wisdom of the Jesus Prayer*, p. 85)

Traditionally, there are two basic ways to pray this prayer, according to Galli and Bell. The first method is known as the "Prayer of the Heart," commonly practiced in the Eastern Orthodoxy's mystic tradition. The pray-er sits alone, looking down at his or her "heart" (the center of their being). Emptying one's mind of all other thoughts, the petitioner concentrates on the words of the prayer while repeating it silently—over and over. The involvement of a spiritual director is recommended when using this prayer method.

The second use of the Jesus Prayer is known as the "Prayer of Daily Life." In this method, the prayer is repeated silently or vocally at the beginning and the end of prayer. It might be prayed on the way to work, at lunch, during a coffee break, prior to retiring at night, and so on. The challenge of this method is to keep the praying meaningful and God-centered.

The Jesus Prayer may be spoken or prayed in silence. It always is prayed slowly and thoughtfully, normally with many seconds—even minutes—between repetitions.

Setting: individuals

Level: intermediate, intense

Time: long

Lectio Divina

Lectio divina, a form of praying the Scriptures, is a time-tested technique for experiencing God with both head and heart. The origins of *lectio divina* are monastic, but today this prayer format is being practiced by a large variety of people.

Benedict of Nursia (A.D. 480-547) began meditating four hours a day on the Scriptures, especially the Psalms. His practice soon became common in many monasteries. In the twelfth century, Guigo II further developed the various facets of "praying the Scriptures" and gave us the practice as we know it today.

The process has four basic steps with two important "bookends":

Bookend One: Select a time and place where you will be comfortable and uninterrupted. Begin with a period of silence. Prepare your heart to hear the Word properly. Express this desire to God in prayer. Share with God your desire to have his Word influence your life.

Step One: Read (*lectio*) a portion of Scripture. You can select a passage of your own choosing, use a Bible reading guide, or follow the monastic practice of selecting a book of Scripture to read through (not necessarily in one sitting). Set aside your commentary. Ignore the marginal comments and footnotes. Simply read the passage slowly. Expect God to underscore a word, phrase, or verse to speak directly to your heart. In the reading, the Word is received as a personal word from God ("What is God saying to me?") rather than a theological reading ("What is the exegesis of this passage?"). Reread the verses again slowly. Don't rush it.

Step Two: Reflect for a few moments on the word, phrase, or verse the Lord underscored. This is meditating (*meditatio*) on Scripture: How is God asking me to receive and implement this word? What memories, images, feelings, thoughts, hymns, or other Scripture passages does it bring to mind? What does the passage say about my heart, my character, my family, or my ministry? The monks described this aspect of the process as *ruminatio*, or rumination.

Step Three: Respond to the word or phrase. This is the time for Scripture to touch your heart. Ask youself: What am I feeling—joy, anticipation, lament, confession? How is the passage challenging me to pray? Respond in prayer to what you have heard God say in prayer (*oratio*). Brad Long says, "This *oratio*, or prayer of the heart, is a moving of the Holy Spirit, who melts us; and we begin to respond in awe, joy, and peace."

Step Four: Simply receive the presence of God. This is a time to be still and rest. This phase of contemplation (*contemplatio*) is simply enjoying the company of God. We can be encouraged, nourished, convicted, and comforted. This phase is a great time for contemplative prayer.

Bookend Two: Incorporate what you believe God has been saying to you. Throughout the day, ask the Holy Spirit to help you live the insights of the Scripture God gave to you in the morning.

Dorn Marmion, a Benedictine monk from Ireland (1858-1923), defined *lectio divina* this way: "We read *(lectio)* under the eye of God *(meditatio)* until the heart is touched *(oratio)* and leaps to flame *(contemplatio)*" (Thelma Hall, *Too Deep for Words*, p. 44).

lectio divina in a group

While *lectio divina* is a very personal and prayerful reading of Scripture, it can also be done effectively in small groups and even in corporate worship.

To do *lectio divina* in a small group, prepare by centering yourself in God's presence. Breathe gently. Offer a prayer for the group's openness to God's Spirit.

Bookend One: Open with a word of prayer asking God to still your noises and prepare you to hear his voice.

Step One—Reading. The first reader reads the passage twice, the second time more slowly. Be alert to a phrase or word that invites your attention. Share your phrase or word with the group.

Step Two—Reflecting: A second reader reads the passage again. Pay attention to the image or feeling that arises from your phrase or word. Speak your image or feeling to the group.

Step Three—Responding: A third reader reads the passage a fourth time. Be aware of how you experience God around your image or feeling as it relates to your phrase or word. Listen and respond to your image, feeling, phrase, or word for an extended amount of time. How is God present in and through this? You may sense God's reminder of being with you through a call, challenge, or other impression. You may find it helpful to journal your feelings and thoughts. Share your experience of God with the group.

Step Four—Resting/receiving. Commune alone with God during an extended silence. The leader concludes this time by speaking "Amen."

Bookend Two: This bookend can be done in several ways. Group members can hold each other accountable for implementing what God has pointed out; the group can spend time in prayer asking God to help them; the group can spend time in silence while members write down on an index card how they will follow through, and so on.

—Adapted from Tom Schwanda, "Praying the Scriptures with Head and Heart," *The Banner* (Nov. 9, 1998, pp. 24-26).

See page 366 for a corporate worship service built around *lectio divina*.

Setting: individuals, families/households, small groups

Level: intermediate, intense

Time: medium, long

Resources

Clifford Bajema, *At One with Jesus: Rediscovering the Secret of Lectio Divina* (Grand Rapids, MI: CRC Publications, 1998).

Thelma Hall, *Too Deep for Words: Rediscovering Lectio Divina* (New York: Paulist Press, 1988).

Listening Prayer

Listening to the voice of God is a major theme throughout Scripture. Yet it is often the forgotten part of prayer. Prayer is sometimes broken down into four parts: we speak, God listens, God speaks, we listen. In his book *Whole Prayer*, Walter Wangerin notes that our praying isn't complete until we have adequately listened to God.

Jesus listened to God, and he taught us that it is important for us to listen to God as well. This is evident throughout the gospels, but particularly in John 8:

- "What I have heard from him I tell the world" (John 8:26).

- "You are determined to kill me, a man who has told you the truth that I heard from God" (John 8:40).

- "He who belongs to God hears what God says" (John 8:47).

The primary way we hear God is through the Scriptures, God's inspired Word (Rom. 10:17; 2 Tim. 3:16-17; 2 Pet. 1:21). People cannot hear God if they do not read his Word. But God also speaks in other ways:
- through the conscience (the inner voice of God) (see Rom. 2:14-15).

> You can't build a relationship on one-way speeches. You need frequent, sustained, intimate contact between two persons, both of whom speak and both of whom listen. . . . Listening to God speak through his Holy Spirit is not only normal, it is essential.
> —Bill Hybels, *Too Busy Not to Pray*

- through believers worshiping together as the Holy Spirit offers a word from the Lord (see 1 Kings 19:12-13; 1 Cor. 14:1-5).

- through godly people (see 2 Tim. 1:5).

- through the creation (see Ps. 8; 19; Rom. 1:18-20).

It is important to remember that these messages are always subject to the Scriptures. They are not in addition to Scripture, nor are they equivalent to Scripture. Neither are they intended for universal application. Rather, they are individual (directed to a specific person, group, church, or ministry), timely (in answer to a prayer or a specific prompting of the Holy Spirit to do something), and specific (meant for a specific time and place).

ways to develop our listening

1. **Pose a question.** Write down the question in your journal as clearly as possible. Then begin to look for an answer. Keep the question in mind as you read and study Scripture, as you participate in your small group, as you pray, and as you talk with other Christians. The answer will come, not always as expected, but it *will* come if we are listening. If we don't ask the question, we are often unaware that God is speaking to us.

2. **Write a letter.** After a sustained period of silence and meditation, begin writing yourself a letter from God. While this may, at first, seem simply like your own thoughts, you may—upon reading and rereading it—discover a word from God: a truth of Scripture that addresses a nagging question; a word of encouragement when you are discouraged; a word of challenge to move you into ministry; a word of comfort when you feel despair.

3. **Address a problem.** In your morning devotions, ask God about resolving a particular problem. Be as clear about the issue as possible. Then try to remain conscious of God's voice throughout the day. Sometimes God speaks through mental pictures; sometimes he breaks into our thoughts; sometimes he speaks to us logically; sometimes he makes himself clear as we write. God often speaks through our giftedness.

4. *Lectio divina.* If you want to hear God speaking to you, set aside a block of undisturbed time. After selecting a passage of Scripture, simply follow the four basic steps of *lectio divina* (see pp. 73-74).

5. **Watch for God's promptings.**

   - Sometimes we wake up in the middle of the night for no apparent reason. Is God prompting us to pray for someone in particular? Follow that prompting.

   - Sometimes in the middle of our well-planned schedule, a space is created (the plane is delayed, an appointment doesn't show, an activity is completed quicker than anticipated). Instead of simply moving on to the next item, or immediately filling the space with more activity, ask God if he created the space so you might spend more time with him.

   - In the midst of a busy day we may get an inclination to call someone with a word of encouragement. Respond to that feeling.

   - In the middle of praying with your small group, God may prompt you to pray something or to say something following the prayer. Follow the prompting. (For example, after a time of prayer with the church staff, our prayer coordinator said she believed God was telling her we should lay hands on and bless the senior pastor. The rest of the staff agreed and offered to the pastor some much-needed encouragement in a difficult time.)

6. **Practice silence.** When our lives are "noisy" (filled with activities, demands, issues, stresses, and so on) it is difficult to hear God. In order to hear God we need to slow down physically and mentally and spend some time in silence. (The options mentioned under Contemplative Prayer, pp. 54-55, can help prepare you to hear God speaking.)

validating what we hear

When we hear something, we should always ask if it is from God before we act on it. The primary tool for determining God's voice—in contrast to all the other voices we hear—is Scripture. If what we "hear" contradicts God's written Word in any way, it is not a word from God.

In some cases, however, testing the "word" against the Word remains inconclusive. So God has also given us additional validating tests.

- A "word" from God will always reflect God and always give God glory. The Lord's word always brings the focus to himself, never to us.

- A "word" from God will always resonate with other believers. When God answers an inquiry, addresses our petitions, or calls us to a new adventure in faith/ministry, he seldom gives his "word" only to one person.

- A "word" from God will always resonate with intercessors that have been praying for a similar "word." For example, if a church's intercessors are all praying about beginning a certain ministry at the church, God does not say "yes" to some, "no" to others, and "wait" to still others.

- A "word" from God is always relevant to the time and issues at hand. God seldom reveals himself months or years before necessary; nor does he speak to issues that have since disappeared.

Terry Teykl, a national prayer leader, suggests we can know a "word" is God's voice if it

- reflects his nature,
- resonates with Scripture,
- promotes salvation in the city,
- addresses the sins of the community,
- fosters unity in the corporate body of Christ,
- offers mercy and forgiveness,
- challenges and builds our faith, and
- builds Christ's church.

Setting: individuals, small groups

Level: intermediate

Time: medium, long

Resources

Charles Coleman, *That Voice Behind You— God's Guidance in Daily Decisions* (Neptune, NJ: Loizeaux Brothers, 1991).

Cindy Jacobs, *The Voice of God* (Ventura, CA: Regal Books, 1995).

Peter Lord, *Hearing God* (Grand Rapids, MI: Baker Book House, 1988).

C. Peter Wagner, *Praying with Power* (Ventura, CA: Regal Books, 1997).

Lord's Prayer Pattern

While many prayer formats have been introduced over the centuries, the format Jesus taught should continue to guide our daily prayers. By spending about ten minutes with each petition, this format can easily fill an hour.

Here are some ideas:

"Our Father in heaven"

Praise—Expressing my love to God. This is a call to praise. Use words from Scripture, particularly the psalms, prayers, and promises. Include two kinds of praise: adoration for who God is and thanksgiving for what God has done.

"Hallowed be your name"

Piety—Committing myself to holiness before a holy God. This is a call to worship. Spend time in silence and/or in continued praise for who God is and what God has done. Celebrate God by using his many names and attributes. Confess your failure to make his name holy in your life.

"Your kingdom come"

Purpose—Recognizing God's purpose and will for my life. This is a call to pledge allegiance to God and his kingdom. Pray that you will be able to hear and obey God's will and authority in your life. Pray for your pastors, church leaders, and teachers. Pray for your unchurched neighbors who need to know the Lord. Pray that God's church and kingdom will grow; that people will confess God's name; that God's sovereignty will be recognized throughout the world.

"Your will be done on earth as it is in heaven"

Practice—Committing to doing God's will for my life. This is a pledge of your submission to God. Ask God to make you open to doing his will, to empower you to make the world a better place to live. Pray for your community. Pray against abortion, pornography, crime, abuses, and other evils.

"Give us today our daily bread"

Provision—Depending on God to provide for all my needs. Ask God for his provision. Be specific. Pray for spiritual, physical, emotional, professional, and financial needs. Ask God to bless your family and your work. Ask God to provide a solution to world hunger and poverty.

"Forgive us our debts, as we also have forgiven our debtors"

Pardon—Asking God to forgive my sins. Ask God to reveal your sin (Ps. 139). Confess the sins he brings to mind (Prov. 28:13). Make restitution if necessary (Matt. 5:23-24). Receive God's forgiveness (1 John 1:9). Ask God to teach you forgiveness that you might receive forgiveness and be forgiving. Forgive those who have done you an injustice. Ask God for his grace. Thank God for his grace.

"Lead us not into temptation, but deliver us from the evil one"
Protection—Keeping me from temptation. Ask God to provide you with a hedge of protection. Ask for deliverance from whatever evil might be lurking about. Ask for a dependent spirit to trust God's protection. Ask for help finding peace in the midst of chaos. Ask to be covered with the armor of God.

"For yours is the kingdom and the power and the glory forever"
Power—Acknowledging God as the source of all power. This is an opportunity to express your total and absolute dependence on God. Thank God that he has invited you into his presence to be builders of his kingdom (2 Tim. 4:18), to be filled with his power (Ps. 68:35), and to revel in his glory (2 Cor. 3:18). No prayer is complete without recognition of your full dependence on God's grace for everything.

"Amen"
Peace—Everything is in God's hand. Following your "amen," spend a few moments reflecting on your prayer time and listening for God's response.

Setting: individuals, families/households, small groups, large groups, congregations

Level: initial, intermediate, intense

Time: short, medium, long, extended

Resource

The Bensen Music Group has a CD entitled *The Lord's Prayer* that includes one song for each of the sections noted above. It is available at most Christian bookstores or through Bensen, 365 Great Circle Road, Nashville, TN 37228 or in Canada through R.G. Mitchell Family Bookstores, 565 Gordon Baker Road, Willowdale, ON M2H 2W2.

Monastic Prayer

In the fifteenth century, spirituality followed the cultural trend toward personalism and privatization; it became highly personal, largely internal, and essentially subjective. Monastic traditions evolved with this trend, lending nicely to the practice of personal spirituality, and they offer formats for personal prayer that are still widely used today.

the monastic cycle of prayer

In the fourteenth and fifteenth centuries, monastic spirituality set a pattern of prayer that was followed on a daily basis beginning early in the morning. This eight-part pattern was laid out in the Book of Hours.

4:00 a.m.—Matins
Matins simply means "morning." This first prayer of the morning focuses on our creation by God and re-creation in Jesus Christ. Ruminate on the fact that our Creator, who came to redeem us, was rejected. Pray that Jesus, the Creator and Redeemer, will be present in your thoughts and actions throughout the day.

5:00 a.m.—Lauds
Lauds means "praise." Praise is an integral part of the Christian life. Praise God for both blessings and hardships. Ruminate on the praise passages of the psalms and other Scriptures.

6:00 a.m.—Prime
Prime means "first." Prime is the first of the "little prayers" (the prayers between morning prayer and evening prayer). Ruminate on how Jesus stood before Pilate and those who accused him. Pray for God's presence and grace.

9:00 a.m.—Tierce
Tierce means "third." This is prayer at the third hour of the day. Ruminate on how the crowds mocked and ridiculed Jesus. Pray for God's protection in times of trouble.

Noon—Sext
Sext means "sixth." This is prayer at the sixth hour of the day (noon). Ruminate on how Jesus was nailed to the cross and suffered a cruel death. Pray for God's power to save you in your hour of death (or when walking through the shadow of death).

3:00 p.m.—Nones
Nones means "ninth." This is prayer at the ninth hour of the day. Ruminate on how Jesus was pierced in his side, indicating that he had completed ("finished") everything the Father required of him. Pray that God might provide for every one of your needs.

6:00 p.m.—Evensong (or Vespers)
Evensong signals evening—having

prayed from dawn to dusk symbolizes prayer from birth to death and reminds us that all our time is in the Lord's hand. Ruminate on how Jesus was taken down from the cross and our sins were left nailed to the cross. Thank God for his provision—for daily forgiveness and daily food.

9:00 p.m.—Compline
Compline means "complete." These are the prayers said before retiring to bed. Jesus was entombed; his work was finished; his resurrection awaited the morning—a new day. Ruminate on how you identify with this process in your spiritual life. Pray thanksgiving for God's presence and ministry to you throughout the day. Morning awaits.

Praying in this order retells the story of our creation, fall, and redemption. This format can be used as a daily routine or expanded for a daily retreat. The schedule can also be stretched over a week as follows:

Sunday	*Matins*
Monday	*Lauds*
Tuesday	*Prime*
Wednesday	*Tierce*
Thursday	*Sext*
Friday	*Nones*
Saturday	*Evensong* and *Compline*

ruminatio

Ruminatio was probably the most widely used prayer form in fifteenth-century England. *Ruminatio*, a close relative of *lectio divina* (see pp. 73-74), literally means "meditation," "contemplation," and "reflection."

While *lectio divina* normally took place in a communal setting (usually monastic), and emphasized a rational, objective understanding of the text, *ruminato* emphasized a more personal, subjective approach.

statio

Statio is the monastic practice of "pausing" in order to create space for God between our busy activities. Joan Chit-tishter describes it as "the practice of stopping one thing before beginning another." It is the time between times, the cure for the revolving-door mentality. The word "station" literally refers to a monk's place in line as he proceeded to worship—a silent procession to prepare one's heart for what would follow.

....

Setting: individuals

Level: intermediate

Time: short periods throughout the day or an extended commitment if used in retreat form
....

Resource
The Prymer: The Prayer Book of the Medieval Era Adapted for Contemporary Use, translated and adapted by Robert E. Webber (Cape Cod, MA: Paraclete Press, 2000).

Musical Prayers

Silent and spoken prayers are not the only prayer options. Many prayers have been set to music. Many songs and hymns are prayers. We achieve a special kind of harmonization with God and the fellowship of believers when we join our hearts and voices and lift them in prayer to him.

Consider singing your prayers. Consider using "ascriptive" songs (songs addressed directly to God) rather than "descriptive" songs (songs about God). Consider singing your confession as well as your praise. Consider singing in personal worship as well as well as in corporate worship.

Looking in any hymnal's topical index will produce numerous ideas for using songs as prayers. Here is a list to get you started:

"Benediction" (TH 730)
"Be Still and Know" (SFL 225)
"Be Still, My Soul" (TWC 530)
"Be Thou My Vision" (*Renew!* 151)
"Day by Day" (SFL 221)
"Father, We Love You" (PsH 634)
"Fill My Cup" (PH 350)
"I Worship You, O Lord" (PsH 30)
"Kum Ba Yah" (SFL 53)
"Listen to My Cry, Lord" (PsH 61)
"Lord, Be Glorfied" (SFL 71)
"Lord, Have Mercy upon Us" (PsH 258)
"Lord, I Lift Your Name on High" (*Renew!* 4)
"Lord, Listen to Your Children Praying" (PsH 625)
"The Lord's Prayer" (PsH 207, TWC 632)
"O Christ, the Lamb of God" (PsH 257)
"Open My Eyes, That I May See" (TWC 557)
"Open Our Eyes, Lord" (TWC 536)
"Precious Lord, Take My Hand" (PsH 493)
"Psalm 5" (*Renew!* 104)
"Sanctuary" (*Renew!* 185)
"Spirit of the Living God" (PsH 424)
"Spirit of God, Who Dwells Within My Heart" (PsH 419)
"You Are My Hiding Place" (*Renew!* 107)

The songs listed above can be found in the following sources:

- *Psalter Hymnal* (PsH), © 1987, CRC Publications (1-800-333-8300)
- *Songs for LiFE* (SFL), © 1994, CRC Publications (1-800-333-8300)
- *Renew!* (*Renew!*), © 1995, Hope Publishing Company
- *The Presbyterian Hymnal* (PH), © 1990, Westminster/John Knox Press
- *Trinity Hymnal* (TH), © 1990, Great Commission Publications, Inc.
- *The Worshiping Church* (TWC), © 1990, Hope Publishing Company

Setting: individuals, families/households, small groups, large groups, congregations

Level: initial, intermediate

Time: short, medium, long, extended

Names of God

There are many names for God in the Old Testament that illustrate God's nature and work. These names can serve as an outline for prayer and can be used in any order. You may simply focus on the one or two names that speak to you at a particular time. Alternatively, you may use the entire list for a prolonged time of prayer.

Jehovah (Yahweh) (cf. Ex. 3:14)
Meaning: The Lord Is the Self-existent One
   Thank God for being the "immortal, invisible, God-only-God."

Jireh (cf. Gen. 22:14)
Meaning: The Lord Is My Provider
   Praise God for his strength, wisdom, guidance, daily sustenance.

Mekoddish (cf. Lev. 20:8)
Meaning: The Lord Is My Sanctification
   Petition/praise God for his encouragement when you feel useless and unwanted.

Nissi (cf. Ex. 17:15)
Meaning: The Lord Is My Banner
   Petition/praise God for his victory in your daily conflicts and battles.

Rapha (cf. Ex. 15:26)
Meaning: The Lord Is My Healer
   Petition/praise God for his healing when you are physically sick, emotionally hopeless, and/or spiritually broken.

Rohi (cf. Ps. 23:1)
Meaning: The Lord Is My Shepherd
   Petition/praise God for direction, guidance, and protection on the journey.

Shalom (cf. Judg. 6:24)
Meaning: The Lord Is My Peace
   Petition/praise God for relief from worry, anger, and inner struggles.

Shammah (cf. Jer. 23:23)
Meaning: The Lord Is Present with Me
   Petition/praise God for his presence when you feel alone, abandoned, or forgotten.

Tsidkenu (cf. Jer. 23:6)
Meaning: God Is My Righteousness
   Petition/praise God for his forgiveness and grace when you feel dirty, guilty, accused, and unworthy.

Setting: individuals, families/households, small groups, large groups, congregations

Level: initial, intermediate

Time: short, medium, long, extended

One-Word Prayers

One-word prayers, sometimes called "popcorn prayers," work best in a small group setting with pray-ers who are intentional about their praying. Having chosen one or more designated themes (for example, confession, thanksgiving, adoration, caring, friendship, service, celebration) ahead of time, the leader opens with a short prayer and then offers a sentence to be completed by the pray-ers with one word or a short phrase. For example:

"Lord, I thank you for _____."
"Lord, I love you because _____."
"Lord, I celebrate your _____."
"Lord, I need your _____."
"Lord, help me to be more _____."
"Lord, thank you for being _____."

The leader also closes the prayer time with a short prayer.

One-word prayers are often used to assist people who are learning to pray aloud. In this situation, begin with a leading sentence that can be completed with one-word answers. After people feel comfortable praying in that format, offer a lead sentence that must be completed with a short phrase. When people are comfortable offering short sentences, provide a topic and encourage people to offer a complete sentence prayer.

Setting: individuals, families/households, small groups, large groups

Level: initial

Time: short, medium, long

P.R.A.Y.

There are a number of acronyms that can guide prayer. The National Day of Prayer Committee promotes the use of P.R.A.Y.

praise

Honor God for who he is and what he has done.
"Enter his gates with thanksgiving and his courts with praise; give thanks to him and praise his name" (Ps. 100:4). Focus on God. Forget about yourself and your needs. Give God the honor he deserves. This can be done silently or aloud, with spoken words or with song. When we praise God, we draw close to him by acknowledging his sovereignty and our dependency. Praise is always appropriate as we come into God's presence.

repent

Confess personal and corporate sins.
"If I had cherished sin in my heart, the Lord would not have listened" (Ps. 66:18). Tell God you are sorry. Confess your ungodly thoughts, words, and deeds. Unrepentant sinners have difficulty standing in the presence of a holy God because sin builds walls between us and God. Repentance offers us God's listening ear and makes us recipients of God's grace and forgiveness.

ask

Include petitions and intercessions.
"All my longings lie open before you, O LORD; my sighing is not hidden from you" (Ps. 38:9). Envision Jesus sitting next to you. He offers you the opportunity to talk about and ask for anything. Ask your questions; share your concerns. God's Word promises that he will not only listen to, but answer every prayer.

yield

Submit to the direction of the Holy Spirit.
"Show me the way I should go, for to you I lift up my soul" (Ps. 143:8). Having offered our needs and requests to God, we leave them there. While we may bring them again and again, we trust that God will answer them—in his time. We also submit our lives to his answers—including the possible "no." Wait, watch, and listen for God to move. Are you willing to trust God?

Some people add two letters to the acronym to make it "P.R.A.Y.E.R.":

expect

Anticipate that God will answer your prayer.
"Ask and it will be given to you, seek and you will find, knock and the door will be opened to you" (Matt. 7:7-8). This is the

time of waiting on the Lord with expectation. Ask the Lord to help you receive his answer and offer thanksgiving to him in anticipation of his response.

rejoice

Praise God for who he is and what he will do.
"Rejoice in the Lord always. I will say it again: Rejoice! . . . Do not be anxious about anything, but in everything, by prayer and petition, with thanksgiving, present your requests to God" (Phil. 4:4, 6). Thank God for answering prayer—for answers you have already witnessed as well as those you know to be forthcoming.

....

Setting: individuals, families/households, small groups, large groups, congregations

Level: initial, intermediate, intense

Time: short, medium, long, extended

....

Resource
The National Day of Prayer Committee, along with Youth for Christ and Creative Youth Resources, makes P.R.A.Y. bracelets that serve as a prayer reminder and guide. Call 1-800-444-8828.

Prayer of Discernment

(for Decision-Making)

This prayer format is based on the discernment cycle of St. Ignatius of Loyola. It is designed for waiting on the Lord in order to discern his will.

framing the discernment question

- Let the silence deepen around you. Enter into it. Express and renew your desire to do God's will, to follow God's call in your decision. Do not rush. Simply turn your attention to God as you experience God and address your desire to God.

- Describe for yourself an issue in your life.

- Elaborate in your journal the components of the decision you face.

- Frame the decision as concisely as you can, if possible as a question that can be answered yes or no (for example, "Should I take the new job that has been offered to me?").

- Bring the issue and your process thus far to God, and attend to any sense that arises in you.

approaching a decision through rational process

- Renew your desire to follow God's call.

- Begin to turn your potential decision over in your mind. Make a list of pros and cons.

- Reflect on each list in turn, beginning with the cons.

- Journal about how the decision appears now that you have generated these lists.

- Weigh the lists carefully. Frame a tentative decision.

- Renew your desire to follow God's call. Notice what happens when you place your tentative decision next to your desire to follow God.

approaching a decision through intuition

- Renew your desire to follow God's call.

- Become quiet and let your consciousness be open to your depths.

- Permit images to float freely. Write them down as they come to you.

- Does one image seem to capture the decision you face better than others? Which image(s) has a righteousness? A freshness? A creativity? An energy?

- Journal about what new options the image(s) might suggest.

- Speak with God about what emerges from this process.

approaching a decision through imagination

- Renew your desire to follow God's call.

- Return to your deep silence and focus your attention.

- Use your imagination to enter one (or two) of the images you wrote down in the last reflection period; or visualize one option to which your decision could take you.

- Imagine yourself choosing the option to which your intuition points. Journal about what you visualize.

- Imagine yourself taking a different path. Journal about what path opens up and where it takes you.

- Answer the following:

  — Which course flowed most freely?

  — Which excited me the most?

  — Which seemed right to me?

  — Which has the most connection with my personal history?

approaching a decision through religious affections

- Spend a few moments—as long as you need—allowing yourself to become aware of God's presence, God's love, and God's care for you.

- Renew your desire to follow God's call.

- Examine the tentative direction to see if it produces consolation—a sense of increasing faith, hope, love, and peace with God, others, and yourself. Or does it produce desolation, restlessness, discouragement, heaviness, and a disinclination to proceed?

- Make a tentative decision based on your experience of consolation or desolation.

- Test your decision over time.

testing a discerned decision

- No one test can by itself prove the rightness or wrongness of a decision. However, over time, a well-discerned decision remains firm. Look for confirmation in the general direction suggested by a number of questions.

  — Does the decision continue to "sit well"?

  — Does the consolation remain?

  — Does the "fruit of the Spirit" (Gal. 5:22) appear in my life?

  — Do I have the energy and the courage to proceed?

  — Do others I know well confirm the decision?

  — Is it in accord with the biblical witness?

  — Does it strengthen my personal commitment, for example, to my family?

Setting: individuals

Level: intense

Time: long

Resource

The Spiritual Exercises of Saint Ignatius of Loyola, trans. Pierre Wolff (Liguori, MO: Liguori Publications, 1997).

The Prayer of *Examen*

The Prayer of *Examen* (*examen* refers to the weight indicator on a scale), named and defined by Saint Ignatius of Loyola, is borne of the idea of accurately weighing or assessing a situation or issue.

Ignatius, in explaining his "awareness *examen,*" encouraged people to look specifically for "openings" (opportunities to hear God, times to witness his grace, and so on) and "blocks" (hindrances to hearing God, moments of brokenness, and so on). Richard Foster, in his book *Prayer: Finding the Heart's True Home,* describes these two aspects of prayer "like two sides of a door"—one side he identifies as the "*examen* of consciousness," the other, "the *examen* of conscience."

With the *examen* of consciousness, a person selects a defined period of time to prayerfully reflect on certain events to discover what God may be saying to him or her. For example, following a worship service, a parent might ask family members around the dinner table, "What was God saying to you during worship today?" Or at the end of the day, a person could ask, "What was God saying to me in that fight with my spouse?" After a mission project with the youth group, the leader could ask the group to spend some time prayerfully asking God to reveal what he was trying to teach them through the experience. Around the campfire on the last evening of a camping trip with your small group, you could ask, "What has God been saying to us in our time here together?" (If using the *examen* of consciousness in a small group,

invite the pray-ers to share their insights after a period of silent reflection—a minimum of five to ten minutes, depending on the nature of the group.)

The second side of the door, the *examen* of conscience, is where we ask God to uncover those areas in our lives that prevent us from hearing God fully and obeying him completely. In this prayer we ask God to expose in us whatever it is that keeps us from being who he wants us to be. This is a very personal, individual, aspect of *examen.* These are the areas of our life that need confessing, forgiveness, and healing. There are a variety of ways to enter the examen of conscience: Martin Luther used the Ten Commandments and the Lord's Prayer as a pattern for prayerful examination of his life. Some people journal. Others go on a weekly or monthly personal retreat. Some arrive early for worship on Sunday to sit in the worship center and pray.

The Prayer of *Examen* is always personal. It does not seek to discover God's word for someone else or request that God bring to light someone else's sin.

Setting: individuals

Level: intense

Time: medium, long

Resources

Richard Foster, *Prayer: Finding the Heart's True Home* (San Francisco: Harper, 1992).

The Spiritual Exercises of Saint Ignatius of Loyola, trans. Pierre Wolff (Liguori, MO: Liguori Publications, 1997).

Prayer Imaging

This prayer format requires pray-ers to use their imagination. It works well with children and adolescents and also with new Christians. Participants must be relaxed, passive, and able to experience a new situation. The primary responsibility for the effectiveness of this prayer format lies with the leader.

In his book *Alive in Christ: The Dynamic Process of Spiritual Formation* (Upper Room, 1984, pp. 118-120), Maxie Dunnam explains how this prayer format works. Begin by selecting a narrative Scripture passage. Gospel stories work well. Some good ones to use are

- the storm on the Sea of Galilee (Mark 4:35-41)
- the party at Simon's house (Luke 7:36-50)
- the woman caught in adultery (John 8:1-11)
- the healing of the blind man (John 9:1-25)

While the leader slowly reads the passage aloud, participants close their eyes and picture (recreate) the scene in their imagination. The leader slowly reads the passage several more times as appropriate.

Between each reading, the leader pauses for a period of silence during which the participants are encouraged to "replay" the scene in their mind—to picture themselves as a part of the scene, to join the dialogue, to participate in the action, and to listen carefully to Jesus.

After a period of time, the participants gather in small groups where they are encouraged to share their feelings, thoughts, and reactions: What did they learn? What was God saying to them? Participants should avoid moralizing, finding clever applications, drawing theological conclusions, discussing how someone felt, or telling people how they ought to feel after being confronted by the passage.

Prayer imaging works well with small groups and in retreat settings where longer periods of prayer and reflection are possible.

....

Setting: individuals, families/households, small groups, large groups, congregations

Level: initial, intermediate

Time: medium, long

....

Prayer Journaling

Many pray-ers keep a prayer journal—a written record of their prayers—and have found that it adds depth to their prayer life. A journal is an honest record of an intimate relationship between a believer and his or her Lord.

Prayer journals can take a number of forms. Some prayer journals are simply a record of the pray-er's written-out prayers. While this is somewhat time-consuming, it provides an excellent resource for personal prayer as the author can re-pray the prayers again and again.

Some people collect the prayers of others in their prayer journal. They take classic prayers, prayer songs/hymns, and prayers they have heard others pray, record the prayers in their journal, and use the prayers during their personal prayer time.

Another format of prayer journaling is to write yourself a letter from God (see Listening Prayer, pp. 75-76).

Some journals are simply lists of intercessions and petitions. As answers to prayer are received, they are recorded in the journal. As new prayer needs come up, they are added. This ongoing prayer list is always available and provides "proof" that God answers prayer.

Some people use a prayer journal to note prayer "insights"—concepts and wisdom about prayer gleaned while reading books or articles, listening to sermons, talking with other intercessors, and/or attending prayer conferences.

Many prayer journals are combinations of the above, and often are records of a person's regular devotion time. In this case, the journal may be organized into several sections, or it can be one continuous chapter—distinguished only by the date at the top of the page. Such a journal can include

Another form of "journaling" your prayers is to express them through various art forms—painting, songwriting, sculpting, dancing, writing poems or stories. These can be personal, private expressions of your prayers, or you many want to share them to enrich another's prayer life as well as your own.

- personal worship (reflections)
- personally written prayers
- copied prayers (from other Christians, from songs, from Scripture)
- prayer request lists
- Scripture verses
- reflections on scriptural prayers/readings
- prayer insights and lessons learned
- issues of spiritual warfare
- attacks by the enemy—struggles, dreams, temptations
- answers to prayer

If you decide to journal, write in it regularly. Daily is ideal; several times a week is preferable; and once a week is minimal. Write what you hear the Lord encouraging

Like a lathe, a journal forces us inward to the heart of the wood.

—Virginia Stem Owens

you to write. You do not need to write pages each time. In fact, a few sentences daily is often more helpful than paragraphs once a week. Sometimes you may write only a line or two; other times you may write pages.

Normally, write whatever comes to mind: feelings, insights, confessions, experiences, arguments, ideas, and prayers. Keep your journal protected. It should be available only to you (and to God).

Setting: individuals

Level: initial, intermediate, intense

Time: medium, long

Resources

Ronald Klug, *How to Keep a Spiritual Journal* (Minneapolis: Augsburg Fortress, 1993).

Richard Peace, *Spiritual Journaling: Recording Your Journey Toward God* (Colorado Springs, CO: NavPress, 1999).

Prayer Journeying

Prayer journeying requires that participants use their imagination. This prayer format must be led by one who has a close walk with God and a sense of creativity. While similar to prayer imaging, prayer journeying does not focus on a Scripture passage in the same way.

At first, this prayer format should be leader directed. After participants have experienced it a few times, it can also be effectively incorporated into one's personal devotions.

While prayer journeying is very personal, it is normally used in small groups. It is especially effective with older children and adolescents, and is often used in retreat settings where the atmosphere and schedule are unhurried.

the process

The prayer begins with the leader asking people to close their eyes and to begin imagining themselves in a particular environment. This may be a beautiful, quiet, solitary setting such as walking on a deserted beach, standing on the porch of a mountain cabin, or sitting snugly by a fire. With people who have used this prayer format before, the leader might lead participants beside a grave (to address our eternity), onto a small boat in a raging river (to underscore our trust level), or into a mountainous evergreen in the midst of a thunderstorm (awe at God's power). The leader must be descriptive. The more details (descriptions, sounds, etc.) the leader can add, the clearer the picture will be for the pray-ers. The leader should describe things that appeal to the senses—touch, sight, hearing, smell, taste—without telling the pray-ers how to feel.

Jesus must always be the central figure; he is always the recipient of our prayers. The leader should help participants to encounter Jesus. Participants should be invited to discuss (silently) with Jesus what is happening in their lives, to admit how they have failed him, to ask for his assistance, to acknowledge his power, and to listen carefully to him. The discussion should be in keeping with the journey; that is, after being out in a small boat on a raging river the discussion would appropriately be focused on faith questions ("Do you trust Jesus to save you?"). On some occasions, spend some time simply enjoying being with Jesus (for example, sitting side by side near a fire).

The leader should bring the journey to a close. If you are in a small group or in a retreat setting, offer the opportunity for people to discuss their experience.

Setting: individuals, small groups

Level: intermediate

Time: short, medium

Prayer-Summit Style

Over the past several years, International Renewal Ministries has been responsible for sponsoring hundreds of Pastors' Prayer Summits throughout North America and in more than thirty other countries. During these four-day retreats, pastors and church leaders come together with no other agenda than to seek God. At each prayer summit, anywhere from twenty to several hundred pastors worship, pray, and grow closer to God.

In their desire to seek God, a unique prayer format has developed. Participants sit in a circle (if there are too many people to sit in one large circle, concentric circles are formed). After a time of prayer for God's guidance and additional prayers for God's protection, participants are encouraged to participate in one of three ways:

- **Praying.** All prayers are to be directed to God. Prayers of praise, thanksgiving, and adoration are encouraged. Some time may also be set aside for confession. Prayers of intercession and petition are generally discouraged.

- **Reading Scripture.** Participants are encouraged to share Scripture that God brings to mind. Sometimes the person reading the Scripture follows the reading with a prayer or a song.

- **Singing.** Participants may introduce a song that God brings to mind by beginning to sing it. Others join in. Normally these songs are sung from memory; songbooks and instruments are not used.

This style of prayer usually takes an extended period of time (a minimum of sixty minutes and often extending for several hours). It works best in a retreat setting or in a small group setting where members are comfortable with each other. It also works well for prayer services where people can sit in a circle.

It is important for the leader to explain the prayer format before beginning and to answer any questions people might have. Do not overlook the initial prayers for protection and for God's guidance. Both are imperative. Before using this prayer form, it would be beneficial for the leader to have participated in a prayer summit.

Setting: small groups, large groups, congregations

Level: intermediate, intense

Time: long, extended

Resources

Joe Aldrich, *Prayer Summits* (Portland, OR: Multnomah Press, 1992).

International Renewal Ministries
8435 N.E. Gilison St.
Portland, OR 97220
503-251-6455
fax: 503-254-1268
e-mail: irm@multnomah.edu
www.multnomah.edu

the Psalms

In an article in *Discipleship Journal* ("Patterns for Prayer," May/June 1997), Young Life Director Howard Baker shares how the book of Psalms not only influenced his life but also taught him how to pray. He notes four important truths about the Psalms and prayer:

1. "The psalms teach us to pray honestly." Prayer should not merely be a polite, superficial conversation, but an intimate, passionate expression of what is happening in our hearts.

2. "The psalms teach us to pray comprehensively." The book of Psalms, Israel's worship book, calls us to pray—not according to a manageable and predictable formula, but as real life unfolds, with all of its issues and all of its emotions.

3. "The psalms teach us to pray in a God-centered way." Praying the psalms prevents our prayers from being self-centered and self-absorbed.

4. "The psalms teach us to pray responsively." Like parents require a response from their children, the psalms can be our response to God. Praying the psalms helps to connect our present-day issues with God and his Word. All of life calls for our response.

praying the psalms individually

Praying through the book of Psalms in personal prayer times has long been a tradition in the church. While it has been neglected for decades, the tradition seems to be making a comeback. There are a number of ways to pray the Psalms individually:

- Divide the psalms into fifty equal parts and pray three psalms each day (one for morning, one for noon, and one for evening).

- Pray one psalm each day. (Psalm 119 can be broken into twenty-two parts). This process takes about five months to complete.

- Some reserve psalm praying for Sunday when they have more time, preferring to focus on other prayer formats during the week. In this schedule, the psalms may be divided into fifty-two or fifty-three parts, and one section prayed each Sunday. Or, simply pray one psalm each Sunday.

When praying a psalm, simply read the psalm. Pause. Reflect. Then re-read the psalm. Take one verse at a time. Pause. Reflect. Let the words of the psalmist become your prayer. Use the outline of the psalm to share your heart with the Lord. It may be helpful to use a simple commentary or study Bible to learn the background of the psalm. Also, consider reading the psalm in more than one translation, including a more contemporary translation like *The Message* by Eugene Peterson.

praying the psalms in small groups

Praying the psalms can be very meaningful in small groups. With a short psalm, each person can pray over the same verse (silently or aloud) before moving on to the next verse. With a longer psalm, take turns reading the verses, having the reader identify the primary teaching/truth of the verse and offer a word of prayer (petition, thanksgiving, confession, and so on) in response to it.

For example (from Psalm 145):

145:1—"I will exalt you, my God the King; I will praise your name for ever and ever." *Father, we celebrate you. You are great. You give us strength, and we will celebrate and rejoice in who you are.*

145:2—"Every day I will praise you and extol your name for ever and ever." *Father, your name is always on our lips. We praise you and promise to keep praising you all the time.*

145:3—"Great is the Lord and most worthy of praise; his greatness no one can fathom." *Father, we praise you because you deserve to be praised. The things you have done are so great we cannot always understand. Thank you for creating the world; thank you for the great gift of Jesus Christ; thank you for calling us to salvation. Father, you are beyond our understanding.*

Continue in the same way with the remaining verses of the psalm.

praying the psalms in corporate worship

Although they can be used individually and in small groups, the Psalms were written primarily for corporate worship. They were used extensively by God's people in both the Old and New Testaments. Worshipers learned to pray personally by praying together; they learned to pray together by being led in prayer. For example (from Psalm 23):

Great Shepherd, we are like sheep, easily frightened. We want to see that you are beside us, leading us in the right paths; but our eyes cannot turn away from our broken bodies, broken families, and broken dreams. But today we have enough to believe, at least, that we are your sheep. So to you we cry out, asking you to restore our souls.

Find all in your sanctuary today who are passing through the dark valley of grief. We pray for *[insert names of those in your congregation]* . . .

—M. Craig Barnes, *Leadership* (Spring 1999), p. 52

Setting: individuals, families/households, small groups, large groups, congregations

Level: intermediate

Time: short, medium

Resources

John Calvin, *Heart Aflame: Daily Readings from Calvin on the Psalms* (Phillipsburg, NJ: P&R Publishing, 1999).

Victor Parachin, *Daily Strength: One Year in the Psalms* (Liguori, MO: Liguori Publications, 1996).

Praying the Scriptures

Praying the Scriptures, like praying the psalms, has a long tradition in the church. The process is similar to praying the psalms:

- First, read the selected passage of Scripture—reading it aloud allows you to both vocalize and listen to the passage.

- Return to the beginning and re-read the Scripture a phrase or verse at a time—pausing to turn the passage into a prayer. Apply it to your life and circumstances.

- Move through a book at a time—pausing at each paragraph/story. Record your discoveries in a prayer journal.

examples

In John 17, Jesus prays for himself, for other leaders, and for all believers.

For yourself:

17:2—Pray for the blessing of salvation, eternal life.

17:5—Pray for the privilege of dwelling in the presence of God.

For other leaders:

17:6—Pray for the privilege of belonging to God.

17:8—Pray for the privilege of believing God.

17:10—Pray for the opportunity to receive all God's blessings.

17:11—Pray for protection from worldly enticements.

17:13—Pray for the full measure of God's joy.

17:15—Pray for protection from the evil one.

For all believers:

17:20—Pray for unity of mission among believers.

17:24—Pray for a growing walk with Jesus Christ.

17:25-26—Pray for courage to share the gospel.

Zechariah 3 is a great passage to confess sin and/or bring comfort to someone dealing with sin.

3:1—"Father, like Joshua, I stand before you. The devil accuses me of sin. I feel the weight and guilt of what I've done."

3:2—"Thank you for intervening in my life and plucking me out of the consuming fire of sin."

3:3—"Lord, I have looked in the mirror and see the filthy rags I wear. My sin has tarnished my life."

3:4—"Lord, I bring my sins to you. I lay them at your feet. Lord, thank you for the clean garments that you have given me to wear."

3:5—"Lord, thank you for the 'turban' on my head. May I wear it to bring attention to what you have done in my life. May others see it and be directed to you."

3:7—"Lord, thank you for cleansing me and now using me in your kingdom. Give me the strength to walk in your ways; give me clarity of your will so I can follow it; give me a place so I may stand with your people."

Setting: individuals, families/households, small groups, large groups, congregations

Level: intermediate

Time: short, medium

Repetitive Prayer

Repetitive prayer is a lost prayer format. In our driven society, repetition has received a bad rap. "Been there, done that" says that repetition is a waste of time. We suspect repetition is redundant: "If God didn't hear it the first time, why would he hear it the second, fifth, or fiftieth time?"

Yet think about this: You bounce a child on your leg; when you stop bouncing, the first thing the child says is, "Do it again, do it again." In a child's mind, if it is enjoyable, it is worth doing over and over and over again. Unfortunately, in our prayer lives we have lost much of our childlike eagerness.

Repetitive prayer is a powerful way to communicate with God:

- The angels praised God with continued repetitions: "Holy, holy, holy, is the Lord Almighty; the whole earth is full of his glory" (Isa. 6:3).

- The Old Testament worship and prayer book (the book of Psalms) frequently uses repetition. Consider Psalm 136, for example.

- The church fathers used the Jesus Prayer (see pp. 71-72) as well as other prayer repetitions (for example, "Holy Father, Holy Son, Holy Spirit, teach me to serve you" and "Lord, Jesus, you are my light in my world; enlighten my darkness").

the process

Find a quiet, secluded place. Select a verse from Scripture or a short prayer (see above), or pray the prayer God is laying on your heart. Pray the prayer slowly and audibly. Pause for reflection and listening. Continue this cycle as long as possible.

While this prayer format seems simplistic, the benefit is the opportunity to spend time in the presence of God and to watch God work in your life.

Note: Some people confuse repetitive prayer with "vain repetition" or mantras. Like repetitive prayer, a mantra is repeated over and over; unlike repetitive prayer, a mantra is usually a meaningless sound or word. Likewise, a "vain repetition" is a phrase that initially may have been meaningful, but over a period of time has lost its meaning. Remember, the prayer must be meaningful—or don't use it.

Setting: individuals

Level: intermediate

Time: medium, long

The Salvation Prayer

The Salvation Prayer is a prayer offered when a person accepts Jesus as Savior and Lord. This is a prayer most believers pray only once for themselves, but all believers should be familiar with it as they have opportunities to lead others to Jesus.

When a person has heard the gospel message and desires to accept its promises, you may want to ask, "Do you wish to receive the gift of eternal life that God is offering to you now by receiving Jesus Christ as your personal Savior and Lord?" You may also want to clarify what the commitment involves:

- accepting the death and resurrection of Jesus Christ as the only way to take away your sin and bring you into a relationship with God;

- acknowledging that you are a sinner, confessing your sins, and promising to live a new life in Christ; and

- surrendering your life to Jesus Christ and making him Lord of your daily living as an act of gratitude and thanksgiving for what he has done for you.

When the person is ready to make a verbal commitment, pray that commitment to God. This Prayer of Salvation normally involves three parts:

1. Pray for the person.

Father, I thank you that _____ is ready to accept you as her Savior and Lord. I thank you that you are willing to offer her eternal life as a gift of your Son, Jesus Christ. Give her the faith to trust in your promises. Forgive her as she confesses her sin. Give her the presence and the power of your Spirit today. Welcome her into your family.

2. Pray with the person.

Ask the person to repeat each line after you.

(For adults) Jesus, I want you to come and take over my life. / I have sinned. / I have been trying to be good on my own and have not done so well. / I need you. / I am ready to place my complete trust in you and accept you as my Savior. / I believe that you died on the cross to be the Savior from my sin. / I believe that you rose from the dead to be the Lord of my life. / Thank you for forgiving my sins. / Thank you for dying to give me real life. / I offer you my whole life. / Help me to live for you.

(For children) Dear Jesus, Thank you for dying on the cross to take away my sin. / Thank you for making me God's child. / I know that I don't deserve that, because I've done lots of things that don't please you. / But I trust your promise, and I want to live

my life for you. / Please come into my life and be my Savior and Lord. / Show me how to live, and give me your Spirit so I'll do what you want me to do. / Help me when I do the things that you do not want me to do. / Keep me trusting you every day. (Leading a Child to Jesus, CRC Publications, 2000)

3. Pray for the person (assurance of pardon).

Father, you have heard the prayer that _____ has prayed. Thank you for forgiving her sins. Give her the confidence that you have now forgiven each one of them, that you have accepted her into your family, and that you love her. Make your promise that "If we confess our sins you will be faithful and just and forgive us our sins and cleanse us from all unrighteousness" a reality for her life. Give her the strength to follow you; give her the peace that you are now in control of her life. In Jesus' name, Amen.

Just as the road leads a person to making this commitment, so the road continues beyond this point in a person's faith journey. Be sure to help the new Christian understand how she can continue to grow in her newfound faith—by spending time with God in prayer and in God's Word, by attending worship with other Christians, by publicly confessing her faith, by sharing the good news with others, and so on. Also be sure to celebrate! What a joyous occasion when someone accepts God's gracious gift of salvation! Give assurance of Jesus' love and acceptance and of your continued prayers.

Setting: individuals, small groups

Level: intermediate

Time: short

Silence

Silence in prayer can take on as many different meanings as there are people who practice it. For some people, silent prayer is praying without speaking audibly. For others, silence is their role in prayer as someone else verbalizes a prayer. For some, silent prayer is active—they are earnestly "agreeing" with the pray-er; for others, silent prayer is simply a doorway for a wandering mind.

Historically, silence was not defined as praying silently, nor was it listening to someone else pray. Silence was listening for God: the Quakers, for example, use silence as a form of spiritual discipline—sitting together silently in a spartan room for hours at a time—waiting and listening for the Spirit of God to move and speak. The classic monastery also provided an avenue for the monk to conform his life to the Word of God through silence.

> **The fruit of silence is prayer; the fruit of prayer is faith; the fruit of faith is love; the fruit of love is service; the fruit of service is peace.**
> **—Mother Teresa**

Silence is a form of fasting—fasting from words, busyness, and noise in order to focus on God. It takes on many different forms:

- spending a breakfast in silence
- spending a day in silence
- going on a three- or four-day silent retreat
- reading in a quiet place—the Scriptures, a meditative work of a church father, a book by a contemplative, and so on
- taking a walk (solitude includes most of the dynamics of silence)

Listening for God (see Listening Prayer, pp. 75-77) is difficult—it requires an absence of distractions. It requires silence. E. Stanley Jones suggested ending our spoken prayers with "And now, God, is there anything you want to say to me?" followed by a time of silence.

Silence can effectively be included within another prayer format. It makes excellent "bookends" to other prayer forms: silence at the beginning to focus our hearts and minds on God, and silence at the end, as Jones recommends, to listen for God's response.

Setting: individuals, families/households, small groups, large groups, congregations

Level: initial, intermediate

Time: short, medium, long, extended

Resources

Thomas Merton, *Thoughts on Solitude* (New York: Noonday Press, 1999).

Walter Wangerin, *Whole Prayer: Speaking and Listening to God* (Grand Rapids, MI: Zondervan, 1999).

Spontaneous Prayer

In many traditions, praying spontaneously is a way of being open to the Holy Spirit. Spontaneous prayer is not praying because it is your turn or because you feel the pressure to pray after everyone else has done so. Spontaneous prayer is simply praying when and how the Holy Spirit leads—often in the context of a prayer cell, a prayer meeting, or a designated time in a worship service.

In some contexts, spontaneous prayer offers the opportunity for a person to pray at any time—but not while someone else is praying. In other contexts, spontaneous prayer means a person is encouraged to pray at any time—even while others are praying. In the first context, the prayer time may have much silence—opportunities for participants to listen to God, to hear what he is asking them to pray, and then to pray it. In the second context, while an individual should periodically pause to listen to God, the room will seldom be quiet. The first context works best with groups no larger than twenty-four (if the group is larger than this, divide into smaller groups). In the second context, spontaneous prayer can be used in any size group.

Spontaneous prayer also happens outside an organized group setting. The idea behind spontaneous prayer is that when the Spirit prompts you to pray, pray. Hence, you should constantly be open, alert, and sensitive to the opportunities to pray . . .

- When someone shares with you they have had a bad week, offer to pray for them—right then and there.

- When someone tells you they have just been diagnosed with cancer, pray with them.

- When the Spirit places the name of a neighbor or coworker in your mind, pray for them.

- When you drive by an automobile accident and someone appears injured, pray for them.

Spontaneous prayer doesn't have a set formula; all it requires is a heart open to the Spirit's leading. Spontaneous pray-ers pray on the telephone, face-to-face, over the Internet, and through snail mail. Spontaneous pray-ers pray in offices, schools, factories, and malls. Spontaneous pray-ers pray audibly and silently.

Setting: individuals, families/households, small groups, large groups, congregations

Level: initial, intermediate

Time: short, medium, long, extended

Resources

Cindy Jacobs, *The Voice of God* (Ventura, CA: Regal Books, 1995).

Charles Stanley, *How to Listen to God* (Nashville: Oliver Nelson Books, 1985).

Warfare Prayer

Spiritual warfare is real war, with real battles and real casualties. Warfare prayer is a necessary part of waging the battles; it is necessary for the fulfilling of the Great Commission. Warfare prayer is confrontational prayer.

We must realize that when we start praying for God to bring people into his kingdom, we are praying that they will leave another kingdom—Satan's kingdom. And Satan is not happy about this. He is willing to go to war. While we must realistically understand that not every negative, harmful, or difficult thing that happens in our lives is spiritual warfare, much of it is. Tom White, well-known speaker and author in the area of spiritual warfare, lists the many kinds of attacks Satan makes against spiritual leaders, evangelists, intercessors, and churches (*Spiritual Warfare and Kingdom Advancement*, Presbyterian and Reformed Renewal Ministries International, 1993, p. 113):

- personal weaknesses
- curses, hexes, and spells from those in the occult
- physical illness
- diminished devotional life
- division or breakdown in relationships
- resistance to important ministry
- depression and discouragement
- barrages of fear
- confused thoughts and battles with doubt
- opposition from persons amenable to demonic control

White also points out that these satanic attacks come in at least two levels of intensity:

1. **The Primary Level.** This level of temptation comes from our sinful human nature (Rom. 7:18), which is the primary influence that causes us to sin. The solution is sanctification (Rom. 6:6).

2. **The Secondary Level.** At this level Satan and his legions entice believers and entrap unbelievers.

Specific warfare tactics against believers include

- temptation—internal enticement to evil (see Matt. 4:1). Solution: resistance (see James 4:7; 1 Pet. 5:9).

- flaming arrows—external temptations to sin (see Eph. 6:16). Solution: put on the armor of God (see Eph. 6:13-18).

Specific warfare tactics against unbelievers include

- control—dominance by deception and disobedience (see 1 John 5:19; Rev. 12:9; Eph. 2:2) and control by evil spirits (see Matt. 8:28-33). Solution: salvation (see Col. 1:13-14).

- lingering warfare—clinging spirits, oppression, possession (see Acts 10:38). Solution: deliverance (see Acts 10:38).

preparing for battle

Warfare prayer begins quietly—in personal preparation—"basic training" for what is to come. The training begins in one's own heart, soul, mind, and strength and in relationships with others. It is characterized by repentance and reconciliation. We cannot fight enemies we detest with one hand while refusing to let go of them with the other. (For example, we cannot pray against immorality, pornography, and sexual abuse while keeping inappropriate literature in our homes or visiting immoral websites.) It is our unrepentant sin that supplies the strength for satanic strongholds in our personal lives, in our churches, in our cities. To adequately prepare for spiritual battle, we must first declare war on our own sin. When Christ is our sole focus—when we have been equipped with the armor of God (Eph. 6)—then we are ready for battle.

the levels of spiritual warfare

Warfare prayer commonly occurs at three levels. The first level is called **ground level.** At this level, we assist other Christians to become free to join the battle. Ground level warfare is associated with individual bondage and/or demonization; it is the routine casting out of demons—including lust, greed, bitterness, complaining, gossip, and so on. This level is also called "deliverance." With some basic training and a devoted, holy life, most believers can participate effectively in ground-level warfare. Unfortunately, deliverance is a ministry often overlooked by many churches in the Western world.

The second level of spiritual warfare is known as the **occult level.** This is an intentional interruption designed to cancel the workings of the evil world. It involves intercessory confrontations with demonic forces operating through Satanism, witchcraft, shamanism, esoteric philosophies, and any number of similar occult vehicles. Intercessors come together to break strong-

holds—to confess corporate sins, to pray against pride, hypersensitivity, divisiveness, disunity, accusation, prejudice, judgmentalism, fear, lust, and other sins. While this is a significant and powerful ministry, it is usually done quietly behind the scenes. Again, most believers who are living holy lives, can—with some training and experience—participate in this level of spiritual warfare.

The third level of spiritual warfare—the **strategic level**—deals with "principalities and powers." It is a frightening level of warfare. Casualties—even physical deaths—are not uncommon. Unless intercessors are thoroughly trained, are protected by other experienced intercessors, and understand the risks, they should not attempt to battle at this level. As a result, when we talk about doing spiritual warfare we are *not* recommending participating—even dabbling—at this level. (This level should be reserved for intercessors with experience and adequate spiritual cover.)

weapons for spiritual warfare

God has given us spiritual weapons, and we must use them wisely. Spiritual warfare requires discipline (sticking with this lifetime battle), discretion (knowing where to battle), determination (knowing how to battle), and discernment (distinguishing God's voice from other voices).

Three essential weapons are available to all Christians:

1. **The authority of the name of Jesus.** Jesus said, "Until now you have not asked for anything in my name. Ask and you will receive" (John 16:24). Jesus has been given "all authority." Employ Jesus' name with authority as you pray for the lost; against demons, principalities, and powers; and against Satan's strongholds.

2. **The authority of the blood of Jesus.** It is the shed blood of Jesus that makes salvation possible. The Bible says, "In [Christ] we have redemption through his blood" (Eph. 1:7), and, "They overcame

[Satan] by the blood of the Lamb" (Rev. 12:11).

3. **The authority of our testimony.** We can overcome by "the word of our testimony" (Rev. 12:11). Bring God's Word into your praying—it is "the sword of the Spirit" (Eph. 6:17).

guidelines for waging spiritual warfare

Terry Teykl offers the following guidelines for those interested in becoming involved in spiritual warfare:

1. Don't be trigger happy; not everything is an evil force. Spiritual warfare should only be done as a last resort; it is never a "quick fix" for a first encounter. Before you engage, study to gain understanding. Seek the wisdom of other godly men and women who have done it with good results.

2. Before you go after the rats, try taking out the garbage. Evil can only reside where there is sin, so do all you can to address the sin issues in your home/church/city. You may find that when you get rid of the garbage, the rats leave without an argument.

3. Make no kamikaze flights. Warfare is not meant to be a solo act; it demands a united front. Prayers of eviction are best served under the covering of the city-wide church.

4. Prepare with prayer and fasting (John 9:29). This ensures that you go into battle under God's authority, not your own. The lower you can humble yourself, the greater your chances for victory since God's power is made perfect in our weakness.

5. Be sensitive to God's leading about time and place. Spiritual warfare is not designed to be public entertainment. It is real; it is serious; and it can be dangerous. Charging out into the street before the light turns green is a good way to get run over.

6. Focus on Jesus, not the critters. You do not need to do an inordinate amount of "binding" and "casting out" because the name of Jesus is omnipotent. The resurrection notarized the ultimate eviction notice that was served at Calvary.

7. Cover and seal the encounter with free-flowing praise. The Lord inhabits the praises of his people, which is why praise that magnifies Jesus is so offensive to Satan. As the Holy Spirit comes in response to praise, his presence displaces evil.

8. Never allow warfare to become an end in itself. This is not a hobby or an extracurricular activity. The objective must always be to set captives free so that Jesus is glorified and his reign is established in lives and cities.

9. Maintain an attitude of humility; God is in the driver's seat. The Almighty Creator of the universe does not require your help to dismantle a stronghold. However, because he loves you, he will occasionally allow you to put your hands next to his on the steering wheel. To respond with arrogance or pride would be foolish.

10. Keep in mind the "onion principle." When you peel off one layer, you may find another underneath that looks just like it. Sin and evil often grow like an onion—you may peel away a crime problem and discover a deeper issue of racism. Behind racism may be a layer of disunity. And beneath the disunity may be a hard core of pride. Go one step at a time.

—From *Blueprint for the House of Prayer*, © 1999, Prayer Point Press, 1-888-656-6067, www.prayerpointpress.com. Used by permission.

warning

There is no clear precedent in Scripture for direct confrontation with principalities and powers. Never attempt to confront spirits alone, or without a group of advanced intercessors.

....

Setting: small groups, large groups, congregations

Level: intense

Time: long, extended

....

Resources

Francis Frangipane, *Discerning of Spirits* (New York: Arrow Publications, 1994).

Calvin Miller, *Disarming the Darkness: A Guide to Spiritual Warfare*. (Grand Rapids, MI: Zondervan, 1998).

Jeff Stam, *Straight Talk About Spiritual Warfare: What the Bible Teaches, What you Need to Know* (Grand Rapids, MI: CRC Publications, 1999).

George Otis, *Informed Intercession* (Ventura, CA: Regal Books, 1999).

C. Peter Wagner, *Confronting the Powers* (Ventura, CA: Regal Books, 1996).

———. *Engaging the Enemy* (Ventura, CA: Regal Books, 1991).

———. *Warfare Prayer* (Ventura, CA: Regal Books, 1992).

Weekly Pattern for Prayer

Numerous prayer aids are available to remind us of the important things to pray for and to guide our discipline of prayer throughout the week. Following are two examples.

how to pray through the week (based on acts 1:8)

Sunday Focus: Your Church

"You will receive power when the Holy Spirit comes on you . . ."

- Invite the Holy Spirit within your gathering of believers.
- Trust God to speak to and bless you through your pastor.
- Trust God to provide professions and reaffirmations of faith.
- Ask the Lord for a seeker-sensitive atmosphere.
- Praise God for those who labor in the harvest.

You will receive power when the Holy Spirit comes on you; and you will be my witnesses in Jerusalem, and in all Judea and Samaria, and to the ends of the earth.
—Acts 1:8

Monday Focus: Your Family and Sphere of Influence

". . . and you will be my witnesses in Jerusalem . . ."

- Intercede for your family members' needs and concerns.
- Claim salvation for relatives and friends who don't know Christ.
- Pray for your children.
- Pray for forgiveness, healing, and reconciliation for past hurts and sins.
- Pray for three people within your sphere of influence.
- Thank the Lord for working in your family.

Tuesday Focus: Unity in the Body

". . . and in all Judea . . ."

- Pray John 17 for the churches in your community.
- Ask God for relational and racial healing.
- Repent of the corporate sins in your community.
- Glorify Jesus for a breakthrough in unity.

Wednesday Focus: Regional Evangelism

". . . and Samaria . . ."

- Ask God to give your neighbors a hunger for the gospel.
- Pray for intercultural ministries.
- Ask God to raise up church planters as evangelists.

- Pray that these leaders will model Christ's ministry.
- Thank God for souls saved and churches planted.
- Pray for local schools, businesses, and neighborhoods.

Thursday Focus: Global Evangelism

". . . and to the ends of the earth."

- Pray for missionaries and national church workers.
- Repent of attitudes or actions that impede mission in your nation.
- Intercede for missionaries on home assignment.
- Remember those involved in recent world tragedies.
- Praise God that Matthew 28:18-20 is being fulfilled.

Friday Focus: Unreached People Groups

". . . and to the ends of the earth."

- Pray for unreached people groups worldwide.
- Intercede for one of the "world windows" (see p. 277).
- Pray against strongholds that hinder the gospel.
- Thank God for the promise of Matthew 24:14.

Saturday Focus: Your Personal Needs

"You will receive power when the Holy Spirit comes on you."

- Pray the Lord's Prayer for yourself.
- Forgive those who have offended you.
- Make the prayers of Ephesians 1 and 3 yours.
- Appropriate Philippians 4:19 for your needs.
- Bless the Lord for his faithfulness in your life.

—Christian and Missionary Alliance materials

how to pray through the week

Sunday Focus: Your Church

- Pray for leaders—pastors, staff, elders and/or deacons.
- Pray for small groups and their leaders.
- Pray for your outreach, education, and prayer ministries.
- Pray for spiritual and numerical growth.
- Pray for anointed and powerful worship.

Monday Focus: Evangelism in Your Community

- Ask God to bless the Lighthouses in your congregation.
- Ask God to help you build good relationships with your neighbors.
- Pray for police officers, firefighters, schools, and government officials.
- Pray that your coworkers may be open to the gospel.

Tuesday Focus: Families and Individuals

- Thank God for your parents.
- Thank God for your spouse.
- Ask God to protect your children and bring them salvation.
- Ask God to allow you to forgive (and forget) previous sins and heal lingering pain.

Wednesday Focus: Material Needs

- Thank God or ask God for gainful employment.
- Thank God for your residence, food, and clothing.
- Ask God to continue to bless you financially.
- Ask God to bless your giving.

Thursday Focus: Unity

- Pray for healing between races.

- Pray for denominational cooperation.

- Pray for opportunities for believers to come together: Jesus March, prayer walks, and so on.

- Pray for unity in the worldwide church.

Friday Focus: The World

- Pray for national and international crises; for military hotspots.

- Pray for your nation and the world—for leaders, for peace, and for economic stability.

- Pray for missions, missionaries, and a rich harvest.

Saturday Focus: For Release from Addictions and Strongholds

- Pray against rampant use of drugs and alcohol.

- Pray against spiritual strongholds in your community—materialism, greed, complaining, pride, prejudice, and so on.

- Pray for the Holy Spirit's presence in your life as you prepare for worship.

Setting: individuals, families/households

Level: initial

Time: short, medium

Written Prayer

In our "hurry-up" society, few people take the time to write out their prayers. But it is a discipline worth observing.

Many people have discovered the benefits of this practice. You may find that in writing out your prayers your mind wanders less and you aren't as apt to doze off. You may find that it is a great spiritual blessing to go back and reread your prayers of previous days.

the process

- Start with a clean sheet of paper or the next clean page in your prayer journal.

- Begin with a time of silence. Ask for the Holy Spirit's presence and assistance in "forming your prayer."

- Let you heart, soul, and mind "go." That is, when writing out your prayers, write out the thoughts God places before you.

- When finished, pray (reread) the prayer. Add to or delete from it as appropriate.

- Reflect quietly on the words the Spirit gave you.

Setting: individuals

Level: initial

Time: short, medium

Section 2

THE LEADER'S PRAYER LIFE

THE LEADER'S PRAYER LIFE

(*Note:* While the references in this section are primarily to pastors, the discussion applies to all church leaders—staff members, prayer leaders, church planters, missionaries, servant ministry leaders, church education leaders, and so on.)

It becomes clear that a certain unavailability is essential for the spiritual life of the minister. I am not trying to build a religious argument for a game of golf, a trip to a conference, a cruise to the Caribbean, or a sabbatical. These arguments have been made and they all strike me as quite unconvincing in the midst of our suffering world. No, I would like to make a plea for prayer as the creative way of being unavailable.

How would it sound when the question, "Can I speak to the minister?" is not answered by "I am sorry, he has someone in his office" but by "I am sorry, he is praying"? When someone says, "The minister is unavailable because this is his day of solitude, this is his day in the hermitage, this is his desert day," could that not be a consoling ministry? What it says is that the minister is unavailable to others, but because he is with God, and God alone—the God who is our God.

—Henri J. M. Nouwen, *The Living Reminder* (Seabury Press, 1977)

John Throop, an Episcopal priest, takes the illustration of Henri Nouwen one step further when he reflects on a call from a business executive to the Episcopal Bishop of Chicago. The bishop's secretary answered: "I'm sorry, the bishop is not able to come to the phone right now, he's praying." "Praying!?" was the response. "He should be working!"

The response isn't surprising. Somehow in the last two thousand years—since the apostles reminded the church that the primary work of the pastoral leader is "prayer and the ministry of the word" (Acts 6:4)—we have disassociated prayer from the work of the church's leaders. Yet if a congregation is to become a praying church, it must be born out of the heart of a praying pastor and leadership team. When the church sees the pastor's passion for prayer as the disciples saw Jesus' passion for prayer, they too will ask, "Teach us to pray."

Prayer is the primary way in which leaders accomplish their tasks.
—Alvin Vander Griend

There are two primary facets to the leader's prayer life. The most obvious is the personal prayer life *of* the leader. Is the leader spending time in prayer? Is he or she walking closely with the Lord? The second important facet of a leader's prayer life is the prayers offered *for* the leader. Are his or her needs being lifted up in daily prayer by those who share in the ministry? Both facets are imperative for the effective ministry of Christ's church.

the leader's personal prayer life

It is important for the pastor's prayer life to be strong and vital. However, a recent survey taken at a pastors' conference in Dallas indicated that 95 percent of the pastors prayed less than five minutes a day. Some years ago, C. Peter Wagner surveyed almost six hundred pastors across the United States to learn about their prayer life; he found that the average time these pastors spent in prayer each day was twenty-two minutes and that 57 percent prayed less than twenty minutes per day (*Ministries Today*, November/December, 1992).

The reasons for this deficiency of prayer are not unlike the reasons other Christians pray so little:

- Many church leaders have insufficient time set aside for prayer.

- The diversity of tasks in ministry makes scheduling unpredictable.

- Prayer easily falls by the wayside under the pressures of the job.

- Prayer can lose its freshness for pastors, and they can lose interest in prayer.

- Many church leaders have a strained relationship with God. High stress, low pay, and constant criticism can deal a devastating blow to a pastor's relationship with his or her "boss."

- Many church leaders do not know how to pray. Few seminaries teach a course on prayer.

- Many pastors lack accountability, especially in their prayer life. Pastors, as leaders, are often loners.

- Many church members do not prioritize prayer, so they think a pastor ought to be "working" instead of "wasting his time praying."

Tragically, prayer is not the top priority for many North American pastors. By contrast, in Korea, home of six of the ten largest churches in the world, the average pastor prays ninety minutes a day. To build praying churches, church leaders must become serious about their personal prayer lives.

some practical suggestions

- Put prayer in your job description. Clarify with your leadership board that prayer is an important facet of a leader's responsibility. It was the apostles' first priority (Acts 6:4).

- Put prayer on your day planner. If possible, select the same time each day so you can build the "habit" of prayer. Protect your time with the Lord.

- Keep a prayer journal. This is a good way to keep track of God's answers and of how God is working in your life in answer to prayer.

- Vary your prayer pattern. Learn to use a variety of prayer formats. Prayer is designed to be the joy of our relationship with the Lord—not a duty.

- Study the Scriptures' teaching on prayer. Preaching regularly on prayer requires regular study on prayer.

- Read (or re-read) a couple of books on prayer every year.

- Attend a Pastor's Prayer Summit in your area.

- Join a small prayer group.

- Take a day each month for a personal prayer retreat.

- Pray regularly with other church and ministry leaders in your community—ideally across denominational and ethnic lines.

- Pray with your spouse daily.

- Schedule counseling appointments early. When they arrive, explain that you will see them in twenty minutes and encourage them to spend time in the prayer room (or worship center) praying for wisdom and guidance.

- Set aside a specific place to pray—such as a prayer closet, a special chair, a pillow in the corner of your study—that regularly calls you to prayer.

the leader's prayer support

Being supported by prayer throughout the week is as important as the pastor's own prayer life. In fact, C. Peter Wagner has said, "Even though my personal prayer life is sometimes lacking, my prayer life is wonderful because of the prayers of my prayer warriors." Prayer support is especially important for leaders. The apostle Paul frequently asked the church to pray for him (cf. Rom. 15:30; Eph. 6:19; Col. 4:3-4; 1 Thess. 5:25; 2 Thess. 3:1-2). And in 1 Timothy 2:1-2, Paul specifically encourages Timothy to pray for leaders.

According to *Church Growth* (Winter 1991), leaders need more prayer for five reasons:

- They have been given more responsibility and accountability by God.

- Satan turns up the heat on those with more responsibility, especially in the areas of money, sex, and power.

- Satanists, New Agers, occult leaders, and others focus their evil attacks specifically on pastors and church leaders.

- Since leaders have greater influence, they take down more people when they fall.

- Because of their visibility, church leaders are subject to gossip and criticism.

Like an automobile needs continual care, especially if it is to run at peak performance, pastors and church leaders need a Pastor's Intercessory Team ("PIT Crew") to keep them working at high efficiency—blessed, protected, and encouraged.

I have heard John Maxwell's story of how a total stranger walked into his office one afternoon and said that God had appointed him to simply pray for John. In my own twenty-five years of pastoral ministry, I have had hundreds of singles, couples, small groups, even entire families "step into my office." On one occasion—after a particularly difficult board meeting—an elder knocked at my door. He had stopped by my study for no other reason than to pray for me and to offer a word of encouragement. It happened once. I will never forget it. It continues to encourage me. One of the greatest disappointments in ministry is recalling those who "promised" to pray but who never did, or those who prayed a few times and then forgot. Initially it may have been a genuine offer, but eventually you could tell—in them, in me, and in the ministry—that the praying had stopped.

In addition to providing encouragement, a congregation that prays for its pastor reaps other benefits:

- The pastor receives added spiritual protection from temptation and moral failure.

- Intercessors receive insights from God to share with the pastor.

A Prayer for Pastors

O Lord God, I beseech you to give to your church, both now and at all times, pastors and teachers after your own heart, those who shall bring the sheep of Christ into his fold, and who, through the influence of your good Spirit, shall feed them with saving knowledge and understanding.

Make every preacher of your Word know and always remember that he who plants is nothing, nor he who waters, but you are all in all, who alone can give the increase.

Let none of them vainly presume on their skill and ability to do any good and obtain any success by their preaching, but let them all humbly wait for and obtain the aids of your graces to enable them to dispense the Word of Life, and let your blessing render their preaching happily successful to the souls of those who hear them. Amen.

—August Hermann Francke (1725)

- Prayer keeps people attuned to the leader—they gain insight into the leader's needs and feel a part of the ministry.

- Praying for church leaders bridges the gap between leaders and members, builds unity in the congregation, and decreases criticism of the leadership.

some practical suggestions

- Recruit intercessors for a prayer shield (see pp. 131-133). Always look for additional intercessors.

- Support, encourage, and appreciate your prayer shield members.

- Adopt an "open door prayer policy" and encourage members to stop in to pray for you and other staff members.

- Place some books in your prayer room that teach people how to pray for their pastor.

- Teach an adult education course on how to pray for leaders.

- Have each Sunday school class "adopt a pastor" or staff member.

- Join the worship prayer team before the worship service so they can pray for you.

- Put pictures of the church's leaders in your prayer room.

- Borrow a church member's cottage or cabin for a short prayer retreat.

- Have a lay leader pray specifically for the pastor during worship.

- Have a few people designated to pray—during worship—while the pastor is preaching.

- Ask the leadership board to spend time at their monthly meetings praying for the pastor.

- Put the phrase "pray for your pastor" in the bulletin and newsletter periodically.

- Ask your members to say a prayer for church leaders every time they pass the church building during the week.

some cautions

- Be cautious of building a close relationship with intercessors of the opposite sex.

- Be cautious of "intercessors" who want to get close to the pastor for reasons other than prayer.

- Be cautious of "intercessors" who attempt to control the leader ("God says you should . . .").

- Be cautious of building your team too quickly. Having quality intercessors (people with high commitment and the spiritual gift of intercession) you can trust is far more important than a large quantity of intercessors.

prayer ideas for pastor appreciation day (or month)

- Invite people to write prayers and send them to the pastor.

- Invite people to come early for worship and pray for the pastor.

- Conduct a twenty-four–hour prayer vigil for the pastor.

- Have the elders lay hands on and pray for the pastor during worship.

- Have a guest pastor speak on how to pray for your pastor.

- Ask people to leave a prayer on the pastor's voicemail.

Resources

Rueben P. Job and Norman Shawchuck, *A Guide to Prayer for Ministers and Other Servants* (Nashville: Upper Room, 1983).

John Maxwell, *Partners in Prayer* (Nashville: Thomas Nelson, 1996).

Reggie McNeal, *A Work of the Heart: Understanding How God Shapes Spiritual Leaders* (San Francisco: Jossey-Bass, 2000).

Terry Muck, *Liberating the Leader's Prayer Life* (Nashville: Word, 1985).

Terry Tekyl, *Preyed On or Prayed For: Hedging in Your Pastor with Prayer* (Anderson, IN: Bristol Books, 1993).

Alvin Vander Griend, *The Praying Church Sourcebook* (Grand Rapids, MI: CRC Publications, 1997).

Intercessory Top Ten List

The list of people, needs, and items for which a pastor can pray is almost endless. While it is imperative to keep a running list of these needs and to pray for them throughout the week, some pastors use a "top ten" list of prayer needs.

Items can be placed on the list for a week at a time. This list can be

- placed in the sidebar of your daily/weekly planner.

- made into a bookmark and inserted in your Bible.

- written on a specially designed business card (see sample).

Items that can be placed on the list include

- your spouse, children, parents
- church leaders and staff members
- ministries of the church
- those in your church community with specific needs
- neighboring ministers
- upcoming responsibilities

- non-Christian neighbors
- national, regional, local government
- area schools, businesses, services

The list could obviously go on and on. One important thing to remember, however, is to be as specific as possible.

(front)

My Top Ten Prayer List

Week of _____

1. _____

2. _____

3. _____

4. _____

(back)

5. _____

6. _____

7. _____

8. _____

9. _____

10. _____

Leading a Meeting by Prayer

One of the most difficult challenges of ministry is to incorporate meaningful prayer into a board or committee meeting. Traditionally, prayer serves as the "book-ends" for the meeting—a short prayer opens the meeting and a shorter prayer closes it. In between, prayer is often forgotten.

The Sleepy Hollow Presbyterian Church of San Anselmo, California, working with the San Francisco Seminary Youth Ministry and Spirituality Project, developed a way to emphasize prayer in a meeting:

Opening Prayer	Usually includes time for silence.
Check-in	A brief (5-10 minutes) opportunity for people to communicate the baggage they bring to the meeting.
Lectio Divina	After a time of silence, a Bible passage is read two or three times. Members listen for a word or phrase that "shimmers" or "sticks." After a few more minutes of silence, each member shares the word or image and what it means for him or her.
Openings and Blocks	One member shares "openings" (where they have sensed God's presence or movement in the previous meeting) and "blocks" (where God's movement felt blocked or shut out). This is followed by prayerful reflections by the rest of the group.
Assignments/Planning	Every other week, the group spends a longer time noticing the various openings and how they may inform programming and planning.
Closing Prayer	Offering up gratitude and listening for common themes in the meeting.

At Calvary Christian Reformed Church in Wyoming, Michigan, we have modified this format to incorporate more prayer into our board meetings:

Opening Prayer	A brief opening prayer to ask for God's guidance and protection.
Teaching	The nature of this teaching varies. It can include *lectio divina*, a biblical teaching on prayer, a presentation about caregiving or another important topic, and so on.
Prayer	This is an extended time of prayer (30-60 minutes) that can be structured in a number of ways:

- Using one of the prayer formats described in Section 1 of this book.
- Inviting each person to write a prayer need—personal or communal—on an index card and passing the cards out; each person prays for the prayer need they have been handed.
- Dividing into smaller groups (4-5 members) for a time of prayer and mutual encouragement.
- Using open-ended questions that encourage sharing, such as "The hardest thing about being on this committee is . . ." or "The first time Christ felt 'real' to me was . . ." or "The best memory of my childhood is . . ."

Business	Minutes, discussion, decision-making, pertinent matters.
Groups	Our board breaks into three respective groups: elders, deacons, and shepherds (caregivers and small group leaders).
Districts	One elder, one deacon, and two to five shepherds discuss matters pertaining to members in the geographic district they have been assigned. They also spend time in prayer for these members.
Closing	The meeting ends with the group gathered together for a brief closing prayer.

We have discovered that by engaging in biblical meditation, silence, and other contemplative prayer practices

- God, rather than our opinions and interests, becomes the focus.

- we are reminded the ministry belongs to God.

- seeking God's will takes precedence over asking God to bless our plans.

- the pressure to always make the "right" decision decreases.

- we grow together in unity.

- we grow spiritually.

- we model the importance of Scripture and prayer.

Resource

For additional information on the San Francisco Youth Ministry and Spirituality Project, contact:

San Francisco Theological Seminary
2 Kensington Road
San Anselmo, CA 94960-2905
415-258-6500; 800-447-8820
fax: 415-258-6509
e-mail: ymsp@sfts.edu
www.sfts.edu/subyouthe.html

Pastor's Prayer Group

A pastor's prayer group is a gathering of pastors who come together to pray for revival, reconciliation, and repentance in their city. This involves focusing on the problems and strongholds in their city, as well as praying for protection on the leaders, schools, businesses, police force, firefighters, and rescue personnel, and on the churches and their pastors.

A pastor's prayer group may be comprised of pastors from the same denomination or pastors from the same community. The benefits of interdenominational, cross-cultural prayer are significant:

- It unites pastors and their congregations.

- It helps pastors to appreciate other denominational, cultural, and ethnic blessings.

- It provides a base of unity to pray for revival, evangelism, and spiritual awakening in a community or city.

- It provides a hedge of protection over the city's spiritual leaders and their families.

- It provides an example of unity for the churches the pastors serve.

- It provides some accountability for pastors' personal prayer lives.

- It serves as the foundation for city-wide prayer initiatives: National Day of Prayer, Pastor's Prayer Summits, Concerts of Prayer, Marches for Jesus, and so on.

Pastors invited to join the group should

- believe in Jesus Christ as their Lord and Savior.

- believe in the power of prayer.

- be committed to unity among other pastors.

- be willing to follow the leading of the Holy Spirit.

- encourage other pastors to join in prayer.

When pastors come together to pray, most of the time should be spent praying—for each other, for their city, and for the lost. The pastors should be encouraged to pray as they are accustomed to—and to respect those who pray in a different manner. Also, consider varying the format of the prayer time, using such prayer formats as A.C.T.S. (see p. 38), *lectio divina* (see pp. 73-74), Summit Style (see p. 95), and Bidding Prayer (see pp. 47-48).

warnings

- Keep prayers vertical; leave the sermons in the study.

- Stay focused on prayer.

- Keep to the designated time.

other opportunities

- Have each pastor select another pastor in the city each week, make an appointment, and visit their office for the purpose of praying with them.

- Adopt three-way partnerships. In the Dallas/Fort Worth area, pastors have joined a "P-by-P" (Prayer by Phone) ministry. For pastors whose phones allow for three-way calling, a call is initiated each week for the triad to pray together over the phone. Some pastors' spouses are also involved in a P-by-P designed exclusively for them.

- Pray for a pastor/church in your area each Sunday morning, list them in your bulletin, and have church members send cards of appreciation to that church and pastor.

- Mandate a prayer team from your church to pray for another church. Each week they should make an appointment to visit a neighboring pastor to pray with him or her. The following Sunday they should arrive early and, with prior permission, pray for the worship service, and then worship with the church. That evening (or the following Sunday) they can share with their own church the blessings they have experienced.

Pastor's Prayer Partners

In 1981, sixty-year-old Bill Klassen walked into the office of a young man he had never met before who was pastoring a church he had never attended before. His agenda was simple: "I believe God has called me—a layman—to disciple, encourage, and pray for pastors. The reason I came here today was so that I could pray for you." And they prayed together.

The pastor Bill Klassen began praying for was John Maxwell, the pastor of Skyline Wesleyan Church in San Diego, California. Over the next few years as Bill prayed for John, the church more than tripled in size, the annual giving multiplied almost seven times, and the prayer partner ministry grew to 120 intercessors. Bill Klassen continues to pray for John Maxwell.

For a pastor, having one or more prayer partners—individuals (of the same gender as the pastor) who will commit to regularly praying with and for the pastor—is imperative. Whether contact is made one-on-one or in a small group, over the phone or over breakfast, Saturday morning or Sunday evening, this is an essential component of the pastor's ministry.

Pastors, recognizing the value of their prayer partners, should keep their partner(s) well informed—whether through a newsletter, a special phone line, or another method—and should affirm their partners' work by holding monthly get-togethers or an annual retreat.

Resource

John Maxwell, *Partners in Prayer* (Nashville: Thomas Nelson, 1996).

Pastor's Prayer Plan

We try to find time in our daily schedule for God—for prayer, for Bible study, for reflection. Sometimes we are successful; often we are not. Yet *all* of our time belongs to God, and God expects to be not merely an appointment on our calendar, but the priority of our life. So what do we do?

The Connection Planner (see sample on page 126) suggests that our spiritual life will be transformed by submitting the seven basic relationships in our life to God, acknowledging that all of our time belongs to God, and prioritizing our time in the Word and in prayer.

It is not how well you manage your time that determines your success in life; it is how well you manage your relationships—your connections to God and others.

—Unknown

By following this daily planner, you will

- focus on seven primary relationships.

- read through Scripture.

- have the opportunity to memorize a verse of Scripture a day.

- reflect on a question or two each day.

- keep a record of your prayer petitions and the answers God provides.

- have a growing recognition that your entire day belongs to the Lord.

Resource

The Connection Series is available in three levels—adult, student, and early childhood—as a bound book or in three-ring binder format from

The Bible League
16801 Van Dam Road
South Holland, IL 60473-2600
800-334-7017
www.connectionclub.com

DECEMBER 25

1999	2000	2001
Sat	Mon	Tue

John 1:14 — *And Christ became a human being and lived here on earth among us and was full of loving forgiveness and truth. And some of us have seen his glory — the glory of the only Son of the heavenly Father! (TLB)*

Treat others with compassion and forgiveness as Jesus did, and they will see Jesus in you.

What are you doing to reveal your relationship with God to others?

Ronald Pineda, Philippines

2 Jn. - Jude
According to Jude's epistle, who disputed with Satan over the body of Moses?

Rev. 16
What container holds God's wrath on the earth?

Rev. 3
What church was neither hot nor cold?

Prayers for the seven connections:

1 Personal

2 Marriage/Friend

3 Family

4 Small Group/Friends

5 Church

6 Kingdom

7 World

• *Whom can you share your walk with today?*

Thanksgiving / Praise:

Confession:

✓	Prayer (To Do) List	I Cor. 10:31

©1998 LifeNet 21, Inc.

—Reprinted with permission of The Bible League, 1-800-334-7017, www.connectionclub.com.

Pastors' Prayer Summits

Several years ago, Joe Aldrich, president of Multnomah Bible College, invited a number of pastors along the Oregon coast to a four-day retreat where the only agenda was to "wait on God." Since then, International Renewal Ministries has sponsored hundreds of Pastors' Prayer Summits each year throughout the United States and Canada and more than thirty other countries.

Prayer summits are designed to call the pastors of a city or region together to pray—across denominational, cultural, racial, and other lines. Because of confidentiality issues, summits are normally limited to pastors of local congregations. Because of the dynamics of vulnerability, confession, and sharing, summits are normally gender-specific (although some summits have been held with couples).

A typical summit begins on Monday with lunch and concludes Thursday at noon. There are extended times of communal worship and prayer (see Prayer-Summit Style, p. 95), as well as time for personal communion with the Lord, time for fellowship and networking with other pastors from the city or community, and some time for rest and recreation.

Resources

Joe Aldrich, *Prayer Summits* (Portland, OR: Multnomah Press, 1992).

International Renewal Ministries
8435 N.E. Gilison St.
Portland, OR 97220
503-251-6455
fax: 503-254-1268
www.multnomah.edu

Pastor's Small Group

Every pastor ought to be in at least one small group. Small groups provide fellowship, accountability, and encouragement. They are also a primary incubator for spiritual growth—for studying the Word and for prayer.

There are various types of small groups. Each type has its benefits and its liabilities. Although it involves a significant investment of time, some pastors are involved in all three primary types.

staff small group

In medium and large churches that have multiple staff members, the pastor can be involved with the staff in a weekly Bible study and prayer time. In very large churches, staff members can meet together as departments (for example, the entire youth staff meets together weekly for Bible study and prayer).

Benefits:

- Helps build a sense of teamwork and unity of purpose.

- Guarantees that each staff member will spend time in the Word and in prayer at least weekly.

- Gives the staff an opportunity to pray about the issues of ministry.

- Provides a model for the congregation.

Liabilities:

- Confidentiality may be an issue. Pastors are not at liberty to discuss some issues with others and should be cautious about the confessions they share.

non-staff small group

This type of small group comes in a number of forms.

Some pastors enjoy meeting with a group of their fellow church members.

Benefits:

- Provides an immediate affinity—people have ownership in the church and a commitment to the pastor.

Liabilities:

- Some things are not open for discussion in this context because of confidentiality issues.

- The pastor still remains the pastor to the other group members (that is, the pastor continues to live the role and may have difficulty being accepted as a peer).

- If there is trouble in the church, the trouble may come into the group.

Some pastors prefer to be in a small group comprised of people other than their church members.

Benefits:
- Allows the pastor to share openly with other group members.

Liabilities:
- This may be a difficult group to assemble and maintain unless group members have something else in common.

Some pastors prefer to be in a same-gender group.

Benefits:
- May serve as an accountability group that can deal with issues not often acceptable in a mixed-gender group.

Liabilities:
- The range of fellowship is limited.

Some pastors prefer to be in a mixed-gender group.

Benefits:
- The range of fellowship is wide open.
- Provides the pastor with an opportunity to be in a small group with his or her spouse.

Liabilities:
- Some items are inappropriate for a mixed-gender group to deal with.

Note: Ideally, a pastor should be in a same-gender group for accountability and a mixed-gender group for fellowship and caregiving. Both types of groups can be involved in Bible study and service.

pastor's small group

This small group comes in two types: a group of other pastors from the same denomination or a group of other pastors in the same community or city (see Pastor's Prayer Group, pp. 122-123).

Personal Retreats

Periodic retreats promote spiritual growth and physical refreshment. Increasingly, pastors are setting aside a day each month to focus their attention on this important part of their ministry.

Pastor Frank H. Billman of Somerton United Methodist Church in Philadelphia, Pennsylvania, recommends:

> Write prayer retreats into your schedule on a regular (monthly or quarterly) basis. Get away from the office for a day or a half-day to get in touch with God and yourself, and pray for the congregation. Go to another church, a retreat center, or a park. Advertise your prayer retreats ahead of time. This allows people to pray for you. Invite people to write down specific requests for which they would like you to pray. Ask them to put their requests in an envelope marked "Confidential—Prayer retreat." Tell them you will open the envelope on the retreat, pray for the request, destroy the papers, and tell no one the contents. This way people are more willing to share deep needs that they might be unwilling to share in person or with anyone else.
>
> —*Net Results*, January 1997

In planning a prayer retreat, pastors should remember that retreat time has two important components: spiritual exercise and physical recreation.

spiritual exercises

- Read a book of the Bible (use *lectio divina*, see pp. 73-74).

- Pray through your church directory.

- Read a book on prayer.

- Enjoy God's creation by taking a walk—in the woods, on the beach, in the desert, through the city.

- Fast and pray for direction and guidance.

- Worship, using CDs or tapes.

- Listen for God.

- Journal.

physical recreation

- Rest; take a short nap.

- Go for a walk or a run.

- Read a short book for enjoyment (avoid news magazines and newspapers).

- Go swimming or sit in a hot tub.

- Do whatever relaxes you (avoid television, radio, news).

Resources

See the section on Prayer Retreats for additional information and sample retreat schedules.

Prayer Shield

(*Note*: This is written for the pastor's perspective; for additional insights from the church's perspective, see pp. 214-217.)

A prayer shield is one of the most significant ministries a pastor can develop in his or her congregation. Unfortunately, this ministry is frequently overlooked for a number of reasons:

- Some pastors do not understand its necessity to daily ministry.

- This ministry is directed at pastors and their families, and they may be hesitant to promote something that might appear self-serving.

- Some pastors hesitate to admit they need prayer.

- Some pastors prefer not to share their needs with others.

- Some pastors are afraid of becoming too involved with intercessors. High-level intercessors can have a significant impact; they often receive significant answers, discernments, and insights from God. This can be intimidating or humbling—emotions that some pastors would rather not deal with.

> **It takes prayer in the pulpit and prayer in the pew to make preaching arresting, life-giving, and soul-saving.**
> **—E. M. Bounds**

- Some pastors think they are no different than any other believer. Unfortunately, leaders in the church are generally attacked with far more regularity and force than other believers.

As a result, few pastors encourage their congregation to begin this ministry, so most members do not understand its value to daily ministry or the extent to which their pastor needs such intercession.

In his book *Prayer Shield*, C. Peter Wagner speaks about three basic levels of intercessors for leaders:

- **Level Three intercessors** have a distant relationship with the leader. In some cases, these intercessors have never even met the person(s) they are praying for. For example, many people have prayed for Billy Graham on a daily basis and yet have never met him; many others pray for missionaries they have never met.

- **Level Two intercessors** have a casual relationship with the leader. There is some regular two-way contact, although it may not be one-on-one, intensive, or sustained over any length of time. This may include, for example, Sunday morning worship attendees who pray for their pastor.

- **Level One intercessors** have a very close relationship with the person they are praying for, which allows them to pray for items that are personal and possibly confidential. These people have personal contact on a regular basis.

Identifying your prayer shield intercessors

Pastors should know that some intercessors will respond to a general appeal; some need to be personally invited; and a few will be led by God through their prayers to step forward. Following are some ideas for identifying those who can form a pastor's prayer shield.

- In *Possessing the Gates of the Enemy*, Cindy Jacobs uses Jesus' words in Matthew 7:7 as an outline for building a prayer shield:

  —**ASK** the Lord to set aside personal prayer partners on your behalf.

  —**SEEK** out those whom you feel would pray for you on a regular basis.

  —**KNOCK**—contact those on your potential prayer partner list.

- One pastor bought twenty-five books on intercession (*Prayer Shield* by C. Peter Wagner is a good one) and announced that the books were in his study. Anyone willing to commit to pray for him for an hour a week could sign their name and take a book after the service. All the books disappeared. He then called the intercessors together to talk with them and train them.

- Enlist every member of the church to pray for the pastor(s) for one minute every day (for example, at noon) or at the beginning of your morning service.

  Intercessors who have been identified should

- love the pastor.

- want to be used by God, but also be willing to be a team player.

- have a passion for or the gift of intercession, or both.

- have integrity and maturity and be respected in the church.

- be able to keep a confidence (violation of confidentiality requires immediate dismissal from the Prayer Shield team).

caring for your intercessors

While much of the intercessors' work will be unseen, it is important that the pastor not take their prayers for granted. There are a number of things pastors can do to care for and show appreciation for their intercessors:

- Provide regular training in prayer.

- Maintain regular contact; provide intercessors with a monthly prayer calendar. In some cases, the prayer concerns shared with the different levels may vary.

- Trust your intercessors—especially Level One intercessors—and listen carefully to what they are hearing from God.

- Hold personal interviews with each Level One intercessor and every intercessor privileged with confidential requests.

- Pray regularly for your intercessors—and, if you don't have a Level One intercessor, pray that God will send you one.

- Gather your intercessors together over a meal for a time of fellowship.

- Express your appreciation for their work and encourage their prayer life by giving them a book on prayer.

- Send a thank-you card.

cautions

- Be cautious of intercessors of the opposite gender; Level One intercessors should be of the same gender as the leader.

- Be cautious of "intercessors" who want to get close to the pastor for reasons other than to pray.

- Be cautious of "intercessors" who try to control the leader ("God says you should . . .").

- Be cautious of playing the numbers game. Having quality intercessors (people with high commitment and the spiritual gift of intercession) is far more important than the quantity of intercessors.

- Be cautious of building your team too fast.

Resource

C. Peter Wagner, *Prayer Shield: How to Intercede for Pastors, Christian Leaders, and Others on the Spiritual Frontlines* (Ventura, CA: Gospel Light, 1997).

It is important for members of the congregation to pray for their leaders. It is also important for church leaders to pray for their congregation. Pastors commonly pray for church members who are going through crises. But pastors also need to intercede for their church's members when things are going well. A pastor's prayers for his or her congregation are for daily protection, guidance, and blessing. Such prayers must be intentional, systematic, and regular.

options

- Pastor John Kerssies of Redeemer Christian Reformed Church in Sarnia, Ontario, uses this method in his personal devotions:

    On each page of my church directory are listed about eight to ten families/members. Each morning I make it a point to pray for those listed on one page; the next morning I go to the next page; and so on. In the opening pages of the directory are the names of persons serving in the various church ministries. I take time to pray for them as well.

    This method forces me to pray for every member of my church at least twice a month. I think about them, reflect on their needs, and plan to visit them in the future if my schedule allows. It helps me be less critical of those whose views I do not fully share. It helps to concretely thank the Lord much more for the positive elements within my congregation. It makes me more conscious of the riches that we treasure together in the Lord.

- Pastor John Throop of St. Simon's Episcopal Church in Arlington Heights, Illinois, takes his calendar and assigns one member/family their own day. When "their" day comes, Throop remembers them specifically in his devotions throughout the day. He writes them a personal letter, letting them know he has been praying for them throughout the day and asking them to continue to remember him in prayer.

- Divide the directory into seven equal sections—one for each day of the week. In a large church divide it into thirty equal sections—one for each day of the month. If there are multiple pastors, divide the list among the pastors and rotate lists each month.

- Pray for the congregation in the worship center. During the week, begin on one side of the worship center and, stopping by each row, pray for the people who often sit in those seats.

Praying with Your Leaders

Some months ago, our congregation faced a small financial crisis. We decided to call our leaders to a month of prayer and fasting, asking God for discernment and guidance. At the end of the month, we asked each member of our leadership team (forty elders, shepherds, and deacons) to write down on index cards what they felt the Lord was saying to them in answer to their prayers. The response was amazing:

- A couple of people admitted that they had not fasted and prayed enough to discover God's leading.

- Over half of the people wrote down answers that resonated with each other—that is, they provided a unified direction for the church. We understood this as God's leading.

- A number of people submitted other scenarios—in most cases the same opinions they held before they prayed.

James, the leader of the early church in Jerusalem, understood the importance of praying leaders. He writes, "If any of you lacks wisdom, he should ask God, who gives generously to all without finding fault, and it will be given to him" (James 1:5).

Jesus is the head of the church. So the task of church leaders is not to exchange opinions, debate certain issues, or even to take votes. Majority "rule" is not the goal of church leadership. A church leader's responsibility is to discover what God wants and then to lead the people into God's will by example, teaching, and encouragement. This requires significant prayer.

All too often, however, prayer serves simply as a "call to order" and the "motion to adjourn" or as a request for God to bless the human agenda. Much of what happens in leadership meetings is based on discussing the facts and exercising our "God-given" judgment.

Since prayer is a vital part of leadership, prayer must be a vital part of leaders' meetings. Extended time for prayer must be scheduled into meetings; placing prayer at the beginning of a meeting underscores its priority, reminds us that Christ is the head of the church, sets the proper atmosphere for discussion, and prevents running out of time for prayer at the end.

When leaders come together to seek the face of the Lord, to lay out their concerns and genuinely seek his will, and to ask for strength to make the right decisions, the church begins to move. Ask God to teach you to pray. Then allow God to teach you by practicing prayer.

Writing in *Leadership* (March/April 1982, p. 10), Richard Lane says that his elders recognized God was calling them to be men of prayer and God's Word. They began meeting together each Friday morning at 6:00 a.m. for ninety minutes of praise, prayer, and sharing. The congregation found out about it and "as a result, between seventy and eighty requests come in each week for the elders to pray about."

practical ideas

- Assign each leader a specific prayer concern/issue (pass out index cards with a prayer need written on them).

- Break into groups of three or four and pray for each other and various ministries of the church.

- Schedule a prayer retreat for your leadership team. Teach prayer and pray together.

- Spend time going through a book on prayer a chapter at a time.

- Call a meeting with no other agenda than to spend time together in prayer.

- Leave the prayer time open for each person to pray. Encourage people to participate. This is corporate prayer.

- Vary the format of prayer.

- Give people permission to ask for prayer at any time during a meeting; when prayer is requested the debate should cease and prayer should be made.

- Before making a decision, spend time in prayer about it; for strategic decisions, consider spending a month in prayer.

- Don't hasten the prayer time to get to the agenda—prayer is the agenda.

- Encourage prayer to be genuine. Avoid flowery language. Express your heart simply.

- Make sure all the prayers are vertical—directed to God (No preaching allowed!).

- Do not use the prayer time to manipulate others or to seek God's approval for a personal agenda.

Note: For more ideas, see Leading a Meeting by Prayer, pages 120-121.

Staff Prayer

For several years, our staff meeting lasted the entire morning. Then someone suggested that if we were asking our congregation to pray, the staff should set aside time to study Scripture and to pray. We wondered how we could add ninety minutes and still get all the work done. To our amazement, we discovered that after spending time in the Word and in prayer, we still had plenty of time to complete all our work.

Every church with multiple staff members needs a regular staff meeting that includes a season of prayer. While some staffs meet for devotions on a daily basis, most churches have a weekly prayer time for staff members. In some cases the prayer time is held in connection with the staff meeting; in other cases a separate time is selected.

If devotions are held daily, they are usually limited to fifteen to thirty minutes. At least once a week, the prayer time should be extended. If the staff meets once a week for prayer, the time should also be extended.

The prayer time should include

- prayer for the congregation (crises, illnesses, and praying through the directory) and for unity
- prayer for worship
- prayer for ministries and their leaders
- prayer for the staff and their families
- prayer for upcoming special events
- prayer for effective evangelism and for the lost
- prayer for the presence and power of the Holy Spirit

In addition to spending time praying, a staff may want to enrich its prayer life by working through a book on prayer, such as Terry Teykl's *Acts 29: Fifty Days of Prayer to Invite the Holy Spirit*; by going through a book of the Bible using *lectio divina*; or by encouraging staff members to spend personal time with the Lord—literally building it into the workweek. (For example, College Hill Presbyterian Church in Cincinnati reserves every Wednesday morning from 11:00 until noon as a "Quiet Time to the Lord." During this time, the desks are vacant, the computers are quiet, the phones are on voicemail, meetings are set aside, and staff members meet with God.)

Note: For more ideas, see Leading a Meeting by Prayer, pages 120-121.

Section 3

PRAYER MINISTRY IDEAS

IMPLEMENTING A PRAYER MINISTRY

While building a house of prayer is not simply a program, it does have programmatic dynamics. There is recruiting to be done, people to be trained, structures to be put in place, schedules to keep, paperwork to be completed, and evaluations to be filled out. Programs are not inherently bad—unless the reason for doing them is lost. While prayer is more than a program, building a house of prayer involves selecting some prayer ministries and programs that involve believers in intentional prayer.

determining ministries

It is clear that there are no predetermined prayer ministries a church should begin, and that developing a praying church involves far more than adding a few prayer ministries. However, becoming a house of prayer does require an intentional plan.

The first priority is to raise up prayer leadership. The New Testament apostles filled this role. Ideally, the pastors of the church will feel a similar calling to "give [their] attention to prayer and the ministry of the word" (Acts 6:4). While it is imperative for pastors to model the priority of prayer in their private and public lives, the administration of a prayer ministry can be delegated to other gifted leaders in the church. As churches grow and the emphasis on specializing increases, more and more churches are appointing prayer coordina-

tors. While these often are volunteer positions, they remain opportunities of considerable responsibility. (For more information on qualifications and responsibilities, see pp. 180-184.) Thus, it is important that such an appointment be made only after considerable prayer and seeking God's will for the direction of your church. As the prayer ministry develops and more ministries are added, additional leaders should be added to form a prayer ministry team.

When a church begins to earnestly seek God and his will, the spiritual attacks will intensify. While the church is the target for these spiritual attacks, the pastor and his family are the "bull's-eye." Pastors and other leaders need to be protected. Beginning a Prayer Shield ministry (see pp. 131-133 and 214-217) is a good way to ensure this protection. Recruit people who are willing to pray for the pastor and leaders of your church every day.

Worship is a significant part of the church's purpose and identity. In addition to leaders, worship is a primary target for spiritual attack. Thus, praying for your church's worship services is an important part of ministry (see pp. 229-232). Pray before, during, and following worship for spiritual protection, the Spirit's presence, anointed preaching, receptive hearts, enhanced fellowship, visitors, and so on.

Pray for your church members (Eph. 6:18). Begin with one or two ministries that provide prayer, support, and encouragement for church members and fellow believers. A

Prayer Chain (see pp. 176-179) is helpful for those in crisis. A Prayer Team (see pp. 221-222) can visit those who are in the hospital or rest homes and those who are confined to their homes. A team of intercessors can Pray Through the Directory (see pp. 233-234) each week. Prayer Calendars (see p. 175) can unify a congregation's daily prayer focus throughout the month.

Becoming a praying church requires both an inward and an outward focus; remember also to pray for the lost. This section outlines ministries with a primarily inward focus. Section 4, Harvest Prayer Ideas, details ministries that intentionally and actively pray for the lost.

Part of becoming a house of prayer is ensuring that your church knows how to pray. Develop opportunities for people to learn about and practice prayer. This might include building a Prayer Library (see p. 197) of books, videos, and CDs on prayer; offering a School of Prayer (see pp. 235-236); holding regular Prayer Retreats (see p. 207); or sponsoring an annual Prayer Emphasis Week/Month (see pp. 186-187) with opportunities for people to be trained in prayer.

When these basic ministries are in place and functioning well, consider adding ministries as the Lord leads in areas of greatest need, interest, and members' giftedness. This section is a list of possible prayer ministries. Obviously, no church will use all of them. Your congregation, leaders, and intercessors should pray about which to incorporate. Selecting the ministries that are appropriate for your church should be based on

- the direction God is leading.

- your congregation's mission and vision.

- the needs of the community in which God has placed you.

- the spiritual gifts and interests of your members.

These are not four different factors, but four facets of the same factor. For example, God will not lead you into areas where your members have no spiritual gifts, nor into an area of ministry that meets no needs.

developing ministries

Start slowly. Begin with ministries that do not involve structure or paradigm changes; no one will object to beginning a small prayer group. Upgrade current prayer ministries; if you have a prayer-chain ministry, look at how you could make it more effective and involve more people.

Develop one idea at a time. Make sure a ministry is effective and has adequate leadership and participation before developing a new ministry. Note that the goal of developing a house of prayer is not to have the most ministries in place, but to develop effective prayer ministries that involve a growing number of participants and meet a growing number of needs.

Each of the ministries in this section fits into one of four categories:

An **initial ministry** is one of the first ministries to consider implementing in your congregation. Once these basic, fundamental ministries are in place, consider adding additional ministries as the need arises and as God leads. Seven ministries in this section have been designated as initial: Prayer Meeting, Prayer Room, Prayer Shield, Prayer Teams, Praying for Worship, Prayer Warriors, and School of Prayer. Most of these initial ministries require one volunteer leader to supervise.

A **simple ministry** is fairly easy to start, involves minimal training of participants, and requires little maintainance. One prayer team member can supervise several simple ministries.

An **intermediate ministry** involves some planning time, takes more effort to get started and to recruit participants, necessitates basic training of participants, and requires regular attention to maintain. One team member can supervise one or two intermediate ministries.

An **intense ministry** requires adequate planning time, considerable start-up and recruiting time, regular training and encouragement of participants, and considerable attention to maintain. One prayer team member, especially if that person is a volunteer, should not be responsible for more than one intense ministry.

Some of the prayer ministries in this section may sound similar and may overlap with other prayer ministries. Feel free to use these ministries to create your own prayer ministries that reflect your church and community.

recruiting participants

One of the most difficult aspects of developing and maintaining a prayer ministry is recruiting people to pray. While Christians believe in the necessity and power of prayer, people are busy—bombarded with endless opportunities and responsibilities. Unfortunately, prayer is often relegated to the bottom of the priority list. (Once a believer has developed a meaningful prayer life the priority changes—but the pressures of life and the spiritual warfare seldom do.) As a result, recruiting is a constant challenge. Here are some suggestions for recruiting intercessors for your prayer ministry:

- Pray. Ask God to bring more intercessors into the prayer ministry.

- Have people regularly share with your congregation how God is working in their life in answer to prayer. One of the best recruiting "tools" is answered prayer.

- Keep prayer request cards easily accessible (for example, in the bulletin, in the friendship pad, and/or in the pews).

- Advertise prayer events in the bulletin and/or newsletter, on worship screens or TV monitors.

- Have a "recruiting" drive during prayer emphasis week/month.

- Produce a brochure that describes all the aspects of your prayer ministry—include phone numbers for additional information and a commitment card for people to become involved. Place the brochure in the bulletin at least twice a year, hand it out at new member classes, and put it in your church's brochure rack.

appreciating your participants

One of the most overlooked aspects of developing and maintaining a prayer ministry is appreciating people who are involved in the prayer ministry. While intercessors do not covet recognition, everyone needs appreciation. Below are some suggestions for appreciating intercessors in your prayer ministry.

- Have an annual Prayer Ministry Appreciation Banquet (or even a simple luncheon). Some churches hold an annual banquet for all their volunteers; in this case, prayer ministry participants could be included.

- Appreciate and recognize intercessors during an annual commissioning service.

- Place a note of appreciation in the bulletin and/or newsletter. List your intercessors by name.

- Send notes of appreciation regularly. Thanksgiving, Easter, and the National Day of Prayer make excellent opportunities to thank those who are praying.

- When your prayer team meets, always express some words of appreciation.

- Make periodic phone calls to express appreciation.

- Have the pastor(s) stop in during prayer events and offer a word of appreciation.

Abrahamic Blessing

Abraham had a close walk with the Lord and the Lord blessed him (Gen. 24:1). The Abrahamic blessing ministry is a ministry that prays for economic blessing for the purpose of providing

- opportunities for meaningful employment.

- monetary blessing in order to give proportionately to God's church and kingdom.

- a testimony to God's faithfulness to the community.

To start, collect business cards from church members. Place the cards in a small notebook designed to hold business cards or into a Rolodex business card file. (Cards should be inserted in protective sleeves because of repeated use.)

Gather a prayer team to meet weekly to pray for God's blessing on these individuals, their families, and their businesses.

Keep the list updated. Add new business cards as they become available. Contact the businesses quarterly to remind them that you are praying for them.

options

- Several business cards could be solicited from each person and multiple books made up for pray-ers to keep in their home and pray for daily or weekly. The group could then continue to meet weekly or decide to meet only once a month to pray together.

- Place the notebook or card file in your church's prayer room. One prayer station could be designated for "Abrahamic Blessing." People could be encouraged to come in throughout the week and pray through the listings.

- Invite business people to give their testimonies in church periodically to illustrate how God answers prayer.

- Collect business cards from your community and pray over them that God will bless your community.

- Prayerwalk neighborhood businesses as well as businesses in which members are involved. Write cards to the owners, leaders, and employees of the businesses.

how to pray for the workplace

- Ask for God's blessing on the place of business (Matt. 7:7-11).

- Ask God to identify and unify the Christians in the workplace (John 17).

- Ask God to bring salvation to the business leaders (Mark 3:13-14).

- Ask God to maintain business integrity and to provide wisdom for the decisions that are made (Prov. 1:7).

- Ask God to keep the employees safe while on the job (Ps. 91:11-12).

- Ask God to shield workers from job-related stress (John 14:1; Col. 3:15).

- Ask God to make work a joy, to center hearts on service instead of self, on contentment instead of personal gain (1 Thess. 4:11-12).

- Ask God to bless employees' physical health, family stability, emotional well-being, and spiritual life.

- Ask Christ to become Lord of the workplace.

- Ask God to bless the customers served by the employees.

- Thank God for gainful employment, for meaningful labor, and for economic success.

Ministry category: simple

Adopt-a-Leader

The Michigan Family Forum has promoted the Adopt-a-Leader ministry for many years. Its goal is to pair intercessors with city, county, and state officials. (National leaders could also be included.) This can be a ministry initiated by an individual church, by cooperating churches in a city, or by associating with an organization in your state or province that promotes an "adopt-a-leader" type ministry.

Begin by determining your church's type of involvement. Will you pray for local officials, county officials, state officials, national officials, or a combination? Will you allow the pray-ers to select the person they will be praying for, or will the prayer ministry simply assign intercessors to leaders?

When pairings have been assigned or chosen, provide each participant with the name of their official, his or her particular role in government, and as much information about his or her job and family as is available. Periodically, intercessors should send a Prayer-a-Gram (see pp. 189-190) or encouraging note to the official for whom they are praying.

Ministry category: simple

Resources

An Adopt-a-Leader Prayer Calendar is available from:

Michigan Family Forum
P.O. 15216
Lansing, MI 48901-5216
517-374-1171

An Adopt-a-Leader Prayer Kit is available from:

National Day of Prayer Committee
P.O. Box 15616
Colorado Springs, CO 80935-5616
719-531-3379
fax: 719-548-4520
e-mail: ndptf@aol.com

Blessing Homes

In many cultures and traditions, the "blessing" of a new home is both a spiritual and social event to which family, friends, and neighbors are invited. A home is more than simply a place to eat and sleep; it is a place where dreams are formed, children are born and nurtured, and marriages are sustained. As a result, blessing a home seems natural. Considered to be the forerunner to the common "housewarming," house blessing is increasingly becoming a tradition that crosses religious and denominational lines. More families are requesting blessings to create peace and sanctuary in their home.

Although one prayer can be offered to cover everything in the house, normally individual prayers are said as the celebrants walk through the home. Each prayer is tailored to the function of the room and its contents. Prayers are said for the child who will sleep in the bedroom, for the information received in the television room, for the family bonding that takes place across the table in the kitchen. Prayers are said asking God to bless, hallow, and fill the home with his grace. Prayers are offered for the health, joy, and happiness of all who visit the home. Prayers are offered to keep hurt, harm, and danger away. Prayers are also offered outside in the yard; frequently intercessors walk the outside boundaries of the yard as a dedication to the Lord.

While a house blessing can be as brief as a few minutes, some last an hour or more, followed by a time of fellowship. Often guests bring a food item to share.

In the sphere of spiritual warfare, it is not uncommon for demons to stay in a home, even after the previous residents have left. Scripture readings, prayers, singing, and dedicating the home to Jesus create an uncomfortable atmosphere for demons to remain. If the home is known to be occupied by demons, additional measures may be taken (see Warfare Prayer, pp. 105-108).

Ministry category: intermediate

Resources

Max Lucado, *The Great House of God* (Nashville: Word, 1997).

Robert Munger, *My Heart, Christ's Home* (InterVarsity, 1992).

Church Pierce and Rebecca Wagner Sytsema, *Ridding Your Home of Spiritual Darkness* (Colorado Springs: Wagner Publications, Inc., 2000).

Bulletin Panel

Dedicate one panel of your bulletin for prayer items: petitions, intercessions, answers, and thanksgivings (see sample).

Encourage your congregation to keep the bulletin (or just that panel) in their Bible, in their devotional book, or on the refrigerator as a daily reminder to pray for the needs of your church family.

Ministry category: simple

Welcome to Calvary

We're glad you are here to worship today. Join us in the Fellowship Room for a cup of coffee after worship this morning. Throughout the week we have activities for adults, teens and children, and you are welcome to attend them as well. See the descriptions in this brochure or receive more information at our fellowship time. Guest mailboxes are located near the Information Center.

Church Family News and Prayer Reminders

Please remember in prayer and with a card our Calvary Members who need our support and encouragement.
Praise the Lord, O my soul; all my inmost being, praise his holy name" **Psalm 103:1**

Prayer needs and prayers of thanksgiving:
Give thanks to God for answered prayers that there were no serious Y2K problems. Praise God for His faithfulness.
Betty Swieringa will have tests on Jan. 26 to find out the cause of her dizziness. Pray that the results of the tests will show that her condition is treatable and that she will feel better soon.
Pray for **Diane Koster**. Diane continues her dialysis three times a week. She also is having a problem with her sight. Pray for daily strength and encourage her with your prayers and cards. Pray for Ken who cares for her daily.
Pray for members of our congregation who have **extended family** with difficult health problems. Pray for healing and strength for each individual.
Pray for the ministries meeting at Calvary this week: Council, Weekly Prayer Meeting, Cadets, Gems, Yesterday Youth Family Fun Night. Pray that these ministries will be effective and that many will become involved in serving our Lord.
Pray that our Pastors may be granted discernment and wisdom in maintaining and nurturing all relationships in family, church, and community.
Missionaries: Pray for **Bill and Diana Steele** as they continue to minister in Guinea, West Africa. Pray for a good stable political situation and for freedom of ministry.
Continue to pray for your neighbor, co-workers who are unchurched. Pray that you will have opportunities to share the love of the Lord with them.
Pray for the "What if it's True?" campaign. Pray that we will effectively influence our neighbors, co-workers, friends and family members for Christ. Ask Him for the grace to pray through for His will be accomplished.
In China, persecution of Christians and incredible church growth are realities as we begin this new millenium. Prayer is urgently needed for tens of thousands of new believers there, and for those persecuted for their faith. Pray also for Christian Reformed missionaries who teach in universities across this great land.
Pray for Rev. Jeff Schmidt and congregation of the United Wesleyan church in Wyoming. Pray for them as they care and reach out to each other and their community.

Children's Prayer Ministry

Childhood is the best time to learn to pray. While the Scriptures place the primary responsibility for the training and nurturing of children with the parents (Deut. 6:1-9), the church plays a supportive role. Ideally, one member of your prayer leadership team should have a passion for integrating prayer into your children's ministry.

One of the most effective ways to teach is by modeling—letting children see and hear you pray. Encourage parents to take their children along to the worship services, healing services, prayer meetings, prayer vigils, prayerwalks, and so on as soon as they are old enough to understand. Encourage children to participate in prayer by having them lead prayer during worship or soliciting prayer requests during worship.

Consider holding a class for parents in how to build a praying family or how to teach children to pray. Provide materials encouraging parents to pray with their children regularly. A family prayer calendar, unlike the adult prayer calendar (p. 175), is an activity for the family to do together. Encourage the children to fill in the calendar with prayer requests regarding things that are of concern and relevance to them.

young children (ages 2-5)

- Teach children to pray at an early age. In toddler nursery, break into small groups (one adult with three to five children) and spend a few moments in prayer together. Encourage them to participate.

- Teach the Hand of Prayer format (p. 64) or others adaptable for children.

- Give the children a large piece of construction paper with the dates of the month drawn in. Have them cut and paste items for prayer onto their calendar, take them home, and pray for the items they pasted onto each day.

> **"Whoever welcomes a little child like this in my name welcomes me. . . . See that you do not look down on one of these little ones."**
> **—Matthew 18:5, 10**

- Use "echo prayers"—the leader says a sentence or phrase, and the children repeat it.

elementary school children (ages 6-12)

- At the start of the church school season give a prayer journal to each child and show the children how to record personal requests, praises, and answers to prayer. Then ask them to bring the journal to class each week and talk about answers they have received.

- Hold a prayer service for children concurrent with the adult prayer service. Design the service specifically for them.

- In church school, keep a prayer board on the wall or a prayer box in the corner, or set up a prayer station in the corner.

- Take the children on a prayerwalk.

- Encourage children to pray short sentence prayers in their church school classroom.

- Teach a few age-appropriate prayer forms. Assist children in becoming comfortable with silence, sentence prayers, and praying in front of others.

- Bring a video of the previous night's television news broadcast or the front page of a recent local newspaper to your church school class. Spend a few minutes praying for some of the needs mentioned.

teens (ages 13-18)

- Hold a prayer service for teenage youth concurrent with the adult prayer service. Design the service for youth.

- Take your class to a local nursing home and spend time praying with and for the residents.

- Take the young people on a prayerwalk.

- Teach the youth a few appropriate prayer forms and a variety of prayer positions.

family (at home)

- Record the daily family prayers in a notebook. Record and celebrate answers.

- Use some of the small group prayer activities (see Small Group Prayer, p. 242) for family devotions.

- Designate a prayer garden/family altar away from the dinner table where the family can go to pray (for example, an empty room, by the fireplace, in the den, and so on).

Ministry category: intermediate

The Colorado Springs church community held a Children's Prayer Walk that more than a thousand children attended. Rather than walking the children through a community, they walked through a local park set up with multiple stations: a fire engine, police car, ambulance, city maintenance truck, miniature chapel, airplane, and so on. At each station, the needs of that area were explained and the children were led in a brief prayer for that area (for example, at the ambulance they prayed for those who are sick and those who take care of the sick). Then the children had their "passport" stamped. The prayer walk was concluded by asking each child to fill out a prayer request and attach it to a helium-filled balloon. These balloons were released during a short time of worship.

Resources

Books

Lenae Bulthuis, *It's Me, Jesus: My Prayer Diary* (Grand Rapids, MI: CRC Publications, 2000).

Roberta Hromas, *52 Simple Ways to Teach Your Child to Pray* (Nashville: Thomas Nelson, 1991).

Carolyn Luetje and Meg Marcrander, *Face to Face with God in Your Home: Guiding Children and Youth in Prayer* (Minneapolis: Augsburg Fortress, 1995).

Gertrude Mueller Nelson, *To Dance with God: Family Ritual and Community Celebration* (Mahwah, NJ: Paulist Press, 1987).

Mike and Mary Nappa, *52 Fun Prayer Adventures* (Minneapolis: Augsburg Fortress, 1996).

Quin Sherrer and Ruthanne Garlock, *How to Pray for Your Children* (Ventura, CA: Gospel Light, 1998).

Alvin Vander Griend, *The Praying Church Sourcebook* (Grand Rapids, MI: CRC Publications, 1997).

Video

Prayerwalking for Kids (7 minutes). Joey and Fawn Parish. Ventura, CA. 805-650-3511.

Organizations
Esther Network International
854 Conniston Road
West Palm Beach, FL 33405
407-832-6490

National Children's Prayer Network
c/o Lin Story
P.O. Box 9683
Washington, DC 20016

(This is a network of children in Christian schools and home schools who have committed to pray for their church leaders.)

Magazine
PrayKids! (by the publishers of *Pray!*
 magazine)
3820 N. 30th St.
Colorado Springs, CO 80909
800-355-7788
www.praymag.com

Community Prayer Lunch

A community prayer lunch is a regular (weekly or monthly) opportunity for people to come together to eat and pray. In some communities it works well to rotate the location. In other communities the location may remain the same. Usually the hour-long luncheon is held at a church facility. It is open to members of the community: businesspersons, school administrators, pastors, government officials, and so on.

A sample format might be:

Lunch—Because buffets can take too much time, it is best for lunch to be served.

Speaker—Keep the presentation short—no more than ten to fifteen minutes. Invite a variety of speakers: government officials, pastors, school administrators, businesspersons. Keep the theme on prayer, revival, and community. Permit people to eat while the speaker is talking.

Prayer Time—Spend at least twenty minutes in prayer, varying the format (see Section 1, Prayer Formats).

Set a nominal fee to help cover the cost of the lunch and speaker.

Ministry category: intermediate

Cradle-a-Child

Cradle-a-Child was initiated by the Second Baptist Church of Houston to pray for their daycare and preschool ministries, to cover the children in prayer, and to pray for the children's families.

Each child enrolled in their daycare center and preschool program is matched with an intercessor for a predetermined period of time (for example, a calendar year, a school year, a semester). Since many of the children come from non-Christian homes, this is a significant way for parents and families to receive the blessings of prayer.

The Cradle-a-Child coordinator distributes application forms to the congregation and informs the children's parents about the ministry. Each intercessor is matched with a child and receives the first name and birth date of the child. The parent is given the first name and phone number of the intercessor with an invitation to call the intercessor about specific prayer needs. Intercessors are discouraged from initiating phone conversations and personal contact.

options

- With permission from the parent(s), invite the intercessors, the children, and their parent(s) and/or guardian to attend an "intercessors lunch" at the beginning of the year, at the end of the year, or both. This allows the intercessor to visualize the child and parent and to pray more knowledgeably. Do not take this step without parental involvement and consent.

- If you do not have a daycare ministry at your church, this ministry can work very effectively with a daycare in your community. The coordinator for this ministry and the daycare administrator must work closely together.

- While intercessors are discouraged from initiating contact with the child and parent(s), a parent may contact the intercessor. Since a parent may contact an intercessor, the intercessor should be prepared to provide additional caring, deal with a crisis situation, and possibly lead someone to Jesus.

Ministry category: intermediate

Resources

For additional information on Cradle-a-Child contact:

Prayer Ministry
Second Baptist Church
6400 Woodway
Houston, TX 77057

Jill Griffith, *How to Have a Dynamic Church Prayer Ministry* (Colorado Springs: Wagner Publications, Inc., 1999). (Jill Griffith is the former director of prayer ministries at Second Baptist Church, Houston.)

Dial-a-Prayer

An average of one hundred people every day dial the Dial-a-Prayer number at First Reformed Church in Berwyn, Illinois. They hear a two- to three-minute recorded message and prayer prepared by the church's pastor. The message and prayer are changed daily.

Judging from the responses, Dial-a-Prayer reaches people from a variety of ethnic, economic, and religious backgrounds. The church advertises its ministry in the local newspapers and on bus-stop benches near the church. The church's advertising budget for this ministry is several thousand dollars a year.

Ministry category: intermediate

Resource

First Reformed Church
1900 S. Oak Park Ave.
Berwyn, IL 60402

Elder Care Ministry

An elder care ministry is made up of teams of elders who assist the pastoral staff by providing additional pastoral care to members of the church and community who are ill, have a special need, or are going through a crisis. These teams normally consist of two elders. Some churches also use elders who are not actively serving; others team up a husband and wife (where at least one of them is an elder).

Typically, the elder team reads an appropriate passage of Scripture, offers words of encouragement, and intercedes for the person. When appropriate, teams also anoint the sick with oil (see James 5:14) or administer communion.

The key to an effective care ministry team is adequate training. Teams should not be sent out without preparation. Some churches train their elders using Stephen Ministry materials or denominational materials. Some churches develop their own training materials. If churches decide to develop their own training materials, those resources should include

- the stated mission and goals of the program.

- a list of appropriate Scripture passages and how to use them.

- training in various forms of prayer (such as warfare prayer, deliverance, praying in agreement, and the Salvation Prayer).

- opportunities to develop listening skills.

- instruction in appropriate theology (including familiarity with the church's stand on divorce, abuse, public sins, death, and so on).

- how to administer communion.

- a form for recording the calls that are made.

In addition to classroom instruction, new care ministry members should receive on-the-job training from the pastor or an experienced care ministry team member. This training involves three basic steps:

- Observe the experienced team member as they minister.

- Participate in the call as appropriate.

- Take leadership for the entire visit.

In some churches, teams are assigned to certain people (for example, people who are chronically ill, elderly, shut-ins) and are expected to visit them regularly and provide for their long-term spiritual care. This duty is sometimes assigned to trained Stephen Ministers. Other churches reserve elder care teams for crisis situations: sickness, loss of employment, death in the family, domestic violence, and so on. Some churches have

Are any among you sick? They should call for the elders of the church and have them pray over them, anointing them with oil in the name of the Lord.
—James 5:14

teams that deal with specific issues, for example, a team to assist those who are grieving, a team for people having marital difficulties, or a team for those facing surgery.

Jim Kok, director of Care Ministries at the Crystal Cathedral in Garden Grove, California, offers the following recommendations:

- Before going in, pray that the Lord will use you to listen carefully, care appropriately, and pray sensitively.

- Talk to God personally about what the [hurting] person is experiencing right now. For example: "Lord, John and Mary are brokenhearted over this great loss. It seems so senseless. They wonder how life can ever be good again. They hurt so badly. We know that you are with them in this, your arms embrace them, your heart hurts with theirs. . . . May they feel your presence today and in the agonizing days to come. Walk with them through this valley of the shadow of death. In their sorrow, fear, and anger over this awful accident, help them to support each other."

- Personal prayer (as contrasted with a more formal, classical style) is emotionally powerful. Be prepared for tears. Not only theirs, but yours too. Both are okay and good.

- Taking their hand in yours for prayer has great meaning for all involved.

- Avoid promptly departing after prayer. Often the thoughts and feelings elicited by the prayer require your presence a little longer (in other words, pray in the middle of your time together, not at the end).

- Mention names in the prayer—the names of those grieving and the one(s) grieved.

- If personal, conversational prayer is not possible for you, focus the prayer on the immediate circumstances; avoid homilizing and theologizing

through prayer. The Lord's Prayer can be used effectively also, especially in conjunction with your own prayer.

When the training is completed, consider commissioning team members in a worship service. This not only recognizes the gifts and responsibilities of the teams, it also alerts the church members to this ministry so they can pray for it and use it, if necessary.

Provide the care teams with a church "business card" that can be left at the conclusion of the visit. This card gives the team credibility as representatives from the church (this is especially important when calling on members of the community). Team members should write their names and phone numbers on the card so the recipient can call if further needs arise.

Ministry category: intermediate

Resources

Bjorn Pedersen, *Face to Face with God in Your Church: Establishing a Prayer Ministry* (Minneapolis: Augsburg Fortress, 1995).

Alvin Vander Griend, *The Praying Church Sourcebook* (Grand Rapids, MI: CRC Publications, 1997).

E-mail Prayer

Prayer, like almost everything else, has gone "high-tech." The Internet provides a fast and effective way to exchange prayer requests and prayer needs with other intercessors. Prayer needs from around the world appear at your doorstep in seconds; prayer requests can be sent to thousands of Christians simultaneously.

This type of ministry can happen in a variety of ways:

- A local prayer leader can e-mail hundreds, even thousands of people simultaneously with up-to-the-minute prayer requests. Like a prayer chain, people in the congregation can sign up to be on the list. Insert their e-mail addresses in your computer address book, form a group of all those interested in prayer updates, and simply send your prayer e-mail to everyone in the group.

- Form a small prayer group (or add this opportunity to your current small group) and communicate your prayer needs via the Internet. These needs can be printed out and attached to your refrigerator or placed in your Bible for reference.

- Set up a church chat room that is designed as a prayer room. Publish the location and invite people to log on for prayer. (Unless you have special software, all persons in the chat room must use the same on-line service.)

some guidelines

- When originating an e-mail, include the date and an original location in the body of the text. Dates and original e-mail addresses tend to get lost as electronic mail is forwarded.

- In preparing an e-mail prayer request, remember once you send it, you have no control over where it goes, who will read it, and how the information will be used (or even changed).

- Keep the request as simple, short, and clear as possible.

- Do not use personal names unless you have their permission. (In some countries and contexts using a person's name can seriously jeopardize that person's life.)

- Before forwarding an e-mail prayer request, verify the request, original date, and need. If the message is old, or if there is no way to verify its validity, don't forward it.

- Forward prayer requests to people you know and trust—and only to people you know will pray for the requests.

Ministry category: simple

Ministry of Deliverance

While the presence of demons and evil spirits is a commonly accepted fact in many cultures and regions of the world, it is an idea that has largely been ignored on the North American landscape. Increasingly North Americans are recognizing the presence and effects of demonic bondage, yet most are ill-equipped to handle such situations.

Roger Barrier writes:

Today our church sponsors a deliverance ministry, which developed because people sought help for problems that could only be described as demonic. As we began caring for these folks, some in our congregation were upset. Some were convinced that demons existed only in the first-century world. Others were indignant; most were ignorant of spiritual warfare issues. A turning point came when our counseling pastor . . . added spiritual warfare to his tools for helping people, [and] discovered that people who were not helped in any other way began finding victory. . . . It needs to be done—but carefully and wisely.

—"When the Force Is Against You," *Leadership*, Winter 1999, pp. 82-85

starting a deliverance ministry

It is important to have a plan for starting such a ministry. The first priority is to pray. Does God want your church to begin a deliverance ministry? Invite the entire congregation to be involved in a season of prayer for seeking God's will in this matter.

If your church is called to a ministry of deliverance, learn as much as possible about it. Read books; consult with another church that already has a deliverance ministry. Study the procedures for binding demons—not the demons themselves.

Explain this ministry to the church leadership and to the congregation. Ask your church to pray for God to identify deliverance "team members." It is important that no one attempt to do a deliverance ministry alone; the team should have three to four "up-front" members, and six to twelve "behind the scenes" members. Team members should lead holy lives, as they will become targets of spiritual attack.

Provide training for your team members. Invite an experienced deliverance team member from another church to provide training, or obtain permission to bring your team members to another experienced church to participate in their training. Some of the training should be "on the job"—that is, your team members should have the experience of actually participating in deliverance before they are sent out on their own.

the procedure

The initial step is determining if the person is ready for deliverance. Two questions must be asked:

1. Does the person have an evil spirit/ demon? This is normally determined in three ways:

   - Observation. If the spirit manifests itself, it becomes clearly evident.

   - Written questionnaire. The person should complete an extensive survey that asks appropriate questions to determine if demons are present and to determine their nature.

   - Interview. In some cases the questionnaire may be given orally; in other cases additional questions are asked for clarification.

   Many people with a demon admit to unsuccessfully trying to overcome their difficulty by themselves; to feeling hopeless and discouraged; to hearing a voice telling them to do something bad; or to having a history of occult practices (palm reading, witchcraft, astrology, and so on), addiction, sexual immorality, or other deliberate sin.

   Demons usually enter because someone left the door open. These doors may be hereditary, the result of a continuous or deliberate sin, or the result of strongholds such a bitterness, fear, judgment, and pride.

2. Does the person want to be delivered? Is he or she serious about breaking bad habits, renouncing sin, or breaking off certain relationships? Is he or she committed to living a holy life, to "walking in the light"?

   Once these questions have been answered, the next step is extended prayer.

1. Begin by asking for God's presence, protection, and power while the team is with the person. Seek God's guidance before continuing.

   Dear heavenly Father, we acknowledge your presence in this room and in our lives. You are the only omniscient, omnipotent, and omnipresent God. We are dependent upon you, for apart from you we can do nothing. We stand in the truth that all authority in heaven and on earth has been given to the resurrected Christ, and because we are in Christ, we share that authority in order to make disciples and set captives free. We ask you to fill us with your Holy Spirit and lead us into all truth. We pray for your complete protection and for your guidance. In Jesus' name. Amen.

   —Neil Anderson, *The Steps to Freedom in Christ*, p. 2

2. Bind the evil spirit; command it not to manifest itself during this time.

   Now, in the mighty name of Jesus, I bind, muzzle and gag every evil spirit present in the heart and life of (name). I say you are forbidden to manifest or cause discomfort, and you will leave when I command you to do so! Holy Spirit, please come and accompany us as we pray together and guide all our thoughts, conversation, and prayer, in Jesus' name. Amen.

   —Doris Wagner, *How to Cast Out Demons*, p. 103

3. Offer prayers for deliverance of the known, identifiable demons.

   In the name of the Father, the Son, and the Holy Spirit, I break all ungodly spirit, soul, and body ties that have been established between you and (name). I sever that linking supernaturally and ask God to remove from you all influence of (name), and draw back to yourself every part that has been wrongfully tied in bondage to (name).

At this point pray specifically against the sins, strongholds, and demons that have been identified.

I now speak directly to every evil spirit that has taken advantage of this ungodly soul tie. You no longer have any rights here and I order you to leave now without hurting or harming (name) or any other person, and without going into any other member of the family. In Jesus' name. Amen.

—Peter Horrobin, *Healing Through Deliverance: The Practical Ministry*, p. 238

Remember that evil spirits are cast out in the name of Jesus and that they hate anything associated with his light; so reading Scripture, offering worship and praise, and praying are powerful weapons.

Finally, offer a concluding prayer asking for God's blessing. Also, remember that one victory doesn't mean the war is over; the person must keep the door closed and live a faithful life.

Ministry category: intense

Resources

Neil Anderson, *Helping Others Find Freedom in Christ* (Ventura, CA: Regal, 1997).

———. *The Steps to Freedom in Christ* (Ventura, CA: Gospel Light, 2000).

Peter Horrobin, *Healing Through Deliverance: The Practical Ministry*, vols. 1 and 2 (Willowdale, ON: R.G. Mitchell Family Books, 2000).

Doris Wagner, *How to Cast Out Demons: A Beginner's Guide* (Colorado Springs: Wagner Publications, Inc., 1999).

Ministry of Intercession

Frequently the phrase "ministry of intercession" is used generically to include a variety of prayer ministries. In fact, in its purest form, intercession is simply praying for others. Most of the ministries identified in this book meet that qualification.

types of intercessors

A **general intercessor** is an eager pray-er—willing to pray through a prayer guide, participate as a prayer partner, and work through the prayer stations in the prayer room. General intercessors participate joyfully in prayer opportunities. About one of every ten people have the spiritual gift of intercession. These people can be assigned a specific area or ministry in the church to pray for daily—such as children and youth and their ministries, pastors and church leaders and their families, the worship ministries, evangelism, short- and long-term healing needs, singles, seniors, marriages, and so on.

A **crisis intercessor** prays fervently in a crisis situation. If someone is sick or dying, if someone has been in an automobile accident, if there is trouble at church, if a crime has been committed, crisis intercessors can't wait to enter their prayer closet or go to the bedside. Crisis intercessors love to be where the action is.

A **personal intercessor** is a special person. Personal intercessors pray for pastors, leaders, and specific people with such tenacity they will "wear the devil out." C. Peter Wagner, in his book *Prayer Shield,* identifies three levels of personal intercessors (see p. 131 for an explanation of the levels).

A **warfare intercessor** is explained more fully under Warfare Prayer (see pp. 105-108).

Prophetic intercessors are beginning to gain more attention. These intercessors focus on the listening side of prayer; they receive special insights into an issue, problem, or teaching. For example, the prophet Elijah was able to "see" things that were not revealed to the average person (see 2 Kings 6:12-18).

characteristics of a ministry of intercession

It is intentional. The church has developed a plan to discover, develop, and deploy intercessors to pray for specific issues at a designated time.

It is inclusive. People tend to pray differently. Some prefer to pray silently, alone, and seated. Others prefer praying aloud, in groups, standing. Some pray softly; others pray loudly. Some speak; others wail. All are welcome in the ministry of intercession.

It is imperative. The intercessors pray for urgent needs and thank God for his timely answers.

It is intense. Intercessors pray daily. Some may pray in the prayer room, some in their homes, some during their commute to work, some on the job. But people are praying day after day after day.

It is inspired. Intercessors, filled with the Holy Spirit, are passionate about their relationship with the Lord, fervent in their petitions for other's needs, and confident that God will answer.

identifying intercessors in your church

Since this is a critical ministry, intercessors should be selected carefully and share the following qualifications:

- is fully devoted to Jesus Christ
- is an active member of the church (a regular attender and faithful giver)
- firmly embraces the mission of the church
- is willing to submit to pastoral leadership
- is a team player
- displays a servant attitude and teachable spirit
- is able to keep a confidence
- is respected both inside and outside of the church
- lives a life of holiness and integrity before the Lord
- has a meaningful prayer life (the gift of intercession is helpful, but not required)

The responsibilities of a participant in the ministry of intercession might include

- praying for the pastor, other leaders, and church members at least daily.
- praying as requested by the pastor via personal written contact.
- listening to God for direction.

Areas for which an intercessor can pray can span a wide spectrum. Some intercessors are willing to receive assignments; others feel they have received their assignment from God. Possibilities include the senior pastor and other staff members, church leaders, church members, visitors, the lost, evangelism efforts, neighboring churches, God's creation, the city, those who are ill or grieving, prisons and jails, and so on.

Once your church has identified its intercessors, they should be trained. Offer regular opportunities for learning about and practicing prayer; make resources on prayer readily available. Consider putting a notebook in your church's prayer room that is updated regularly or sending to your intercessors a weekly "prayer paper" that lists intercessory needs.

how to pray for intercessory needs

- Begin by focusing on God (use Scripture, a hymn, a CD).
- Still the noises inside—offer them to God.
- Spend time in personal confession.
- Thank God for his presence in your life.
- Ask God for protection for yourself and your family and friends.
- Use the guide to intercession.
- Conclude by thanking God for his answers.

Ministry category: intermediate

Moms in Touch

In 1984, Fern Nichols, a mother living in Abbotsford, British Columbia, felt the need to pray for her two oldest children as they entered junior high school. Nichols invited another mother to pray with her. The following week, five mothers gathered to pray that God would protect their children from peer pressure and kids selling drugs. Four years later, Nichols appeared with James Dobson on a Focus on the Family broadcast. As a result of sharing her story and passion to pray for her children, more than 20,000 mothers requested assistance to start praying for their children. The Moms in Touch ministry was born.

Today across North America, thousands of mothers, grandmothers, and others willing to pray for a specific child and school gather weekly for one hour of concentrated prayer. In groups as small as two, in schools or homes or churches, they pray for their children, their schools, their teachers and administrators. Primarily using the A.C.T.S. format as a guide, they pray

- that their education may be guided by biblical values and morals.

- for their salvation and that they will have the conviction to stand boldly for their faith.

- for spiritual and physical protection (especially in light of the upsurge of school violence).

The goal of Moms in Touch is to raise up mothers to intercede for every school in North America and, ultimately, around the world. People considering forming such a group should register with Moms in Touch.

Ministry category: intermediate

Resource

For more information, contact

Moms in Touch
P.O. Box 1120
Poway, CA 92074-1120
619-486-4065

Monthly Prayer Focus

This ministry designates a particular prayer focus for each month. Designations can be set on a yearly basis and can be changed as appropriate. A sample annual designation follows:

January. Pray for a spiritual harvest. Ask God to raise up harvesters, church planters, and missionaries. Pray for those who are currently doing these tasks. Pray for protection, for energy and courage, and for fruit from their labors. Pray that God will bring in an abundant harvest this year.

February. This is the month of Valentine's Day. Focus on relationships—husband and wife, parent and child, friend and friend, neighbor and neighbor, employer and employee, servant and Master. Ask God to bless these relationships and keep them healthy and vibrant.

March. March is planting time. The farmers are in their fields tilling and planting. Ask God to send the appropriate sun, warmth, and rain. Pray for a rich and bountiful harvest—not only to supply the economic needs of the farmer, but also to provide the necessary food to feed the world.

April. Easter often falls in April. During Resurrection Month, pray for those who do not yet know the gospel of Jesus Christ. Pray that Christ may "come alive" in their hearts. Pray for your neighbors, coworkers, and relatives, that they might believe in Jesus.

May. The American National Day of Prayer falls on the first Thursday of May. Thank God for the freedoms North Americans enjoy. Pray for your elected and appointed officials at all levels of government.

June. June is commonly known as the month for weddings. Pray for the marriages in your congregation and community. Pray for those who are dating, engaged, newly married, married with children, and so on.

July. July is vacation month. Pray for those taking a break from their work that they might be refreshed and renewed. Pray that over the summer months, believers will not abandon their spiritual disciplines, but use these opportunities to share the gospel and be refreshed for another season of ministry.

August. August is the traditional "back to school" month. Focus your prayers on teachers and students. Include administrators, faculty, and students at all levels from preschool to university. Remember those in public, charter, private, parochial, and home schools.

September. This is the month when most church programs and ministries begin after a slower summer season.

Pray for each of these ministries, for their leaders, and for those who will be influenced by their ministry.

October. October is Clergy Appreciation Month. During this month pray for God's protection on your pastor and his or her family, thank God for faithful pastoral leadership, and lift up your pastor's personal and professional needs.

November. November is the month for national, state, and local elections in the United States. This month could be set aside to pray for government leaders—those currently in office, those completing a term of service, and those newly elected to office. Or, Thanksgiving Day in the United States falls into this month. Select thirty things for which you are thankful and remember one of them in your prayers each day.

December. December is a month of Christmas celebrations, parties, and family times. It is also a time of intense loneliness for those without families, and an especially difficult time for those who have lost loved ones during the past year. Remember those who are alone during the holiday season.

At the beginning of the month, place a prayer focus card (see p. 188) in each bulletin or place them in members' mailboxes. Ask the pastor to remember the focus during each worship service and to encourage members to be praying for the focus during the week. Use a church bulletin board in a high traffic area to highlight the focus of the month.

Ministry category: simple

National Day of Prayer (United States)

In 1952, the U.S. Congress passed a joint resolution declaring that the United States would observe a National Day of Prayer every year. Not until 1988 was a specific day—the first Thursday in May—established.

While many churches tend to celebrate the Day of Prayer as individual congregations, the goal is to bring churches and communities together to pray for their cities, states, and country. If your church or a group of churches in your area will be participating, register your prayer service with the National Day of Prayer Task Force (see below).

A church can be involved at a variety of levels:

- Distribute a prayer guide to church members on the Sunday before the Day of Prayer. Ask them to pray throughout the day (for example, the first five minutes of each waking hour) and/or during their lunch hour.

- Open your sanctuary or prayer room from 6 A.M. to 10:00 P.M. and invite church members and those who live in your church's community to come and pray.

- Hold a prayer breakfast.

- Participate in (or organize) a prayer service at noon at city hall.

- Hold a youth or children's prayer rally.

- Hold a twenty-four–hour prayer vigil (midnight to midnight) where people sign up for specific times.

- Hold a prayer service—either at noon or in the early evening—that uses the Concert of Prayer format (see pp. 339-340). Often several churches in an area cooperate to make this a community service.

- Join the National Day of Prayer Broadcast via satellite or the Internet.

- Run radio spots about the importance of prayer or provide radio spots of actual prayers.

- Invite all the prayer ministries to come together—for breakfast, for example.

- Invite all those involved in all of your prayer ministries as well as those being prayed for (for example, Shield a Badge, Moms in Touch, Cradle-a-Child) to come together for a time of prayer.

how to pray for your nation

(fill in the names of appropriate persons)

Your Nation
Ask God to protect, direct, give wisdom to, and bless . . .
The President/Prime Minister: _____
The Vice President: _____
Members of Legislature/Parliament: _____
Supreme Court Justices: _____
Advisors/staff: _____

Your State/Province
Ask God to protect, direct, give wisdom to, and bless . . .
The Governor/Premier: _____
The Lieutenant Governor: _____
Legislative Members: _____
Supreme Court Justices: _____
Advisors/staff: _____

Your County
Ask God to protect, direct, give wisdom to, and bless . . .
Commissioners: _____
The County Clerk: _____
Advisors/staff: _____

City/Township
Ask God to protect, direct, give wisdom to, and bless . . .
The Mayor: _____
The Township Supervisor: _____
Council members: _____
Advisors/staff: _____
Schools: _____
Police officers, firefighters, and emergency personnel
Businesses and commerce
Poor, homeless, oppressed people
Spiritually lost people

Ministry category: intermediate

Resources

Alvin Vander Griend, *The Praying Church Sourcebook* (Grand Rapids, MI: CRC Publications, 1997).

National Day of Prayer Task Force
P.O. Box 15616
Colorado Springs, CO 80935-5616
719-531-3379
fax: 719-548-4520
e-mail: ndptf@aol.com

National Prayer Day Broadcast
c/o Robert Bakke
901 E. 78th St.
Minneapolis, MN 55420-1300
612-853-1758
fax: 612-853-8488
e-mail: efca@compuserve.com
www.concertofprayer.org

Parents' Prayer Program

Parents cherish their children and want only the very best for them. While parents remember their children in their prayers, many also realize that their prayers soon become repetitive and superficial. Challenged one Sunday to pray more intentionally for his children—that they would develop strong morals, evidence the fruit of the Spirit, and that a suitable marriage partner would be prepared for them—Bob Hostetler developed the following calendar for praying for his children (*Focus on the Family*, Feb. 2000, pp. 18-19):

1. **Salvation**
   Lord, let salvation spring up within my children, that they may obtain the salvation that is in Christ Jesus, with eternal glory. (Isa. 45:8; 1 Tim. 2:10)

2. **Growth in grace**
   I pray that my children may grow in the grace and knowledge of our Lord and Savior Jesus Christ. (2 Pet. 3:18)

3. **Love**
   Grant, Lord, that my children may learn to live a life of love, through the Spirit who dwells in them. (Gal. 5:25; Eph. 5:2)

4. **Honesty and integrity**
   May integrity and honesty be their virtue and their protection. (Ps. 25:21)

5. **Self-control**
   God, help my children not to be like many others around them, but let them be alert and self-controlled in all they do. (1 Thess. 5:6)

6. **Love for God's Word**
   May my children grow to find your Word more precious than much pure gold and sweeter than honey from the comb. (Ps. 19:10)

7. **Justice**
   God, help my children to love justice as you do and act justly in all they do. (Ps. 11:7; Mic. 6:8)

8. **Mercy**
   May my children always be merciful, just as their Father is merciful. (Luke 6:36)

9. **Respect (for self, others, authority)**
   God, grant that my children may show proper respect to everyone, as your Word commands. (1 Pet. 2:17)

10. **Biblical self-esteem**
    Help my children to develop a strong self-esteem that is rooted in the realization that they are God's workmanship, created in Christ Jesus. (Eph. 2:10)

11. **Faithfulness**
    Let love and faithfulness never leave my children, but bind these twin virtues around their necks and write them on the tablet of their hearts. (Prov. 3:3)

12. **Courage**
    May my children always be strong and courageous in their character and in their actions. (Deut. 31:6)

13. **Purity**
    Create in them a pure heart, O God, and let that purity of heart be shown in their actions. (Ps. 51:10)

14. **Kindness**
    Lord, may my children always try to be kind to each other and to everyone else. (1 Thess. 5:15)

15. **Generosity**
    Grant that my children may be generous and willing to share, and so lay up treasure for themselves as a firm foundation for the coming age. (1 Tim. 6:18-19)

> After several days of praying through this list, I discovered an additional benefit to the prayer program: as I prayed with my children each night, the Lord brought to mind the subject I'd prayed for that morning, and I would repeat my request in Aubrey and Aaron's hearing. Before long, they began to echo my praying and poured out their own hearts in prayer for the very virtues and qualities I desired to see in them. Thus, my simple prayer program not only changed how I prayed but also how my children prayed and—by God's grace—how they live as well.
>
> **—Bob Hostetler**

16. **Peace-loving**
    God, let my children make every effort to do what leads to peace. (Rom. 14:19)

17. **Joy**
    May my children be filled with the joy given by the Holy Spirit. (1 Thess. 1:6)

18. **Perseverance**
    Lord, teach my children perseverance in all they do, and help them especially to run with perseverance the race marked out for them. (Heb. 12:1)

19. **Humility**
    God, please cultivate in my children the ability to show true humility toward all. (Titus 3:2)

20. **Compassion**
    Lord, please clothe my children with the virtue of compassion. (Col. 3:12)

21. **Responsibility**
    Grant that my children may learn responsibility, for each one should carry his own load. (Gal. 6:5)

22. **Contentment**
    God, teach my children the secret of being content in any and every situation, through him who gives them strength. (Phil. 4:12-13)

23. **Faith**
    I pray that faith will find root and grow in my children's hearts, that by faith they may gain what has been promised to them. (Luke 17:5-6; Heb. 11:1-40)

24. **A servant's heart**
    God, please help my children to develop servants' hearts, that they may serve wholeheartedly, as if they were serving the Lord and not people. (Eph. 6:7)

25. **Hope**
    May the God of hope grant that my children may overflow with hope and hopefulness by the power of the Holy Spirit. (Rom. 15:13)

26. **Willingness and ability to work**
    Teach my children, Lord, to value work and to work at it with all their heart, as working for the Lord, not for other people. (Col. 3:23)

27. **Passion for God**
    Lord, please instill in my children a soul that clings passionately to you. (Ps. 63:8)

28. **Self-discipline**
    God, I pray that my children may acquire a disciplined and prudent life, doing what is right and just and fair. (Prov. 1:3)

29. **Prayerfulness**
    Grant, Lord, that my children's lives may be marked by prayerfulness, that they may learn to pray in the Spirit on all occasions with all kinds of prayers and requests. (Eph. 6:18)

30. **Gratitude**

    Help my children to live lives that are always overflowing with thankfulness and always giving thanks to God the Father for everything, in the name of our Lord Jesus Christ. (Eph. 5:20; Col. 2:7)

31. **A heart for missions**

    Lord, please help my children to develop a desire to see your glory declared among the nations, your marvelous deeds among all peoples. (Ps. 96:3)

    —Reprinted by permission of Bob Hostetler.

options

1. Encourage all the parents in your congregation to use this prayer guide monthly. As children grow older, they could be encouraged to participate in the prayer—perhaps as a bedtime ritual.

2. Invite parents to come together once a week or once a month to pray for their children.

3. Set aside a time in your worship service during which several parents lead the congregation in prayer for several of these items.

4. Remember one item in the pastoral prayer each week.

5. Invite the youth leaders to join in prayer for the young people using many of these items.

Ministry category: simple

Pledge-a-Prayer

Many churches support their general budget, building fund, and missionaries through a "pledge card" system. Consider asking your congregation to "pledge" their prayer support to the church on an annual (or semiannual) basis.

Have pledge cards printed (see the sample below). Keep it simple; offer a few basic opportunities. Someone must collect the completed cards, compile them, and pass along the names of those interested to each prayer ministry's coordinator for follow-up. The pledge cards work especially well in connection with a prayer emphasis week/month, a prayer retreat, or a prayer breakfast.

Ministry category: simple

Prayer Pledge Card

For January 1 through June 30, 20____

"Again, I tell you that if two of you on earth agree about anything you ask for, it will be done for you by my Father in heaven" (Matt. 18:19).

_____I commit to pray one hour each week in the prayer room. (Prayer Room Ministry)

_____I commit to pray daily for my pastor. (Prayer Shield Ministry)

_____I commit to staffing the prayer room during one worship service a month. (Prayer Room Ministry)

_____I commit to pray for a minimum of one hour a day at home. (Prayer Warrior Ministry)

_____I commit to pray for five of my neighbors for five minutes a day. (Lighthouse Ministry)

_____I commit to placing a prayer box at _____ and providing the follow-up ministry. (Prayer Box Ministry)

Signed _____

Phone_____

Pray at the Polls

One of the most important days on the community calendar is "election day." Candidates vie for leadership positions, judges are elected to the bench, and ballot proposals are decided. The results of the elections influence our daily lives for years to come.

The goal of Pray at the Polls is to cover every polling site in prayer. This is not a political movement, but one approach to following the prescription of 2 Chronicles 7:14—"If my people, who are called by my name, will humble themselves and pray and seek my face and turn from their wicked ways, then will I hear from heaven and will forgive their sin and heal their land."

options

1. Provide a prayer focus card (see p. 188) to members of your congregation to pray through while they are waiting in line to vote. (See National Day of Prayer, pp. 165-166, for suggestions.)

2. Mobilize your prayer warriors and/or intercessors to prayerwalk the polls in your precinct or area.

3. Get a voter card/absentee ballot with all of the candidates and pray over them at your weekly prayer meeting.

Ministry category: intermediate

Resource
Pray at the Polls
Shepherd's Prayer Ministry
11875 W. Eagle Lake Drive
Maple Grove, MN 55369

Prayer Board

In order to encourage people to pray and to promote the prayer ministries of the church, some churches put up a "prayer board" in a high traffic area. On the prayer board, place some or all of the following:

- Information about upcoming prayer events.

- Reviews of new books available on prayer.

- Large sheets of white paper over the board with an invitation for people to write their prayer requests on the board.

- Filled-in prayer request cards that people can take home and pray for throughout the week. They can then exchange them the following Sunday. (Answered requests are celebrated in worship and removed.)

- The monthly prayer focus (see pp. 163-164).

- The names of church staff with the names of ten individuals or families in the congregation for whom that staff member will be praying during the coming week. The individuals and families are invited to write in specific requests beside their name.

With a little imagination, a visible prayer board can be a real prayer encourager.

Ministry category: initial

Prayer Breakfast

Prayer breakfasts are often held in conjunction with mission emphasis week, Lent, and the National Day of Prayer. Increasingly, churches hold monthly, and even weekly, prayer breakfasts (see also Community Prayer Lunch, p. 151).

The key to a successful prayer breakfast is to keep it simple, focused, and enjoyable. With a little preparation, a prayer breakfast can be held at the church. If the breakfast is held at a local restaurant, reserve a separate room and place the food order in advance. Be sure to schedule your breakfast early enough to accommodate those who work. The breakfast and prayer time usually last about forty minutes. (For example, a forty-minute breakfast beginning at 7:00 will still allow most people to be to work by 8:00.) When the breakfast is held on Saturday, it can start later (for example, 8:00 A.M.) and can last sixty to seventy-five minutes, allowing more time for a speaker, for worship, and so on.

While many prayer breakfasts include a short meditation or teaching on prayer or a testimonial, the primary goal of a prayer breakfast is prayer. The prayer focus may vary from month to month—for example, Thanksgiving in November; confession in Lent; students, teachers, and schools in September; and so on. (See Monthly Prayer Focus, pp. 163-164 for additional ideas.)

There are many possible prayer formats. Prayers can be led from the podium, offered silently, shared in pairs or triads or at each table, and so on. Some churches like to give people the opportunity to pray individually; some prefer to have a concert of prayer (see pp. 339-340). Use a variety of formats from section 1.

sample schedule

Welcome
Breakfast
Special music (optional)
Testimony (optional)
Short message/meditation/teaching on prayer
Prayer around the table
Dismissal

community prayer breakfast

While most prayer breakfasts are held within the local church, community prayer breakfasts are becoming more common. With promotion (see sample on next page), food arrangements for a larger group, and a more complex program, a community prayer breakfast creates more work; but it is often worth the effort. Community prayer breakfasts often include a speaker and usually last about an hour. (See Community Prayer Lunch, p. 151, for further ideas.)

Ministry category: intermediate

We want to appreciate YOU
for building our church through PRAYER

Continental Breakfast

Saturday, December 4
8:00 a.m. – 9:45 a.m.
in Calvary's Fellowship Room

Featuring Special Guest: Jim Heethuis
<u>Choosing a Daily Connection to God</u>
Deliberate "How to's" in deepening your walk with God

**Use the enclosed card to RSVP by December 1
or call Donna Fisher at 245-8847.**

Continental Prayer Breakfast

Saturday, December 4
8:00 a.m. – 9:45 a.m.

_____
will be attending
(friends, spouse or family members are welcome)

Return to the Information Center or call Donna Fisher at 245-8847.

Prayer Calendar

A prayer calendar is simply a monthly calendar filled in with prayer requests for each day.

The calendar format can vary considerably:

- List families and individuals in the congregation and repeat these names throughout the year.

- Place the names of individuals on their birthdays and couples on their anniversaries.

- List the various ministries of the church—Sunday school, missions, youth groups, pastors, social justice, boys' and girls' clubs, small groups, prayer, outreach, and so on.

Some prayer calendars suggest prayer topics for specific days:

- Sunday—prayers for worship, unity

- Monday—prayers for the pastors, leaders

- Tuesday—prayers for church ministries: outreach (first week), discipleship (second week), caring (third week), small groups (fourth week)

- Wednesday—prayers for people groups: children, youth, singles, couples/marriages, elderly

- Thursday—prayers for individual members of the congregation

- Friday—prayers for neighbors, the lost

- Saturday—prayers for personal spiritual growth

Some churches produce a professionally printed calendar annually and sell them as a ministry fundraiser. Others photocopy a computer-generated calendar and insert it in the Sunday bulletin. Some simply list the date followed by the prayer request.

Ministry category: intermediate

Prayer Chain

Prayer chains effectively enhance congregational prayer and are often one of the first prayer ministries started in a church. By design, they involve a significant number of people, require minimal investment from the participant, and provide a regular organized prayer base for the church. An effective prayer chain often can reveal additional intercessors in the church, stir an increased passion for prayer throughout the congregation, and raise a growing awareness of God's answers to prayer.

There are two primary kinds of prayer chains: the continuous prayer chain and the informative prayer chain.

continuous prayer chain

The continuous prayer chain is designed to have people praying around the clock. Members can sign up to pray for 20- to 30-minute intervals throughout the day and night. These prayer chains can be continued for just a day or two (see Prayer Vigil, pp. 225-226), or they can continue for as long as a year. With 30-minute prayer times, at least 48 people are needed for round-the-clock prayer. Some people may be willing to do this seven times a week, others only once a week.

While many churches have a prayer room and encourage people to pray there, most churches—primarily for convenience and safety—allow people to pray at home or at work. If you plan to start such a ministry,

begin slowly. Start with a 12-hour time slot two days a week and increase the time as God leads and as intercessors become available. Add night hours in the prayer room only if a sufficient number of people are available to assure the safety of the intercessors.

The continuous prayer chain handles a variety of prayer requests:

- Permanent requests, such as requests for unity in the church, protection for the pastor and leaders, effectiveness for the church's ministries, salvation for the lost.

- Urgent needs, such as requests that are of such a nature that they should be included in prayer every half hour.

- Temporary requests, such as requests for physical health, physical needs, financial needs, spiritual needs.

- Spiritual requests, such as requests for the salvation of loved ones, friends, and neighbors; requests for healing certain marriages and families.

informative prayer chain

The informative prayer chain, the more common type of prayer chain, is a sort of "alarm system" activated when a special need arises. (Sometimes churches limit it to emergency needs.) When someone becomes aware of a special need for prayer, they contact the prayer chain coordinator. The coordinator calls two or three people. Each of these people calls one person who calls the next "link" in the chain. The chain continues until everyone who signed on (or in some cases, the entire congregation) has been informed and is praying. In this ministry, each pray-er should commit to praying for a minimum of five minutes each hour for the six to twelve hours following the initial phone call.

Some churches break their informative prayer chain into two chains: a "basic" prayer chain that operates from 8 A.M. until 10 P.M. and a "24-hour" chain, which involves people who are willing to be contacted any time, day or night.

options and suggestions

- To ensure accuracy, participants should write the message down while on the phone and repeat what they have written to the caller. When the phone call is completed, and before calling the next "link" in the chain, they should spend a few moments in prayer. Messages should be kept simple and provide only enough information to enable people to pray effectively. If a person is not home, the caller temporarily skips to the next person on the chain. People should fill in the missing "links" as soon as possible.

- Keeping a prayer chain going can be difficult. People often are not home, and the details of the message often change by the time it reaches the end of the chain. First Baptist Church of Gozaburg, Nebraska, solved this problem by purchasing an automated voice mail system designed for telemarketing campaigns. It assures that prayer requests and updates are passed along accurately.

- In some rural areas and small towns where everyone seems to know each other, neighboring churches have come together and formed a multichurch prayer chain.

- Some churches have multiple prayer chains serving different purposes. One church has a continuous prayer chain for unsaved people; they keep praying until they have confirmation of the person's salvation. Another church has six prayer chains—one each for pastors, outreach, healing, deliverance, salvation, and finances. Another church has divided (multiplied, actually) their prayer chains by life stage; they have prayer chains for children, youth, adults, and seniors.

- In one church, the prayer chain is a group of women. The first woman in each chain is the leader of ten women. The leaders meet weekly for prayer, invite their members to their homes two to three times a year to build unity, and regularly send notes of encouragement. The last woman on the list is the anchor. When she receives the message she calls the leader and relays the message. This way the leader is assured the message made it all the way through intact.

- Some churches have multiple prayer chains determined by when the people can be reached at home. For example, one chain involves people who can be reached at home during the day (7:00 A.M.-5:00 P.M.); another for late afternoon and early evening (5:00 P.M.-10 P.M.); and a third for overnight (10 P.M.-7:00 A.M.). Other churches use the Internet to link intercessors.

- In some churches the informative prayer chain is limited to emergencies; in other churches, all information such as births, deaths, outreach programs, important decisions being made by the church, and so on are passed along. In some churches the chain is activated on Wednesday and includes reminders of prayer needs that people may already have been informed about.

- It is important to activate the prayer chain again when a prayer is answered in order to share the answer to prayer and to request prayers of thanksgiving.

- Ideally, the prayer chain should have multiple leaders in case one leader is not available when a request comes in.

Ministry category: simple

Resource

Alvin Vander Griend, *The Praying Church Sourcebook* (Grand Rapids, MI: CRC Publications, 1997).

Prayer Chain

Coordinators:
(Please call one of the following to activate the Prayer Chain)

_____/_____

_____/_____

_____/_____
              (Name)   (Phone)

Chain One	Chain Two	Chain Three	Chain Four

Captains

_____/_____ _____/_____ _____/_____ _____/_____

Members

_____/_____ _____/_____ _____/_____ _____/_____

_____/_____ _____/_____ _____/_____ _____/_____

_____/_____ _____/_____ _____/_____ _____/_____

_____/_____ _____/_____ _____/_____ _____/_____

_____/_____ _____/_____ _____/_____ _____/_____

_____/_____ _____/_____ _____/_____ _____/_____

_____/_____ _____/_____ _____/_____ _____/_____

_____/_____ _____/_____ _____/_____ _____/_____

_____/_____ _____/_____ _____/_____ _____/_____

_____/_____ _____/_____ _____/_____ _____/_____

_____/_____ _____/_____ _____/_____ _____/_____

Anchor

_____/_____ _____/_____ _____/_____ _____/_____

Notes
- If you have a prayer request, please call one of the prayer chain coordinators to activate the chain.
- If you are unable to reach the person immediately below you, please continue down the chain until you can continue the link. Please continue calling the person immediately below you until you make contact.
- If you are the anchor, please contact your captain when you have received a prayer request.

Prayer Coordinator

While the primary "prayer coordinator" is the Holy Spirit, every church enhances its ministry when it appoints a prayer coordinator or a prayer coordinating team. A prayer coordinator serves as the organizer of prayer activities, the promoter of prayer, and the primary encourager for building a prayer ministry in the church. Simply stated, a prayer coordinator's responsibility is to help make the church a house of prayer. It may be a part-time or full-time paid position or a volunteer position. Either way, a prayer coordinator is an essential person in the development of a praying church. Appointing a prayer coordinator indicates that the church is serious about prayer—that prayer is as important as preaching, pastoral care, evangelism, and education—and ensures that prayer will not be forgotten in the ministry of the church.

qualifications

While a passion for prayer is an obvious prerequisite for the job, certain qualifications and spiritual gifts are necessary, such as:

- has a confirmation of God's call to this ministry
- supports the senior pastor's leadership
- understands and supports the mission and vision of the local church
- works well as a team member with other ministry leaders
- has spiritual maturity (not a new Christian)

- practices personal integrity
- has a strong personal prayer life
- possesses the spiritual gifts of organization/administration, encouragement, and discernment and the ability to plan, delegate, lead, and communicate.
- is respected in the congregation and community
- has sufficient time to do the job well
- is a good listener and a good speaker
- has a passion for the lost
- is self-motivated
- has a biblical understanding of prayer (the conviction that prayer changes things)
- is not the senior pastor, but willing to follow the senior pastor's leadership
- has a servant's heart and leadership style (willingness to work behind the scenes without a lot of accolades; a teachable spirit)

appointment

The prayer coordinator should be appointed by the elders and accountable to the senior pastor.

responsibilities

1. **Pray**—for strength and wisdom and for others to come alongside to assist in building the prayer ministry.

2. **Build a prayer team.** The ministry of prayer is difficult to do alone. Initially, it may take time for people to understand the necessity of a prayer ministry and to become involved. With only a handful of people coming together for prayer on a weekly basis, it can be a discouraging task. The best members of the team will probably not volunteer; they will probably have to be asked. Prayer team members should be chosen as carefully as the prayer coordinator.

   Qualifications for a prayer team member:

   - spiritual maturity
   - a passion for the lost
   - a sense of calling by God
   - a team player
   - a strong personal prayer life
   - gifts of leadership and encouragement

   The team should meet at least six to eight times a year (more at first, maybe less often once the ministry is running well).

3. **Enlist the support of the pastor and leaders** of the church. Encourage them to become actively involved in some facet of the prayer ministry.

4. **Develop an overall prayer strategy** that outlines the purpose (mission statement), goals, and objectives of the prayer ministry (and its subministries), as well as a proposed strategy for accomplishing them.

   Once the prayer priorities are set, begin with a couple of simple prayer ministries (don't add too many, too fast). For each prayer ministry you add, find a person who is willing to accept the responsibility for that ministry in line with their spiritual gifts. Add this person to your leadership team.

   A comprehensive prayer strategy should train believers to pray in the following areas:

   - prayer shield for the pastor(s) and church leaders
   - their personal relationship with God
   - marriage and family ministries
   - small group prayer
   - prayer ministries to support needs of the members
   - praying for leaders in church, business, government
   - community prayer involvement
   - a worldwide prayer consciousness

5. **Recruit, train, and encourage people in your prayer ministry.** Some recruiting suggestions:

   - Identify people in your church with the gift of intercession.

   - Use personal testimonies of what God is doing in answer to prayer (initially you may want to use "outside" examples, but people from within your own church will be most effective).

   - Set a "term" of involvement. Terms are normally for one year, but may be longer. Allow people to complete their term and be appreciated. This builds a sense of accomplishment. People can be invited to sign up again (even right away).

   - Offer choices. Not everyone is interested in the same type of prayer ministry. As a result, not everyone will respond to the same recruiting approach.

   Some training suggestions:

   - Offer adult education classes in prayer at your church (see School of Prayer, pp. 235-236).

   - Attend regional prayer training events as a prayer team.

   - Invite the prayer coordinator from another church with a growing prayer ministry to meet with your groups.

   - Purchase tapes and books on prayer, pass them around, and discuss them together.

Some appreciation suggestions:

- Send thank-you notes.

- Sponsor a periodic complimentary prayer breakfast with a short teaching on prayer and some prayer time.

- Commission the church intercessors in a worship service.

6. **Begin building your prayer ministry.** Set such priorities as

- developing a Prayer Shield ministry to protect your leaders.

- praying for the lost. Become a Lighthouse church.

- encouraging more prayer in worship. Encourage people to share their answers as well as their needs.

- initiating a ministry to pray for special needs in your church (for example, prayer chain, elder prayer teams, and so on).

- designating a place to pray. A prayer room, set aside for personal and/or small group prayer, is essential for building a strong prayer ministry (see Prayer Room, pp. 208-212).

Some suggestions:

- Develop only one prayer ministry at a time.

- Add new ministries as the Lord calls you, clarifies the need, and provides the leadership.

- Work within the existing church structure—leadership, committees, staff, teachers, small groups, and ministry leaders—to integrate prayer throughout the ministry of the church.

- Establish a prayer resource library.

7. **Expand your ministry beyond your church.** Network with other prayer leaders in nearby churches—plan some community prayer activities. Consider becoming involved in at least one national and/or worldwide prayer initiative annually.

8. **Evaluate your prayer ministry regularly.**

prayer coordinator networks

An increasing number of denominations are appointing denominational prayer coordinators to assist and network with local church prayer coordinators. A national association also serves the same purpose. Church prayer leaders need mutual support and encouragement. As a result, an increasing number of cities and regions are forming networks of church prayer coordinators that cross denominational and cultural lines.

Ministry category: intense

Resources

Church Prayer Coordinator's Start-Up Packet (Bridge Builders International Leadership Network, P.O. 31415, Phoenix, AZ 85046-1415. 1-602-789-1111).

Alvin Vander Griend, *The Praying Church Sourcebook* (Grand Rapids, MI: CRC Publications, 1997).

Prayer Watch International
(This is an extended, intensive training.)
P.O. Box 3705
Flagstaff, AZ 86003-3705
520-526-7779
fax: 520-522-0101
e-mail: bjornpray@aol.com

Annual Local Church Prayer Leader's
   Conference
World Prayer Center
11005 Hwy 83
Colorado Springs, CO 80921
719-268-8210
fax: 719-594-6707
e-mail: NALCPL@cswpc.net

National Association of Local Church
   Prayer Leaders
World Prayer Center
11005 Hwy 83
Colorado Springs, CO 80921
719-268-8210
fax: 719-594-6707
e-mail: NALCPL@cswpc.net
(Annual membership is $25.)

sample job descriptions

Job Description
Calvary Church Prayer Coordinator

Purpose: The mission of the Congregational Prayer Coordinator is to encourage, facilitate, and enhance the practice of prayer and intercession (including prayer for the lost) in Calvary Church.

Goals
1. Develop a prayer leadership team. Each team member is responsible for one or more prayer ministries in the church.
2. Identify, train, and network those in the church with the gift of intercession.
3. Increase the frequency, consistency, and intensity of prayer in the ministry of the church, among the church staff and leaders, in the worship and fellowship of the congregation, and in the lives of individual members.
4. Promote participation in local, regional, denominational, and national prayer initiatives.

Responsibilities
1. Work closely and cooperatively with the (senior) pastor and the church's leadership to plan, implement, and enhance the church's prayer ministry.
2. Hold regular meetings (at least quarterly) of the prayer team to coordinate current prayer ministries, to discuss and develop new prayer ministries as God leads, and to intercede for the ministry and members.
3. Coordinate Calvary's Prayer Warriors: identify, train, and network those with the gift of intercession.
4. Promote the practice of prayer in all aspects of Calvary's ministry—among the leaders, members, and community; within worship, small groups, and team meetings; both personally and corporately.
5. Supervise and coordinate the prayer room and prayer line.
6. Assist the senior pastor in providing a strong prayer shield.
7. Intercede daily for Calvary Church.
8. Oversee the Lighthouse ministry.
9. Coordinate the Tuesday evening prayer meeting.
10. Promote participation in local (for example, pastor prayer groups, intrachurch teaching opportunities), regional (for example, crusades, Pastor's Prayer Summits, multiple church events), denominational (for example, annual days of prayer, Prayers for the Harvest), and national prayer initiatives (for example, National Day of Prayer, PrayUSA, Mission America, DAWN).

Qualities
1. Has a personal relationship with God through Jesus Christ.
2. Is a person of prayer.
3. Desires to strengthen fellow believers' personal walk with God as well as bring in the lost to be discipled.
4. Is willing to be a team player and to submit to the authority of the senior pastor.
5. Possesses the spiritual gifts of leadership, administration, encouragement, and intercession.
6. Has a passion for intercession and evangelism.

Line of Authority
Directly responsible to the Senior Pastor.

Job Description
Grace and Peace Fellowship Prayer Coordinator

Ministry Responsibilities
1. Develop a vision, yearly budget, and yearly strategy.
2. Plan and lead the weekly Saturday prayer gathering.
3. Train others in intercession.
4. Meet monthly with the prayer warriors to plan concerts of prayer, coordinate prayer ministry at altar calls, develop a prayer chain, etc.
5. Regularly pray for the Sunday service and those involved.
6. Meet monthly with the program ministry team.
7. Seek to grow in knowledge and expertise by reading relevant materials and attending seminars, etc.

Other Responsibilities (requiring senior pastor direction and/or approval)
1. Oversee special services, such as concerts of prayer.
2. Cooperate with evangelism director and cell leaders regarding congregational needs.
3. Lead some services.
4. Be the main contact with prayer directors from other churches.

Church Requirements
1. Be in or lead a cell group.
2. Attend all church services and prayer meetings.

Extent of Authority
1. Recruit, train, deploy, and nurture helpers under your ministry.
2. Dismiss helpers who hinder the ministry.
3. Discipline helpers under your ministry (only with the consent of the senior pastor).
4. Spend the annual budget (assuming funds can be released per bookkeeper and/or senior pastor).
5. In the event that your ministry conflicts with another church event, you are to do your ministry unless directed not to do so by the senior pastor.
6. You may rebuke, correct, or even expel any uncooperative person under your care.

Prayer Driving

Prayerwalking and Marches for Jesus have become popular among Christians in many cities. As a variation, some churches have started a prayer driving ministry.

Chris Halls, a pastor in Niagara Falls, Ontario, reports on the first-ever Car Prayer Rally in his city. Intercessors gathered with a fleet of cars at a local shopping mall (a neutral site is best if multiple churches are involved). They were given instructions on where to drive and what to pray for. Appropriate Scriptures and a detailed route were also included. The motor route included tourist sites, the local high school, the police station, city hall, poorer areas of town, the local newspaper office, local radio and television stations, hospitals, the business district, high crime areas (such as streets with prostitutes, x-rated theaters, drug houses), prisons, and churches. At each stop the intercessors prayed for specific needs related to that site. They gathered together again at the end of the evening over refreshments at a local church, and realized they had encircled the entire city and blessed it in the name of the Lord.

Prayer driving allows intercessors the opportunity to cover a long distance and visit many locations in a short period of time. It's an excellent way to involve those whose disabilities might prevent them from prayerwalking. It is also a safer way to pray in certain areas of the city. Ideally, each car should have three or four intercessors. Cars should go in pairs, and no more than two cars should visit a site at any given time.

Ministry category: intermediate

Prayer Emphasis Week (or Month)

In *The Praying Church Sourcebook* (CRC Publications, 1997), Alvin Vander Griend notes that Dutch Reformed churches traditionally held a ten-day prayer emphasis "week" from Ascension Day to Pentecost. This was a time for people to confess their sins and return to God.

Many churches, in addition to having the traditional mission emphasis week, also have prayer emphasis weeks. (Some churches, because of the benefits they've experienced with a prayer emphasis week, have broadened their prayer emphasis to last a month.) In contrast to the Dutch Reformed tradition, most of these weeks are held in the fall as the church year begins. Holding a prayer emphasis week in the fall has some practical advantages:

- It helps in setting goals for the year and renewing vision.

- It provides an opportunity for people to make personal commitments to the various prayer ministries.

- It can introduce the theme for the year and related devotions.

- A time of confession is appropriate at the beginning of a new church year.

A prayer emphasis week (or month) is an intentional period of time set aside to underscore the importance of prayer, to focus on teaching about prayer, to spend time in prayer, and to celebrate God's answers to prayer. The prayer emphasis week may include the following:

- Sunday messages on prayer.

- A concert of prayer (see pp. 339-340).

- Seminars on prayer.

- A prayer breakfast (see pp. 173-174).

- A prayer vigil (see pp. 225-226).

- Prayer focus cards (see p. 188).

- A midweek prayer service.

- A guide to family prayer.

- A study to be used in small groups or Sunday school.

- Testimonies during worship services of how God answers prayer.

- A solemn assembly (see p. 358).

- Introduction of a new prayer ministry.

- Opportunities for people to join a prayer ministry (see Pledge-a-Prayer, p. 170).

- Education in and experiences of some new forms of prayer (see section 1).

- An overnight prayer retreat (see section 7).

options and suggestions

- Consider beginning with an eight-day format (Sunday through the following

Sunday). Conclude on the second Sunday with a special service of testimonies and sharing.

- In planning your prayer emphasis week, start small. Don't over-schedule. Begin with a few activities you can do well.

- Make this time consistent by using the same month or week each year.

- Consider using people from both inside (pastor, prayer team, intercessors) and outside your church.

- If repeating this on an annual basis, continue the prayer ministries that were helpful, discontinue those that were not, and add new ones each year. Do not base your evaluation solely on attendance.

Ministry: intermediate

Resources

Bjorn Pedersen, *Face to Face with God in Your Church: Establishing a Prayer Ministry* (Minneapolis: Augsburg Fortress, 1995).

Alvin Vander Griend, *The Praying Church Sourcebook* (Grand Rapids, MI: CRC Publications, 1997).

Focus Cards

A prayer focus card is a bookmark or small card that not only reminds people to pray, it also offers assistance in how to pray effectively.

Cards can be designed on a computer, copied onto heavier paper, and laminated (if the card is intended to last longer than a month). They can be placed in the worship bulletin or mailed with a monthly prayer calendar; they can be given to everyone in the church or directed just to those who have signed up to pray.

Prayer focus cards can be provided monthly or developed around the liturgical season, a sermon series, or special needs as they arise through the year. The possibilities for prayer focus cards are endless. Cards can developed for use throughout the year on topics such as

- How to pray for your pastor
- How to pray for your church
- How to pray for your children
- How to pray for your spouse
- How to pray for political leaders
- How to pray for missionaries
- How to pray for business owners
- How to pray for persecuted Christians

Or for special issues in the congregation, such as

- How to pray for a new pastor
- How to pray for stewardship week
- How to pray for the capital fund drive
- How to pray for the new building program

Or for special people groups, such as

- How to pray for teachers and students
- How to pray for farmers
- How to pray for police officers, firefighters, emergency technicians
- How to pray for government officials
- How to pray for military personnel
- How to pray for our children
- How to pray for marriages
- How to pray for the lost

Or, place the outline of a new prayer format on a focus card. Many of the ideas in this book can be adapted and made into prayer focus cards.

options and suggestions

- In developing a card, talk with people in the group being prayed for. For example, when preparing a focus card on how to pray for teachers, ask a teacher to help design the card.

- Make all the prayer cards the same size (this will encourage people to save them and refer back to them).

- Keep a prayer focus card rack. As cards are developed, place them in the rack for people to take, use, and share.

Ministry category: intermediate

Prayer-a-Grams

The prayer-a-gram ministry was begun to support and encourage missionaries. Over the years, however, it has been used very effectively in other aspects of prayer ministry. The idea is simple: send a note to someone you have prayed for or are praying for to let them know they are in your prayers. Prayer-a-grams are key in communicating the commitment of the body of Christ to pray for people in their time of crisis or need. People cherish such notes and cards of encouragement, sometimes keeping them for months, even years.

The options and opportunities are almost endless. One church has a prayer team that prays for inactive members; after praying, they send a prayer-a-gram. Houses of Prayer Everywhere (H.O.P.E.) encourages praying for your neighbors and sending periodic prayer-a-grams to neighbors who have been prayed for. Some churches have a prayer partner ministry for college students that involves follow-up with a prayer-a-gram.

Prayer-a-grams can be used in all types of situations:

- Make cards available in worshipers' seats, so they can write a prayer-a-gram during a worship service after praying for people in the pastoral prayer.

- Use prayer-a-grams to remind local and national leaders that people are praying for them.

- Send notes of encouragement to those in the armed forces.

- Use them as a way to minister to those in prison.

- Follow up virtually any prayer ministry effort with prayer-a-grams: Shield-a-Badge, Cradle-a-Child, Prayer Shield, and so on.

Prayer-a-grams can be professionally designed and printed, made in-house with a computer and a quality copy machine, or purchased ready-made (see Resources, below). If designing or making your own, consider the following suggestions:

- Prayer-a-grams can be postcards (which are less confidential) or small notecards with envelopes.

- They should be easily identified with the church and should include the church's logo, address, phone, e-mail address and website (if applicable).

- It is helpful to place an appropriate Scripture verse on the card.

- Use quality materials and bright colors.

In writing out the prayer-a-gram, keep the following in mind:

- Begin by asking the Lord to guide you as you write the note.

- Keep the note relatively short—no more than a paragraph or two.

- Keep the note encouraging. Include, if appropriate, a Scripture promise.

- Don't sign your full name. Use your first name only. If there are others writing prayer-a-grams with the same name, use your first name and last initial.

- If the prayer-a-gram is in response to a prayer need that has been made known in worship or over the telephone, send it in a timely manner.

Ministry category: simple

Resources

Houses of Prayer Everywhere (H.O.P.E.) offers a colorful prayer greeting card to send a prayer to a neighbor or friend. Three different cards are available. (1-800-217-5200)

Prayer-a-grams can be purchased from:

Harvest Prayer Ministries
11991 E. Davis Ave.
Brazil, IN 47834
812-443-5800
fax: 812-443-5505
e-mail: harvestprayer@email.com
www.harvestprayer.com

Prayer Guides

Many people don't always know what to pray for. Others need help recalling the many prayer concerns from their church and its ministries. The publication and distribution of a regular prayer guide can be helpful. A prayer guide is similar to a prayer calendar, but offers more information about each prayer request than is possible to fit on a calendar. And, unlike a prayer calendar, a prayer guide asks that people remember all of the needs listed for the entire week or month.

Many churches publish weekly or monthly prayer guides. In addition, some denominations publish monthly or quarterly prayer guides containing denominational needs. Some prayer guides are printed in the bulletin; others are printed separately.

Prayer guides can be used in a variety of venues:

- in the various prayer ministries
- in the opening and closing of meetings
- in the church's small groups
- in family devotions
- in personal devotions

Some churches develop multiple prayer guides—a special guide for the prayer shield intercessors, another for the prayer warriors, and a general prayer guide for everyone in the congregation. Some churches have special guides for the seniors, youth, children, and Lighthouse intercessors.

Prayer guides can take a number of forms:

- bulletin panel (see p. 147)
- prayer calendar (see p. 175)
- prayer focus cards (see p. 188)
- bookmarks
- tri-fold brochures

In using prayer guides, remember:

- Prayer guides should be small so they can easily be posted on a bulletin board, taped to the refrigerator, or used as a bookmark in a Bible. In order to be most effective, prayer guides must be highly visible throughout the week.

- Prayer guides should include answers to previous prayer requests (opportunities for praising God) as well as prayer concerns. It is important to publicize and praise God for the answers he provides.

- Prayer guides should be published regularly, preferably weekly, so that the information is current.

- Members of the congregation should be encouraged to submit prayer requests for the prayer guide.

- Include a variety of requests. Intercessory prayer can be about many things.

- Prayer guides should be handed out, inserted into the bulletins, or placed in church mailboxes. When prayer guides are left on a table to be picked up, they seldom are taken.

- The pastor and other leaders must model the use of the guides. The pastor should use the prayer guide in worship.

- Be careful to maintain confidentiality on the prayer guides. No one knows where the guide will end up.

- Be as specific as possible, yet give only sufficient information to pray appropriately.

- Include items for praising God as well as petitioning God.

Ministry category: simple

Resource

Alvin Vander Griend, *The Praying Church Sourcebook* (Grand Rapids, MI: CRC Publications, 1997).

sample prayer guide

Prayer Guide

Community Church
Week of September 10

Scripture

For I am convinced that neither death nor life, neither angels nor demons, neither the present nor the future, nor any powers, neither height nor depth, nor anything else in all creation, will be able to separate us from the love of God that is in Christ Jesus our Lord.

—Romans 8:38-39

Prayer Meditation

Father, we thank you that nothing will ever separate us from your love and your presence. Give us the confidence that we can boldly follow you in obedience knowing that we will always be loved by you. Give us the assurance that your love extends to those we love and lift up to you in prayer. Continue to surround us with your arms and hold us close to your heart. Amen.

Prayer Requests

- Pray for Don D. whose wife passed away last week.

- Pray for those who have left for college and are now separated from their families.

- Pray for the twelfth graders who will be working at the City Coffee House this week with people who have been separated from their loved ones and homes.

- Pray for a member of the congregation who has recently separated from his wife and family. Pray for reconciliation and restoration.

- Pray for Mary S., who lost her job this past week due to downsizing by her employer.

Blessing

Lord, keep us close to you. Keep us safe and secure under the umbrella of your love. May our walk today bring us closer and closer to you. Amen.

Prayer for Healing

Paul Cedar, pastor of Lake Avenue Congregational Church in Pasadena, California, tells of a time he preached on James 5:14-15:

> Is any one of you sick? He should call the elders of the church to pray over him and anoint him with oil in the name of the Lord. And the prayer offered in faith will make the sick person well.

Moved by what he read, he announced that after each worship service, the pastoral team and elders would be available to pray for those needing physical, emotional, or spiritual healing. All those desiring prayer were invited to the prayer room after the service. People responded. Three months after his message, an average of twenty-five people each Sunday were requesting healing prayer.

God heals the sick. In fact, throughout the early church, prayer and healing are found side by side. Consider the following passages:

> Peter sent them all out of the room; then he got down on his knees and prayed. Turning toward the dead woman, he said, "Tabitha, get up." She opened her eyes, and seeing Peter she sat up. (Acts 9:40)

> [Publius's] father was sick in bed, suffering from fever and dysentery. Paul went in to see him and, after prayer, placed his hands on him and healed him. (Acts 28:8)

The definition of *heal* is "to make whole." Becoming whole involves every aspect of a person's being—physical, emotional, and spiritual. Thus, a healing ministry prays for people who desire healing of body, soul, or spirit. Praying for the physically sick, the emotionally troubled, and the spiritually searching is a powerful statement of faith—because the outcome rests with God, not with us. While God sometimes chooses to heal immediately and instantaneously, most healing prayers are answered over a period of time—and ultimately will come to completion on the Day of the Lord.

basic principles for developing a healing prayer ministry

- A healing prayer ministry involves elders and/or intercessors (in keeping with the word from James) who are trained and authorized to pray, anoint with oil, and lay on hands. Many churches have healing ministry prayer teams that make hospital and emergency room visits, offer prayers of deliverance, and visit shut-ins.

- When introducing this ministry to your church, go slowly. Consider holding classes on healing prayer (for example, on the history, theory, and practice of healing prayer). Or, preach a series of messages on prayers for healing.

- The prayer team must believe in the power and effectiveness of prayer, that God desires healing, and that God brings healing through prayer.

- A healing prayer ministry is not a faith healing ministry. Jesus—only Jesus—heals. The level of one's faith does not determine or manipulate God's response. (Some people are reluctant to receive this ministry because they fear that if nothing happens, they will be left wondering, "What is wrong with me? Is my faith that weak?")

- The primary activity of healing prayer is listening. As one intercedes for a hurting person, the intercessor must listen for a word from the Lord, for the Holy Spirit's direction, and for how to proceed.

- Healing prayer involves submitting to the Lord. Is God asking us to change an attitude? Change a behavior? Sever a harmful relationship?

- Healing prayer involves claiming the promises God has made to us—promises about salvation (the ultimate healing), spiritual healing, emotional healing, and physical healing (see 1 Pet. 2:24).

- One must acknowledge the value of redemptive suffering. Some suffering carries God's redemptive purpose with it. One pastor has said, "Every time an unbeliever gets cancer a believer gets cancer so the world can see the difference." When it becomes clear that God is using this illness in this way, we can change our prayers for comfort, strength, and peace.

- Healing prayer is done in the presence of the person. True, God is powerful enough to heal "long distance," but a face-to-face visit—in the prayer room at church, at a bedside in the hospital, or sitting around a kitchen table—contains some important healing ingredients:

  — There is an expression of love.

  — There is the opportunity to touch the person. Touch communicates caring and love. Holding hands during prayer is a very "healing" experience.

  — When multiple people gather for prayer, the presence of God becomes very real ("For where two or three come together in my name, there am I with them" [Matt. 18:20]).

  — The person who is being prayed for becomes personally involved in the prayer. Their faith is strengthened.

  — A prayer team gives the opportunity for a variety of spiritual gifts to be used: discernment, wisdom, and knowledge, as well as faith.

- Ministry must address the whole person (body, mind, soul, and spirit).

A Prayer of Surrender

Loving Father, I surrender to you today with all my heart and soul. Please come into my heart in a deeper way. I say "Yes" to you today. I open all the secret places of my heart to you and say, "Come on in."

Jesus, you are Lord of my whole life. I believe in you and receive you as my Lord and Savior. I hold nothing back.

Holy Spirit, bring me to a deeper conversion to the person of Jesus Christ.

I surrender all to you: my health, my family, my resources, my occupation, skills, relationships, time management, successes, and failures. I release it and let it go. I surrender my understanding of how things ought to be, my choices and my will. I surrender to you the promises I have kept and the promises I have failed to keep. I surrender my weaknesses and strengths to you. I surrender my emotions, my fears, my insecurities, my sexuality. . . .

Lord, I surrender my entire life to you, the past, the present, and the future. In sickness and in health, in life and in death, I belong to you. Amen.

—Linda Schubert, *Miracle Hour: A Method of Prayer That Will Change Your Life* (Queenship Publishing Co., 1997), pp. 12-13

- God works through unity (Matt. 18:19-20). The prayer team must work together as a team. Jesus' prayer for all believers (John 17) is that "they may be brought to complete unity to let the world know that you sent me and have loved them even as you have loved me."

the process

Writing in *Authority to Heal* (InterVarsity Press, 1987), Ken Blue outlines the simple five-step method used by the Vineyard Church to pray for the sick.

1. **Interview.** This step is simply for gathering information from which to make some important decisions. Ask the who, what, when, where, and how questions as sensitively as possible. Is sin involved? Which sin? How?

2. **Strategize.** Based on the interview, some decisions can be made on how to proceed. While few of us would presume to be physicians, many "illnesses" have nonmedical sources. If a thorough medical examination has ruled out physical ailments, the nonmedical sources become increasingly plausible. Many headaches, some allergies, asthma, and lower back pain, as well as some gastric problems and skin diseases, can be caused by anxiety, guilt, bitterness, and anger. Unresolved emotional experiences can also trigger physiological problems. Paul Tournier, in *The Healing of Persons* (HarperCollins, 1983), indicates that spiritual unrest, emotional trauma, and damaged relationships underlie many chronic and serious illnesses.

3. **Pray.** Pray specifically. Pray for God's intervention. Pray for healing of a specific disease, ailment, or pain. The length of prayer is seldom significant. The faith of the person being prayed for is seldom the determining factor. The faith of those who pray is a significant factor.

4. **Assess the results.** Keep in touch with the person prayed for. If healing occurs, thank God. If the healing has begun, but is yet incomplete, keep praying. Healing—especially emotional healing—often comes gradually. If healing is still not occurring, keep praying.

5. **Follow up.** God provides us additional resources. People who have been prayed for should continue to seek medical help, counseling, and encouragement.

healing prayer services

Many healing ministries include periodic healing services (see p. 375). Periodical, often quarterly, services devote much time to praying for physical, emotional, and spiritual healing. Other churches offer the opportunity to come to the front of the church each week to receive a special prayer for healing.

Healing services could also include opportunities such as the following:

- The pastor prays for the sick on behalf of the congregation; people remain seated/kneeling.

- Worshipers break into small groups of three or four and pray for each other or for those with shared needs.

- People are invited to meet with a trained prayer team member. In this case, remember that women are normally more open to sharing with another woman, and men generally feel freer talking with another man.

- People are invited to come to the front of the sanctuary, kneel, and be prayed for (and possibly be anointed with oil by the elders).

Ministry category: intense

Resources

Richard J. Beckmen, *Praying for Wholeness and Healing* (Minneapolis: Augsburg Fortress, 1995).

Ken Blue, *Authority to Heal* (Downers Grove, IL: InterVarsity Press, 1987).

Alvin Vander Griend, *The Praying Church Sourcebook* (Grand Rapids, MI: CRC Publications, 1997).

C. Peter Wagner, *How to Have a Healing Ministry Without Making Your Church Sick* (Ventura, CA: Regal Books, 1988).

John Wimber, *Power Healing—The Vineyard Model* (New York: Harper and Row, 1987).

The International Order of St. Luke
P.O. Box 13701
San Antonio, TX 78213
512-492-5222

Prayer Library

Every church should begin building a prayer resource library on a separate shelf in the church library or in the church's prayer room. The resources should be visible and easily accessible for church members', small groups', and prayer leaders' use.

Items to include in a prayer library are

- books
- videos
- audiocassettes (see Prayer Tape Ministry, p. 220)
- brochures and pamphlets
- notebooks from conferences

The following list will get you started:

Henry Blackaby, *Experiencing God* (Nashville: Broadman and Holman, 1998).

David Bryant, *Concerts of Prayer* (Ventura, CA: Regal Books, 1988).

Paul Yongii Cho, *Prayer: Key to Revival* (Waco, TX: Word, 1984).

Jim Cymbala, *Fresh Wind, Fresh Fire* (Grand Rapids, MI: Zondervan, 1997).

Charles Finney, *Prevailing Prayer* (Grand Rapids, MI: Kregel, 1965).

Richard Foster, *Prayer: Finding the Heart's True Home* (San Francisco: Harper, 1992).

Jill Griffith, *How to Have a Dynamic Prayer Ministry* (Colorado Springs: Wagner Publications, Inc., 1999).

Bill Hybels, *Too Busy Not to Pray* (Downers Grove, IL: InterVarsity, 1988).

Cindy Jacobs, *Possessing the Gates of the Enemy* (Fairfax, VA: Chosen Books Publishing Co., 1994).

Larry Lea, *Could You Not Tarry One Hour?* (Altamonte Springs, FL: Creation House, 1987).

C. S. Lewis, *Letters to Malcolm: Chiefly on Prayer* (Harcourt Brace, 1983).

Max Lucado, *The Great House of God* (Waco, TX: Word, 1997).

John Maxwell, *Partners in Prayer* (Nashville: Thomas Nelson, 1996).

Henri Nouwen, *Out of Solitude* (Notre Dame, IN: Ave Maria Press, 1984).

Bjorn Pedersen, *Face to Face with God in Your Church: Establishing a Prayer Ministry* (Minneapolis: Augsburg Fortress, 1995)

Don Postema, *Space for God: Study and Practice of Spirituality and Prayer* (Grand Rapids, MI: CRC Publications, 1997).

Dutch Sheets, *Intercessory Prayer: How God Can Use Your Prayers to Move Heaven and Earth* (Ventura, CA: Regal Books, 1997).

Terry Teykl, *Acts 29: Blueprint for the House of Prayer* (Muncie, IN: Prayer Point Press).

Alvin Vander Griend, *The Praying Church Sourcebook* (Grand Rapids, MI: CRC Publications, 1997).

C. Peter Wagner, *Praying with Power* (Ventura, CA: Regal Books, 1997).

Walter Wangerin, *Whole Prayer: Speaking and Listening to God* (Grand Rapids, MI: Zondervan, 1998).

Ministry category: initial

Prayer Meeting

A prayer meeting (or prayer service) is a gathering of a congregation, a segment of the congregation, or multiple congregations for a time of extended prayer. Most prayer meetings are modified worship services—including a time of praise, teaching, and perhaps an offering. But most of the time is spent in prayer.

In some churches the concept of a prayer meeting is little more than a forgotten tradition. In the latter half of the nineteenth century, pastors slowly took over because people assumed pastors were more qualified to lead the prayer service. This move, unfortunately, weakened interest in prayer. The prayer meeting became message-centered and people stopped coming. In addition, the prayer meeting's traditional emphasis on missions—the spread of the gospel—was lost. The prayer meeting became much more inwardly focused.

As a result, many prayer meetings today are weighted heavily on teaching rather than praying. Lay participation is down. Results are few.

However, prayer meetings are reviving, and in some cases the prayer meeting is the lifeblood of the church. More and more churches are holding weekly prayer meetings. And, whether the meeting involves ten people or one thousand people, whether it lasts for one hour or three hours, whether it's held at church or in a home, it can be an integral part of the vitality of the church.

types of prayer meetings

Prayer meetings come in a variety of forms, although most can be placed in one of four categories: (1) regular (weekly) church prayer meetings, (2) special prayer meetings, (3) critical need prayer meetings, and (4) home prayer meetings.

Many churches hold weekly prayer meetings. In many settings these are relatively small groups (ten to thirty people); in some settings, like New York's Brooklyn Tabernacle, they involve almost 2,000 people. While many of these are held on Wednesday evening, some churches select other nights of the week. Some weeks there may be a specific focus; other weeks wider scopes of need are prayed for. These services last from one to three hours.

Special prayer meetings are often called on a national or denominational level. The World Day of Prayer is held the first Thursday in March for churches belonging to the National Association of Evangelicals. The first Thursday in May is set aside as a National Day of Prayer in the United States. The International Day of Prayer for the Persecuted Church calls believers around the world to unite in prayer during November. Many of these calls to prayer offer churches the opportunity to unite as congregations as well as to join with other churches across denominational lines to celebrate their unity in Christ.

Critical need prayer meetings are held in response to critical needs. These meetings are often called in times of sickness, drought, and war. But they may also be called when moral indiscretion hits a church leader, when finances are in trouble, when factions disrupt church unity, when a fire has damaged the facility, when the church faces an important decision, and so on. These prayer meetings are designed around one primary need.

Many churches encourage prayer meetings in local homes. These meetings are, by design, small and informal. Six to ten people join together in the intimacy of a living room to pray. Some of these prayer groups are actually small groups that meet weekly or biweekly. Others may be Lighthouses in the community with people coming together to pray for their neighbors.

In his book *Fresh Wind, Fresh Fire,* Jim Cymbala tells of a pastor who once observed: "You can tell how popular a church is by who comes on Sunday morning. You can tell how popular the pastor is by who comes on Sunday night. But you can tell how popular Jesus is by who comes to the prayer meeting" (p. 28).

In *The Praying Church Sourcebook* (CRC Publications, 1997) Alvin Vander Griend distinguishes between "maintenance-style" prayer meetings and "frontline" prayer meetings. A maintenance-style prayer meeting is aimed at preserving the status quo of the church— the existing life and ministry of the congregation. Visibly, the prayer is primarily for the church's internal needs. Unfortunately, people often do not come to such inwardly focused meetings expecting God to change them, their church, or their relationship with the community. By contrast, people come to a frontline prayer meeting expecting God not only to encounter them there, but also to change them. A frontline prayer meeting balances the church's needs and the community's needs—including prayer for the lost.

integrating a prayer meeting into your church

If a church decides to hold regular prayer meetings, the meetings should play a significant role in the church's ministry. This can be accomplished by doing a number of things.

First, choose a night for the prayer meeting. Many churches have a family night on, say, Wednesday, with scheduled classes, choir, and youth activities—and an optional prayer meeting for adults. Ideally, however, the prayer meeting should be the *only* thing happening that night at the church (unless an additional youth prayer service or children's prayer service is held simultaneously). Designating one night for prayer—and only prayer—underscores the importance of prayer.

Promote the prayer meeting at every opportunity. After Sunday worship, invite the congregation to come back for the prayer service later in the week. Share testimonies of what God is doing at the prayer meeting. Advertise the meetings in the bulletin and on a bulletin board.

Prioritize the prayer meeting. Pastors, church leaders, and staff should be visible at the prayer meeting each week. If they are not interested in meeting for prayer, if they are not thoroughly convinced prayer will make a difference, few others will be. Initiating and maintaining group participation in a prayer meeting is often a challenge. Involve your leadership.

Consider holding a simultaneous prayer meeting for youth and children. This can communicate to young people both the church's priority on prayer and the church's value of its younger members.

Pray for the presence and anointing of God's Spirit on the prayer meeting. While it is important to spend some time planning the meeting, more time should be spent praying for the meeting. People want to be where hearts are being changed, sins are being confessed, lives are being healed, the

Holy Spirit is moving, and answers to prayer are being received.

prayer meeting formats

While the format for a prayer meeting is normally highly influenced by a church's tradition, the prayer leaders should

- help people focus their attention on God through worship.

- lead simple songs or Scripture choruses that people know or are easy to learn.

- read Scriptures that praise and worship God.

- have someone lead in a prayer of praise and adoration, invite people to come to the front, or encourage people to pray aloud from their seats.

- share answers to prayer. Celebrate them. Thank God for them.

- allow people to share their personal needs by filling out prayer cards or by sharing in small groups or in the larger meeting.

- pray. Remember, however, to keep the meeting moving. Avoid praying too long at one time. Vary the format.

- balance the prayers between church (internal) items and community (mission) items.

- include a short reflection or meditation if your time together is more than an hour.

A prayer meeting that involves multiple churches carries a few different dynamics:

- Welcome—State the reason or focus for coming together.

- Worship—A time to quiet the mind from the day's activities and focus on God.

- Silent reflection—A time to quiet the heart. Participants may be invited to record their prayer needs.

- Prayer time—Use a variety of formats.

- Closing—Encourage people to continue praying personally or in small groups, leaving as they feel ready.

Sample Prayer Meeting from the Brooklyn Tabernacle

(People are asked to enter silently, preparing for an attitude of prayer.)

Participants congregate at the front of church to pray aloud.

Song: "Surely the Presence"

More individual, spontaneous prayer.

Song: "Mine Eyes Have Seen the Glory"

More spontaneous prayer.

Song: "O Lord, You're Beautiful" (sung repeatedly)

Announcements

Participants divide into pairs to pray for revival.

Song: "O Lord, You're Beautiful" (sung repeatedly)

Prayer cards that were filled out during the Sunday service are passed out to pray over.

Message: "Rejoice: Unhappy Christians Are a Contradiction"

Song: "O Lord, You're Beautiful" (repeated many times)

Conclude with "Amen, Amen."

Ministry category: initial

Resources

Jim Cymbala, *Fresh Wind, Fresh Fire* (Grand Rapids, MI: Zondervan, 1997).

Alvin Vander Griend, *The Praying Church Sourcebook* (Grand Rapids, MI: CRC Publications, 1997).

Prayer Newsletter

Many churches publish a monthly newsletter for all participants in the prayer ministry and/or members of the congregation.

When producing a newsletter, consider including the following:

- a note from the prayer coordinator
- a brief teaching or devotional on prayer
- the schedule of upcoming prayer ministries
- encouragement to continue praying
- open slots available in your various prayer ministries
- articles on prayer (with copyright permission), quotations about prayer, prayers of various people, and so on
- short reviews on new books about prayer that are available in your prayer library
- prayer requests
- answers to prayer
- a short article highlighting one prayer ministry each month

Ministry category: intermediate

Resources

Prayer
This prayer newsletter/bulletin insert (see sample on next page) is available bimonthly from:

Faith Alive Christian Resources
2850 Kalamazoo Ave. SE
Grand Rapids, MI 49509
800-777-7270
www.FaithAliveResources.org

Lighthouse
This evangelistic prayer newsletter/ bulletin insert is available bimonthly from:

H.O.P.E.
455 W. Springhill Drive
Terre Haute, IN 47802
800-217-5200
fax: 812-235-6646
www.hopeministries.org

The Harvest Messenger
This teaching newsletter on prayer is published by

Harvest Prayer Ministries
455 W. Springhill Drive
Terre Haute, IN 47802

Prayer

Urging faithful, powerful,
and effective prayer

"House of Prayer" Now Open in Vancouver

Five Vancouver, British Columbia, area churches have leased a 3,200-square foot building for continuous prayer and worship, 24 hours a day, seven days a week. Known as the "House of Prayer," the five churches in this project include The Dwelling Place, First Century Church Metrotown, Church of Zion, Harvest City Church, and Point Grey Community Church.

The House of Prayer officially opened in late January and offered workshops on spiritual warfare, intimacy with God, and worship. It will also host training sessions for prayer and worship leaders throughout the year.

—*Intercessors for Canada*,
February/March 2001

*Prayer honors God;
it dishonors self.*

What If . . .

What if, starting tomorrow morning, the only things that continued to exist were the things that you thanked God for? Did you thank him for the toothpaste? Then no more toothpaste. Did you thank him for air to breathe? And what about the lungs that make breathing possible? Oops! No more lungs and no more air. Did you thank him for your abilities, your finances, all the bills you have to pay and the ability to pay them, your talents, gifts, hobbies, and interests? Sorry, they'll all disappear.

If you think about that little scenario, it gets across the idea that everything we have and do is dependent upon God. Try to make thanksgiving and acknowledgment part of the very air you breathe. It may just keep that air around a little longer!

—*The Praying Church Sourcebook*,
(CRC Publications)

How to Pray for President Bush

As you intercede for President Bush or for the leader of any nation, consider these seven suggestions:

- Ask God to hide him and his family from satanic attack.
- Ask God to fill him with the spirit of wisdom and revelation (Eph. 1:17-18).
- Pray that he will raise the standard of morality in our nation such that people will want to emulate.
- Pray that he will endeavor to restore the sanctity of life, of families, and of divine order (Eph. 5:22-6:4).
- Ask God to give him strategic insight and godly wisdom in foreign affairs.
- Pray that he will be a God-fearing man and recognize his accountability to the Lord for every decision and action he takes (Prov. 9:10).
- Pray that he will have courage to resist manipulation, pressure, and the fear of people (Prov. 29:25; 2 Tim. 1:7).

The Christian who says his prayers to men will not get answers from God.

What Hinders Your Prayers?

Your prayers are hindered . . .

. . . if you are rejecting truth (Prov. 28:9).
. . . if you have pride (2 Chron. 7:14).
. . . if your heart is hard (Zech. 7:12-13; Jer. 17:9).
. . . if you lack compassion (Prov. 21:13).
. . . if you hold on to unconfessed sin (Ps. 66:18).
. . . if you ask with wrong motives (James 4:3).
. . . if you have broken relationships (1 Pet. 3:7).
. . . if your lifestyle is sinful (Is. 59:2).
. . . if your prayers are empty words (Matt. 6:7).
. . . if you refuse forgiveness (Matt. 6:14-15).
. . . if you harbor hypocrisy (Luke 18:9-14).
. . . if you are double-minded, unstable (James 1:5-8).
. . . if you set idols in your heart (Ezek. 14:3; 1 John 2:15-17).

—*Pray!*, January/February 1999

Prayer Pager Ministry

Using telephone pagers is a unique way to let people know that others are praying for them. A church can purchase a few pagers and offer them to shut-ins, those who are hospitalized, those with terminal illnesses, those in crisis, and so on. The name and pager number of the person(s) who receive the pager are printed in the church bulletin, and the congregation is encouraged to pray for the person and then dial the pager number. When the pager rings or vibrates, the person knows they have been prayed for. When someone calls the pager, instead of leaving their phone number for a return call, they simply dial a predetermined number and hang up.

Some churches assign a number to each intercessor. Other churches use a coded message:

- God bless you ("bless" is "25377")
- Thinking of you ("think" is "84465")
- Get well ("438 9355")
- Praying for you ("praying" is "7729464")

Generally, it is helpful to give a letter of explanation to the person who is receiving the pager. Here's a sample letter:

Dear [name],

This is not just an ordinary pager. This is a "Prayer Pager."

We have given your pager number to many of your family and friends. You must keep your pager on and with you at all times. Every time it goes off, it indicates that someone is praying for you. They will enter the code 516, which represents James 5:16, "Pray for one another, so that you may be healed. The prayer of the righteous is powerful and effective."

We thought it would be an encouragement to you to be physically reminded through your pager of all those who love you and are praying for you. Your pager number is 123-456-7890, and it has statewide range. We love you and pray for you every day.

This ministry offers endless possibilities. It can be helpful for those whose family and friends are separated by distance and cannot make daily visits. It is useful when a member of the congregation is hospitalized at a distance from the church. Third Christian Reformed Church in Denver, Colorado, gives its high school students pagers and a prayer partner, who dials the number at least once a day after praying for the student. Using pagers with a Prayer Partner ministry (see pp. 204-205) opens up many additional opportunities for partners to connect.

Ministry category: simple

Prayer Partners

Prayer partners are simply two people paired together for the purpose of receiving specific, focused prayer over a long period of time (usually three to twelve months). This ministry has two basic categories.

In a **one-way partnership** one partner promises to pray for the other partner. For example, at the Christian Church of San Angelo, Texas, members of the seniors' Sunday school class make a three-month commitment to pray for their church's high school students. After three months, each senior can opt out of the ministry, choose to pray for someone else, or keep praying for the same teen. To help the seniors pray appropriately, the young people fill out questionnaires listing their school schedule, goals for the year, and specific prayer requests. Some of the seniors periodically send cards, reminding the teens they are being prayed for daily.

In *Bridgebuilders* (Fall 1999), Terry Teykl tells of the "Adopt a Teen" ministry of the Englewood Baptist Church in Rocky Mount, North Carolina. This church has over one hundred teens being prayed for daily by a partner in their "Petitioners" ministry. The church takes a picture of each teenager, then asks the teenager to write their name, school, class, phone number, address, and specific requests on the back. The pictures are distributed to those who have committed to pray for the teens. The "adoptive" partners are encouraged to call once a week to receive new requests and answers.

One-way partnerships can work in many situations, such as with college students, those who are in the armed forces, Sunday school teachers, missionaries, and so on.

In a **two-way partnership** both partners promise to pray for each other. This too can work in a variety of situations. Students in a middle school or high school youth group can be paired together and encouraged to regularly connect regarding new requests and answers to prayer. Those in a small group or Bible study can partner with each other. Church staff members can pair up. On a larger scale, the entire congregation can be paired according to life-stage (seniors with seniors, single parents with single parents, college students, and so on). For a fun option, prayer partners can remain secret from each other, to be revealed at the end of the specified time during a dinner or luncheon.

options and suggestions

- With a two-way partnership ministry, it isn't necessary for partners to be paired up. A person can be praying for one person while receiving prayers from another person. This is convenient in groups that have an odd number of people.

- Normally, it is a good idea for men to partner with men, women with women.

- Don't hesitate to include children in this ministry. They can pray for a sibling, for their parents, or for a classmate.

- Participation should always be voluntary, always for a stated period of time, and always renewable by agreement of both parties.

- Partners can stay in touch by e-mail, postcards or letters, periodic phone calls, pagers, and so on. They may even schedule a specific time each week to pray together—either face to face or over the phone.

Ministry category: simple

Prayer Request Box

Taking verbal prayer requests during a worship service or prayer meeting is a common practice among many churches. But many people are still intimidated by having to speak aloud in public or having people know the origin of their prayer request.

Being sensitive to these issues, some churches place a prayer request box in the church foyer. Prayer cards are available near the box for people to fill out. This method offers people who otherwise might not share their prayer request an opportunity to do so quietly and comfortably.

The box should be checked before each worship service or prayer meeting.

Ministry category: simple

PRAYER REQUEST: _____

_____

_____

_____

_____

Your prayer request will be prayed for by Calvary's Weekly Prayer Meeting which meets on Tuesday evenings in the Prayer Room as well as Calvary's Prayer Warriors.

(Prayer requests of a confidential nature should be given to Marge DeYoung or Donna Fisher to be passed onto the Prayer Warriors of our church.)

May we send this person a note of encouragement?
　　☐ Yes　　☐ No

Name of person making request: _____
Phone: _____　Date: _____
Type of request:　☐ First time　　☐ Update

"Do not be anxious about anything, but in everything by prayer and petition with thanksgiving present your requests to God. And the peace of God, which transcends all understanding, will guard your hearts and your minds in Christ Jesus"　--Phillippians 4:6-7

Prayer Retreat

Participating in a prayer retreat—either as an individual or with a group—can have a major impact on a believer's spiritual life. While personal retreats take minimum advance planning (except to reserve a time and location), a group retreat takes more planning. Depending on the size of the group and the length of the retreat, a small committee (three to five people) should begin planning four to six months in advance.

A retreat, in the classical sense, is an extended time away from daily routines in order to spend time alone with the Lord. Unfortunately, we frequently confuse a retreat with a seminar or conference. A seminar is primarily cognitive, while a retreat is highly reflective.

Retreating is important in the prayer ministry of the congregation. In addition to encouraging personal retreats, consider holding an annual retreat for the following groups:

- youth (high school and middle school can have their retreats together or separately depending on the size of the group)
- men
- women
- parents
- seniors
- elders and deacons or leadership board
- staff
- participants in a particular ministry

See section 7 of this book, "Prayer Retreats," for ideas and suggestions for planning a retreat.

Ministry category: intense

Resource
Alvin Vander Griend, *The Praying Church Sourcebook* (Grand Rapids, MI: CRC Publications, 1997).

Prayer Room

A designated prayer room is an essential ministry for any praying church. Our church buildings commonly include spaces for worship, administration, youth, education, fellowship, food preparation, maintenance, and storage. It is only fitting that a room be designated for the primary task of the church—prayer. Thousands of churches are designating prayer rooms, many of which are open twenty-four hours a day, seven days a week.

Designating a prayer room visibly underscores the significance of prayer in your church. While some prayer rooms are designed to provide a quiet place for people to come and pray as they are led, many prayer rooms are bustling centers of activity and ministry. In addition to lending visibility to prayer, providing a model for prayer, and being a center for the prayer ministry, a prayer room also provides

- a place for prayer cells to meet.

- a place for longer times of prayer, such as prayer vigils.

- a location for a telephone prayer ministry.

- a room that is always available for prayer activities.

- a place where answers to prayer can be posted and shared.

- a location to post the prayer opportunities, ministries, and activities of the church.

- a visible witness to guests that your church is serious about being a house of prayer.

Prayer rooms are designed to focus our praying in three different areas. While all of these areas will not fully develop immediately, all three are important for balance and growth.

- First, the prayer room is *a place to worship and pray* to God.

- The prayer room is also *a center for intercessory prayer*—where people "stand in the gap" on behalf of the body of Christ.

- Finally, prayer in the prayer room must include *outwardly directed prayer*—that is, evangelistic, community-centered prayer.

In recent years, there has been a trend that prayer rooms are not limited to churches. In some areas intercessors are crossing denominational lines to provide 'round-the-clock prayer in prayer rooms at local hospitals, near police stations, in malls, and so on. These various prayer rooms often have a director and are staffed by members of the participating churches.

how to set up a prayer room ministry

1. Begin by praying. Ask God what kind of prayer room ministry he wants and to share his timing with you. Ask God to raise up a few leaders willing to accept the responsibility of coordinating this ministry.

2. When the time appears right and the leaders are in place, begin to meet together to pray and organize. While some churches have part- or full-time paid prayer directors, most churches use volunteer leaders. When volunteers are used, it is best to have a team of leaders in place.

3. Develop a statement of purpose. What is the goal and intent of your prayer room? At this point, some decisions need to be made. For example, Will your prayer room include a telephone ministry? Will you staff your prayer room twenty-four hours a day, seven days a week?

   Will your prayer room use prayer stations? How many? How will they be designated—at tables, in card files, in baskets, in a Rolodex file? Which stations will you maintain—worship, confession, your city, missions, your congregation, your pastors, those who are ill, thanksgiving, businesses?

   How will you staff the prayer room—especially on Sundays? That is, will you have people trained in healing prayer, salvation prayer, and intercession in the room (in addition to those who are praying) to assist walk-ins? If so, will it be less disruptive to have an adjoining room where walk-ins can be assisted?

   Will you design your room for limited or for long-term intercession? Some churches have designed prayer rooms for people who desire an extended time to seek the Lord. The room, almost a mini-retreat center, has a sleeper sofa (or cot), a microwave, a small refrigerator, a comfortable chair, a kneeling bench, and a Bible (no phone). In many churches that have such a room, another "typical" prayer room is available.

   Will the prayer room be a central "dispatch" for administering pastoral care in the church? In an increasing number of churches, all crisis and ongoing pastoral needs are called into the prayer room. The person on duty then calls for the appropriate care—a pastor, a small group member, a Stephen Minister, and so on—for follow-up.

4. Promote use of the prayer room in the bulletin, from the pulpit, on bulletin boards, in the newsletter, and in new member classes.

5. Recruit intercessors to staff the prayer room.

6. Have a service of dedication for your prayer room.

7. Commission your intercessors once or twice a year.

8. Regularly share with the congregation what's happening in the prayer room.

9. Consider holding a prayer vigil in the prayer room periodically and inviting the entire church to participate. This helps familiarize people with the prayer room ministry.

how to set up a prayer room

Prayer rooms, like churches, can differ considerably. Here are a few suggestions to consider when planning your prayer room. It should be

- **large enough.** Typically the room should be at least as large as a good-size living room. Some churches have a small prayer closet. These are useful for individual prayer, but their adaptability is quite limited. The room should be large enough to meet the goals of the prayer ministry.

- **comfortable.** It should be an inviting place for veteran intercessors as well as for newcomers. Make pillows available to facilitate kneeling. Ideally, a restroom will be nearby. If the prayer room will be open around the clock, ideally it will have its own heating/cooling system.

- **inspirational.** Place inspirational artwork in the room: serene paintings, sculptures, photographs, plaques, simple banners in soft colors with few or no words, and so on. Use a table or floor lamp with low wattage bulbs to provide a conducive atmosphere for prayer. Avoid overhead lights.

- **accessible.** The room should be easily accessible and highly visible. Many churches locate them directly by the main entrance (this is beneficial throughout the week) or adjacent to the worship center (this is ideal for Sundays). Ideally, the prayer room should have an outside entrance—or at least people should be able to access the prayer room without having access to the entire building.

- **safe.** Since people will be entering the building at all hours of day and night, security is a significant factor. The entrance should be well lit, clearly visible, and safe.

- **functional.** A prayer room's furnishings should be conducive to prayer. These items might include kneeling benches, folding chairs, study carols or tables for prayer stations, a bookcase containing books relating to prayer (see Prayer Library, p. 197), a map of the world and/or the local area, a telephone, a large bulletin board for announcements and schedules, a card filing system or Rolodex file for keeping prayer requests and answers, a computer, prayer focus cards (see p. 188), a copy of the church directory, and so on.

- **exclusive.** Once a room has been designated a prayer room, resist the temptation to use it for anything except activities that promote prayer.

how to staff a prayer room ministry

Recruiting

If the prayer room ministry is perceived by the members as a significant ministry in the church, recruiting participants will be easier than if people consider it just another program. As a result, recruiting should not occur only once or twice a year, but continually throughout the year. Here are some specific ideas:

- Add recruitment of additional intercessors to the permanent prayer list. Pray for more participants.

- Encourage your pastor to get involved and to lead by example.

- Promote the prayer room from the pulpit, in the church newsletter, in the bulletin, in the monthly prayer newsletter.

- Introduce the prayer room ministry during the new member class and include the prayer room in the tour.

- Make signing up easy. Periodically place slips in the bulletin that can be filled out and dropped in the offering plate. Post a sign-up sheet near the prayer room or in a high traffic area. Invite people to call the prayer room coordinator.

- Provide some basic training. For many people, spending an hour in prayer is overwhelming.

- Allow people to sign up for an initial commitment of three months. This way they can see if it is a ministry God is calling them to before they sign on for a longer period of time.

- Ask people to share testimonies of being in the prayer room.

- Put posters around the church promoting the opportunity to pray.

- Hold a one-day training and prayer vigil for anyone who may be interested before asking them to make a commitment.

- Have Sunday school classes tour the prayer room or hold their class in the prayer room. Ask the prayer coordinator to explain the prayer room briefly.

- Explain the purpose of the prayer room during a worship service, followed by a commitment service during which people are encouraged to sign up.

- Provide an opportunity for people to tour the prayer room periodically through the year.

- Appoint "day captains"—one for each day of the week—who are responsible for recruiting intercessors to fill their day.

Praying

- Establish a routine for intercessors when they come to pray. This promotes accountability and ensures that people who have been promised prayer are receiving it.

- Have intercessors sign in when they arrive and sign out when they leave. Encourage intercessors who are not able to fulfill their commitment to find a substitute.

- Set up prayer stations and ask intercessors to spend five to ten minutes at a station. In lieu of prayer stations, have an organized system for prayer—such as a Rolodex file, wire baskets, notebook, or photo album divided into three categories: current requests, ongoing requests, and answers to prayer.

- Each intercessor should spend some time thanking God for answers to prayer. Keep answers to prayers in

Young Ik Yoo of Global Mission Church in Silver Spring, Maryland, tells how one church started an effective prayer room ministry:

Our pastors formed a group of key leaders to develop a prayer ministry. The team designated an intercessory room and gathered training manuals, prayer request cards, recruitment cards, weekly schedule charts, card file boxes, prayer postcards with stamps, a calendar, a church members' directory, Kleenex, and a bulletin board to post announcements. The group also added a telephone and answering machine with a separate number, and printed business cards listing that number.

One month before the launch, the pastor preached a series of messages on prayer; church members were asked to dedicate at least one hour per week to prayer (on a specified day and time for four months). The intercessors were trained in how to enter the prayer room, answer the phone, and utilize the prayer cards.

At the appointed time, the intercessor enters the prayer room, signs in, and spends a few minutes in meditative prayer. Then he or she moves through several stations. At one station are the weekly church ministry prayer requests. At another are the emergency prayer requests. Other stations include files of visitors, new members, and the unsaved; general prayer request cards; and cards for missionaries. The intercessor also answers the phone during the prayer time. While the intercessor does not counsel, he or she may offer appropriate verses of Scripture and prayer.

front of the congregation constantly—from the pulpit, in newsletters, on bulletin boards, in the bulletin, through testimonials, and so on.

- If your prayer room is a 'round-the-clock drop-in center and/or "central dispatch center," be sure to train your staff in how to pray with people and how to identify the next place to refer people who need to see a pastor, a counselor, an intercessory prayer team, and so on. If this is the purpose of your center, you should always have at least two people staffing the room—for safety reasons and for managing the flow of traffic.

- Especially on Sundays, when walk-ins are likely to happen, you may want to staff the room with people who have been trained in various types of prayer—healing prayer, intercessory prayer, salvation prayer, and so on.

Ministry category: initial

Resources

Jill Griffith, *How to Have a Dynamic Prayer Ministry* (Colorado Springs: Wagner Publications, Inc., 1999).

Terry Teykl, *Making Room to Pray: How to Start and Maintain a Prayer Room in Your Church* (Muncie, IN: Prayer Point Press).

Terry Teykl, *Prayer Room Policies for Intercessors* (Muncie, IN: Prayer Point Press).

Alvin Vander Griend, *The Praying Church Sourcebook* (Grand Rapids, MI: CRC Publications, 1997).

C. Peter Wagner, *Churches That Pray* (Ventura, CA: Regal Books, 1993).

The Prayer Room Network
P.O. Box 63060
Colorado Springs, CO 80962-3060
800-689-5961
fax: 719-262-9920
e-mail: prn@wpccs.org

The Prayer Room Network, a ministry of the World Prayer Center, is designed to mobilize and coordinate effective prayer by linking local prayer rooms throughout the nation.

Prayer Session

Prayer sessions encourage people to pray by providing opportunities for focused, group prayer. Some prayer sessions are organized around a prayer focus (for example, prayer for missionaries) or by a group's affinity for certain topics (for example, young people praying over youth issues).

Prayer sessions are distinguished from triads and small groups by their size: they can involve large groups of a hundred or more people. However, prayer sessions are not prayer meetings; they differ in their regularity and focus. Prayer sessions meet as necessary; prayer meetings usually meet weekly. Prayer sessions have a specific focus; prayer meetings normally deal with a variety of needs. A prayer session is also different from a worship service. Very little time is spent singing, and there usually is no offering or preaching.

Here are some examples of prayer sessions:

- A Christian school annually brings people—students, faculty, and parents—together to pray before the school year begins. This is an hour of focused prayer for the coming school year.

- A group of women annually hold a one-day (9 A.M.-3 A.M.) prayer session to pray for mission fields and missionaries.

- Those involved in a church's Lighthouse ministry come together monthly to pray for the ministry, for the Lighthouses, and that God will hear the prayers for their neighbors.

- Prior to the invasion of Iraq by allied forces in the Persian Gulf War, hundreds of churches held special prayer sessions.

- A congregation gathers to ask God for vision and direction (before the church embarks on a planning process).

- At the beginning of a spiritual emphasis week or month, a church gathers to pray for spiritual growth.

Ministry category: intermediate

Prayer Shield

(*Note:* This is written for the church's perspective; for additional insights from the pastor/leader's perspective, see pp. 131-133.)

One of the most important prayer ministries in any church is consistent and earnest prayer for the church's leaders. In 1 Thessalonians 5:25, the apostle Paul pleads, "Pray for us." Regular, intentional prayer for the pastor(s) should be one of the first ministries initiated in a church.

Pastors, church leaders, and Christian workers are primary targets of spiritual attacks. More than one million clergy—pastors and Christian workers—currently serve more than 400,000 churches and servant ministries in North America. The enemy is looking to discourage and discredit each one—including your pastor. While the church is a prime target for Satan's strategic attacks, the pastor is at the bull's-eye of that target. Satan knows if he defeats the leader, the followers often scatter.

At the same time, pastors grow tired under the weight of ministry. They work long hours and normally wear multiple hats—preacher, leader, manager, pastor, counselor, fundraiser, worship leader, discipler, evangelist, administrator, and more. And leaders, by nature of their position, usually struggle alone.

Praying for your pastors on a daily basis provides a hedge of protection around them, their families, and their ministry; helps sustains them in ministry; and opens up God's blessing on their ministry. A pastor should not be in ministry without daily prayer protection. Serious ministry requires serious protection.

identifying prayer shield intercessors

Prayer shield intercessors should be sought through prayer. Pastors should ask God to raise up a support team to pray for them. Some churches place an announcement in their bulletin inviting people to join the prayer shield. Other churches, if the responsibilities will be greater or if issues of confidentiality will be present, conduct interviews with each potential intercessor.

A list of intercessor qualifications might include

- a passion for the Lord. Are they fully devoted to God?

- a love for the pastor. Do they genuinely love the pastor or do they just seek to be in the inner circle?

- a love for the church. Do they wish to see the church grow in effectiveness and numbers? Are they open to the changes prayer might bring?

- a servant attitude. Are they willing to remain behind the scenes and be part of a team?

- trustworthiness with issues of confidentiality. Can they keep a confidence?

- integrity. Are the pray-ers above reproach? Are they respected in the church community?

Some churches identify three levels of intercessors (see p. 131) and thus offer the opportunity for different levels of commitment. Other churches identify prayer partners for each church staff member and/or for their missionaries.

In any case, encourage prayer shield members to commit for a predetermined period of time. Initially a three-month commitment may be appropriate. Then, by mutual assessment, the commitment can be renewed for up to a year. Encourage people to renew their commitments annually.

maintaining the prayer shield

It is important for prayer shield members to meet. This can be done as infrequently as annually—perhaps in a retreat format that includes some basic training—or as often as weekly. This time together could include

- a time of fellowship with the pastor.

- praying for the pastor (including laying on of hands or a blessing).

- a short teaching about intercession.

- sharing of answers to prayer.

- mutual encouragement.

While some pastors provide a monthly prayer guide, newsletter, or calendar for their prayer shield members, other churches use a more generic guide for prayer. Ideally, prayer shield members should have both the pastor's (specific) guide and a more generic guide available. One of the following formats can be selected for an entire year, or the formats may be rotated each month.

How to Pray for Your Pastor (1)

John Maxwell, in *Partners in Prayer* (Thomas Nelson, 1996), encourages people to pray for the top seven needs of a pastor:

Sunday	Rest and strength (Ps. 23)
Monday	Intimacy with God (2 Cor. 13:14)
Tuesday	Family (Eph. 4:32)
Wednesday	Ministry effectiveness (Eph. 4:11-13)
Thursday	Obedience to God (Luke 9:23-24)
Friday	Leadership (Rom. 12:6-8)
Saturday	Wisdom (James 1:5)

How to Pray for Your Pastor (2)

Intercessors can pray for all of these items every day, pray for one a day on a rotating basis, or select one or more each day as the Lord leads.

Abiding in Christ (John 15:5)
Bearing fruit (John 15:8)
Industriousness (Col. 4:13)
Listening to the Spirit (Gal. 5:25)
A loving spirit (1 Cor. 13)
Obedience to God's will (Rom. 12:1-2)
Purity (1 Tim. 5:22)
A servant attitude (Phil. 2:1-5)
Submission to authority (Heb. 13:17)
A thankful attitude (Phil. 4:8)
A vital prayer life (1 Thess. 5:25)
Wisdom (James 1:5)

How to Pray for Your Pastor (3)

In *Your Pastor: Preyed On or Prayed For?* (Prayer Point Press, 1993), Terry Teykl writes that when Larry Lea pastored the Church on the Rock he gave the following instructions to his intercessors on how to pray for him as their pastor:

Pray that your pastor's private life will be as strong as his public life.
Pray that nothing will violate the anointing from without or from within.
Pray that the Lord will send in a great harvest of souls from the north, south, east, and west.
Pray that the pastor will be delivered from unreasonably negative people.
Pray that the Lord will bless the church financially so the pastor can focus on ministry.
Pray that the Lord will place a hedge of protection around the pastor's family.

How to Pray for Your Pastor (4)

Shield your pastor from "head to toe," covering him or her with prayer as the armor of God does (see Eph. 6:10-20). There is one "garment" for each day of the week.

The helmet of salvation. Ask God to protect your pastors' head—their thoughts, ideas, dreams. Ask that God guide their plans, vision, and sermon preparation and that they may know their sins are forgiven in Jesus. Pray that their mind may be continually renewed by a focus on God's gift of salvation and grace. Pray for discernment, wisdom, guidance, and strength.

The belt of truth. Ask God to keep your pastors constantly in God's Word, sensitive to God's direction and will, and able to speak the truth boldly. Pray that their relationships with spouse, children, and friends may be satisfying and provide a strong witness.

The breastplate of righteousness. Pray that your pastors may seek God with their whole heart. Pray that they will place Jesus on the throne of their life and that God will protect their heart with diligence. Ask God to bless them with physical, emotional, and financial well-being.

Feet fitted with the gospel. Ask God to help your pastors walk in ways that are obedient and pleasing to God, to keep their feet on solid ground, to keep them from straying, to lead them where God wants them to go, and to send them with eagerness into the world with the gospel.

The shield of faith. Ask God to guard your pastors from discouragement, unreasonably negative people, and temptation. Ask God to protect their ministry, family, and personal walk with God. Pray that God will enable them to lead with integrity, live with confidence, and love with grace.

The sword of the Spirit. Ask God to give your pastors boldness in preaching, the willingness to confront in counseling situations, and a desire to follow the leading of the Spirit regardless of the cost.

Prayer. Ask God to give your pastors a passionate devotional life, to protect their quiet time with God, to clearly answer their prayers, and to bring fruit into their ministry.

options

- Some churches ask every member to pray for their pastor for five minutes every day at noon; others ask their members to sign up to pray for the pastor on a specific day.

- Some churches also pray for pastors of neighboring churches. Members can be assigned to pray for other pastors, or the prayer shield members can do this when they join for prayer.

- During special times of crisis, encourage your prayer shield intercessors to join together in fasting and prayer.

Ministry category: initial

Resources

John Maxwell, *Partners in Prayer* (Nashville: Thomas Nelson, 1996).

Terry Teykl, *Your Pastor: Preyed On or Prayed For?* (Muncie, IN: Prayer Point Press, 1997).

Alvin Vander Griend, *The Praying Church Sourcebook* (Grand Rapids, MI: CRC Publications, 1997).

C. Peter Wagner, *Prayer Shield* (Ventura, CA: Regal, 1992).

Prayer Support Group

A prayer support group is a small group of believers with a common concern who meet regularly for fellowship, mutual support, and prayer. In contrast to the traditional support group, this group emphasizes prayer.

There are three basic ingredients necessary to make these groups work:

1. *The affinity of the members.* Those participating should have a common understanding, passion, and personal investment in the issue that brings them together.

2. *The deep commitment of the members.* Group members make a personal commitment in the lives of the others in the group. They find strength and encouragement from being together, learn to trust each other, and often build relationships that sustain them apart from the group.

3. *The understanding that this is not a therapy group.* It does not require an expert to lead it. While people share their experiences, advice is minimal. They meet to pray. And prayer makes a significant impact.

The format for the group should be kept fairly simple. A typical ninety-minute session could be divided into three sections:

- a time for welcoming and introducing new members, fellowship, and catch-ing up on each other's lives since the last meeting.

- focused sharing on the common issue as a foundation for prayer.

- prayer time. At least half of the time you spend together should be spent in prayer.

Prayer support groups need one person to facilitate, to keep the group on track. Leadership can be given to one person or rotated through the group. Periodically, you may want to invite an expert on the topic to share with the group.

Prayer support groups can be formed around any number of issues:

- parents of ADHD or ADD children
- people affected by cancer (or any other specific disease, or those with a terminal disease)
- people who have lost spouses
- people with an addicted spouse (drugs, alcohol, pornography)
- parents of unbelieving children
- parents of teenagers
- parents of preschoolers
- couples struggling with infertility
- parents of children with disabilities
- single parents
- singles
- newly married couples

Because of the nature of these groups, they require a high commitment to confidentiality. The significance of keeping the group "stuff" in the group should be reinforced each time a new member joins. At the same time, while there are some dynamics that might encourage these to be closed groups, every effort should be made to keep them open to new members.

Ministry category: intermediate

Resource

Alvin Vander Griend, *The Praying Church Sourcebook* (Grand Rapids, MI: CRC Publications, 1997).

Prayer Tape Ministry

Many people have an opportunity to listen to audio tapes while commuting to work or traveling. By building a collection of tape resources that can be loaned out for teaching and encouragement, your church can help people make good use of their driving time by learning more about prayer.

Consider placing the following tapes in your loaning library:

- your pastor's messages on prayer
- other pastors' messages on prayer
- audio training courses
- devotionals and prayers taped by a reader at the church (permission must be obtained from the original source of these devotions and prayers)
- articles read on tape by local readers (again, permission is required)

Note that taped messages preached by your pastor can be sold for a nominal fee with their permission as long as the messages do not contain copyrighted material (for example, a copyrighted hymn, special music, or a lengthy quotation). Taped messages from other pastors or conference speakers should be purchased from the respective church or conference. Using your own tape recorder, without permission, could violate copyright laws.

Ministry category: simple

Prayer Team Ministry

A prayer team ministry is similar to the elder care ministry (see pp. 154-155). The major difference is that the elder care ministry focuses on the church membership while the prayer team ministers primarily in the community.

Prayer teams provide

- a listening ear to hear what people are saying and to hear what God is asking you to pray for.

- the offer to pray specifically without "preaching" or giving advice.

- a word of encouragement.

- spiritual direction.

Prayer teams can function in a variety of settings, including

- **hospitals.** Prayer teams can assist personnel in hospitals without a chaplain by visiting with patients who request a spiritual visit. In addition, members of the congregation can submit names of neighbors and friends who are in the hospital.

- **prisons.** With proper clearance, many prisons and halfway houses will allow church personnel to have prayer with inmates.

- **malls.** In teams of two, prayer teams can roam the mall striking up conversations with mallwalkers, shoppers, students, and employees.

- **rest homes and rehabilitation centers.** Teams can visit individuals who have been referred by members of the church or the facility itself.

- **the community.** Prayer teams can prayerwalk the neighborhood around the church or follow up on needs referred to the church by social service agencies. Or, set up a prayer booth at the county fair to offer prayer to anyone who might stop.

identifying and utilizing your prayer teams

A prayer team should be made up of people with the gifts of intercession, compassion, and/or discernment. Teams are normally two persons of the same sex, although married couples can serve effectively as prayer teams. Another option is for a small group, as part of its ministry, to divide into prayer teams and go out into the community once or twice a month.

One of the benefits of this prayer ministry is its flexibility. Teams can go out individually (for example, one team visits the hospital every Tuesday evening, another team goes to the county jail on Sunday afternoon, and so on) or all together (such as sending out four teams to a hospice center every Friday evening).

In order to make the congregation aware of the prayer teams' work, announcements offering the services of the teams should be printed regularly in the bulletin. Members of the church should be encouraged to provide referrals. Consider offering a central number for people to call in their referrals.

training your prayer teams

Training is necessary for effective ministry in a variety of situations. It could be provided during the regular meetings of the prayer teams, or special training sessions may be scheduled annually.

The best training is provided on-the-job, where an apprentice member is teamed with an experienced team member. Training should also include some instruction on the biblical teaching about prayer and listening, as well as education about passages that offer comfort and encouragement. Be sure to review the policies and procedures for participating on the prayer team, and address practical questions and answers (such as when it is appropriate to anoint with oil, lay on hands, or break a confidence). Team members should also be asked to sign a statement of confidentiality.

It is important to remember that prayer teams are not counseling teams. Although prayer teams may provide some direction, the purpose of the prayer team is not to solve the issues brought for prayer—but to pray about them.

Ministry category: initial

Resource

Alvin Vander Griend, *The Praying Church Sourcebook* (Grand Rapids, MI: CRC Publications, 1997).

Prayer Triplets

Prayer triplets are three households—families with children, couples, or singles—who commit to pray together weekly. The primary purpose of the prayer triplet is to provide all households in the congregation an opportunity to pray regularly with two other households.

Because this ministry usually involves a small number of people praying together, it is a low-risk step into organized prayer for those who are uncomfortable praying with others. It also allows people with busy schedules to participate. As a result, it may include people who might otherwise not be involved in a prayer ministry; therefore, introduce this ministry carefully, with pastoral support, and give the congregation plenty of information and time to think about signing up.

Groups are formed when members of the congregation sign a commitment card to become involved in the ministry for a specified amount of time—often three or six months. The commitment involves promising to pray daily for the two other households and to maintain personal contact by mail, e-mail, or telephone at least weekly.

After people have returned their commitment cards, the prayer team or triplet ministry coordinator can form the groups. While forming groups can be done in a variety of ways, it should always be done carefully. Consider placing people in a similar geographic location together; be intentional about mixing people—such as pairing newer members with longer-term members, singles with couples and families, younger members with older members. It can be beneficial to rotate the groups every year or so.

prayer triplet activities

After the coordinator of this ministry has formed the triplets, he or she may want to inform people of their group members via a letter that may also contain some basic information about each other. It may also be helpful to include a focus card (see sample on p. 224) or other prayer guide to help people pray for their group members.

In addition to the initial commitment to pray for each other daily and to maintain contact at least weekly, some triplets, as they become more familiar with each other, may desire to regularly meet together for prayer. If so, they should determine their expectations and renew their commitment in consultation with the prayer coordinator. Eventually, triplets may also want to expand their prayer focus, perhaps by praying for one or two specific seekers, or a teacher, or students in the church, and so on.

Be sure to provide opportunities for people to share what has been happening in their prayer triplets—as long as they don't breach confidentiality. Allow for testimonies during worship, or reserve a space in the bulletin or newsletter for people to give thanksgiving and share stories.

How to Pray for Another Believer

Pray for their relationship with God.
— That they will know and experience God's presence, love, and grace.
— That they will be open to God's leading, vision, and direction.
— That they will allow God to heal their hurts, mend broken relationships, and grow them spiritually.
— That God will use them to bring him honor and glory and make an impact for his kingdom.

Pray for their physical well-being.
— That God will protect them from physical injury, illness, and disease.
— That God will provide them meaningful and gainful employment, and healthy working relationships.
— That God will give them time for recreation and relaxation.
— That God will bless their relationships: friendships, marriage, parent-child relationships, and so on.

Pray for their participation in the church.
— That they will support the vision, pastor, and leaders of the church.
— That their fellowship with other believers will be supportive and encouraging.
— That they will continue (or begin) to use their spiritual gifts in ministry and that God will bless them for it.
— That they will be sensitive to others' needs—at church, in their neighborhood, at work, in their extended family.

Pray for their commitment to prayer.
— That God will keep them faithful to their daily commitment.
— That God will provide answers to their prayers.

Ministry: simple

Resource
Alvin Vander Griend, *The Praying Church Sourcebook* (Grand Rapids, MI: CRC Publications, 1997).

Prayer Vigil

Traditionally, a prayer vigil is keeping "vigilance"; that is, "keeping awake and alert" throughout the day or night prior to a religious feast. Today the term describes any concentrated prayer time during which a group of believers meet for a predetermined period of time to pray about specific needs. A vigil is premised on the assurance that if believers earnestly seek the face of God, God will answer their prayer.

Prayer vigils are most commonly held during local or national crises—such as praying for healing from a life-threatening illness or for a country hit by a natural disaster—or in connection with special days, such as New Year's Day and Easter. Many churches also hold a prayer vigil prior to making a major decision or before a significant event in the life of the church (such as a new building addition or a stewardship drive). Although a prayer vigil is an intensive, saturated prayer initiative, it can still take a variety of forms.

prayer vigil formats

- Some prayer vigils are held for two to three days, others for eight hours. Some are held during the day, others go on through the night.

- In some prayer vigils all the participants pray together; in others the group divides into small groups of pray-ers. During extended prayer vigils there may be times when people pray alone.

- During some prayer vigils people come and go as necessary; in others participants are present the entire time.

- Most vigils have a specific focus; however, some are simply held quarterly or monthly to pray for immediate needs.

- Some prayer vigils are held independent of any other event; other vigils are held to provide protection for other events. A group of prayer warriors, for example, keeps vigil prior to and throughout each Promise Keepers event.

- For extended prayer vigils, people are usually scheduled to pray in thirty- to sixty-minute blocks; each person commits to praying for a specific block of time, perhaps even more than once during the vigil. During shorter vigils (eight to twelve hours), participants are more commonly present throughout the entire event.

- While most prayer vigils are held at the church (or another central location), some are designed to allow people to pray from other locations. Some vigils are intentionally held in a home or retreat setting.

examples

- In Acts 12, believers came together to pray for the apostle Peter, who had been imprisoned. Gathered inside a home, "the church was earnestly praying to God for him" (Acts 12:5). God answered this vigil of prayer in a miraculous way by sending an angel to release Peter from prison.

- One church held a twenty-four–hour prayer vigil to pray for its city's police force. Within two months, several police officers began to attend their church and were baptized. Within six months the violent crime rate in the city dropped over 80 percent.

- In 1995, Pakistani evangelist Javed Albert established a routine he calls "Tarry Nights" to counter powerful demonic influences associated with shrine pilgrimages and witchcraft activity. These prayer and praise vigils begin at 9:00 P.M. on Thursday and Saturday evenings and continue until dawn (George Otis, *Informed Intercession*, p. 58).

planning a prayer vigil

- Start small. Consider starting with a short (eight-hour) vigil during which people may come and go; as your church becomes familiar with prayer vigils, you may extend the length.

- Announce the prayer vigil at least a month in advance to allow people time to clear their schedule. Ask your pastor to explain the vigil from the pulpit and invite the congregation to participate.

- Prepare a guide for prayer that explains how the prayer vigil works, describes the responsibilities of the participants, includes a list of items for prayer or a prayer focus card, and so on.

- Prepare an outline of the schedule for the vigil. Be sure to schedule periodic, light refreshment breaks; if the vigil goes throught the night, consider concluding with breakfast.

- During the vigil, encourage people to pray aloud, but also affirm their desire to observe or pray silently.

- Include time for worship that involves music and/or appropriate readings of Scripture or devotionals.

- Close the vigil with a time of praise and celebration.

- Do not be disappointed if the initial participation seems low. Many churches' vigils start small, with three or four people. But as the word spreads, subsequent vigils tend to grow. Approximately five percent participation of the adult membership is an appropriate goal.

Ministry category: intermediate

Resources

David Bryant, *Concerts of Prayer* (Ventura, CA: Regal Books, 1988).

Alvin Vander Griend, *The Praying Church Sourcebook* (Grand Rapids, MI: CRC Publications, 1997).

Prayer Wall

Many churches attempt to provide prayer twenty-four hours a day, seven days a week; this ends up being 168 one-hour blocks, which are filled by individuals, families, and small groups committed to prayer. Keeping track of such a prayer effort can be an organizational nightmare. As a result, many churches build a prayer wall.

The prayer wall is located on an actual wall in the prayer room or another highly visible place. The wall is divided into seven columns—one for each day of the week—and twelve to twenty-four rows—depending on how many hours the church decides to cover in prayer. As people commit to pray, their name is posted on the wall in the time block they have chosen.

Since many people make a three-month commitment, names on the wall may change fairly frequently. As a result, the wall should accommodate such changes easily. Some churches actually paint the columns and rows onto a smooth wall; names can then be taped or poster-puttied to the wall. Other churches have painted a wall with chalkboard paint or covered the wall with a marker-board; names can easily be written and erased when changes are made. Other churches put 168 slots on a wall, into which can be inserted a small plastic plaque with the person's name written or engraved on it.

The purpose of the prayer wall may vary; the focus should be determined in advance. However, it's also possible to have more than one prayer wall to serve different focuses, or to change the focus of the wall periodically (but not too frequently). The wall can be used in connection with a prayer room ministry; it can be for general needs, for the church's members and ministries, for the church's neighborhood, for missions, and so on.

Ministry category: intermediate

Prayer Warriors

Prayer warriors are a group of spiritually gifted intercessors (see Ministry of Intercession, pp. 160-161) who feel called by God to make prayer for their church their primary ministry.

Prayer warriors pray daily for the needs of the church and its pastor, mission, members, and so on, that the Lord places before them. They normally spend one to twenty hours a week in prayer—a major commitment.

People with the gift of intercession and a passion for prayer are encouraged to sign a pledge card that offers different levels of commitment for intercession:

Level One: People who are willing to pray for ten minutes each day (or one hour a week).

Level Two: People who are willing to pray for an hour each day (or a minimum of five hours per week).

Level Three: People who are willing to pray for more than an hour a day (or a minimum of ten hours per week).

When people join this ministry, request a three-month commitment. When renewing they can recommit for six to twelve months.

Publish a weekly or biweekly list of prayer needs to be distributed to the prayer warriors. The intercessors should be aware that the list may include prayer requests from the congregation that are highly confidential and cannot currently be shared with the entire congregation. Items should be divided into at least two major sections: current prayer needs and answers to prayer.

These prayer issues might include

- people going through personal crisis, such as hospitalization, illness, or unemployment.

- those going through marriage or family crises or other difficult family issues.

- people in need of spiritual healing.

- those who are unsaved.

- people who are grieving.

- births and other reasons for rejoicing.

- thanksgiving for answered prayers.

Being a prayer warrior is a "behind the scenes" ministry. Since prayer warriors do not get much public recognition, the prayer coordinator should be conscientious about offering encouragement and appreciation.

Ministry category: initial

Prayer for Worship

The worship service is the "main event" in most churches. Yet few worship services are adequately bathed in prayer. The purpose of a prayer for worship ministry is to ask God to prepare worshipers; to protect the worship environment from distraction; and to promote a spirit of praise, healing, and fellowship prior to the worship service, during the worship service, and following the worship service.

Charles Spurgeon had a group of intercessors praying in the basement, below his pulpit, whenever he preached. He called it his "furnace room." In fact, churches that have instituted prayers for worship indicate that services tend to run more smoothly, that messages become more powerful, and that church members make a greater investment in the service.

the parts of worship prayer

There are three primary aspects in praying for a worship service. Each different aspect normally involves a different group of intercessors.

1. Pre-prayer

During the week, these people pray on a pre-assigned day for the services the following Sunday. All members of the congregation are encouraged to spend five minutes around their Saturday evening meal (before or after) specifically praying for the service the following day. In order to encourage this practice, a section of the bulletin titled "Next Sunday" contains a brief description of the morning and evening services so people can pray effectively.

Early Sunday morning a small group, a ministry team, or a specific group of interested people come to the church at least an hour early to pray for the service. They may want to prayerwalk the sanctuary, pausing at various places to pray for what will happen during the service (for example, laying hands on the seats and asking that each worshiper will sense God's presence, or kneeling on the platform and asking God to bless the worship leaders and pastor). In addition, a focus card like the one on page 230 can be provided to every member of the church.

2. Leadership prayer

Invite all of the participants in the worship service to come together for prayer. This would include the pastor(s), instrumentalists, worship leaders, and technicians. It could also include ushers, greeters, childcare attendants, and parking lot attendants. If these groups are not meeting together for prayer, the individual ministries should meet separately for prayer. The size of the group is usually the determining factor.

How to Pray Before a Worship Service

- While driving to church, pray for safety for those who will be driving to church.

- Seeing the church sign, pray that God will allow others to "see" the sign and be convicted to come.

- Walking from the car to the front door, pray that everyone will come with a receptive heart.

- Entering the welcome area, pray that everyone who comes will be warmly welcomed.

- Entering the worship center, ask God to send a rich measure of his Spirit to bless the worship that will soon take place.

This can be done quietly in a room near the worship center or on the platform. Participants should feel free to pray for any aspect of the worship service—including things which are of particular concern to their participation.

3. Concurrent prayer

This is the time for prayer that begins shortly before worship, continues through the time of worship, and concludes shortly after the conclusion of worship. Invite those who gather for this part of the ministry to sign in, and provide them with copies of the worship service and with a guide or focus card (see sample on p. 231) for how to pray for a worship service. Include a time of worship in your prayer time.

At the conclusion of the service, encourage the pray-ers to record in a book anything the Lord was showing the group during the prayer time. Have the group sign out.

recruiting people to pray for the worship service

- Assign a member of your prayer ministry leadership team to this ministry.

- Regularly encourage your members to become worship intercessors. This can be done from the pulpit, through periodical testimonies from pray-ers, in the newsletter, on bulletin boards, and in the bulletin.

- Offer a variety of commitment options; encourage people to volunteer once a quarter, once a month, twice a month, or weekly.

- Invite an existing small group to pray during worship three or four times a year. Provide training in this type of prayer to small group leaders at your regular small group training sessions.

- Assign this ministry to board members and staff members; provide them with adequate training.

- During the summer months when intercessors seem harder to find (and schedules are harder to keep), consider placing a prayer insert in 10 percent of the bulletins requesting people to pray for the service while in the service (see the sample insert on p. 232).

- Assign people to the prayer room, just as you assign nursery attendants, for a Sunday or two during the year. In addition to those assigned, have a couple of experienced intercessors present to lead the prayer time.

- In churches that have an established 'round-the-clock prayer ministry, the focus can change on Sunday to praying for the worship.

Ministry category: initial

How to Pray for a Worship Service

Scripture
— Read the Scripture passage noted in the bulletin for today's sermon.

Adoration
— Praise God for entering our place of worship.
— Adore God for who he is: loving, gracious, holy, just, compassionate, and so on.
— Sing a song of praise.

Silence
— Wait in silence for a few moments—listening to God for his wisdom to pray for today's worship service.

Prayer for the worship service
— Pray for excitement, worship, and praise to take place, that God might be honored and glorified throughout the worship time.
— Ask the Holy Spirit to prepare the heart of every worshiper so the music, message, and prayers might speak to them. Ask the Spirit to assist people in setting aside any distracting "noises." Ask God for teachable hearts.
— Request the manifestation of God's presence in the services (Ps. 22:3).
— Pray for visitors. Pray that they will feel welcomed and loved. Pray that God will open their eyes and convict their hearts about Jesus Christ. Pray that they might desire to become a part of God's family.
— Pray for a spirit of thanksgiving in the musicians and singers (Ps. 100:4). Speak blessings over the choir and worship leaders. Pray they will effectively lead people into worship. Pray that they will illustrate the joy of the Lord.
— Ask the Holy Spirit to protect and anoint the pastor so he or she will boldly preach the Word.
— Pray for many hearts to be open to receiving the message, for hearts to be stirred. Ask the Holy Spirit to loosen a spirit of conviction for sin and a desire for conversion in the worship service.
— Ask God to bind unbelief and doubt, as well as apathy to the glory of God.
— Pray for physical and emotional healing to come to people throughout the congregation.
— Pray for biblical worship—that which includes the emotions as well as reason. Rebuke the spirit of entertainment and any meaningless religious routines.

Thanksgiving
— Ask God to give people a spirit of worship and thanksgiving throughout the coming week and to apply what the Spirit has convicted them of in worship.
— Thank God for his faithfulness in answering your prayers.
— Thank God for a wonderful opportunity to worship, and ask God that this might be the beginning of revival across your nation.
— Thank God for any specific words/answers/insights God revealed while you were praying.

You have been "randomly selected"
to be a

WORSHIP PRAYER SERVANT

and we hope you will accept this awesome privilege
to pray for the worship service today.

Twenty of these inserts have been placed at random in today's bulletins. Since you have received one, you are invited to pray for today's worship service. You do not need to close your eyes or go elsewhere. Pray as you participate in worship.

Here are some prayer suggestions:

- As you await the start of worship, pray for spiritual protection around this place. Ask God to remove all that distracts and to turn hearts to him. Pray that the worship may be done in spirit and in truth.

- Pray for the worship leaders as they lead in music. Pray blessings on the musicians.

- As people turn to greet one another, pray for courage and kindness. Pray that each person will sense God's love and welcome to worship.

- Pray for those involved in a special ministry: music, baptism, profession of faith, testimony, and so on.

- Praise God for the opportunity to give gifts back to him. Pray for cheerful giving during the offering.

- Ask the Holy Spirit to loosen a spirit of conviction of sin and a desire for conversion.

- Ask God to prepare hearts and instill hunger for the reading of his Word.

- Ask for God's anointing of the Holy Spirit upon the pastor. Pray for open hearts to receive the preaching of the Word.

- As you receive the departing blessing, pray that this blessing will be passed on to others as people fellowship together and enter the world as God's witnesses.

Praying Through the Directory

Praying through the directory simply means using the church's directory of members as a guide to pray specifically for one person, one household, one family at a time. It can be an excellent ministry for the pastor, for other church leaders, for a specific prayer group, for small groups, for new members of a congregation (there is no better way to get to know the congregation than to pray for them!), and so on.

Depending on the size of the church and the number of people committed to praying through the directory, every person can be prayed for once a month or as often as every day.

There are a number of ways that this ministry can happen:

- One person who commits to praying through the directory can simply pray for a few names or households each day, with the goal being to work through the directory in a month or two.

- At the beginning of each month, place 28 to 31 membership lists in the back of church. Number each list from 1 to 28/31 (depending on the number of days in that month), and invite people to take one and, on the date specified, to pray through the directory.

- Produce and distribute a monthly prayer calendar. By simply placing four singles/couples/families/households on a day, about 120 households can be prayed for. If your church is larger, consider making multiple calendars so that every month, everyone is prayed for.

- In your prayer room, create a prayer station with the specific purpose of praying through the directory on a continual basis. Have intercessors simply place a sticky note where they left off so the next person can pick it up.

> Catherine Rood, in *The Breakthrough Intercessor,* writes: "During a recent quiet time, I was challenged to pray for our congregation, person by person. I reluctantly picked up the church directory. There were so many names there and I couldn't put a face on many of those people. But I began to pray for each by name. I wrote the prayer in my journal.
>
> "At church, I asked around, 'Who is so-and-so?' When I met them, they became real people to me because I had prayed for them. Occasionally, I would mention to one of them, 'Oh, by the way, I was praying for you on Tuesday.'
>
> "'You were?' Each was surprised; some were incredulous, others asked why. Always I was thanked for my prayers. And I realized that my heart was becoming tangled up with people who, six months before, had been nothing more to me than sterile type on a directory page. Not any longer!"

- If the pastor, staff, or an organized ministry team is praying through the directory, consider sending out note-cards (see Prayer-a-Grams, pp. 189-190) letting people know they have been prayed for.

Ministry category: intermediate

School of Prayer

School implies learning, intentionality, and goals. A school of prayer is designed to provide a structured, organized curriculum to promote the teaching and practice of prayer in order to bring people into a closer walk with the Lord.

A school of prayer can take on a variety of formats:

1. A seven-week, three-season (fall, winter, spring) curriculum which runs concurrently with adult education ministry or as part of the adult education offerings.

2. Periodical weekend retreats. These retreats can be Friday evening and Saturday morning; all day Saturday; or Saturday evening through Sunday noon. Some churches also hold special sessions beginning Sunday afternoon through Sunday evening.

3. Dedicate one or two months a year as School of Prayer Month. Provide a specific curriculum and request each small group in your church to spend those months discussing and practicing prayer.

4. Preach extensively on prayer. If prayer is to be significant in your church's ministry it must be significant in your church's preaching. This necessitates a sermon series each year or frequent preaching on prayer throughout the year.

5. Teach prayer through one-on-one discipling relationships. While a one-on-one relationship is highly recommended for training *all* believers, it is often an impossible task. As a result, most churches emphasize one-on-one relationships with new Christians. Prayer should be an extensive part of this relationship—both teaching prayer and praying together.

In every format, emphasize training that is experiential—actually spend time praying!

options for curriculum materials

Curricula on prayer may come from a number of sources:

- Use resources from your denomination.

- Use resources from other denominations.

- Use resources from other churches in your denomination or community.

- Study a book on prayer. (Many include study guides.)

- Develop your own course(s).

Prayer curricula topics may also vary widely:

- Bible prayers (a Bible study of prayers in the Bible)

- Bible pray-ers (a Bible study of the prayer life of biblical characters who prayed, such as Daniel)

- "Changing the World Through Prayer" (an interactive seminar by Bill Bright)

- Classic prayer forms (a study of the prayers of historical religious figures and/or a study of various classic prayer formats)

- Healing prayer (try the book *Power Healing* by John Wimber)

- Intercessory prayer (try *Intercessory Prayer* by Dutch Sheets or *The Workbook of Intercessory Prayer* by Maxie Dunnam)

- The Lord's Prayer (try *The Great House of God* by Max Lucado)

- Practicing the presence of God (try *Space for God* by Don Postema)

- Prayer formats (see section 1 of this book)

Whatever prayer education your church chooses to offer, be sure to offer a variety of formats: classroom, retreat, video, conferences, seminars, banquets with a teaching and prayer time, special guest speakers, and so on. Also, repeat courses that were helpful at different times and in different formats so that more people have opportunity to take it. If your church is small or if you are just beginning your prayer ministry, consider joining with another church or a few other churches to offer a school of prayer for your collective memberships.

Ministry category: initial

Resources

Bjorn Pedersen, *Face to Face with God in Your Church: Establishing a Prayer Ministry* (Minneapolis: Augsburg Fortress, 1995).

Alvin Vander Griend, *The Praying Church Sourcebook* (Grand Rapids, MI: CRC Publications, 1997).

Secret Intercessors

Secret Intercessors is a form of prayer partner ministry (see pp. 204-205) in which the intercessor remains unknown to the person for whom he or she is praying.

People who wish to participate in this ministry fill out an information card (see sample on next page) that includes their name, address, and any special requests for prayer they have. The coordinator of this ministry collects the cards, determines the pairings (either intentionally or randomly), and distributes each person's card to his or her assigned partner. On the reverse side of each card is a statement of commitment that the partners sign, signifying their commitment to pray for the person on their card for a set period of time.

At the end of each year, hold a special worship service, dinner, or celebration to reveal prayer partners.

Ministry category: simple

My Request for Prayer

Name: _____

Address: _____

_____

Special requests/Needs: _____

_____

_____

_____

_____

_____

My Commitment to Pray

I promise to pray for my assigned prayer partner every day for one year, from July 1, 20____, through June 31, 20____.

I promise to encourage my prayer partner periodically with cards and notes.

I promise not to disclose the identity of my prayer partner to anyone nor my identity to my prayer partner until the appropriate time.

Signed: _____

See You at the Pole

See You at the Pole is a national movement that had its beginning at a Burleson, Texas, youth retreat in 1990. At the retreat, youth leaders handed each student a marble and asked, "What is hindering your relationship with Jesus Christ?" Then, one by one, each student placed his or her marble—representing an issue keeping them from God—at the foot of a large wooden cross as a gesture of repentance.

After this spiritually emotional event, the students decided to pray for themselves and their friends. Going to each of the three high schools represented in their group, they gathered around the flagpoles and prayed that God would visit the school.

Shortly thereafter, in a meeting of youth leaders who were discussing how they could motivate Christian students to pray, one of the leaders used the example of the Burleson group. The idea took off, and one morning the following September more than 45,000 students in four states gathered around more than 1,200 flagpoles. Since then See You at the Pole has become an international student movement held around the world one morning every September.

Doug Clark, director of Field Ministries for the National Network of Youth Ministries, the organization that oversees See You at the Pole, describes this event: "Groups meet for forty-five minutes before school. Some sing. Some have a student leader. Some simply join hands and pray. Although many youth leaders actively encourage students to participate, the prayer time is student-initiated and student-led." Students pray for their school, teachers, administration and staff; for their friends, families, government, and nation; and for those who do not know Christ.

The time at the pole is normally divided between singing, reading Scripture, hearing testimonies, and offering general prayers in the large group and then more specific prayers in small groups. The goal of this ministry is to be present on every school campus. Students planning a SYATP prayer service should register at the address below and file a report on www.syatp.com.

As a courtesy, students should notify their administrators of SYATP plans at their school.

Ministry category: intermediate

Resources
See You at the Pole
12335 World Trade Dr., Ste. 16
San Diego, CA 92128
e-mail: pray@syatp.com
www.syatp.com

Promotional resources are available from:

National Network of Youth Ministries
P.O. Box 60134
Fort Worth, TX 76115
www.syatp.com

Senior Intercessors

The older members of a congregation are often the congregation's greatest assets. Many of them have the time, flexibility, and wisdom to pray. Unfortunately, this prayer resource is often overlooked.

While many seniors are active and healthy, others are less active and some are confined to their homes. Many seniors have been active in the church most of their lives, but as they get older they feel less useful. However, prayer is a significant part of ministry, and every church needs the prayers of its senior members. Praying gives seniors an important role in the church and allows them to be personally involved without requiring a significant physical commitment.

Seniors can be involved in various prayer ministries, such as

- prayer partners (including being paired with staff members)
- prayer journeys
- Lighthouses of prayer
- praying through the directory
- prayer room participants

Encourage the older members of your church to develop their own prayer ministry. Make sure homebound seniors and nursing home residents are included.

As with any ministry, it is important to keep your intercessors informed. Consider sending a monthly note or newsletter to your seniors to keep them well informed about prayer needs and opportunities, answers to prayer, and training information, and to offer encouragement.

Ministry category: simple

Resource

Alvin Vander Griend, *The Praying Church Sourcebook* (Grand Rapids, MI: CRC Publications, 1997).

Shield a Badge

The Shield a Badge with Prayer ministry was started in 1990 by Jill Griffith, prayer ministry director at the Second Baptist Church of Houston. It was designed to support law enforcement officers and has been duplicated successfully in many cities and counties. Second Baptist Church currently prays for more than 650 Houston police officers and their families each day. One year after starting this ministry, divorces among Houston police officers declined fifty percent and deaths among officers also declined dramatically.

This ministry can involve members of the church, intercessors from other churches, and members of the community. A coordinator should be appointed to represent the ministry in its contact with the police department, to recruit and interview intercessors, and to provide some basic training. Intercessors make a one-year (renewable) commitment to pray for an assigned officer. (Individuals, families, small groups, and church school classes can adopt one or more officers as long as members are willing to pray daily.) They are given only the officer's name, badge number, and the station to which the officer is assigned.

When the assignment has been made, the prayer partner prays daily for the officer's safety on the job, for good judgment in the discharge of his or her responsibilities, for a safe return home, and for the officer's family. Communication from the prayer partner to the officer is important, but should also be limited—contact should only be made through the mail, and not more than four times per year. (One of these pieces should be a letter of introduction.) All correspondence should be sent to the station that employs the officer. Proselytizing is forbidden. It is the officer's option to respond or not.

If an officer leaves his or her station the prayer partner is notified of the change. In some cases another officer may be assigned. When an officer leaves the force, the prayer partner is notified and another officer is assigned. If for some reason the prayer partner cannot fulfill the commitment, they should notify the church coordinator as soon as possible.

In addition to praying for police officers, firefighters and their families could also be included.

Ministry category: intermediate

Resources

Jill Griffith, *How to Have a Dynamic Church Prayer Ministry* (Colorado Springs: Wagner Publications, Inc., 1999).

For more information and materials contact:

Prayer Ministry Office
Second Baptist Church
6400 Woodway
Houston, TX 77057
713-465-3408

Small Group Prayer

A small group prayer ministry is one or more small groups (three to twelve people) whose primary ministry is to pray together.

A small group has a designated leader and members who covenant together to attend each meeting. The covenant should include the following:

- the focus of the group (for children in school, for missionaries, for the lost, for a worship service, and so on)

- the length of commitment (normally three to six months, with the option of making an additional commitment when the previous commitment is fulfilled)

- the time and length of the meetings (for example, Mondays from 8:00 to 9:00 A.M.)

A praying small group may choose to focus on a number of different issues, or a combination of related issues, such as

- the mission and vision of their church.

- their pastor.

- the leaders of their church (such as church staff, elders, deacons, small group leaders, teachers).

- the Sunday and weekday service (see Prayer for Worship, pp. 229-232).

- the ministries of the church.

- specific needs of the church, individual members, and community.

- neighbors (see Evangelistic Prayer, pp. 59-60).

- inactive members.

The focus of a small group should be clearly explained and people should be encouraged to join a group they have an affinity for. Do not assign people to prayer groups.

Some groups agree to use the same prayer format week after week; other groups prefer to vary the praying format. While this issue does not need to be addressed in the group's covenant, the group should discuss this and come to consensus about how the meetings will go.

Ministry category: intermediate

Resource

Alvin Vander Griend, *The Praying Church Sourcebook* (Grand Rapids, MI: CRC Publications, 1997).

Telephone Prayer Ministry

While the telephone may be used as a tool in many prayer ministries, there are two specific prayer ministries whose primary work is done through use of telephone technology.

pre-recorded prayer messages

A prayer line with an answering machine is a helpful way for members of a church to stay updated on the prayer needs of the congregation throughout the week. This is a simple but effective ministry. It is relatively inexpensive, requiring only a separate phone line and an answering machine.

Churches use their messages in different ways:

- Some churches have a recorded Scripture reading, brief message, and prayer.

- Some churches provide a list of prayer requests.

- Some churches provide a list of prayer requests and then offer an opportunity to leave a personal prayer request.

- Some churches offer only an opportunity to leave a request, name, and address or phone number, and a promise to follow up.

In order for this ministry to be meaningful, the answering machine message needs to be changed regularly. A recorded Scripture reading and message should be changed at least weekly; prayer updates should be changed as necessary and at least twice a week. If there is an invitation to leave a message, someone must check the machine daily in order to assure prompt follow-up.

personally monitored phone ministry

A personally answered telephone prayer ministry is an ambitious undertaking. It offers people the opportunity to call in, share their prayer need, and have someone pray with them over the phone. While some ministries limit the time they are open (for example, from 8:00 A.M. to 8:00 P.M., Monday through Saturday), others are available twenty-four hours a day, seven days a week.

There are at least three basic options for managing this kind of ministry:

- Personal staffing of the phone line in the church's prayer room during the hours of operation. If there are frequent calls to the prayer line, this is the most effective option.

- Call forwarding. People are scheduled to answer the phone during hours of operation, but they can remain at home or at another location and calls are forwarded to them at that location.

- A cell phone. Intercessors carry the phone and respond appropriately when it rings. When their shift is complete (anywhere from a day to a week at a time), they pass the cell phone to the next person on the list. This is an excellent method if relatively few calls are received.

Training is important in this prayer ministry. Train the intercessors in standard answering protocol as well as in how to handle calls they may receive. Standard protocol may look something like this:

1. Offer an initial greeting that includes your church's name and an invitation: "How may I pray for you today?"

2. Listen carefully and take notes on a prayer card or in a notebook. Always listen with compassion and understanding; always acknowledge what they are saying. Avoid unnecessary probing, but try to obtain basic information, such as their name, address and/or phone number, whether they belong to a church, and their prayer need.

3. Pray with them. Avoid asking them if they would like to pray. Instead, say something like, "Let me pray about that with you."

4. Conclude the prayer by inviting them to call back—either for additional prayer or to share God's answer to the prayer.

5. Take appropriate follow-up action. This may include mailing information about the issue they are dealing with, having a pastor call on them, passing their need to an intercessory team, mailing them a brief presentation of the gospel, or whatever action you committed to on the phone.

In addition to standard protocol, special protocols should be set up for suicide calls, compulsive (frequent) callers, and calls for benevolence. Each pray-er should also know how to present the gospel and how to lead someone in the salvation prayer.

options and suggestions

- Placing caller ID on the phone line can often be helpful—not only in identifying the caller, but also in dealing with obscene phone calls.

- Place a high value on confidentiality. Breaches in confidentiality should lead to dismissing the person involved.

- Avoid counseling and/or giving advice. Remind callers, if necessary, that this is a prayer line.

- If you promise to continue praying for someone or to follow up with them, keep your promise. The integrity of the ministry depends on it.

- Print business cards that promote the prayer line. These can be passed out by church members. Some churches also use billboards and newspaper advertising to promote their prayer line number. Some churches print small adhesive stickers that can be placed on a phone or magnets that can be displayed on a refrigerator.

- Websites and e-mail addresses can also work in these types of ministries. Prayer chat rooms can also serve a valuable purpose.

Ministry category: initial to intense

Resources

Jill Griffith, *How to Have a Dynamic Prayer Ministry* (Colorado Springs: Wagner Publications, Inc., 1999).

Alvin Vander Griend, *The Praying Church Sourcebook* (Grand Rapids, MI: CRC Publications, 1997).

Section 4

HARVEST PRAYER IDEAS

THE CASE FOR HARVEST PRAYER

No matter how many prayer ministries a church has implemented, no matter how many of its members are regularly involved in prayer initiatives, no matter how well its leaders model a prayerful life, a church that does not pray for those who do not know Jesus Christ will be hard-pressed to call itself a house of prayer. If we profess to believe that prayer changes things, then we'd better be praying that God will change the eternal destiny of our neighbors.

Even if we ignore the fact that harvest prayer is mandated by Scripture—by God— there are enough reasons upon which to build a case for making harvest prayer a priority in any church.

Harvest prayer is God's desire. The apostle Paul wrote: "I urge that requests, prayers, intercessions and thanksgiving be made for everyone. . . . This is good, and pleases God our Savior, who wants everyone to be saved and to come to a knowledge of the truth" (1 Tim. 2:1-3). God desires that all people be saved. And the apostle Paul outlines God's strategy: God's people are to pray for everyone—with requests (praying for people's felt needs), prayers (praying for those items that God calls you to pray about), intercessions ("standing in the gap" for people who cannot or are not praying for themselves), and thanksgiving (celebrating God's acts). When we pray for the salvation of others, God is pleased.

Harvest prayer is essential to the harvest. Jesus himself said, "The harvest is plentiful but the workers are few. Ask the Lord of the harvest, therefore, to send out workers into his harvest field" (Matt. 9:37-38). While saving the lost is solely a work of God, God, in his wisdom, has called on the church to ask for the harvest. So throughout history, the spread of the gospel has paralleled the prevalence of prayer for the lost. When the church prays, there is a great harvest of souls. When the church fails to pray, the harvest is small. Jesus has made it very clear—without prayer there will be insufficient harvesters; without sufficient harvesters there will be an insufficient harvest.

Harvest prayer is spiritual warfare. Whenever the church seeks to draw people out of the kingdom of darkness and into the kingdom of light, Satan attacks. Such spiritual warfare requires a strong prayer base that asks God to release the power of his Word and Spirit. Satan continually places obstacles in the way to discourage the church, frustrate its effort, and discourage prayer; he does not want Christ's church to grow.

In spite of the opposition, churches are increasingly taking up arms, joining the spiritual battle, and invading the kingdom of darkness through prayer. The harvest continues:

- The number of Christians in Africa has risen from 5 percent of the population in 1900 to over half of the population in 2000.

- The church is South America is growing exponentially, with tens of thousands coming to Christ each week.

- More than 30,000 people are coming to Jesus Christ every day in China.

The church in North America, however, is not growing. How many believers today know their neighbors? How many are actively sharing their faith? How many North American Christians spend any significant amount of time praying, and when we pray, how often do we remember to pray for the lost? I fear the numbers are embarrassingly small and, as a result, the church is stagnant. It sometimes seems that Satan is winning the battle on this continent.

Harvest prayer brings answers. Alvin Vander Griend tells of an experiment done by a church in Phoenix, Arizona. Intercessors randomly selected 160 names from the local telephone book and divided the names into two equal groups. For ninety days they prayed for one group of eighty homes. The other eighty homes were not prayed for. After ninety days, they called all 160 homes, identified themselves and their church, and asked for permission to stop by and pray for the family and any needs they might be willing to share. Of the eighty homes for which they didn't pray, only one invited them to come. Of the eighty homes for which they had prayed for three months, sixty-nine invited them to come over; of the sixty-nine, forty-five invited them to come in.

Prayer makes a difference in the harvest because God's promise to answer prayer applies to our prayers for the lost. Jesus said:

I tell you the truth, anyone who has faith in me will do what I have been doing. He will do even greater things than these, because I am going to the Father. And I will do whatever you ask in my name, so that the Son may bring glory to the Father. You may ask me for anything in my name, and I will do it. (John 14:12-14)

We have not because we ask not. James Leggett summarizes God's invitation:

God has given us access to his throne. He has promised to answer our prayers. Let us approach him with our petition for the harvest, fully expecting him to bring men and women into his kingdom. (*WIN*, March 1992)

developing a harvest prayer ministry

In building a praying church, a major focus of prayer must be evangelism and missions. Most churches that consistently reach unsaved people have organized harvest prayer. The ideas that follow in this section are provided for the purpose of making harvest prayer a priority in your church's ministry. Each idea is identified by "ministry category" (see an explanation on pp. 141-142) and by "focus." The focus of a harvest prayer ministry may be on one of four general places: the **local** congregation, a **region** that includes a number of congregations, a **nation,** or the **world.**

When developing or augmenting a harvest prayer ministry, keep the following guidelines in mind:

- Always begin with prayer. Ask God to anoint leaders, clarify the direction, reveal his timing, and supply the intercessors. Do not proceed until after an extended season of prayer by your intercessory team.

- Proceed only with the approval of your pastor and the church leaders.

- Provide a written purpose statement. Make sure your purpose is a God-given one.

- Do not start a harvest prayer ministry with the goal of growing your church numerically, solving your church's financial crisis, making your church appear more spiritual, or competing with the church down the street. Pray out of your compassion for the lost and in obedience to God's command.

- Select or design a ministry in which people of all ages (from children to seniors) and maturity levels (new Christians to mature Christians) can participate. Provide opportunities for people to pray personally, with their families, in small groups, and in large groups such as corporate worship. Provide opportunities for Level One, Level Two, and Level Three intercessors (see p. 131), and offer flexibility so people can pray anytime, anywhere.

- Recognize that prayer ministries for the lost often lead to additional caring about those who are prayed for, and eventually may result in the opportunity to share your testimony or the gospel. Be prepared. Harvest prayer often results in long-term relationships.

- Harvest prayer requires a concerted, consistent effort over a sustained period of time. While some prayers may be answered almost instantly, others may take years before they are answered. The timing is always in God's hand (Eccles. 3:11). Do not begin an evangelistic prayer ministry if you are unable to sustain it.

- Harvest prayer takes place not only in the prayer room or at home, but out in the community itself. Provide a balance of prayer "behind doors" and prayer "outdoors" in the neighborhoods.

- A harvest prayer ministry requires a passion for lost people. While it may begin as a "program," it requires an investment in other people's lives.

- Provide adequate and necessary training that includes how to pray for the lost, how to live lives that reflect Jesus, how to build a relationship with a neighbor, how to share a personal testimony, how to share the gospel, and how to initiate the discipling process.

- Encourage those who are involved in harvest prayer. While most intercessors are not interested in public recog-

nition, encouragement is always appropriate in the form of a note, keeping people appraised of answers, a periodic prayer breakfast, support from the pastor, and so on.

- Celebrate all answers to prayer—both small and large.

How to Pray for the Lost

For yourself, pray
- that you will be open to God's leading.
- that the Lord will provide opportunities for you to influence your unsaved friends.

For your unsaved friends, pray
- that God will draw your friend to himself.
- that they will seek to know God.
- that they will believe the Scriptures.
- that Satan is bound from blinding them to the truth.
- that the Holy Spirit is working in them.
- that they turn from sin.
- that they believe in Jesus Christ as Savior and obey him as Lord.
- that they take root and grow in Christ.

—Southern Heights
Christian Reformed Church,
Kalamazoo, Mich.

Bar Caroling

Encouraging Christians to frequent the neighborhood bar will come as a surprise to some. But an increasing number of churches have recognized the importance of going where the needs are—and local bars and taverns can be filled with people who have needs.

Resurrection Lutheran Church of Des Moines, Washington, goes "bar caroling" each December after their Christmas Eve service. During Advent volunteers receive brief training and meet together for prayer. Following the Christmas Eve service, they begin with a session of prayer, break into groups of six to eight, and carpool to the bars that are open that evening. One member of each group enters the establishment and asks the owner or manager for permission to sing a few carols. If permission is given, the entire group enters, announces their intention of singing a few Christmas carols, and invites the patrons to join by using prepared song sheets.

After singing a verse or two of several familiar carols, they close with "We Wish You a Merry Christmas." When the singing is complete, they thank the patrons for the opportunity to share the story of God's love at Christmas, and they pass out Christmas cards and a small gift (usually a New Testament). The cards include a short greeting, followed by the church's address, worship times, and phone number. As they pass the cards and gifts they listen and offer to pray with the patrons.

This format can work in many different venues: prisons (permission must be received ahead of time), halfway houses, retirement villages, and rest homes.

Ministry category: intermediate

Focus: local

Bookmarks

Using available technology and information, you can create evangelistic prayer bookmarks that list the neighbors of members of your church. On a 3" x 8" piece of paper, list the name and address of a church member. Then list the names and addresses of the two houses on their left, the two houses on their right, and the five houses across the street. This information is available on CD from the Mapping Center for Evangelism (see p. 426) or by using a city directory available at your local library. When the bookmarks are complete, distribute them to church members and encourage people to pray for the nine names and households on their list.

Another church found a unique way to use their brochure rack. The children in their children's ministry drew pictures of mission activities (for example, someone preaching, helping to plant crops, teaching children to read) on 3" x 8" pieces of paper. On a separate 3" x 8" piece of paper, they printed information about one of the missionaries they were supporting, including their names, country in which they were serving, type of ministry, family status, and special requests for prayer. The pictures and information were laminated together—back to back—to form a bookmark. These bookmarks were placed in the brochure racks (one slot for each missionary) and people were invited to take one and remember the missionary in their daily devotions. After thirty days they returned the bookmark and traded it in for another missionary's bookmark. This same idea could be done with the various ministries in your church.

Another way to support your church's missionaries in prayer is to make a bookmark for each missionary, photocopy each bookmark (a color copy machine would be best), and pass them out to the congregation—or insert them in the bulletins. A different missionary could be selected each month, or all the missionaries could be distributed together during a mission emphasis week or month.

Bookmarks can be made for any number of prayer needs. Provide prayer bookmarks for the staff and leaders of the congregation with a short biographical sketch on one side and prayer needs on the other side. Make bookmarks of the special needs in your congregation—sicknesses, children in military or away at college, engagements, first-year marriages, and so on. Or, for every new child born in your congregation, create a bookmark including a picture, their birth date, parents, and other interesting information (birth weight, length, hospital). Distribute them to the congregation when the child is baptized or dedicated. The same thing can be done for people making public profession of faith and for people joining the congregation.

Ministry category: simple

Focus: local, region, nation, world

Church-a-Day

One of the most effective methods of breaking strongholds in a city and opening the door for effective evangelism is for local churches to unite across denominational and racial lines. The single most effective show of unity is to come together to pray.

While many cities hold periodic city-wide prayer meetings (especially in connection with the National Day of Prayer) some communities are discovering the impact of praying for the city every day of the year. Praying for the city involves confession for corporate sin, requests for protection and safety, a blessing on the city's institutions (government, schools, civic organizations, hospitals), and intercession for the salvation of its citizens.

Before launching into this extensive ministry, spend time in prayer. Be sure of God's leading. Begin only with your pastor's blessing and your church's participation. Then invite other churches to participate. Contact the prayer coordinator or pastor of other churches in your community, share what God has laid on your heart, and invite them to participate with you.

When you have identified the churches that will participate (the number should not be less than seven), assign each church the days it will be praying. Depending on how many churches are involved, each church could have from one to fifty-two days each year. Each church can then decide how they will spend that day in prayer for the city. Options include

- dividing the day into time blocks, such as fifteen-, twenty-, thirty-, and sixty-minute segments requiring one to four intercessors for each hour. While the goal may be for the church to be in prayer for twenty-four hours, some churches may only be able to cover twelve or sixteen hours.

- encouraging the congregation to pray throughout the day—at home, at work, at church, and so on—or asking members to pray for five minutes each hour for twelve hours on the day they are assigned.

- asking established small groups to meet together on that day for dinner and then spend one hour in prayer.

- holding a special prayer service in the evening. (Members from other churches could be invited too. In fact, if every church did this, there would be a prayer service in the city every single night of the year.)

- sponsoring a prayer breakfast or prayer lunch on that day.

Ministry category: simple

Focus: local, region, nation, world

Circle of Prayer

A circle of prayer gives us an overview of the people with whom we are connected. God intentionally gives us these connections so that we will pray for these people.

The diagram shows a sample wheel. The seven categories can be modified to meet your individual situation.

Make a wheel like the one above and fill in the blanks with names of people who fall into that category. Cut another circle the same size, and cut out a "pie piece" that is the size of one category. Use a paper fastener to attach the second circle over the first circle; the top

circle should now be able to rotate so that only one category is revealed at a time.

Once the wheel has been made, it can be used in a number of different ways:

- Pray for one section several times throughout the day. This brings you around the wheel in a week.

- Pray through the wheel in a day. Spend five minutes in prayer for each group at two-hour intervals. Or spend five minutes with each group during your quiet time and prayer.

- During family devotions, hand the prayer wheel to one member of the family who prays for the people in one section, turns the wheel to the next section, and hands it to the person next to them. Continue until all seven sections have been prayed for.

Ministry category: simple

Focus: local, region, nation, world

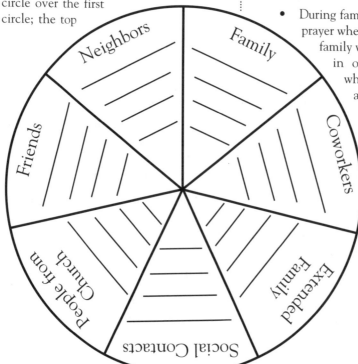

Easter Vigil

On the first Sunday of Lent, invite members of the congregation to write on index cards the names of unsaved loved ones, friends, coworkers, or other acquaintances, along with a short statement of need (such as, "For my brother, John, who has not been walking with the Lord and is now planning marriage to his fifth wife"). Those who have done so may then place the names at the foot of a cross in the front of the sanctuary (or they can be collected by ushers or elders).

During the following week, the prayer ministry team prays for each of these names and writes a Scripture passage (see examples in sidebar) on the back of each card as a word of encouragement to the intercessor who will be continuing to pray for that person.

The following Sunday, invite congregational members to come forward and select one or more cards and to pray for the people on their cards through the remaining weeks of Lent. In addition, encourage the intercessors to attend at least a segment of an Easter vigil service in order to return the name cards and to personally (silently or aloud) pray for those they had been praying for throughout Lent. On Easter morning, provide an opportunity for members of the congregation to share answers to the prayers and celebrate God's blessings.

options

- Divide the names and remember one-sixth of them in public worship each Sunday during Lent (use first names only).

- Make copies of the cards and place them in your prayer room. Staff your prayer room twenty-four hours a day for the seven days preceding Easter to pray for these people.

- Consider sending an Easter card to those for whom you have prayed indicating that you have prayed for them and wishing them a blessed Easter. Include your worship times on the back of the card.

Ministry category: simple

Focus: local

The Lord is not slow in keeping his promise, as some understand slowness. He is patient with you, not wanting anyone to perish, but everyone to come to repentance (2 Pet. 3:9).

Therefore he is able to save completely those who come to God through him, because he always lives to intercede for them (Heb. 7:25).

And everyone who calls on the name of the Lord will be saved (Acts 2:21).

Feed the Hungry

In one city, prior to Thanksgiving, a group of ten churches each recruited an average of twenty-five members to canvass their city's neighborhoods to collect food for a local food bank and to ask if each home would also share one prayer request.

Each volunteer was given forty homes to contact, and more than ninety percent of the residents were willing to participate. In less than two hours, each volunteer collected an average of one hundred pounds of food. More than half the homes contacted were also willing to share a prayer request.

For several weeks the volunteers prayed for these requests, then returned to the homes they had contacted and reported on the success of the food drive. They also left a few gifts in the spirit of the Christmas season—such as a New Testament—and in appreciation for their help.

Note: In some communities it is helpful to send a letter in advance (see your city directory) explaining the "Feed the Hungry" program. A small card inserted inside could request a written prayer need or prayer of thanksgiving. In other communities an advertisement in the daily or weekly newspaper would be sufficient.

Ministry category: intermediate

Focus: local, region

First Friday

Believers around the world are beginning to set aside the first Friday of every month to pray for the lost. Sponsored by Intercessors for America, "First Friday Prayer and Fasting" is an effort to unite hundreds of thousands of intercessors in praying for an abundant harvest.

The prayer focus is twofold:

1. For all to be saved and the Great Commission to be fulfilled; a church for every people, and the gospel for every person.

2. For all elected and appointed officials, men and women in positions of influence, that all people might live worshipful and peaceful lives and be free to witness and preach the gospel.

First Friday is observed by individual Christians, in small groups, and in large groups who pray at various times during the day. The praying takes place at businesses, schools, homes, and churches.

Intercessors for America provides a monthly theme to guide the prayers; the theme can be found on their website: www.ifa-usapray.org or www.national-prayer.org. The organization also encourages participants to consider some form of fasting (such as fasting from lunch, from television, or from dessert) as a way of humbling oneself before the Lord and hearing God's call to pray.

Ministry: simple

Focus: nation

Fishbowl

One church that had become a Lighthouse church (see pp. 260-262) introduced a visual way to encourage members to pray for their neighbors.

The pastor asked the members to write down the names of the unsaved persons they were praying for on cards (see sample card below) and then place them in a large fishbowl. Before each worship service the fishbowl was placed next to the pulpit in the front of the sanctuary. During the prayer time, the pastor drew several cards from the fishbowl and shared their first names and a sentence about the type of prayer being requested.

During the prayer the pastor petitioned: "Lord, I don't know the people whose names appear here, but they are unsaved and I know they matter to you. So we pray now for their salvation. I pray not only for these unsaved persons, but for the members of this congregation who submitted these names and who are praying for them. Together we pray for all those names in this bowl, who are known to you and who matter to you, and for all those who intercede for them."

One variation in implementing this ministry could be to color-code the cards. Ask that congregation members use

- gray cards for those who are unsaved.

- blue cards for those who are praying (the Lighthouses).

- yellow cards for answers to prayer.

In selecting cards to pray for, select several gray cards, at least one blue card, and at least one yellow card.

A fishbowl ministry could also be implemented in a prayer room, and intercessors who use the prayer room can select cards as a guide for their prayer time.

Ministry category: simple

Focus: local, region, nation, world

Name of person submitting request (optional):_____

Date request submitted:_____

Person to be prayed for (first name only):_____

Prayer Focus (include any information to make praying more specific):

Fishnet

Following a sermon or message on the parable of the net from Matthew 14:47-52, pastor Merle Bierma from Cragmor Christian Reformed Church in Colorado Springs invited his congregation to commit themselves to an emerging evangelism and discipleship program called Fishnet.

By accepting the invitation, members committed to the following:

- to personally follow Jesus Christ and live Christian lives,

- to intentionally look for opportunities to build a relationship with an unbeliever,

- to share the gospel regularly,

- to seek to lead at least one person to Jesus Christ each year, and

- to make themselves accountable to another member for prayer and their other commitments.

Bierma provides a monthly newsletter, "Fish Line," that offers training, information, answers to prayer, and encouragement to the more than one hundred men and women in this ministry.

Ministry: simple

Focus: local

Halloween Prayer

For several years, a group of Christians in St. Louis, Missouri, has been using Halloween as an opportunity to bring the community together for prayers of safety and protection. They also use this as an opportunity to pray for people's specific needs.

Participants string white Christmas lights around their homes and turn on all their house lights—making their homes a visual statement of "the light coming into the world" (John 1:9). Donuts, hot chocolate, and cider are served on the front lawn.

Believers offer to pray a prayer for God's protection for everyone who comes and invite their guests to share any other items for prayer. They also hand out small Bibles or New Testaments, bookmarks, and the like.

Ministry category: simple

Focus: local

Jesus Video Project

Pastor Tim Koster of the Good Shepherd Church in Flushing, Michigan, meets with a group of six to seven pastors every week to pray. Through their prayer time, God convinced them to become involved in a ministry together. They selected the Jesus Video Project (see sidebar). Fifteen churches worked together to raise $40,000, enabling them to purchase and mail almost 10,000 videos—one to every residence in the their zip code. Each video was mailed with a letter explaining that the video was a gift—no strings attached. Also enclosed was a list of churches involved, their addresses, worship times, and phone numbers, and a list of "e-mail mentors" they were welcome to contact with any questions or responses.

A "Jesus Video phone line" was installed in one of the churches and monitored by trained believers to field calls that might come in. Yard signs were strategically placed throughout the community to promote the project. However, as Koster explains it, the secret of the entire project was prayer. A continuous prayer vigil was held for 245 hours (ten days) before the mailing. Daily prayer meetings were held for a couple of weeks after the video went out. Most of the responses were overwhelmingly positive; many people requested additional videos so they could send them to family and friends.

The script of the Jesus Video is taken directly from the gospel of Luke. The eighty-three–minute video, capturing the entire life of Christ, was filmed in the Holy Land. At the conclusion of the video, viewers are invited to pray a prayer of faith and commitment.

Research has shown that for every two videos distributed, one person prays the faith prayer at the end. This amazing response is the result of the foundation of prayer before, during, and after the videos are distributed. More than five million households over North America have received it. It is a simple, effective, non-offensive way to share the gospel with your neighbor.

To order the video, contact:

Jesus Video Project
24600 Arrowhead Springs Road
San Bernadino, CA 92414
www.jesusvideo.org
1-888-Jesus-36

Videos are also available in Spanish.

---

options

- In some communities, believers prayer-walk the community before distributing the film.

- In many communities, the video is personally distributed (or hung on doors) instead of being mailed.

Ministry category: intermediate

Focus: local, region, nation, world

Lighthouses

Jesus said, "Let your light shine before men, that they may see your good deeds and praise your Father in heaven" (Matt. 5:16). You can follow Jesus' command by making your home a Lighthouse—a "gathering of two or more believers in Jesus' name for the purpose of praying for, caring about, and sharing Christ with their neighbors and others in their sphere of influence." The primary focus of a Lighthouse is to establish the presence of Christ in that household's neighborhood. But Lighthouses are also being established in churches, businesses, schools, and other settings.

The Lighthouse Prayer Movement is a fast-growing evangelistic phenomenon promoted in North America by Mission America, in cooperation with Campus Crusade for Christ, H.O.P.E. Ministries, Harvest Evangelism, Promise Keepers, and the Jesus Video Project. They are working together to "light our streets, light our cities, and light our nations." In North America, more than seventy-one denominations and over three hundred servant-ministries are partnering together in this ministry. The goal is to have 100,000 "Lighthouse churches," each with an average of thirty Lighthouses in their community, for a total of three million Lighthouses each praying for their neighbors. The ultimate goal is that every home in North America will be prayed for every day!

The Lighthouse ministry is based on three biblical concepts:

- **Praying for your neighbor.** "Devote yourselves to prayer, being watchful and thankful. And pray also for us, too, that God may open a door for our message, so that we may proclaim the mystery of Christ. . . . Be wise in the way you act toward outsiders; make the most of every opportunity. Let your conversation be always full of grace, seasoned with salt, so that you may know how to answer everyone" (Col. 4:2-6).

- **Letting your light shine.** "You are the light of the world. . . . Let your light shine before men, that they may see your good deeds and praise your Father in heaven" (Matt. 5:14, 16).

- **The home as the center of spirituality.** "They broke bread in their homes and ate together with glad and sincere hearts. . ." (Acts 2:46). "Day after day, in the temple courts and from house to house, they never stopped teaching and proclaiming the good news that Jesus is the Christ" (Acts 5:42).

three basic components

Prayer. One of the most important aspects of a Lighthouse is prayer. Stand in the doorway of your home and look in all directions. Those who live to the left, to the right, in front, and behind are your neighbors. Pray for them, for your community, for coworkers and friends. Pray for the people God puts on your heart and places around you—and observe the Lord at work. Prayerwalk through your neighborhood. Gather with other neighbors at a scheduled time during the week. Distribute brochures or door hangers encouraging people to share prayer requests with you. Place a decal in your window to identify your home as a Lighthouse of prayer.

Care. People respond to expressions of care and compassion. Seek ways to show your neighbors that you care, and offer to pray for their respective needs. Organize a block party or neighborhood barbecue. Share your talents and interests such as sports, woodworking, gardening, yardwork, cars, and so on. Do a lot of listening. This kind of caring is designed to be neighborly, gracious, and reconciling. Reach out and get acquainted with people. Be approachable, accepting, and encouraging. Simple acts of kindness are normally most effective. Show the love of Christ by being a servant to those for whom you are praying.

The key is talking to God about your neighbor before talking to your neighbor about God.
—Ed Silvoso

Share. Look for opportunities to share your faith. Always be ready to share your testimony. Share a portion of God's Word (when appropriate). Offer the Jesus Video. Hand out devotional guides or nonthreatening brochures. Invite your neighbors to church, to an outreach event, or to a Bible study. Seek natural opportunities to share your faith in Christ.

why lighthouses work

Alvin Vander Griend explains that Lighthouses are effective for the following reasons:

- God gives us *our* neighbors. We could have been born anytime and anyplace. But God, in his wisdom, placed us in this time among these neighbors (see Acts 17:26).

- Our neighbors matter to God. In Luke 15, Jesus shares three parables (the Lost Sheep, the Lost Coin, and the Lost Son). Jesus underscores that those who are "lost" are very important to him. He knows them by name. We often don't know our neighbors. But when we begin praying for the house with the barking dogs, the one with lots of kids, the one with the manicured lawn or beautiful garden, we soon discover we both know them and care about them.

- Neighbors welcome prayer. Currently, in our North American culture, it is acceptable to ask people if we might pray for them. Most are very receptive to the idea; pray-ers are often invited past fences and into homes.

- Lighthouse prayer is very simple to do. The schedule is very flexible. It doesn't require hours of training.

- Although the pastor provides a necessary model, Lighthouse prayer is a lay ministry.

- Lighthouse prayer is a simple program for the church to organize and maintain.

- Lighthouse prayer is an adaptable model. Lighthouses can be formed in homes, apartment complexes, college dorms, businesses, factories, retail stores, and prison cells.

- Lighthouses can be formed in affinity groups, such as Promise Keeper groups, MOPS, Moms in Touch, Shield a Badge, and so on.

- Lighthouse prayer is practical prayer. People pray for felt needs and real needs of people they know (or will soon know).

- Lighthouse prayer enhances relationships and, as a result, is one of the most effective forms of evangelism.

Prayer releases God's grace and power in the lives of our neighbors. Things begin to happen that would not be happening if we were not praying (see James 5:16).

where lighthouses are working

- Southern Heights Christian Reformed Church in Kalamazoo, Michigan, launched an evangelistic endeavor called "Impact 8000." They believe God has called them to spiritually impact one tenth (8,000) of the 80,000 unchurched/underchurched people in their community in the next five years. By "spiritually impact" they mean:

  — to pray faithfully for them.

  — to proactively befriend and care for them.

  — to prayerfully seek to share the good news.

  — to submit a spiritual impact card so others can join the effort to pray for them.

- There are more than 81,000 public schools in the U.S. and tens of thousands more in Canada that have established a Lighthouse ministry. Some organizations' goal is to establish a Lighthouse of prayer on every campus.

- In Crawford County, Illinois, six Lighthouse churches have constructed scores of miniature lighthouses (about 18 inches high) that are placed on the front yards of neighborhood Lighthouses of Prayer. The churches have placed announcements on their church signs and bulletin boards: "Need Prayer? Look for a Lighthouse near you." In another community, Lighthouses place an electric candle in the window as a reminder to the community they are praying for them.

Ministry category: initial, intense

Focus: local

Resources

"How to Start and Sustain a Church Lighthouse Ministry" (H.O.P.E., 1-800-217-5200).

Lighthouse of Prayer Starter Kit (available from Faith Alive Christian Resources, 1-800-333-8300 or www.FaithAliveResources.org).

Alvin Vander Griend, *The Praying Church Sourcebook* (Grand Rapids, MI: CRC Publications, 1997).

Outreach Prayer

For churches that are not accustomed to outreach, Bjorn Pedersen, former pastor of prayer at the Community Church of Joy in Phoenix, Arizona, has a recommendation: Include prayer in non-prayer, fun activities. In his book *Face to Face with God in Your Church: Establishing a Prayer Ministry* (Augsburg Fortress, 1995), Pedersen writes that this is a low-key way to introduce evangelistic prayer to people, to encourage people to pray, and to underscore the importance of prayer in the ministry of the church.

The Community Church of Joy holds an annual "Prayer from the Mountain" trip. The prayer ministry of the church arranges a bus trip to Mt. Agassiz near Flagstaff, Arizona. Participants include church members and regular guests. The trip includes a spectacular chair life ride to a spot overlooking the area west of Flagstaff and north to the Grand Canyon. Participants climb to an altitude of nearly 12,000 feet, and there, at the top of the mountain, they enjoy the scenery, share thoughts about prayer, and pray briefly together. The trip concludes with a picnic and the ride home.

Another activity the church uses is a pool volleyball/prayer party. Sometime in the middle of playing volleyball, they pause for prayer. While the emphasis is on having a good time with each other, the participants also learn something about the importance of prayer.

This approach to evangelistic prayer can be used in activities of all age groups and life stages, and it is a good way to bring new people into the church as well as bring new believers into the church's prayer ministry.

Ministry category: intermediate

Focus: local

Praise Marches

The first March for Jesus was held in 1987 in London at the initiation of Graham Kendrick, a British songwriter; Roger Forster, from Ichthus Fellowship; Lynn Green, with Youth with a Mission (YWAM); and Gerald Coates, founder of Pioneer Team.

Kendrick summarized the purpose of the marches in *March for Jesus:*

> So much of what happens in the church goes on behind closed doors. The once powerful, visible church has become virtually invisible. I have a vision for the church becoming visible again—the "bride on display" if you will. It's time for the bride of Christ to quit hiding and show herself. (Kingsway Publications, 1992, p. 26)

More than 15,000 believers marched in the rain in that first March for Jesus. The following year more than 55,000 walked. By 1990, over 200,000 marched in more than 600 cities in Great Britain alone. That same year the first March for Jesus took place in Austin, Texas. Fifteen thousand believers from 120 churches participated. Since then millions of Christians from different nationalities, cultures, and denominations annually take to the streets singing, praying, and celebrating Jesus. Now each year, believers march in every time zone, filling an entire day with praise. The largest March for Jesus took place in Sao Paulo, Brazil, where, in spite of the fear of persecution, more than 300,000 Christians participated.

While March for Jesus is the most famous and visible praise march, praise marches are nothing new. King David led a praise march into Jerusalem with the return of the ark of the covenant (2 Sam. 6:12-17). And Jesus' triumphal entry into Jerusalem (Matt. 21:1-9) could also be considered a praise march.

A praise march *is not*

- a protest march. It is not a statement against something, but a statement for Someone.

- an issue march. Issues are set aside to center on the person of Jesus Christ.

- a personality celebration. All the focus is on Jesus, not on church or religious leaders.

- a media event. Any publicity is a side benefit.

- an evangelistic crusade, although observers may be introduced to Jesus for the first time.

- a political statement. It is not a show of political force or the endorsement of any candidate or political party.

A praise march *is*

- a celebration of the kingdom of God, a foretaste of the eternal "party" we will be enjoying in heaven.

- designed to bring the body of Christ together in unity, agreement, and worship and to leave the imprint of Jesus on the city.

- a visible manifestation of the worship and prayer ministries of Christ's church.

These goals are accomplished through

- **Praise.** While walking, people worship.

- **Prayer.** Before, during, and following a praise march, prayer plays an important role. Intercession for the city often begins months before the march, with intensive prayer beginning two weeks before the event. In many cases a prayer vigil is held through the night preceding the event. During the event, the march takes on the added dimension of a prayerwalk (see pp. 284-286). After a praise march concludes, there is a season of intercession for the city, for its leaders, and for the lost. There is also a prayer tent at the celebration afterwards.

- **Proclamation.** The gospel is clearly communicated by way of singing throughout the march.

- **Pre-evangelism.** Observers will hear (and become more familiar with) the name of Jesus and witness the passion with which Jesus' followers live.

- **Partying.** During the march, walkers not only sing, they pass out hugs and candy and encourage people to walk with them. After the march, believers often continue to celebrate in a local park with worship, food, games, and fun activities. The party or "celebration" also normally includes a service opportunity: feeding the hungry, visiting the sick and elderly; cleaning up the neighborhood, and so on.

Ministry category: intense

Focus: region, nation, world

Resources

Graham Kendrick, Gerald Coates, Roger Forster, and Lynn Green with Catherine Butcher, *March for Jesus* (Eastbourne, England: Kingsway Publications, 1992)

Graham Kendrick, *Public Praise* (Altamonte Springs, FL: Creation House, 1992).

For more information, contact:

(United States)
March for Jesus USA
P.O. Box 3216
Austin, TX 78764
512-416-0066
e-mail: 104203@compuserve.com
www.mfj.org

(Outside the U.S.)
March for Jesus
P.O. Box 39
Sunbury-on-Thames
Middlesex, England TW16 6PP

Prayer Boxes

Renewal Ministries has taken the traditional "prayer box" that many churches have inside their building and transformed it into an evangelism tool. Recognizing that prayer is currently culturally acceptable, they have developed a small, colorful box that can be placed in the community, such as

- in the office of a local business.
- by the checkout of a retail store.
- in the waiting room of a dentist's or doctor's office.
- by the cashier in a gas station.
- in the lounge of a police or fire station.

People can fill out a prayer card, called a "lift ticket" (see samples on p. 267), and place it in the box. Some churches also place their business cards (containing the phone number for the prayer line) nearby so people can take one. Each week, someone from the church who has "adopted" that box empties it and begins to pray for the requests. These requests may also be shared with the church's prayer team, prayed for in prayer cell groups, or remembered in prayer at the weekly prayer meeting.

Normally, an individual or family or small group adopts a prayer box. "Adopting" a box involves

- checking it at least once a week, removing the prayer requests, and making sure there are sufficient prayer cards ("lift tickets") and church business cards available.

- when "on location," taking the time to talk with (and offer to pray with) the business owner, doctor, dentist, and so on.

- calling those who request a phone call.

- praying for the needs written on the cards.

Ministry category: intermediate

Focus: local, region

Resources

Prepared boxes, a set of "Lift Tickets," and an instructional booklet are available from

Renewal Ministries
2100 N. Carrolton Dr.
Muncie, IN 47304
765-759-5165
fax: 765-759-5857
e-mail: jangof@renewalministries.com

One couple has placed a mailbox by their curb and clearly marked it, "Neighborhood Prayer Requests." Having committed themselves to being a Lighthouse in their community, they wanted to provide their neighbors with a convenient, nonthreatening way to share their requests. Using a typical mailbox mounted a little lower than a standard mailbox, they provide a prayer form and a pencil inside the box. Prayer requests can be anonymous. If people leave a name, address, and phone number, they can be contacted.

LIFT TICKET

Name _____

Phone (Home) _____ (Work) _____

Address _____

☐ Please Call ☐ No Phone Call Necessary

My Prayer Request _____

_____

_____

_____

_____

LIFT TICKET

Name _____

Phone (Home) _____ (Work) _____

Address _____

☐ Please Call ☐ No Phone Call Necessary

My Prayer Request _____

_____

_____

_____

_____

LIFT TICKET

Name _____

Phone (Home) _____ (Work) _____

Address _____

☐ Please Call ☐ No Phone Call Necessary

My Prayer Request _____

_____

_____

_____

_____

—Taken from *Box 3:16 Prayer Evangelism for the Marketplace*. Permission granted by Prayer Point Press, 1-888-656-6067, www.prayerpointpress.com.

Prayer Expeditions

While prayerwalks (see pp. 284-286) focus primarily on communities and praise marches (see pp. 264-265) focus on cities, prayer expeditions focus primarily on regions. In *Churches That Pray* (Regal Books, 1993), C. Peter Wagner tells of a 1992 prayer expedition organized by Roger Forster, Gerald Coates, Lynn Green, and Graham Kendrick (the same group that started March for Jesus, see pp. 264-265) that covered an 800-mile path from London to Berlin. Intercessors from six countries participated. While ten people walked the entire route, as many as thirty others walked portions of the route with them. (While most prayer expeditions involve walking, some prayer expeditions have used airplanes, cars, vans, buses, and ferryboats.)

As the size of the endeavor increases (from communities to cities to regions) so does the spiritual intensity, spiritual warfare, and necessary preparation and organization. Prayer expeditions are normally held only in response to clear mandates from God. They are preceded by thorough spiritual mapping (see *Informed Intercession* by George Otis) that identifies the spiritual strongholds holding back the spread of the gospel. These include personal strongholds (prejudices, lust, greed), ideological strongholds (humanism, new age, racism), social strongholds (injustice, poverty), occultic strongholds (witchcraft, principalities, curses), and sectarian strongholds (denominationalism, isolationism, doctrinal pride).

Spiritual mapping also helps to identify God's redemptive gift for the region. It is important to ask, "Why did God place this region here? What contribution have they been called to make to the building of God's kingdom?" John Dawson, in *Taking Our Cities for God* (Lake Mary, FL: Creation House, 1989), says,

> Determining your city's redemptive gift is even more important than discerning the nature of evil principalities. Principalities rule through perverting the gift of a city in the same way an individual's gift is turned to the enemy's use through sin.

Wagner (*Churches That Pray*, pp. 201ff.) notes four areas where prayer is focused during prayer expeditions:

- Prayers of Repentance—confessing sins of the past, including past generations (2 Chron. 7:14).

- Prayers of Intercession—praying for the salvation of people who occupy the region (Eze. 22:30).

- Prayers of Proclamation—announcing the Word and praising God. This is often done through singing, shouting, and periodically through preaching (Ps. 86:8-9).

- Prayers of Blessing—prayers for healing social, political, economic, and religious wounds.

Ministry category: intense

Focus: region

Resource
C. Peter Wagner, *Churches That Pray* (Ventura, CA: Regal Books, 1993).

Prayer for Churches

In too many communities, churches compete rather than cooperate. Instead of working together, they work separately. It is a masterful plan of the devil. Jesus said, "If a house is divided against itself, that house cannot stand" (Mark 3:25).

Some years ago, the Lord laid it on our hearts that our church should begin praying for the other churches in our city each week during our worship. So each Sunday we pray specifically for a different church, for their pastor, for an effective ministry, for their current members, and for God to grow their church by bringing in the lost.

Two of our driving principles in this ministry—in addition to obeying God's call—are that

- we believe that God will begin moving through our city only when the churches and their leaders come together.

- we believe this kind of praying is one way for our members to realize the body of Christ in our community is larger than just our church.

Each Sunday on our church bulletin's prayer list, we include another church and its pastor. On Monday, we mail a copy of our bulletin along with a short note of encouragement to the pastor to share that our congregation is supporting that church in prayer.

There are many other ways that churches can support each other in prayer, such as

- sending a letter to another church each week with an encouraging word or a blessing.

- sending a few intercessors to another church on a Sunday morning to pray in their parking lot, pray with their pastor before the service, or pray through their worship service.

- placing a list of other pastors and churches in your area in the prayer room or dedicating a prayer station for other pastors and churches in your city.

- praying for other churches in your denomination's classis/presbytery/region.

- praying for new church starts/plants in your denomination.

- praying for world mission churches, either in your denomination or in the country you have "adopted."

Ministry category: intermediate

Focus: region, nation, world

Prayer for Cities

As drug use, social injustice, prostitution, gang violence, and economic depression are increasingly claiming strongholds in cities, an increasing number of churches are being led by God to pray for their cities. Government officials and trained sociologists have offered their solutions. Schools, sports programs, and businesses report minor successes. It is becoming increasingly clear that the only solution for lasting transformation is a spiritual one. Cities need to be reclaimed for the Lord.

In cities like Calgary; Colorado Springs; Hemet, California; and Eugene, Oregon, churches, pastors, and intercessors are coming together to pray for the city. The Southern Baptist Convention has designated three major North American cities (Phoenix, Chicago, and Toronto) for saturated prayer. Another evangelical publication lists 125 U.S. cities where church leaders are coming together regularly to pray for their city.

> When he first came to Calgary, Alberta, to pastor a church, Mike Reitsma heard God's call not only to pastor his church, but also to bring the pastors of Calgary together to pray for the city. In response, Reitsma founded the Calgary Evangelical Ministerial Association, and they started to pray for revival. A few years later, Mike wrote:
>
> > About a year ago, at a prayer retreat, we "heard" God say that we were to gather together for prayer in the fall for twenty-one days. In response, we organized a twenty-one–day prayer initiative, which was attended by an average of sixty pastors. When that was completed, the word we heard was "wait," which we did until God gave a very specific vision for a citywide prayer and praise service to be held on Easter Sunday evening. . . . The Jubilee Auditorium was packed out—and the presence of the Lord was evident. God was honored. Since then we have continued to meet and sense that God is calling us to a concerted time of prayer and intercession for the city. This will be set up in such a way that there is prayer twenty-four hours a day, seven days a week for the city of Calgary. This is a calling to the entire body. However, we are thankful to be part of what God is doing and wants to do in our city.

preparing to pray for your city

Accepting the God-given mandate to pray for your city requires adequate preparation. Consider the following:

- Begin by praying for God's direction. Listen for God's direction. Wait on God's timing. The key factor is to seek the Lord and follow his vision.

- Pray for God's protection. Whenever you seek to bring a city (or person) to Christ, Satan will mount his forces to prevent it.

- Inherent in receiving the Lord's protection is living a holy life. Pastors and leaders involved in praying for their city must live lives of integrity. Repent of personal sin (James 3:13-18), come near to God in holiness (James 4:8), and live humble lives (James 4:6).

- Unity across racial and denominational lines is essential. The pastors of local churches are the spiritual gatekeepers of the city (see 1 Chron. 9:22-27). All Bible-believing churches in the area should be invited and encouraged to participate.

- Churches that become involved must have the approval, blessing, and support of their pastors.

- As God leads, clearly define the boundaries. Limit the scope to one city or metropolitan area.

- Call the pastors together. If the pastors are not united, the churches will not be. If the churches are not united, the praying will be less effective. Encourage pastors to "release" their congregations to come together for prayer and worship.

- Do a thorough spiritual mapping to identify the spiritual strongholds (such as greed, immorality, racism, lust, a critical spirit). Study the history of your area; it often provides insights to identify strongholds or corporate sins that need to be confessed. Spiritual mapping can be done professionally by a spiritual mapping group or by the local churches (see *Informed Intercession* by George Otis).

- After identifying the strongholds of your city, corporately confess the sins of the past and present in your city.

- Identify the intercessors in your city and call them to meet regularly (weekly, bimonthly, monthly, or quarterly) together to pray with the pastors. In order to see your city spiritually transformed, you must sustain fervent corporate intercession.

- Establish a public prayer place that can be open twenty-four hours a day. Equip the room with pertinent information about prayer needs of the city and how to pray. Create a special prayer map for the area. Encourage people from any church to sign up to pray there one hour a week.

- Develop a strategy for your city, using what you have learned from observing other cities, from researching your own city, and from going through various resources on prayer (see the resources listed on p. 273). Develop a unique strategy that uses the unique resources of your city to address your city's unique needs. Share your strategy with every church in your city.

- Appoint a citywide coordinator who will coordinate the churches' activities, provide training, handle public relations, and promote prayer.

- Understand that this is a long-term commitment. City transformation seldom happens overnight.

keys to a successful city prayer ministry

George Otis, president of the Sentinel Group, which has mapped and evaluated numerous cities that have been spiritually transformed, found five key factors in spiritually transforming a city (see his book, *Informed Intercession*, Renew Books, 1999). While all five factors were visible in most of the transformations, the first two appeared in every transformation:

- Preserving leadership (Neh. 6:1-16)
- Fervent, united prayer (John 3:5-10)
- Social reconciliation (Matt. 5:23-24; 18:15-20)
- Public power encounters (Acts 9:32-35)
- Diagnostic research/spiritual mapping (Josh. 18:8-10)

How to Pray for Your City

- Pray as specifically as possible for the leaders, the government, the schools, the businesses, and the lost.

- Pray also against the evil strongholds in your city. Confess and pray against them individually.

- Pray for unity, power, and a spiritual anointing on the churches, pastors, and intercessors in the city.

- Pray for those who do not know Jesus Christ, that they may come to faith.

- Pray that God will give a vision for the city.

Ministry category: initial, intense

Focus: region

Resources

John Dawson, *Taking Our Cities for God* (Lake Mary, FL: Creation House, 1989).

George Otis, *Informed Intercession* (Ventura, CA: Renew Books, 1999).

Terry Teykl, *Blueprint for the House of Prayer: Engaging Your City Through Strategic Prayer* (Muncie, IN: Prayer Point Press, 1997).

DAWN (Discipling a Whole Nation)
7899 Lexington Dr. #200B
Colorado Springs, CO 80920
719-548-7460
fax: 719-548-7475
e-mail: 71102.2745@compuserve.com

CitiReach International
P.O. Box 63120
Colorado Springs, CO 80962-3120
719-528-5770
fax: 719-548-9619
e-mail: CitiReach@cs.com

Prayer for Growth

Joe Vugteveen, pastor of the Trinity Church in Broomall, Pennsylvania, invited his church elders to join him in praying that God would bring into their sphere of influence five new families with whom they could minister in some way. This was a new way of thinking about prayer for many of them, and something they were not accustomed to doing. They declined.

But Pastor Vugteveen persisted. The following month he again raised the issue and challenged them with stronger arguments than before. They finally agreed and began praying as their pastor had been: "God, please send us five new families with whom we can begin to work."

Within the next two and a half weeks, God brought Trinity Church into contact with a number of new families. Exactly five.

Ministry category: simple

Focus: local

Prayer for Missionaries

Many churches hold special worship services and events during mission emphasis week. However, missionaries are in need of prayer support at all times of the year.

One way to accomplish this is to challenge your congregation to spend a week in prayer for a missionary. Churches that support more than one missionary can either divide them among the members of the congregation or give people the opportunity to choose a missionary to pray for. Distribute pictures of the missionary (and his or her family) with helpful information and prayer requests on the back (such as names, children's ages, facts about the ministry, information about the location, special needs, and so on). Ask members of your congregation to pray for at least five to ten minutes a day for their missionary.

Or, instead of limiting this prayer ministry to one week, invite the congregation to pray for a different missionary or mission agency each month. If your church has a prayer room, designate a station for the missionaries your church supports.

Ministry category: initial, simple

Focus: nation, world

How to Pray for a Missionary

Day 1—Their Relationship with God (2 Cor. 13:14)
For a close, daily walk with the Lord.
For the indwelling and power of the Holy Spirit.
For humility, a servant's heart, and teachability.
For protection of their time with the Lord—in the Word, in prayer.
For victory over sin.

Day 2—Physical and Personal Needs (Matt. 6:11)
For good physical and emotional health.
For protection from discouragement, depression, or loneliness.
For adequate financial support; for stewardship opportunities.
For supportive relationships and words of encouragement.
For maintaining Sabbath rhythms, vacation, and times of spiritual renewal.

Day 3—For the Family (Eph. 4:32)
For the safety of the missionary and his or her immediate family.
For the ability to keep the family as a top priority and have quality and quantity time to
   spend with them.
For a strong marriage relationship or a secure single spirit.
For opportunities to connect with family members back home.

Day 4—For Ministry Effectiveness (Eph. 4:11-13)
For answers to prayer.
For an unfettered witness to the gospel.
For a harvest, for visible results.
For growing opportunities to reach lost people with the gospel.
For wisdom and insight.

Day 5—For Leadership (Rom. 12:6-8)
For discerning the culture effectively.
For security in themselves as leaders.
For a life that is pure and holy, for integrity in all their relationships.
For keeping the vision of the ministry in front of them (and those they work with) at all
   times.
For powerful and effective preaching and teaching of the gospel.

Day 6—Working Relationships (1 Thess. 4:11)
For acceptance with their indigenous coworkers.
For cooperation of their sending agency or church mission board.
For cooperation with national workers.
For the opportunity to minister without fear of reprisal or physical danger.
For visa, licenses, and government approvals.

Day 7—For the Country of the Missionary (Dan. 9:3-19)
For a stable political government to provide a stable environment for the gospel.
For the identification of and deliverance from the strongholds.
For forgiveness for the sins of the nation, its leaders, and its people.
For wisdom and protection of those in leadership and government.
For the people of the country—for open hearts.

Prayer for Nations

As the twenty-first century arrived, the world's population surpassed six billion people. According to recent statistics, less than one-third profess to be Christian, about one-fifth are Muslim, more than ten percent are Hindu, and more than five percent are Buddhist, with the remaining population sharing various religious perspectives. Of the 6,703 distinct languages in the world, the full Bible is currently available in only a little more than 300. About 800 have the New Testament in their native language; at least one book of the Bible is available in about 1,000 languages. While these languages currently include about ninety percent of the world's population, more than 400 million people still have no part of the Bible in their language!

In recent years, in an attempt to fulfill the Great Commission, efforts have been underway to saturate the nations of the world with prayer. Many of the nations with a significant percentage of non-Christians fall into the "10/40 Window"—the area of the globe that is between ten and forty degrees north of the equator. Christian Information Services has identified 1,739 people groups that are reached by prayer for the 10/40 Window.

The Christian Information Center and the A.D. 2000 Prayer Track keep lists of unreached people groups and encourage churches to "adopt-a-people" group to pray for daily. If your congregation adopts a people group (or nation) consider the following:

- Research the people group or nation you are praying for.

- Purchase that nation's flag.

- Obtain a detailed map of the country.

- Subscribe to a newspaper from that country.

- Write the nation's embassy for information.

- Request a guidebook from the nation's tourism office.

- Correspond with any missionaries you know in the country.

- Invite individuals from that people group who may be visiting or living (even temporarily) in your community to come and speak to your congregation.

- Build a prayer station into your prayer room for this group of people.

- Structure a worship service around learning about and praying for the nation or people group.

How to Pray for a People Group

Day One: Pray for those in the people group who are already believers. Pray for their protection. Pray for unhindered worship. Pray that God will use them as salt and light.

Day Two: Pray for a rich harvest of people from that nation or people group.

Day Three: Pray for laborers, harvesters, and church planters. Pray for adequate financial support and other resources.

Day Four: Pray for the leaders of this nation/people group, that they will be open to missionary efforts, Christian relief, and development opportunities in their country. Pray for the salvation of their leaders.

Day Five: Pray for stability—political, economic, and social.

Day Six: Pray for the safety of the missionaries, for physical and spiritual protection, and for minimal persecution.

Day Seven: Pray for more intercessors to do spiritual battle on behalf of the nation/people group.

Ministry category: initial, intermediate

Focus: nation, world

Resources

George Otis, *Strongholds of the 10/40 Window* (Seattle: YWAM Publishing, 1995).

Praying Through the 100 Gateway Cities of the 10/40 Window, C. Peter Wagner, Stephen Peters, and Mark Wilson, eds. (Seattle: YWAM Publishing, 1995).

The Unreached Peoples, Patrick Johnstone, John Hanna, and Marti Smith, eds. (Seattle: YWAM Publishing, 1996).

Alvin Vander Griend, *The Praying Church Sourcebook* (Grand Rapids, MI: CRC Publications, 1997).

The Center for World Mission
(for "adopt-a-people" resources)
1605 E. Elizabeth St.
Pasadena, CA 91104
e-mail: missionfrontiers@uscwm.org

The Christian Information Center
c/o World Prayer Center
P.O. 63060
11005 Highway 83 North
Colorado Springs, CO 80962-3060
719-536-9100
e-mail: info@wpccs.org
www.wpccs.org

Prayer Journeys

A prayer journey is an "invasion" by intercessors into a community, city, or region in order to provide spiritual mapping, pray against strongholds, and/or open up the area spiritually to evangelism, revival, and spiritual transformation. As the name suggests, this prayer ministry involves traveling to another (sometimes distant) location in order to pray on-site. But even though the location may be scenic and exciting, a prayer journey is a strategic, high-level prayer initiative—not a vacation. Keep the focus solely on prayer.

Prayer journeys are conducted in a wide variety of situations, such as

- helping a church plant in a new location.

- providing a local congregation with encouragement and assistance with a new evangelism initiative.

- providing a prayer base for a city or region seeking revival and transformation.

- identifying and removing strongholds prior to a major event (such as an evangelistic crusade or praise rally).

- visiting a ministry that a family, small group, or congregation supports financially, especially if that ministry has plateaued or appears to be declining.

- invading a city, region, or nation in order to spiritually map the region

and provide an initial assault on the spiritual strongholds found there.

Prayer journeys are often placed into two categories. An *intercessory prayer journey* involves a team of five to ten members. These teams go on-site, often meeting for prayer with the local intercessory team, sometimes joining with teams from other countries. The season of intercession is intense and extended. A *prophetic prayer journey* is simply the other side of the "two-way" prayer equation. That is, not only are the pray-ers interceding, they are also listening intently for God's response. When they "hear" God, they follow his direction. And, as the Scripture notes, this periodically results in some seemingly strange behavior: God told Ezekiel to lay on his left side for 390 days and on his right side for 40 days (Ezek. 4:12,13); God asked Hosea to marry a prostitute (Hosea 1:2).

options

- Organize a group of retirees from your church (or region) who have a passion for prayer and enjoy traveling together in their motor homes (or travel trailers) and who are willing to go "on location" and pray. These groups stay in a given location for one to four weeks. While the schedules may change depending on the location and the couples involved, a sample day might look like this:

— Two hours of prayer in the morning with members of the church staff.

— Two hours of prayer in the afternoon as a group—including time prayer-walking.

— One hour of prayer after supper along with others from the church and community.

— During the other available hours, they may assist the local church or ministry as appropriate.

• For those who can't make "on location" prayer journeys, make prayer stations in your prayer room that center on other locations. This may involve having multiple prayer stations or having one prayer station where the country, region, or city changes monthly. In this situation, you can pray not only for the city, region, or nation, but also for the intercessors who are on-site.

• Assemble six or more prayer stations in a large room. Hold a prayer vigil and invite the congregation to come for a season of prayer. Invite them to spend at least ten minutes praying for each country/region/ city before moving to the next station.

Ministry category: intense

Focus: local, region, nation, world

Resources

Cindy Jacobs, *Possessing the Gates of the Enemy* (Fairfax, VA: Chosen Books, 1994).

Patrick Johnstone, *Operation World* (Grand Rapids, MI: Zondervan, 1993).

C. Peter Wagner, *Churches That Pray* (Ventura, CA: Regal Books, 1993).

The Macedonian Project
100 Lake Hart Drive, Dept. 4000
Orlando, FL 32832-0100
407-826-2810

Prayer Search

A prayer search is actually just that—a search for prayer requests. Church members, in pairs or triplets, visit homes around the church. They explain that they are from the church and ask if there are any prayer requests for which they can pray. The prayer requests are brought back to the church and prayed for. Following a time of prayer, a postcard or prayer-a-gram (see pp. 189-190) is mailed to the home, letting the household know that their prayer need was prayed for.

After several cards have been sent (one to two months later), the team may return to the home to see if the prayers have been answered and to see if there are additional needs. Ideally this will be the same team so that relationships can begin to develop. (Teams that go out into the neighborhood do not necessarily need to be the intercessory team, but they should be trained in presenting the gospel. As people find out how much the church cares about them, many will be open to hearing more about the gospel.)

This prayer ministry requires a commitment to intercession. Don't promise to pray if you are not going to!

Ministry category: intermediate

Focus: local, region

Prayer Stations

A prayer station is simply a table clearly marked "Prayer Station" that is placed on a busy sidewalk, in a mall, at a fair, at a craft show. This unique approach is being used in New York City and reaping results in places where traditional methods are not.

Christians offering to pray with anyone staff the table. Other Christians stand forty to fifty feet away on both sides of the prayer table and hand out flyers that describe the power and effectiveness of prayer.

According to Nick Savoca, who originated the idea, Christians in New York City have prayed with shoppers outside department stores, with commuters at subway stations, with tourists walking the streets, and with homeless people sitting in parks. All volunteers wear uniform clothing in order to indicate their connection with the prayer station.

People interested in being prayed for are invited to fill out an index card that asks for some basic information. (Be careful not to ask for too much information—usually a first name and the prayer request are sufficient. Additional information requested, such as address or phone number, should be noted as optional). This information assists the pray-er in praying for the person. The person is then given the opportunity to be prayed for immediately—or to simply place their card in a box or bowl—with the promise that they will be prayed for by a prayer team for the next thirty days.

Savoca reports that approximately ten percent of those who stop to request prayer also make a commitment to Christ.

Note: Before implementing this ministry, make appropriate arrangements. Be sure to pay any required fees or file necessary permits to reserve the space.

Ministry category: intermediate

Focus: local, region

Resource

Prayer Station Kits are available from:
YWAM Metro New York
70 New York Ave.
Smithtown, NY 11787
516-366-1000
fax: 516-366-4826
e-mail: ywamnewyork@compuserve.com

The kit includes a video and manual. Churches can also purchase Official Prayer Stations, complete with table and banners.

"Are you angels?" a woman from Spanish Harlem tearfully asked one Prayer Station team. Nick Savoca reports that the team "looked at her a bit strangely and asked her why." She told them that she was very depressed and had left work early with the intention of going home and taking her life. They prayed with her, and she not only decided not to go through with her plan, but she gave her heart to Christ right there on the street.
—*Prayer Track News* (Sept/Oct 1999)

Prayer Triads

Prayer triads were introduced by the Billy Graham Evangelistic Association to pray for Graham's crusades. A prayer triad involves God, three believers or households of believers, and approximately nine unsaved persons. The three Christians (or households) form a prayer cell and pray for nine unbelievers. They pray separately daily, and they pray together once a week. The Graham Association forms prayer triads about six months prior to a crusade. This allows time for the prayer cell to learn more about those for whom they are praying, to build relationships, and to offer an invitation to the crusade.

These triads can work well before a church's evangelism thrust. They should organize four to six months before the event, continue to pray during the event, and meet afterwards to thank God for his faithfulness. This prayer ministry can be initiated by a citywide crusade, a local church, or by an individual with a passion for unsaved neighbors (in the latter case, begin by praying for two other intercessors to join you). The focus can be the local community, the city, the state or province, a nation, or even the world.

Once the participants are in place,

- ask God to reveal to you names you should be praying for. Each member of the triad should have three or four names.

- begin praying daily. Pray for the unsaved people on your list and the six to eight people on your prayer partners' lists.

- look for ways to build bridges between you and the three people on your list. Spend time with them.

- watch for the work of the Holy Spirit in the lives of those you are praying for. Look for opportunities to share your testimony, to invite them to your church or small group, and to offer a gospel presentation.

Ministry category: intermediate

Focus: local, region, nation, world

Resource

Information on Prayer-Mids (similar to Prayer Triads) is available from:

Pray for Spiritual Awakening
Florida Baptist Convention
1230 Hendricks Ave.
Jacksonville, FL 32207
904-396-2351
1-800-266-8584 ext. 8263

valking

Prayerwalking is simply walking through your neighborhood or community and praying for what you see: homes, residents, businesses, and so on. While prayerwalking is often done in pairs, it can include

- one person praying while power-walking each morning.

- a husband and wife out for an evening stroll.

- a Lighthouse prayerwalking its neighborhood.

- a small group participating in an organized Prayer for Cities campaign (see pp. 271-273).

- an entire congregation praying for their community as they go caroling at Christmas.

- a citywide praise march (see pp. 264-265).

In fact, one of the attractive features of prayerwalking is that anyone can do it at any time and at almost any place. As Steve Hawthorne observes in *Prayerwalking: Praying On Site with Insight* (Creation House, 1993), whenever we pray "on-site" our praying seems to take on a different priority—God begins to grow a passion in our heart for the lost and hurting people of the world.

Prayerwalking comes in two primary formats:

- **Spontaneous Prayerwalking.** This is the most common form. Some basic training is helpful, but not necessary. While prayerwalking does involve spiritual warfare, it is normally low level.

- **Synchronized Prayerwalking.** This is simultaneously walking an entire community or city in cooperation with other churches. It is often done in connection with a citywide evangelistic event.

things to consider before beginning

Why are we prayerwalking? What is the purpose of this prayerwalk? Is this prayerwalk to pray for salvation, for an end to violence, for protection, for blessing? Always have a clear purpose in mind. If you are doing a synchronized prayerwalk, always explain the purpose clearly in your promotional material and again before the prayerwalk begins.

What format will we use? Will the participants walk alone, in pairs, or in small groups? Will participants stop in front of each home or just walk slowly by and have prayer on the corners?

Where will we walk? Are we walking the neighborhoods where we live, where we work, where we worship, or where the city's trouble spots are? Each team should have a map of where they will be walking.

When will we go? In a synchronized prayerwalk, the goal is to do it together. Meet for prayer at a central location before (to seek God's blessing) and after (to praise God, share responses, and thank God for his presence) the prayerwalking.

adapting the prayerwalk

While a simple walk through your community is an excellent way to pray for your community, there are many other ways to pray "on site with insight":

- At your job, pray for those whose offices you pass while walking down the hallway; pray for the people, residences, and businesses you see on your lunch break; or pray for the businesses and people you have contact with throughout the day.

- While walking with your child to school or as they sell magazines for school or candy for Little League, pray for the homes, businesses, schools, and other organizations you walk past.

- Prayerwalk your children's schools or the school in your neighborhood, and

> A church in a small New York town decided to canvass its community in a rather novel way. There were no brochures, newsletters, or tracts. No one pressed a single doorbell. All the church did was pray. Street by street, with a red marker and a map, church members prayed weekly for the people on each of the town's forty streets. They named no individuals and prayed only that God would touch the lives of those who lived on a particular street. People started visiting the church "out of the blue." Four families came the Sunday after the church had prayed for their street. The pastor said, "I think some of our people were genuinely surprised by the results. They supported the canvass, but they were amazed when visitors began showing up."

pray for the students, teachers, other parents, and administration.

- While waiting in the doctor's or dentist's office, pray for those who work there and those sitting in the waiting room with you.

- If you are a college student, prayerwalk your campus or dormitory.

- While driving through town, pray for the businesses, homes, and buildings you drive by.

- While waiting in check-out lines, pray for store employees.

prayerwalking with children

Prayerwalking is an excellent evangelistic activity for children. While children can simply be invited to walk along with their parents, this can be a special time to teach children how to pray for their neighbors and begin to develop the "habit" of prayerwalking for them. Some churches hold special prayerwalks just for children. When involving children in a prayerwalk, keep the following in mind:

- Encourage children to keep their eyes and ears open. Teach them what to look for. Ask them to look for what they think God wants them to see and then to pray for those things.

- Stop periodically and ask them what they are seeing and hearing that should be prayed about.

- Encourage children to pray—both silently and audibly—as they feel comfortable.

- Encourage them to pray a Scripture passage that comes to mind.

- Younger children, or those new to this form of prayer, can be assigned a specific target or issue (for example, look for houses that you think might have children your age; look for families you think have only one parent; look for families that appear to be sad and think about why they might be sad).

- Keep a low adult-to-child ratio. Form small groups so children may be more comfortable praying.

- Keep the walk focused and short (sixty minutes is often about right). Conclude with a light snack.

- Ask the children to share their impressions verbally or by drawing.

Ministry category: intermediate to intense

Focus: local, region

Resources

Steve Hawthorne and Graham Kendrick, *Prayerwalking: Praying On Site with Insight* (Lake Mary, FL: Creation House, 1993).

Bjorn Pedersen, *Face to Face with God in Your Church: Establishing a Prayer Ministry* (Minneapolis: Augsburg Fortress, 1995).

Prayerwalking: A Simple Path to Body and Soul Fitness (St. Meinrad, IN: Abbey Press, 1994).

Alvin Vander Griend, *The Praying Church Sourcebook* (Grand Rapids, MI: CRC Publications, 1997).

Prompts for Prayerwalkers
Waymakers
P.O. Box 203131
Austin, TX 78720
512-419-7729

How to Pray While Prayerwalking

Generally
- Ask for forgiveness for crimes, gangs, violence that has occurred.

- Ask God to clean up the neighborhood morally and spiritually.

- Ask God to protect the Christians in the neighborhood, to give them the courage to reveal their Christianity in their community, and to use them as salt and light in the area.

- Ask God to block any plan or strategy of Satan; ask God to send the visible presence of his Spirit.

For Residences
- Ask for God to bless the singles, couples, families with harmony and unity.

- Pray for protection—physically, emotionally and spiritually—especially of the children.

- Pray for the salvation of every person in every home.

- Ask God to bring them to church on Sunday.

For Nonresidences
- Pray that Christians working there may let their light shine.

- Pray for a blessing on legitimate businesses; ask God to bind the strongholds and close up illegitimate and immoral enterprises.

- Pray for physical, emotional, and spiritual health of all who work there.

Restaurant Evangelism

The November 1999 issue of *Reach* (CRC Publications) describes how Karen Pierre-Louis and her husband witness in restaurants. Before leaving the table, they write a personal note on a clean paper napkin, addressing their server by name. Then, in a few sentences, they introduce their server to the greatest Servant; they have learned to present the basic gospel in a short paragraph. If the server seems to be having a frustrating day, they tailor the message accordingly. When appropriate, they build on something the server mentioned in casual conversation. They leave this personal note on the table along with a generous tip.

"Though this takes a few extra minutes at the end of our meal," Karen says, "I have been amazed at how many busy servers stop and read our notes as they retrieve their tips. I find that through this practice I am better able to remember servers' names, so I can greet them when we return to the same restaurant—and so I can pray for them. In an impersonal world such gestures can make an eternal difference."

Restaurant evangelism takes on a variety of forms—and must always be "played by ear." (For example, don't personalize the note if you have not been personable with the server.) Proceed as you sense the Lord leading you.

Ministry category: simple

Focus: local

Staking a Claim Evangelism

Throughout the Old Testament we are reminded that God has territorial interests: one of the great promises of the Old Testament was the promised land. This prayer ministry literally calls for staking out the land, marking it for the Lord, and expanding it (see Isa. 54:2).

In addition to some scriptural precedence, "staking a claim" also has historical significance from the early days in American history when homesteaders would drive stakes into the ground to declare ownership. Staking a claim is a public declaration that the land belongs to the Lord. It is a commitment to "take back the land for Jesus."

In staking your claim, you can select several large rocks or bricks. Paint them. Write a Scripture passage or a simple statement (like "Jesus is Lord") on each one. Or, make some wooden "tent" stakes. One church that used wooden stakes wrote "Jesus is Lord" on the top of the stake and one of the following lines on each of the four sides of the stake:

—Repentance (Matt. 6:22)
—Reconciliation (2 Cor. 5:18)
—Renewal (Rom. 12:12)
—Revival (Ps. 85:6-9)

Then stake your claim. During low traffic times, go to key sites—city hall, a masonic temple, schools, colleges, abortion clinics, pornography sites, major roadways, the airport, the bus station, hospitals, the riverfront, a police station, a courthouse, the boundaries of the city—and "stake" your claim.

Before, during, and after planting the stakes, prayer serves as the central focus. If the location is a demonic stronghold, pray against it; if the location is a service ministry, pray for God's blessing. When laying the stones or driving the stake, have a season of prayer that God will take ownership of that place! Continue to visit the location periodically—to check on your claim—and continue to pray.

Ministry category: intermediate

Focus: local, region

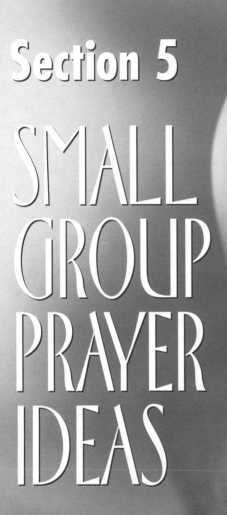

Section 5

SMALL GROUP PRAYER IDEAS

Note: This section offers ideas for integrating prayer into small groups that were not intentionally designed to be "prayer groups." While small groups may be organized for a variety of reasons—service, discipleship, evangelism, fellowship, accountability, support—every small group needs a prayer component.

SMALL GROUP PRAYER

One of the most important places to pray in the church—and often the most overlooked place when designing a prayer ministry—is the small group. As more and more people seek community and spiritual growth through small groups, small groups are becoming increasingly important places to pray. In addition to being a major factor in our personal relationship with God, prayer is vital to our life as a community.

When small groups meet and take prayer seriously, some amazing things begin to happen:

- Group prayer encourages participation. Participation includes prayer. Prayer brings growth.

- Prayer is modeled. Members learn how to pray by observing and participating.

- Praying together encourages members to continue praying outside of the group.

- Relationships grow. Our relationship with God grows because we are spending time with him. Our relationship with the group grows because we are involved in a very intimate activity together.

- Our faith grows as God responds to our prayers. Seeing amazing answers to prayer builds our trust relationship with God.

- Praying together builds community. In small groups we study the Bible because God speaks to us through it. Through prayer, the dialogue continues and is completed. Coming together into God's presence is a group-changing experience.

- Group members begin to care for each other in deeper and more effective ways.

- Prayer opens the door for the Holy Spirit to work in our lives.

- Group members are held accountable for their commitments to pray throughout the week.

- Prayer changes the group dynamics. Complaints, anger, envy, and many other sins seem to disappear after spending time in the presence of God through prayer.

In *Life Together*, Dietrich Bonhoeffer summarizes the importance of praying together when he says: "Where Christians want to live together under the Word of God they may and they should pray together to God in their own words. They have common petitions to bring to God, and they should do so joyfully and confidently. It is, in fact, the most nor-

> **"I tell you that if two of you on earth agree about anything you ask for, it will be done for you by my Father in heaven. For where two or three come together in my name, there I am with them."**
> **—Matthew 18:19-20**

mal thing in the common Christian life to pray together."

building a praying group

Building prayer into small groups takes time, but it is an investment worth making. There are three basic ingredients in building a praying group: the enthusiasm and model of the leader, the study of prayer, and the actual practice of prayer.

Building a praying group begins with the leader. In small group ministry, the adage still holds true: "You cannot teach people what you do not know; you cannot lead people where you have not been." Leaders who are unconvinced of the importance of prayer—of spending one-on-one time with the Lord—will be unable to convince other group members to pray. Small group leaders must spend regular time in the presence of the Lord. In addition to having a personal walk with the Lord, leaders must regularly intercede for the group—before, during, and following meetings. Throughout the week, leaders should pray daily for their group members.

Prayer must be taught with intentionality. When his disciples expressed a need to learn—"Lord, teach us to pray"—Jesus responded to his "small group" with a model of prayer Christians have been using for almost 2,000 years. Small groups offer a unique setting for the teaching of prayer.

A biblical study of prayer is often necessary as a foundation for building a praying group. Many studies are available for this purpose, or leaders may choose to prepare their own outlines. A lesson could include

- studying the prayers of the Bible. One prayer could be highlighted at each meeting, read, reflected on, and even prayed together. The Bible contains many prayers: Hannah (1 Sam. 2), Elijah (1 Kings 18:36-37), David (Ps. 51), Solomon (1 Kings 8:22-53), Jesus (Matt. 26:38-42; John 17), and Paul (Eph. 1:15-23; 3:14-21).

- studying Scripture's teaching about prayer. Jesus taught his disciples the Lord's Prayer (Matt. 6:9-13). Ask group members to focus on one aspect of the prayer each week, then use that focus as the basis for praying together.

- studying the elements of prayer. These include, but are not limited to, adoration, thanksgiving, waiting, petition, intercession, listening, and confession. Discuss one each week. Use appropriate Scripture references.

- studying the list of things God has called us to pray for: leaders, other believers, the lost, the sick, widows and orphans, forgiveness, strength. Select one item for a brief discussion, followed by a time of prayer for that item.

- studying a book on prayer. *Praying from God's Heart* by Lee Braise, *Prayer* by Richard Foster, *Too Busy Not to Pray* by Bill Hybels, and *The Great House of God* by Max Lucado work well for this purpose.

Ultimately, the best way to learn to pray is by praying. Your group must practice praying together. One of the greatest hindrances to learning to pray is that most people believe they already know how. Yet few believers spend much time in prayer. Spending time praying together will be hard work, but the benefits will soon follow.

some guidelines

- Check your physical environment. Try to minimize distractions—children interrupting, a loud television, a ringing telephone or cell phone, a dog barking in the basement.

- Don't always wait until the end of your small group time to pray. Time constraints will adversely affect the prayer time.

- Make sufficient time for prayer. When members sense a hurriedness, it discourages them from participating.

- Variety is very important in small group prayer. Use a different prayer format from meeting to meeting. Periodically introduce a new prayer format to encourage freshness and growth.

- If, in the course of your sharing together, a difficulty or crisis comes to light, stop and pray for it.

- Avoid putting others on the spot. Don't call on anyone to pray unless you've asked permission in advance.

- In introducing a new prayer format or prayer that encourages group participation, give people permission to pray silently.

- Don't expect everyone to pray every time. Don't wait for everyone to participate before concluding the prayer.

- Avoid praying around the circle where people feel pressured to pray.

- Generally, keep prayers in your small group simple.

- Set guidelines for sharing prayer requests, such as length (for example, no more than two minutes), focus (such as "This week we are focusing on our community"), or number (perhaps by inviting people to share "a prayer request or two"). Avoid problem solving.

- Encourage people to follow the "ABCs" (Audible, Brief, and Clear) of prayer.

- Consider appointing a prayer coordinator for your small group.

The ideas presented in this section include recommendations for their use. Some are most appropriate for *children* (8-13 years of age); some work well with *youth* (13-19); some will be more appropriate for *adults*; and some will work in intergenerational groups, like *families*.

Ballooning Prayer

Pass out small pieces of paper or index cards and a balloon for each person. Have each person write a prayer beginning with "Dear Lord, when I feel [stressed, guilty, proud, angry, hurt, depressed, and so on], help me to remember . . ."

Roll or fold the paper and insert it into the balloon. Blow up the balloon and just pinch it shut—do not tie it.

The leader can then say a few words about how stress (or guilt, or pride, and so on) causes us to get all blown up on the outside even though we know that somewhere inside of us there is the Word that helps us put things into perspective.

Everyone should then let go of his or her balloon. Watch them fly. Listen to the air rush out. Each person should recover a balloon (not their own) and remove the paper from inside. The prayer time can be concluded with each person praying for the need expressed on the card.

—Adapted from *Resources for Youth Ministry: Shelter from the Storm* (Board of Youth Ministry of the Missouri Synod Lutheran Church, 1982), p. 6.

Group: youth, adults, families

Christ Candle

Place a large white candle in the center of the circle. This candle represents Jesus Christ, the light of the world. Light the candle and turn the lights out so only the candle provides light.

Explain and practice one of the contemplative prayer formats:

- Centering prayer (see p. 49)
- Contemplative prayer (see p. 54)
- Prayer of *Examen* (see p. 89)
- Jesus Prayer (see p. 71)
- *Lectio divina* (see p. 73)
- Silence (see p. 103)

Practice the prayer form you select for at least fifteen to twenty minutes. If you wish, when finished spend a few minutes discussing the experience.

In addition to representing the presence of Christ during the prayer time, the candle is an encouragement to keep the atmosphere reflective, meditative, and quiet.

Group: youth, adults, families

Empty Chair

In many cell groups (small groups which are designed to grow and then divide) an empty chair is placed in the circle to remind group members of their mission to invite new members to join the group. In many groups, the goal is to invite a non-Christian or underchurched person to fill the chair.

In addition to placing the chair, members should pray over the chair. This can include standing or kneeling around the chair and asking God to fill it; or ask each person in the group to write the name of a potential new member on a slip of paper, place the names on the chair, and pray for the individuals by name.

Group: children, youth, adults, families

Feelings Prayer

Offer each person a pencil and an index card. Ask group members to write one word on the card (mad, happy, sad, scared) that best describes the dominant feeling they have been experiencing the last few days.

Then invite participants to write a one-sentence prayer to God about that feeling—to praise God for that feeling, thank him for understanding it, ask him for his help in dealing with it, and so on.

After a few minutes, invite the group to speak their prayers aloud.

—Adapted from *Resources for Youth Ministry: Sharing Feelings* (Board of Youth Ministry of the Missouri Synod Lutheran Church, 1980), p. 11.

Group: children, youth, adults, families

Hand Squeeze

In this prayer, group members pray for each other. This idea can work a couple different ways:

- Group members may stand, sit, or kneel in a circle holding hands. The leader instructs members to pray silently for the person on either side of them. When the pray-ers are finished they squeeze the hands of the person they have just finished praying for. This simple gesture communicates Christian love and encouragement.

- Everyone sits in a large circle holding hands. The first person begins praying for the person on his or her left (group members should be encouraged to do this either silently or aloud). When finished, the pray-er simply squeezes the hand of the person he or she has just prayed for. The person whose hand has been squeezed prays for the next person, and the prayers continue around the circle.

Group: children, youth, adults, families

Hugging Prayer

Have the members of the group stand in a circle, placing their arms on the shoulders of the people standing on each side of them. Bring the circle in as close as comfort allows.

Remaining in this position, the leader begins the prayer. Other members are encouraged to join in as the Spirit leads. A previously designated member closes with prayer. Following a group "amen," there is a group hug (a tight squeeze).

This is an excellent way to conclude a small group meeting.

Group: children, youth, adults, families

Night of Prayer

Writing in *Discipleship Journal* (no. 98), Keith Wright offers these suggestions for how to use the Night of Prayer format.

As a group, plan to spend a weekend evening—say, from 6:00 P.M. to midnight—in prayer. Include some of the following activities:

Praise. Begin with a time of worship. Nothing ushers people into the presence of God faster than praising him.

Scripture prayers. Spend some time praying Scripture, particularly the Psalms, or use *lectio divina*.

Sanctuary prayers. If a worship service will be held the following day, consider going to your church building and praying through the worship center. Pray by the pulpit for the preaching; by the piano/organ/instruments for the worship and music; by the sound/video board for smooth operation; by the seats for the members and visitors who will sit there; by the doors for the ushers and greeters. If you cannot get into the church, walk the parking lot and pray for those who will be coming to worship.

Silent confession. Offer some personal time for people to confess their sins by themselves. When the group comes back together offer a word of grace from the Scripture or sing together of God's goodness.

Drive-by-prayers. Jump into a van and drive throughout your community. Pray for the schools, churches, nursing homes, and businesses you pass. Or drive by pre-selected homes (such as the homes of shut-ins); you may even consider having a short prayer with the families if it is not too late in the evening.

Prayerwalking. Walk throughout your community or go to a pre-selected place and walk around. Pray appropriately.

Riding the elevator to the top of the tallest building in your city. As you look out over the city, pray for your city.

Reflection. Spend the last half hour reflecting on the experience. Use the last few minutes to thank God. Provide a short celebration with pizza, ice cream sundaes, a dessert, or the like.

The evening can be structured in a variety of ways, but the object is (1) to seek the Lord, (2) to spend extended time in prayer together, (3) to participate in different prayer formats, and (4) to do ministry. Keep an appropriate balance between doing a variety of things and spending sufficient time in each activity you select so people don't feel rushed. Make the evening exciting.

Group: children, youth, adults, families

Personal Prayer

This form of directed or bidding prayer is very simple. One by one, the leader calls the names of all the members of the group, including his or her own, pausing in between each name to allow for group members to pray for that person.

The leader continues to call names until everyone has been prayed for.

Group: youth, adults, families

Polaroid Prayer

Bring a Polaroid camera to your small group. Take a picture of each member, and ask them to write pertinent information on the back, asking them to be as specific as possible when describing their prayer needs.

Place all of the photos in a basket. Have each person select one and commit to pray for the person pictured—at least five minutes daily—until the next meeting. (If you have more than one week between meetings, group members might be encouraged to make contact with the person they are praying for between meetings. This might be for breakfast or lunch, for coffee, or over the phone. This time together should include prayer.) At the next meeting, invite group members to share their prayer experiences and to thank God for his answers to prayer. Then return the pictures to the basket and have group members draw again. Members should select a different photo than the previous month.

If a Polaroid camera is unavailable, simply have people bring pictures of themselves from home. Or, instead of using pictures of themselves, invite group members to bring a picture of someone or something they are currently praying for. Place as much information on the back of the picture as possible.

Another option is to go on an excursion with the camera and take pictures of people and ministries in your church. Bring the pictures to your next meeting, and encourage each group member to take a pic-

ture and intercede for that person or ministry until the next meeting.

Group: children, youth, adults, families

Name:

Phone:

Occupation:

Ministry involvement:

Spiritual gifts:

Specific prayer needs:

Prayer Box

Convert a shoebox (or similar size box) into a prayer box. Encourage group members to write out their prayer requests or prayer needs on small pieces of paper or index cards. Pass the box around and have people insert their requests.

Pass the box again and ask members to draw one request from the box to remember in prayer. Share the requests and, if appropriate, get additional information about the request. Then spend time together praying for each request. (Unselected cards remain in the box for the next meeting.)

If a card is drawn and the request has already been answered, the prayer request becomes a prayer of thanksgiving and gratitude to God.

Following the prayer time, return the cards to the box, and bring the box to the next meeting. Give group members opportunity to add to the box at each meeting.

Group: children, youth, adults, families

Prayer Requests

Most small groups take time for prayer requests, but these often fall into a predictable routine. Vary your prayer request time by announcing two or three categories for prayer. Encourage group members to limit their requests to those categories. Consider these options:

- **Bereavement** (1 Cor. 2:9; 15:55). Pray for those who are dying as well as those who walk with them through the dying process. Pray for those who have recently lost loved ones through death or divorce.

- **Church leaders** (Col. 4:3-4). Pray for the pastors, staff, and leaders of your church.

- **Community concerns** (Jer. 29:7). Pray for your local schools, police force, firefighters, hospitals, government, and so on, and ask for God's intervention with drug problems, racial divisions, greed, violence, and so on.

- **Finances** (Phil. 4:19). Pray for employment, job satisfaction, good stewardship, people in financial crisis, giving to the church.

- **Government leaders** (1 Tim. 2:1-3). Pray for local, state, national, and international leaders.

- **Missions** (Acts 1:8). Pray for missionaries, church planters, harvest fields, and a rich harvest.

- **Protection** (Ps. 4:8; Isa. 43:2). Pray for protection for the group members, their families and loved ones, as well as special prayers for those who will be traveling, are in dangerous situations, or are under spiritual attack.

- **Physical needs** (Ps. 41:3; James 5:14-15). Pray for those who are experiencing short- and long-term physical ailments.

- **Relationships** (Matt. 7:12, Rom. 12:18, Col. 3:15-16). This category can be divided into smaller segments such as parent/child relationships, employer/employee relationships, marriages, friendships, and so on.

- **Salvation** (2 Pet. 3:9). Pray for the lost.

- **Temptations** (1 Cor. 10:13; Heb. 4:15). While people may be reluctant to share personal temptations, they can pray within categories: materialism, lust, greed, drugs, pleasure, overeating, and so on.

—Adapted from Esther Bailey, *Discipleship* (no. 112, p. 94)

Group: youth, adults

Prayer Support

This prayer format is designed to build trust in God within the safe environment of a small group (thus, it is important for there to be a high level of trust between group members). It is particularly helpful in praying for people struggling with fear, with doubts, or with concerns about future events.

Have a group member lie on the floor. The remaining members gather around him or her and literally lift that person into the air (symbolizing their commitment to "lift" this person in prayer throughout the week). While the person is suspended in the air, several group members should offer prayer for this person.

This can be repeated for any number of group members; however, no person should be forced to participate.

Group: youth, adults

Sentence Prayers

Beginning with the leader and proceeding in a predetermined direction around the circle, members are encouraged to pray a one-sentence prayer. Group members should be encouraged to pray silently or aloud.

This process often works best if a prayer focus has been predetermined—such as thanksgiving, petitions, praise, adoration, intercession, and so on—and can be very effective as a response to a time of bidding prayer.

Group: youth, adults

Silent Prayer

In a tight circle (standing, seated, kneeling, even prostrate) have the group pray silently for five to fifteen minutes. The prayer is concluded at the leader's discretion with "amen."

Some groups prefer a more "structured" time of silent prayer. In that case, during the silence, the leader can direct people to pray with simple instructions, such as

- "Pray for the person on your right/ left."
- "Pray for your family."
- "Pray for your neighbors/coworkers/ fellow students."
- "Spend a few moments confessing your sins."
- "Thank God for what he is doing in your life."

Or, spend a few minutes sharing prayer requests and praise before beginning to pray.

This prayer idea works well with the Christ Candle (see p. 294).

Group: youth, adults, families

Spontaneous Prayer

Before beginning, the leader should designate someone to begin and conclude the prayer time. The person who opens the time of prayer should include a prayer for the Spirit's presence and leadership; the person concluding the prayer should be someone who is sensitive to the Spirit's leading.

Between the opening and closing of the prayer is opportunity for silent and spoken prayers from other members in the group. The prayers may be for requests that have been previously shared, for whatever God lays on members' hearts, or focused on a predetermined theme. (While it may seem uncomfortable to some, it is okay for more than one person to pray at the same time.)

Group: children, youth, adults, families

Written Prayers

Many people enjoy the opportunity to read a written prayer that they have had time to think about, so give your group members the opportunity to put some thought into their prayers before praying them together.

Begin your prayer time by giving your group a few minutes to write out their prayers. As with some other small group prayer ideas, you may want to ask that the group focus their prayers on a specific topic, such as interceding for a particular ministry, celebrating a characteristic or attribute of God, offering thanksgiving, and so on. After the prayers have been written, they can be placed in a basket. Each member may take one and pray the prayer on behalf of the author and the group.

Following the prayer time, consider talking about the experience for a few minutes.

Group: children, youth, adults, families

Resources

Approaches to Prayer: A Resource for Groups and Individuals, Henry Morgan, ed. (Harrisburg, PA: Morehouse Publishing, 1993).

Kay Arthur, *Lord, Teach Me to Pray in 28 Days* (Eugene, OR: Harvest House Publishers, 1995).

Arthur Baranowski, *Creating Small Faith Communities: A Plan for Restructuring the Parish and Renewing Catholic Life* (Cincinnati: St. Anthony Messenger Press, 1988).

Bill Donahue, *The Willow Creek Guide to Leading Life-Changing Small Groups* (Grand Rapids, MI: Zondervan, 1994).

Julie Gorman, *Community That Is Christian: A Handbook on Small Groups* (Wheaton, IL: Victor Books, 1993).

Garth Icenogle, *Biblical Foundations for Small Group Ministry: An Intergenerational Approach* (Downer's Grove, IL: InterVarsity Press, 1994).

James Bryan Smith, *A Spiritual Formation Workbook: Small Group Resources for Nurturing Christian Growth* (HarperSan Francisco, 1993).

Alvin Vander Griend, *The Praying Church Sourcebook* (Grand Rapids, MI: CRC Publications, 1997).

Section 6

WORSHIP IDEAS

PRAYER AND WORSHIP

There is an intimate and inseparable connection between prayer and worship. In worship we focus on God: we praise God's name; we offer him our voice, our heart, our whole life; we give God honor and glory. In prayer, we focus on God: we seek his hand and his face; we seek to cultivate an intimacy with God. Our prayer is praise; our praise is prayer.

Worship reflects as well as forms the prayer life of the congregation. Prayer reflects as well as forms the worship life of the congregation. Together, prayer and worship develop a growing intimacy with the Lord, build community in the congregation, and serve as a model and encouragement to our personal prayer and worship. If God's house is to be a house of prayer (Isa. 56:7), we should go to that house to pray.

In a survey of regular church attendees, George Barna discovered that 41 percent had experienced God's presence during a worship service in the last month and 11 percent within the last year. Sadly, however, almost half of those surveyed indicated they had not experienced God in a worship service in the last year. (In fact, an amazing 32 percent indicated they had never experienced the presence of God during worship.) Barna's conclusion: "A significant number of people are not connecting with God" (*A Seminar for Church Leaders: Inward, Outward, and Upward*).

Since many worship services are apparently failing to bring worshipers into the presence of God, we need to take a serious look at worship. When people are asked about their favorite elements in a worship service, singing and preaching often come to mind. Few people mention prayer. Those who do seem to have little positive to say about it: "prayer is boring," "the prayer time does nothing for me," "we pray, but nothing ever comes of it."

For many people prayer has lost its relevance, significance, and power in both their personal and communal lives. Many have experienced unenthusiastic, powerless, and thoughtless praying. Others have understood prayer as simply bringing God a list of their needs and wants.

To assist people in "connecting with God," the prayers of our worship must be heartfelt, meaningful, and powerful. This requires a conscious and conscientious look at the place and priority of prayer in worship. And, in many cases, this may necessitate some changes.

integrating prayer and worship

Worship and prayer must always be fresh and relevant. At the same time, changes in worship can be devastating and can meet with considerable resistance. Many changes are worth the risk and resulting friction so that people can continue to grow spiritually, experience the presence of God, and develop their spiritual gifts in his service. But alienating people in the process significantly decreases the benefits.

In recent decades, some variety and flexibility in prayer have been introduced into the worship service. Oftentimes the key is to make these introductions gradually, giving a congregation time to embrace these elements as an important part of their worship. Following are a number of suggestions for making prayer an integral and vibrant part of your worship service.

- Encourage people, as members of the priesthood of all believers, to pray aloud in public worship. Include men and women, young and old, new and life-long members. This could include requesting people to lead in prayer, to introduce one segment of a bidding prayer, or to pray in concert. A parent could pray for children; a couple celebrating their fiftieth anniversary could pray for marriages; a police officer could pray for the city's police force; a veteran could pray for those in the armed forces.

- Teach regularly about prayer during worship. Intentionally schedule an extended message series on prayer annually or scatter messages on prayer throughout the year. The Heidelberg Catechism provides a wonderful outline for preaching about the Lord's Prayer. Many situations open up opportunities to preach on prayer: prayer services, crisis situations, apparent unanswered prayers, national elections, the persecution of Christians around the world, introducing a new prayer ministry, and so on. In addition, it is imperative that pastors who teach about prayer practice it visibly.

- Use prayer throughout worship. Many shorter prayers are often preferable to one or two longer prayers. Use prayers of adoration, confession, thanksgiving, supplication, and so on.

- Pray for more than local and congregational needs. Include prayers for the community, nation, and world, and for those who do not know the Lord and the missionaries trying to reach them.

- Encourage worshipers to pray before and during the service.

  — While still at home, ask God to prepare your heart for worship. When walking in, pray that God will bless the worship.

  — When seated, pray for the spiritual and physical needs outlined in the bulletin or that you are aware of in the worshipers around you.

  — As you conclude the service, ask that God will use you to touch one life before you leave.

  — As you drive away, thank God for the privilege of worshiping and praising him.

- Bathe the worship of your church in prayer.

  — Pastors should pray as they plan their sermon schedule and prepare their messages.

  — Creative teams and program directors should spend time in prayer as they brainstorm and plan worship services.

  — Worship leaders and musicians should spend time in prayer during rehearsals and on Sunday before providing worship leadership.

  — The leadership board should pray regularly for worship.

  — The congregation should be encouraged to enter the worship center and spend time in prayer for the service that will soon take place.

  — Praise and thanksgiving should be given at the conclusion of the worship—in public, by a prayer team, by worshipers on the way home or around their next meal, or in the small groups that meet following a worship time.

- Introduce people to different prayer formats during worship and encourage them to use the formats in their personal prayer life. Variety avoids the tendency for our prayers to always be the same.

- Teach and encourage worshipers to be pray-ers throughout the worship service. Worship is all about prayer.

- Be open to both planned and spontaneous prayer during worship. For example, if a particular hymn or testimony stirs the congregation, offer a prayer.

some guidelines for praying in worship

Pray seriously. Prepare your prayers. Pastors and worship leaders spend quantity time with message and music preparation; prayers deserve equal attention. Whether you write out your prayers or pray extemporaneously, prayer requires preparation.

Pray significantly—about the important issues. This doesn't mean you should neglect the small issues, but do not forget the significant issues of the Christian life. These might include (but are not limited to) salvation, healing, renewal, justice, confession/forgiveness, comfort, the empowering of the Spirit, the poor and lost.

Pray specifically. Avoid simply praying, "God bless all the missionaries; feed the hungry, right injustice, and empower the poor." Pray for specific situations that you know about. Avoid abstract language. Use verbal pictures and descriptive images.

Pray Scripture. Scripture helps center our praying on the significant issues. Praying prayers written by the church fathers can also assist us in putting words to the "meditations of our heart."

Pray simply. Avoid flowery language. Phrases using big and unnecessary words are often inappropriate attempts to sound "experienced" in prayer. Avoid church jargon—words and phrases that are meaningful only to long-time Christians and make

little or no sense to new and younger believers.

Pray sacredly. Remember, in prayer, you have accepted God's initiation to enter his throne room. Come boldly, but come humbly. Come repentant, but come holy. Come committed to God's will, but come expectantly.

Pray silence. Leave pauses in and around the spoken or sung prayer times to encourage and allow people to pray personally and privately. Include silence periodically in confession, after a sung prayer, or after the reading of Scripture. Use silence to separate various parts of prayer. Normally, keep these periods of silence short—thirty seconds to about two minutes.

Pray "sensorily." Appeal to the various senses to enhance prayer in worship.

specific ideas

- Sing your prayers.

- If a spoken prayer precedes or follows a prayer song, don't interrupt the transition with an injunction (such as "Let's continue our prayer" or "Let us pray"). This underscores that the song is a continuation of the prayer.

- Consider beginning or concluding a spoken prayer with a sung prayer. This allows the congregation to actively participate.

- Periodically use more frequent, shorter prayers in worship instead of one longer prayer.

- Allow people to make the prayers of worship "their" prayers. This can be done through singing, through members verbally speaking, and through a communal "amen."

- Vary the way you address God to fit the context or theme of the service (see Names of God, p. 83). Provide an appropriate atmosphere for prayer—an appropriate song, a time of silence, a reading of God's Word. The address should be appropriate to the prayer that follows.

- Divide into small groups for prayers during a worship service. This can be very effective—but it can also be very intimidating to people who are unfamiliar with it. Introduce this carefully, and allow people to pray silently in the group.

- Balance extemporaneous, written, and scriptural prayers. Balance spoken, sung, and silent prayers. Balance adoration, confession, thanksgiving, lament, and intercession.

Resources

Book of Common Worship (Nashville: Westminster/John Knox Press, 1993).

Hughes Oliphant Old, *Leading in Prayer* (Grand Rapids, MI: Wm. B. Eerdmans, 1995).

So You've Been Asked To Lead in Prayer (Grand Rapids, MI: CRC Publications, 1996).

Alvin Vander Griend, *The Praying Church Sourcebook* (Grand Rapids, MI: CRC Publications, 1997).

PRAYING EMPOWERS PREACHING

Prayer and proclamation go hand in hand. The hand of prayer strengthens and empowers the hand of preaching. E. M. Bounds once said, "The character of our praying will determine the character of our preaching. Light praying makes light preaching."

This is the prayer that takes place in the study throughout the week. From selecting the text, to careful reading, to discerning the voice of God, to crafting the message outline, to interceding for the church in which it will be preached, prayer is an indispensable factor in effective preaching. Richard Foster says, "Prayer is an essential discipline for preaching because it gets us in touch with God, it helps get us in touch with our people, and it helps people get in touch with us."

What does prayer in the study look like? It is not primarily intercession—yet it recognizes that pastors stand "in the gap" between God and his people. It is not primarily petition—although it underscores the pastor's complete dependence on God. It is not primarily about speaking to God; it is about listening to God. It is not simply asking God to give you an "ordained" message outline; it is also praying for the people who will receive the message.

If the pastor's study is a place of prayer throughout the week, worshipers will soon discern that preaching is not only the result of reading books and studying commentaries, of finely crafted sentences and carefully worded illustrations, of impeccable exegesis and the skill of delivery. Preaching is empowered by walking with and talking to God. Without prayer, the message will ring hallow, the power will be weak, and the fruit will be missing.

At the same time, the hand of preaching must inevitably call both the preacher and the worshiper to a growing sense of intimacy and community with God through prayer. Just as praying invigorates preaching; preaching must invigorate our praying. Preaching is designed to point us to God; prayer provides the path to his presence. David Bryant reminds us, "Don't simply preach on prayer; preach on the vision of what we are praying toward."

> **Give me one hundred preachers who fear nothing but sin and desire nothing but God, and I care not a straw whether they be clergy or laity; such alone will shake the gates of hell and set up the kingdom of heaven on earth. God does nothing but in answer to prayer.**
> **—John Wesley**

prayer ideas

- Meet with the worship leaders on Sunday morning prior to the service to pray together. Encourage them to pray quietly for those they are leading in worship.

- Join with a small group and pray over each seat or pew in the worship center before worship.

- Invite (or assign) an elder(s) to stop into your study during the week to pray with you about the service, the message, and the worshipers.

- Preach an annual series on prayer.

sermon ideas

- Series on "Questions People Ask About Prayer"

  — What is Prayer?
  — If God Is Sovereign, Why Pray?
  — Does Prayer Really Change Things?
  — What About Unanswered Prayer?
  — Is Prayer Mostly Talking or Listening?
  — What is Spiritual Warfare?
  — Is Intercession for Everyone or Just for Those with the Gift?

- Prayers of the Bible (see *All the Prayers of the Bible* by Herbert Lockyer)

- Old Testament Pray-ers (for example, Abraham, Joshua, Hannah, Nehemiah, David, Daniel, Job)

- The Eight Prayers of Jesus (Matt. 26:39; 27:46; Luke 10:21; 23:34; 23:46; John 11:41-42; 12:27-28; 17:1-26)

- Paul's Prayer Life

- New Testament Pray-ers

- The Lord's Prayer

- Different Prayer Formats

THE PRAYERS OF WORSHIP
The Opening Prayer

The opening prayer is the first prayer in worship. In some churches, this prayer serves as a request for God's presence. But God is already present. In fact, it is God who invites us to worship, not the worshiper who invites God to come. We enter God's presence in worship: "Let us come before him with thanksgiving. . . . Come, let us bow down in worship, let us kneel before the LORD our Maker" (Ps. 95:2, 6). So, rather, the opening prayer is a prayer for the visible presence, the power, and the action of the Holy Spirit.

At the same time, the opening prayer (where we speak to God) should not be confused with the call to worship (where God speaks to us). Once again, the call, the invitation to worship is God's. Our response to his invitation is to submit in prayer. The opening prayer is a "gathering" prayer.

The ancient pattern of prayer known as the "collect" (kah´-likt) fits well as an opening prayer. A "collect" is a short prayer used to conclude a time of individual prayer and "collects" these prayers into one unified prayer. Since worshipers are often encouraged to prepare for worship through personal prayer, using a "collect" as an opening prayer is most appropriate. There are four basic ingredients:

1. A salutation or address to God (for example, "Almighty God").

2. A celebration of a divine attribute, character trait, or act of God (for example, "who provides for our daily needs").

Select an attribute that resonates with the petition that follows.

3. A petition, often related to the day's theme, followed by a statement of purpose (for example, "Direct our thoughts to your will that we might offer you praise worthy of your holy name").

4. A concluding word of praise or doxology (for example, "through Jesus Christ our Lord, who lives and reigns with you. Amen").

A second prayer form that works well as an opening prayer is known as an "invocation" or *epiclesis* (from *epi-cleo*, meaning "to call upon"). This is an invitation for the Spirit's active presence in worship. John Witvliet of the Calvin Institute for Christian Worship offers a sample:

Lord God,

The power of what we are about to experience is not the result of our creativity, imagination, or insight. It is purely a gift.

May your Spirit work powerfully through this reading of Scripture, the sermon, the celebration of the sacrament.

And because of the Spirit's work, may we be given the grace to see Jesus Christ more clearly through what we are about to do.

Amen.

Opening the worship service with prayer reminds us to expect that the Holy Spirit will be at work, that we will be meeting face to face with God our creator and provider, that we will encounter Jesus Christ—and that all of it is a gift from God.

The Prayer of Adoration and Praise

In many prayer formats (for example, A.C.T.S. and A.W.C.I.P.A.), a major component of the prayer is the adoration and praise of God. We recognize the importance of adoration in our personal praying, but this piece is often missing in our corporate prayers.

Adoration should play a significant part in the "gathering" portion of worship prayer. In style, these prayers are often sung rather than spoken—singing allows the whole congregation to adore and praise God. The subject is always God—his person, purpose, power, people, and presence. Thus, prayers of adoration—whether spoken or sung—must always be directed to God.

examples of songs of adoration

"All Hail King Jesus" (*Renew!* 35)
"Be Merciful to Me, O God" (PsH 57)
"Father, We Love You" (PsH 634)
"Father, I Adore You" (PsH 284)
"For the Beauty of the Earth" (PsH 432)
"I Exalt Thee" (*Renew!* 44)
"I Love You, Lord" (*Renew!* 36, *Sing!*)
"I Worship You, O Lord" (PsH 30)
"In the Presence of Your People" (PsH 160)
"Lord God, Almighty" (*Renew!* 40)
"My Jesus I Love Thee" (PsH 557)
"There's No God as Great/No Hay Dios tan Grande" (PsH 517)
"We Bow Down" (*Renew!* 38, *Sing!*)
"We Will Glorify" (SFL 18, *Sing!*)
"When I Look into Your Holiness" (*Renew!* 41)
"With Grateful Heart My Thanks I Bring" (PsH 183)
"Worthy, You are Worthy" (*Renew!* 43)
"You Are Worthy" (PsH 232)

The songs listed above can be found in the following sources:

- *Psalter Hymnal* (PsH), © 1987, CRC Publications (1-800-333-8300)

- *Songs for LiFE* (SFL), © 1994, CRC Publications (1-800-333-8300)

- *Sing! A New Creation* (*Sing!*), © 2001, CRC Publications (1-800-333-8300)

- *Renew!* (*Renew!*), © 1995, Hope Publishing Company

The Prayer of Confession

Confession has always been a major part of worship as well as a significant ingredient of prayer. John Calvin said, "On every Lord's Day the minister makes a formal confession, in which he represents all as guilty of sin, and supplicates for pardon from the Lord on behalf of all" (*Institutes*, 3.4.11).

The prayer of confession varies from tradition to tradition, from setting to setting, and from season to season. In some traditions the confession is typically sung; in others, the pastor serves as the confessor on behalf of the people; in still others, it is done in silence. In some settings the pastor may lead this prayer; in others, a lay person may offer this prayer; in still others, it may be done in small groups or individually. During Lent, it may be appropriate to spend additional time in confession as we reflect on the fact that our sin sent Jesus Christ to the cross; during the Easter season—as we celebrate the resurrection of Jesus—we might spend less time in confession.

All too often, we hesitate to bring our confessions before God. In doing so, we betray our concern that God might not welcome us, might not hear our litany of failures, might not be gracious enough to forgive our sins. But God has already tipped his hand—he has already guaranteed that if we come he will forgive (1 John 1:9). So a prayer of confession is not a "prayer of groveling," but a prayer of confidence. The prayer of confession is a reminder of the source of our forgiveness and our dependence on God's grace. It is a celebration of a faithful God who is willing to listen even to our disobediences and a gracious God who is willing to forgive our sins. It is a renewal of our commitment to live obedient lives for him.

Some people feel prayers of confession are inappropriate in a worship setting because they seem generic and forced, or serve as a "downer" in an otherwise celebrative service. Not so, says John Witvliet of the Calvin Institute for Christian Worship:

> My response is (1) that there is corporate sin/institutional sin [such as pride, denominationalism, fear, judgmentalism, materialism, racism] that we need to express that none of us as individuals would otherwise think about and (2) that public worship often provides us with patterns for our own personal prayer life.

A typical format for the time of confession might include

- a spoken or sung prayer of confession
- silence
- a declaration or assurance of pardon: a song or an appropriate passage of Scripture
- a hymn or song of gratitude

le litany of
sion

Confession

. . . have been baptized into Christ Jesus were baptized into his death. Therefore, we have been buried with him by baptism into death, so that, just as Christ was raised from the dead by the glory of the Father, so we too might walk in newness of life (Rom. 6:3-4). As we praise God for all the gifts signified by our baptism, let us confess that we have sinned as we have sought to walk in Christ's way.

Let us pray:

Eternal and merciful God,
you have loved us with a love beyond understanding,
and you have set us on paths of righteousness for your name's sake.
Yet, we have strayed from your way;
we have sinned against you in thought, word, and deed,
through what we have done and what we have left undone,
and we have wandered from your pathway.
As we remember the cleansing water of baptism, O God,
we praise you and give you thanks that you forgive us yet again.
Grant us now, we pray, the grace to die daily to sin,
and to rise daily to new life in Christ, who lives and reigns with you,
and in whose strong name we pray. Amen.

Assurance

If we have been united with Christ in a death like his, we will certainly be united with him in a resurrection like his. So you must consider yourselves dead to sin and alive to God in Christ Jesus (Rom. 6:5, 11). Go in peace. Our sins are forgiven.

—Arlo D. Duba, "True Confession," *Reformed Worship* 52, pp. 17-18. © 1999 by CRC Publications. Used by permission.

examples of prayers of confession

Most merciful God,
we confess that we have sinned against you
in thought, word, and deed,
by what we have done,
and by what we have left undone.
We have not loved you with our whole heart;
we have not loved our neighbors as ourselves.
We are truly sorry and we humbly repent.
For the sake of your Son, Jesus Christ,
have mercy on us and forgive us;
that we may delight in your will,
and walk in your ways,
to the glory of your Name. Amen.

—*Book of Common Prayer*, p. 320

Create in me a pure heart, O God,
and renew a steadfast spirit within me.
Do not cast me from your presence
or take your Holy Spirit from me.
Restore to me the joy of your salvation
and grant me a willing spirit, to sustain me.

—Psalm 51:10-12

Heavenly Father, we come before you today to ask your forgiveness and to seek your direction and guidance. We know your Word says, "Woe on those who call evil good," but that is exactly what we have done. We have lost our spiritual equilibrium and reversed our values.

We confess that:

We have ridiculed the absolute truth of your Word and called it pluralism.

We have endorsed perversion and called it an alternative lifestyle.

We have exploited the poor and called it the lottery.

We have neglected the needy and called it self-preservation.

We have rewarded laziness and called it welfare.

We have killed our unborn children and called it choice.

We have shot abortionists and called it justifiable.

We have neglected to discipline our children and called it building self-esteem.

We have abused power and called it political savvy.

We have coveted our neighbor's possessions and called it ambition.

We have polluted the air with profanity and pornography and called it freedom of expression.

We have ridiculed the time-honored values of our forefathers and called it enlightenment.

Search us, O God, and know our hearts today; cleanse us from every sin and set us free. Guide and bless these men and women who have been sent to direct us to the center of your will. I ask it in the name of your Son, the living Savior, Jesus Christ. Amen.

—Joe Wright, prayer of confession to open a new session of the Kansas state legislature

songs of confession

"Change My Heart, O God" (*Renew!* 143, *Sing!*)

"Create in Me a Clean Heart" (SFL 41)

"Forgive Our Sins as We Forgive" (PsH 266)

"God, Be Merciful to Me" (PsH 255)

"Heal Our Land"

"If My People" (*Renew!* 186)

"Kyrie (Lord, Have Mercy upon Us)" (PsH 258, *Sing!*)

"Kyrie Eleison" (*Renew!* 86)

"Lord, Have Mercy" (*Renew!* 84)

"Lord, I Pray" (PsH 268)

"My Jesus, I Love Thee" (PsH 557)

"O Christ, the Lamb of God" (PsH 257)

"Purify My Heart" (*Renew!* 187)

"Sanctuary" (*Renew!* 185)

The songs listed above can be found in the following sources:

- *Psalter Hymnal* (PsH), © 1987, CRC Publications (1-800-333-8300)

- *Songs for LiFE* (SFL), © 1994, CRC Publications (1-800-333-8300)

- *Sing! A New Creation* (*Sing!*), © 2001, CRC Publications (1-800-333-8300

- *Renew!* (*Renew!*), © 1995, Hope Publishing Company

The Prayer of Lament

While there appears to be a growing desire to make worship celebrative, energetic, and upbeat, worship has always served as a reflection of the Christian's life—an expression of the believer's walk with God.

So what do you do when a family loses a child to sudden infant death syndrome, when a young mother is diagnosed with a brain tumor, when a teenager is killed in an automobile accident, when a respected couple announces their impending divorce, when an elder in the church is convicted of sexually abusing a neighborhood child? What do you do when violence strikes your local high school, when a tornado or flood devastates your area, or when your nation becomes involved in armed conflict? Are these situations and tragedies reflected in worship? Do our prayers reflect our life?

One of the obvious responses to such situations is to intercede on behalf of those who have been victimized: to ask God to comfort bereaved parents, to heal a brain tumor, to bring peace to the country, to repair a marriage, to request God's forgiveness and healing. But another option is to lament. John Witvliet, of the Calvin Institute of Christian Worship, notes:

These moments are pastorally more crucial for spiritual formation than a full docket of church education programs. And they occur in the life of many congregations with astonishing regularity. How we handle them may say as much about the gospel we proclaim as a year's worth of sermons.

—"A Time to Weep,"
Reformed Worship 44, p. 22.

Intercession and lament are closely related. Both recognize the pains of humanity, the power of God, and the need to bring the two together. Lament can be intercession—offered on behalf of those in crisis who may not be able to pray. Intercession can be lament—a recognition that something is seriously amiss. But, as John Witvliet says, "Lament is stronger, more poignant. Lament looks at what's wrong square in the face, names it for what it is, and protests against it. . . . Lament prevents intercession from becoming something we take for granted, something we offer glibly" ("A Time to Weep," *Reformed Worship* 45, p. 24). We need laments because there is so much pain in life—physical pain, emotional pain, mental pain, spiritual pain. There is my pain, your pain, the pain of fellow believers, and the pain of the world. This pain is often complicated by the fact that the pain lingers—for weeks, months, or, as in Paul's thorn in the flesh, for a lifetime. We pray, but the prayers seem to fall on deaf ears. We feel abandoned and the doubts begin.

The characters of the Bible lived in this painful world, and Scripture is filled with their expressions of anger, doubt, exasperation, fear, frustration, and pain. While Jeremiah's Lamentations is perhaps the best-known scriptural lament, the psalms also provide us not only with a picture of life's pain but with a model for dealing with it. Witvliet suggests we use the psalms to guide our lament and offers a five-step guide to forming a prayer of lament:

1. Begin with an invocation—a "startling confession that even in times of crisis, we approach a personal and accessible God." Ironically, in the midst of our feelings of abandonment, we seek the God we know and love.

2. Address God "through the picturesque gallery of images used . . . in the psalms. . . . We pray to Yahweh, the rock, the fortress, the hiding place, the bird with encompassing wings. These metaphors are not just theological constructs, but means of directly addressing God. As we pray them, these metaphors shape and reshape how we conceive of God."

3. Bring your theological questions, your intense feelings, your bold lament into your prayers. The psalmists do not mince words. They are direct, honest, and bold. Their prayers are punctuated with question marks and exclamation points.

4. Continue "with specific petition: heal us, free us, save us." Lament leads to petition, petition will lead to praise. "The very attributes for which we praise God are those we invoke in times of need."

5. Finally, express the hope, confidence, and trust God provides, even though they may be muted by the present situation. Lament ultimately looks to the future when our hope is realized.

—"A Time to Weep," *Reformed Worship* 44, pp. 22-23. © 1997 by CRC Publications. Used by permission.

Regardless of the format you use for lament, make sure to complete the cycle of lament—especially remembering to include the petition and praise. Also, avoid "lamenting" quickly. Don't read the psalm too fast; don't say the prayer too quickly. (In some situations, it may be appropriate to structure the entire worship hour around a psalm of lament.)

Another option is to pray a psalm of lament. An appropriate psalm can be used in various ways:

- Read the psalm as your prayer.

- Paraphrase the psalm in your own words to lament your particular situation and needs.

- Read and pray the psalm, pausing periodically to insert your own specific feelings and questions, as in the following example based on Psalm 13:

How long, O Lord? Will you forget me forever?
How long will you hide your face from me?
How long must I bear pain in my soul, and have sorrow in my heart all day long?
How long shall my enemy be exalted over me?

LORD, our Lord,
we feel forgotten.
This abuse rips apart our faith.
The victim, our sister _____, is alone in despair.
How long must this persist?

Consider and answer me, O LORD my God!
Give light to my eyes, or I will sleep the sleep of death,

Scriptural Laments on Everyday Issues

Psalm 3	A crisis of betrayal
Psalm 10	When God is silent
Psalm 13	A crisis of abuse
Psalm 38	A crisis of sickness
Psalm 41	A crisis of sickness
Psalm 51	A crisis of guilt
Psalm 56	When threatened
Psalm 61	A crisis of insecurity
Psalm 69	A crisis of shame
Psalm 71	Afflictions of old age
Psalm 88	A crisis of despair
Psalm 109	When falsely accused
Psalm 139	A crisis of identity
Psalm 142	A crisis of loneliness
Psalm 143	A crisis of oppression

And my enemy will say, "I have prevailed";
My foes will rejoice because I am shaken.

The perpetrator of this abuse is winning!
Please, Lord, stop him!
We cannot bear to see this fool—
the enemy of our sister, and of us—
believe he is successful.

But I trusted in your steadfast love;
My heart shall rejoice in your salvation.
I will sing to the LORD
Because he has dealt bountifully with me.

We long to sing praise,
To have our sister begin to sense your goodness again.
For deep down, we trust in your goodness. Amen.

—John Witvliet, "A Time to Weep," *Reformed Worship* 44, p. 24. © 1997 by CRC Publications. Used by permission.

songs of lament

"Congregational Lament" (PsH 576)
"How Long, O Lord" (*Renew!* 87)
"How Long Will You Forget Me, LORD" (PsH 13)
"Psalm 61: Hear My Cry" (*Renew!* 108)
"Why Has God Forsaken Me?" (TWC 406)

The songs listed above can be found in the following sources:

- *Psalter Hymnal* (PsH), © 1987, CRC Publications (1-800-333-8300)

- *Songs for LiFE* (SFL), © 1994, CRC Publications (1-800-333-8300)

- *Renew!* (*Renew!*), © 1995, Hope Publishing Company

- *The Worshiping Church* (TWC), © 1990, Hope Publishing Company

—John Witvliet, "A Time to Weep," *Reformed Worship* 44 and 45. © 1997 by CRC Publications. Used by permission.

The Prayer of the People

The prayer of the people, sometimes referred to as the intercessory prayer or the pastoral prayer, may be best known as the "long prayer"—so named, no doubt, not only for its length, but also because it has lost much of its meaning. This intercessory prayer is designed to unite the congregation in praying for their needs and the needs of their community. While many different people may participate in this prayer (one after the other, in concert, in small groups, and so on), this is not a collage of different prayers but a single prayer of the congregation.

A prayer of the people has four basic parts:

1. *An acknowledgement of God.* We need to be reminded that God is God—and we are not! Here is an opportunity to celebrate God's attributes, names, and deeds.

2. *A corporate confession of our sin.* If confession has not already been done in the service, this prayer provides the opportunity. If a prayer of confession has already been spoken, this part may be omitted.

3. *Intercession.* Intercession comes with two primary focuses: the needs of the congregation (those submitting to surgery, those going through divorce, those about to be married, those who are pregnant and those who would be, the church's staff and ministry, and so on) and the needs of the world (your local community, your nation, and the entire globe).

4. *Thanksgiving.* One of the most overlooked aspects of prayer is thanksgiving. In addition to thanking God for being God, for being faithful, for caring for and ruling the world, we must remember to thank God for answering our previous prayers.

In order to avoid allowing the pastoral prayer to become routine and lose some of its meaning, consider using some of the following options:

- Invite people to kneel.

- Pray away from the podium or pulpit—symbolically it should take place in the middle of God's people.

- Use a prayer song or hymn before or after the prayer (or pause to pray between each stanza of an appropriate hymn).

- Conclude the prayer with the Lord's Prayer—either spoken in unison or sung together.

- Have worshipers share prayer requests and praise reports before praying (see caution on p. 328).

- Ask different intercessors to pray for different (predetermined) needs or categories; the same people could continue for a month and also share God's answers.

- Have a different elder lead the pastoral prayer each week.

- Vary the format. Use a bidding prayer, an extended time of silence, the A.C.T.S. format (see p. 38), the P.R.A.Y. format (see pp. 85-86), or the Lord's Prayer Pattern (see pp. 78-79).

- Invite people to pray together in unison (the prayer could be written out in the bulletin, projected on a screen, or repeated after the leader).

- Ask worshipers to stand together with hands raised (see 1 Tim. 2:8). This visually indicates they are all joining together in prayer.

- Have the congregation give an audible "amen" at the end of the prayer.

- Place short periods of silence (from fifteen to sixty seconds) between the areas of intercession as an opportunity for worshipers to add their own prayers.

taking prayer requests

In almost every discussion of the pastoral prayer the issue of taking prayer requests and praise reports comes up. While this opportunity is often very meaningful, it can also be a disaster if some basic guidelines are not followed. When introducing this opportunity—and periodically thereafter—spend some time explaining the following cautions:

- Confidentiality must be maintained. It is not uncommon for people to pray publicly for private matters—often betraying confidentiality and privacy issues under the guise of prayer. Encourage people to share personal requests about themselves; but remind them to share personal requests about others only if they have permission to do so.

- Only the first names of non-church members should be shared.

- If permission is received, pray as specifically as possible. Unless the church is small, or everyone knows for whom you are praying, use complete names. Pray for real people.

- Encourage people to share any kind of need so that your prayer is not just a litany of physical needs.

a note of caution for prayer leaders

Pray-ers, especially pastors, should be careful to avoid the following pitfalls:

- *announcements in prayer.* The pastoral prayer is not the medium for making announcements.

- *controversial issues.* Don't ask God to bless your side or perspective on a controversial issue.

- *corrective prayers.* Avoid the temptation to teach or correct theology.

- *generalized prayers.* While portions of the pastoral prayer may be somewhat general, keep the prayer as specific as possible. Pray for real people and real needs.

- *no-confidence prayers.* Pray with boldness. God promises to answer prayer if we believe. Hold God to his promises.

- *oration.* Some people have the unfortunate ability of constructing a prayer so beautiful and flowery that the prayer draws more attention to itself than to God.

- *personal agendas.* Avoid pushing your personal agenda in prayer.

- *summarizing prayer.* If the pastoral prayer follows the message, avoid the temptation to review the message, re-emphasize a point, or even make a point you may have forgotten.

The Prayer for the Offering

This prayer can be offered either before or after the offering. Before the offering, the primary emphasis is to request that God touch our hearts and bless our giving. Following the offering, the prayer is an opportunity to symbolize the dedicating of our tithe to the Lord for his service and the building of his kingdom. In both cases, this prayer underscores the significance of our daily labor and the spiritual act of giving an offering.

The prayer may be offered in a variety of ways. Some examples:

- Have a deacon (or someone who collects the offering) offer the prayer.

- Have someone from the ministry (a leader, participant, or recipient) offer an explanation of the ministry or a testimonial and then offer the prayer.

- Pray while the offering is being received (this can be done silently, verbally, or by singing).

- Place a prayer in the bulletin or on a screen for people to pray in unison.

a prayer before the offering

Father, we worked hard this week in offices and factories, in schools and stores, on the road and in the air. We have worked long hours and hard days. Sometimes we have enjoyed our work; sometimes it has been a burden we have borne. But now we bring the firstfruits of our reward as evidence of our love for you and gratitude to you—for who you are and for everything you have done. Amen.

a prayer after the offering

Father, we offer the fruit of our daily labor for the building of your church, for the expansion of your kingdom, and for the glory of your name. Bless the use of these monies, that they, in turn, will bear much fruit. Amen.

a prayer for the offering from scripture

What shall I return to the LORD for all his bounty to me?
I will lift up the cup of salvation and call on the name of the LORD.
I will offer to you a thanksgiving sacrifice and call on the name of the LORD.
I will pay my vows to the LORD in the presence of all his people,
in the courts of the house of the LORD, in your midst, O Jerusalem (Ps. 116:12-13, 17-19 NRSV).

songs for the offertory prayer

"Father, I Adore You" (PsH 284)
"Have Thine Own Way, Lord" (PsH 287)
"Take My Life and Let It Be" (PsH 288)
"Take My Life That It May Be" (PsH 289)

The songs listed above can be found in the *Psalter Hymnal*, © 1987, CRC Publications (1-800-333-8300).

The Prayer for Illumination

The prayer for illumination is a short prayer offered prior to the reading of Scripture or between the reading of Scripture and the message. This prayer asks the Spirit to bless the reading of the Word, to anoint the pastor who brings the message, and to open the recipients' hearts, minds, and souls to receive the Word of God.

The preaching of God's Word, in the Presbyterian and Reformed tradition, is considered one of the two means of grace (the other is the sacraments). This does not mean that God dispenses grace only in these ways; it does mean God has said this is one of the ways he intentionally and routinely dispenses grace through the Holy Spirit. For John Calvin, the message was not merely some well thought-out reflections to bring inspiration, encouragement, and comfort; but rather a faithful explanation and application of the Word—a direct word from God.

While this prayer is a regular part of worship in some churches and traditions, it is completely omitted in others. Sometimes this prayer is offered by a layperson and sometimes by the clergy. In some traditions, it is more common to sing a hymn to prepare the worshipers' hearts to hear the Word of God.

sample prayers of illumination

Guide us, O God,
by your Word and Spirit,
that in your light we may see light,
in your truth find wisdom,
and in your will discover your peace,
through Jesus Christ our Lord. Amen.

Living God,
help us so to hear your holy Word
that we may truly understand;
that, understanding, we may believe
and believing,
we may follow in all faithfulness and
    obedience,
seeking your honor and glory in all
    that we do;
through Christ our Lord. Amen.

—From the *Source Book of Worship Resources*, volume 2 (Canton, Ohio: Communication Resources, 1996). Printed in *Reformed Worship* 52, p. 20. © 1999 by CRC Publications. Used by permission.

songs of illumination

"Blessed Jesus, at Your Word" (PsH 280)
"Holy Spirit, Mighty God" (PsH 278)
"Open Our Eyes, Lord" (*Renew!* 91, *Sing!*)
"Speak, Lord in the Stillness" (*Renew!* 96)
"Spirit of the Living God" (PsH 424)
"Thy Word" (*Renew!* 94)

The songs listed above can be found in the following sources:

- *Psalter Hymnal* (PsH), © 1987, CRC Publications (1-800-333-8300)

- *Sing! A New Creation* (*Sing!*), © 2001, CRC Publications (1-800-333-8300)

- *Renew!* (*Renew!*), © 1995, Hope Publishing Company

The Prayer of Commitment

The prayer of commitment (sometimes known as the prayer of application or the prayer of invitation) is offered at the conclusion of a message. While the prayer of commitment reflects the message, it is not designed to summarize the major points of the message. This is a prayer asking the Spirit to apply God's Word to our lives, to move us into God's will, and to make our commitment or recommitment of our lives acceptable to the Lord.

Because this prayer is an invitation, it is appropriate to ask for some kind of response from the congregation. Consider the following examples:

- Invite people to come forward for the salvation prayer if they are experiencing crisis.

- Invite people to raise their hands, hug a fellow worshiper, divide into triads and pray, and so on.

- Ask the congregation to respond in song.

songs of commitment

"Here I Am, Lord" (SFL 243, *Sing!*)
"Lead Me, Lord" (*Renew!* 175)
"Make Me a Servant" (TWC 653)
"Send Me, Lord" (SFL 252)
"Take My Life That It May Be" (PsH 289)

The songs listed above can be found in the following sources:

- *Psalter Hymnal* (PsH), © 1987, CRC Publications (1-800-333-8300)

- *Songs for LiFE* (SFL), © 1994, CRC Publications (1-800-333-8300)

- *Sing! A New Creation* (Sing!), © 2001, CRC Publications (1-800-333-8300)

- *Renew!* (*Renew!*), © 1995, Hope Publishing Company

- *The Worshiping Church* (TWC), © 1990, Hope Publishing Company

The Prayer of Consecration

The sacrament of the Lord's Supper is an awesome opportunity to remember Christ's suffering and death, and to be intimately united with him through the bread and the wine. In many traditions, before the bread is broken and the wine is poured, a prayer of consecration is offered. In this prayer, we ask God to prepare hearts and minds to receive the body and blood of Christ.

The sacrament of baptism is an equally awesome opportunity to remember what Jesus did, for we are "buried with him through baptism into death in order that, just as Christ was raised from the dead through the glory of the Father, we too may live a new life" (Rom. 6:4).

A prayer of consecration traditionally involves three parts:

1. Praising God.

2. Remembering God's reconciling work through Jesus Christ.

3. Invoking the presence and power of the Holy Spirit

These three aspects all may be included in one prayer, or they may be broken into three sections and spread throughout the sacrament.

a prayer for the conclusion of the Lord's Supper

Eternal God, heavenly Father,
you have graciously accepted us as living members
of your Son our Savior Jesus Christ,
and you have fed us with spiritual food
in the Sacrament of his Body and Blood.
Send us now into the world in peace,
and grant us strength and courage
to love and serve you
with gladness and singleness of heart;
through Christ our Lord. Amen.

—*Book of Common Prayer*, p. 365

songs of consecration for the Lord's Supper

"God Is Here" (PsH 516)

"He Is Exalted" (*Renew!* 238, *Sing!*)

"Jesus, Remember Me" (PsH 217)

"Jesus, Stand Among Us" (*Renew!* 237)

"Worthy Is Christ/Digno Es Jesus" (PsH 629)

"Worthy Is the Lamb" (*Renew!* 234)

a prayer for the conclusion of baptism

Ever-living God,
in your mercy you promised to be not
only our God,
but also the God of our children.
We thank you for receiving _____ by
baptism.
Keep them always in your love.
Guide them as they grow in faith.
Protect them in all the dangers and
temptations of life.
Bring them to confess Jesus Christ as
their Lord and Savior
and be his faithful disciples to their
life's end;
in the name of Jesus Christ.
Amen.

—*Book of Common Worship*,
pp. 416-417

songs of consecration for baptism

"How Great Is the Love of the Father" (PsH
231)
"I Have Decided to Follow Jesus" (SFL 226)
"Jesus Loves Me" (SFL 61)
"Lift Your Heart to the Lord" (PsH 515)

The songs listed above can be found in the following sources:

- *Psalter Hymnal* (PsH), © 1987, CRC Publications (1-800-333-8300)

- *Songs for LiFE* (SFL), © 1994, CRC Publications (1-800-333-8300)

- *Sing! A New Creation (Sing!)*, © 2001, CRC
Publications (1-800-333-8300)

- *Renew! (Renew!)*, © 1995, Hope Publishing
Company

The Closing Prayer

In many traditions, the final word of worship is the blessing or benediction. While many people see it simply as the signal that the service is over, receiving God's blessing is a beautiful way to conclude worship. This blessing reminds us as we leave that God is in control, that God will be with us wherever we go, and that God will sustain us and provide for us each day.

The closing prayer is optional and, if used, is normally very short. In some churches, the closing prayer is a thanksgiving for God's active presence during worship and a request for his parting blessing. In this case the prayer precedes the blessing. In other churches, God's blessing is offered, and receiving God's blessing provides the people an opportunity to respond.

when the closing prayer precedes the blessing

Prayer

Father, we have worshiped you, expressed our love, offered our thanksgiving, and listened to your Word. As we walk from this place into your world, we ask for your continued presence and blessing upon us. Guide us and guard us as we serve you. In Christ's name, Amen.

Blessing

The grace of our Lord Jesus Christ, the love of God the Father, and the fellowship, power, and presence of the Holy Spirit be with you always. Amen.

when the closing prayer follows the blessing

Blessing

The Lord bless you and keep you. The Lord make his face to shine upon you. The Lord turn his face to you and give you peace.

Prayer

Father, we have worshiped you, expressed our love, offered our thanksgiving, listened to your Word, and been blessed by you. As we walk from this place into your world, we thank you for your grace, your faithfulness, and your love that go with us as we seek to serve you. In Christ's name, Amen.

songs for the closing prayer

"Bind Us Together" (*Renew!* 292)
"Bless His Holy Name" (PsH 627)
"Lord, Bid Your Servant Go in Peace" (*Renew!* 295)

"Lord, Let Us Now Depart in Peace" (TWC 842)

"Praise God, from Whom All Blessings Flow" (PsH 637, 638)

The songs listed above can be found in the following sources:

- *Psalter Hymnal* (PsH), © 1987, CRC Publications (1-800-333-8300)

- *Renew!* (Renew!), © 1995, Hope Publishing Company

- *The Worshiping Church* (TWC), © 1990, Hope Publishing Company

IDEAS FOR WORSHIP SERVICES
An Invitation to Pray

A growing number of churches is offering worshipers the opportunity to continue praying or to be prayed for personally—usually in the front of the church—after the worship concludes. Some churches offer this prayer opportunity following every service; some hold it periodically (for example, the first or last Sunday of each month, at the end of each sermon series, or following an evangelism message); and some when the pastor feels the Spirit's leading.

An invitation for general prayer can be done as follows:

1. Invite worshipers who have a special prayer need to come to the front. The invitation may relate to the message; for example, you might say, "All those who need healing for a physical ailment . . ." or, "All who would like to recommit themselves to being good stewards of their financial resources . . ." or, "All those who are currently involved in the teaching ministry of the church . . ." In making the invitation, indicate that no one will single them out or ask specifically about their need. Invite intercessors in the congregation to come forward to join them—not to interrogate them—but to support and encourage them with their presence.

2. Worshipers should be encouraged to come forward and simply kneel or stand (depending on your facility and tradition) in the front.

3. Following the invitation, give people sufficient time to come to the front. Musicians may play quietly in the background.

4. When those coming to the front have arrived, the pastor or an elder or worship leader should lead in prayer.

5. Invite the people remaining in their seats to join you in a prayer song.

An invitation that will result in one-on-one pairings with an intercessor can follow this procedure:

1. Invite worshipers who have a special prayer need to come to the front. In the invitation, the pastor should indicate that intercessors will join them to hear their prayer need and to offer a personal prayer for them and that they can come regardless of the nature of the need—financial, spiritual, physical, emotional, relational, and so on.

2. People should be encouraged to come forward and simply stand in the front.

3. Following the invitation, give people sufficient time to come to the front. Musicians may play quietly in the background.

4. As those moving to the front arrive, intercessors should come forward to "claim" someone who has a prayer need. It is best to try to match pairs by gender and age.

5. Offer a general prayer to close the service. As the congregation exits, the trained intercessors listen, offer a word of prayer, and provide a word of encouragement or an appropriate Scripture. They should also promise to continue to remember the prayer request. Intercessors should request only enough information about the request to pray appropriately.

6. Normally this form of prayer works best at the conclusion of a service. If scheduled at another time during the service, a song should be sung to allow those in the front of the church to exit from the worship center to a quiet place. They can return to worship during a subsequent song.

7. All information shared is considered confidential unless the person designates otherwise. Serious issues should be referred to a pastor—but only with the person's permission. The only exception to the confidentiality rule is when the information indicates they are thinking of harming themselves or someone else; such information must be shared as soon as possible.

Concert of Prayer

Concerts of prayer are designed to bring believers together across denominational and racial lines for prayer, to focus on spiritual revival and world evangelism, and to celebrate God's movement across the nation in answer to previous prayers.

The word *concert* suggests two pictures. The first is a symphony. Just as instruments blend their voices to make music, a concert of prayer blends voices into a single offering of prayer to God. As an orchestra plays a variety of music—symphonies, overtures, pops—so a concert of prayer includes praise, confession, thanksgiving, intercession. The term *concert* also suggests a "concerted" effort. A concert of prayer is an extended, intentional, united, and sustained commitment to seek God.

Concerts of prayer have their roots in 1750 Scotland, when several Scottish congregations first came together to pray. For more than one hundred years, this concerted effort of multiple congregations was at the root of evangelistic and revival movements.

A concert of prayer is a significant undertaking. Anytime more than one church comes together to worship and pray, advanced planning and coordination are required. Frequently, a neutral site is required to accommodate large numbers of people.

The concert of prayer centers on worship and prayer and is normally broken down into segments. The segments usually include various formats of prayer, and one or more leaders introduce the segments and formats.

David Bryant, director of Concerts of Prayer International, suggests the following program for a concert of prayer:

Celebration (15 minutes)
— Praise with hymns and choruses that focus on awakening and mission
— Reports of God's answers to prayers offered during previous concerts
— Prayers of praise for God's faithfulness, for his kingdom, for his Son

Preparation (20 minutes)
— Welcome to the concert!
— Overview: Why are we here?
— Biblical perspective on the concert's prayer focus
— Preview of the format
— Teaming up in partners and huddles

Prayer of Dedication (5 minutes)
— Commitment to be servants through prayer and to be used in answer to our prayers
— Thanksgiving for the privilege of united prayer and for those with whom we unite
— Invitation for Christ to lead the concert and to pray through us
— Hymn of praise

Seeking for Fullness/Awakening in the Church (30 minutes)
— In partners: for personal revival
— In huddles: for awakening in our local church and ministries

— As a whole: for awakening in the church worldwide
— Pause to listen to God
— Chorus

Seeking for Fulfillment/Mission Among the Nations (30 minutes)
— In partners: for personal ministries
— In huddles: for outreach and mission in our city or campus
— As a whole: for world evangelism
— Pause to listen to God
— Chorus

Testimonies: What has God said to us here? (10 minutes)
— On fullness (awakening)
— On fulfillment (mission)

Grand Finale (10 minutes)
— Offering ourselves to be answers to our prayers and also to live accordingly
— Prayer for God's empowerment in our own lives for ministry
— Prayer for prayer movements locally and worldwide
— Offering praise to God, who will answer our concert of prayer in wonderful ways
— Leave to watch and serve "in concert"

—David Bryant, *Concerts of Prayer,*
© 1988 by Gospel Light/Regal
Books, Ventura, CA 93003.
Used by permission.

Resources

David Bryant, *Concerts of Prayer* (Ventura, CA: Regal Books, 1988).

Alvin Vander Griend, *The Praying Church Sourcebook* (Grand Rapids, MI: CRC Publications, 1997).

Day of Prayer

Designate a Sunday as a "Day of Prayer." This can be done annually (for example, with a prayer emphasis week), biennially, or even quarterly.

A sample schedule might look like this:

10:00-11:30	Morning Worship (includes prayer time and a message on prayer)
12:00	Lunch
1:00-1:30	Worship (singing, Scripture, encouragement, explanation, prayer)
1:30-2:15	Divide into small groups of three or four for prayers for the congregation, illnesses, special needs
2:15-3:00	Bring two to three small groups together—pray for church renewal and revival
3:00-3:30	Individual quiet time for listening and petitioning God for his will and your role in it
3:30-3:45	Break/refreshments/fellowship
3:45-4:30	Same small groups of three or four—prayer for neighbors using the B.L.E.S.S. format (see p. 59)
4:30-5:00	Worship, sharing, closing prayer

Some churches have an evening service. If this is the case, add a light supper between the end of the afternoon prayers and before the evening worship service. In this case, it works well to have a concert of prayer during the evening service.

Headline Prayers

Headline praying is an excellent way to keep your praying relevant; it underscores the intimate link between our prayer life and our lives in the world. Mass media can be a powerful tool for intercession. While many people are offended by the daily news, the media provide a springboard for prayer. The daily newspaper contains dozens of people and circumstances in need of prayer. The front page, the local section, the editorials, letters to the editor, even the obituaries provide issues for intercession.

Designate a member of your prayer team to scan the local paper for prayer needs from your community/region/nation. These can be organized into broad subject areas (for example, neighborhood, city, state, nation, world) and given to the pastor or another prayer leader prior to the worship service. The headlines can be copied onto an overhead projector and used during the service.

Headline prayer is also an effective format for prayer services and prayer groups. Each person can bring one or two newspaper items from the previous week to pray for. At the meeting, each person, in turn, describes the prayer need and then prays, either verbally or silently. If appropriate, a note or postcard can be mailed to the persons prayed for.

Monthly Prayer Emphasis

Many churches have an interest in placing more emphasis on prayer, but the Cadillac (Michigan) Christian Reformed Church is actually doing something about it. They have designated one of their Sunday evening worship services each month as a prayer service.

The service begins with a time of praise, followed by teaching on prayer. Then the congregation is offered three different prayer opportunities:

- Those interested in praying for general prayer requests from the congregation meet in the worship center to pray.

- Those interested in praying for specific needs of the congregation, community, and world meet in the prayer room.

- Those interested in praying for anyone who requests prayer for spiritual, emotional, or physical healing meet in the fellowship room.

It is working well," says the pastor, "because it involves the whole congregation in the foundation-building work of prayer."

A few things to consider when implementing a monthly prayer emphasis:

- Many additional rooms and areas of prayer could be used in such a service—such as praying for the youth in the youth room, for the educational ministries in a classroom, for hospitality in the kitchen, and so on.

- Each prayer location should have a handout listing prayer needs for that area. This allows people to pray meaningfully both at church and at home.

- It is helpful to have a designated leader at each location to help facilitate the praying.

- Consider taking a few minutes at each location to briefly share additional prayer requests.

Passing the Pad

Some churches use a "prayer pad" that worshipers pass down the rows at a designated time in the worship service. The pad contains a form on which people can write their prayer requests and specify what kind of prayer they would like (perhaps by a checklist including "prayer during worship," "given to prayer warriors," "shared with pastors," and so on).

Some smaller churches pass one pad—beginning at the start of the service—from the front to the back of the sanctuary; the list is then photocopied and distributed as people leave worship.

As an alternative, on the first Sunday of the month, pass a blank prayer calendar (see p. 175) and invite people to write down anything they would like prayer for, such as birthdays, anniversaries, upcoming hospitalizations or surgeries, school activities, and so on.

Prayer Chain

This prayer chain is a visual chain that will brighten up your home and the church's worship center as well as call attention to the large amount of daily prayer needed within a local congregation.

As a family activity, write prayers on strips of colored paper and place them in a jar. These can include the prayer needs from your church's bulletin, neighborhood prayer needs, names of people in your community you are praying for, and needs your children bring home from school. Each day pull one out, pray for it as a family, and loop it together to form a paper chain. (Make sure the printed side is out so you can continue to read them.)

As a church activity, write the prayer items listed in your bulletin or shared during the worship prayer time on strips of colored construction paper. These prayer requests can then be added to the chain following each service. The chain can be strung throughout the worship center or the church. As an option, color-code the prayers (for example, prayers for healing in green, prayers of thanksgiving in blue, prayers for the lost in red, prayers for the nation in yellow, answers to prayer in orange, and so on). Or, place a variety of colored paper strips in each bulletin on the first Sunday of the month and ask people to fill out as many as appropriate and place them in the offering plate.

Constructing a prayer chain has several benefits:

- It reminds people of the many needs to take to God in prayer.

- It encourages worshipers to pray for others.

- It can be coordinated with a specific prayer challenge. For example:

  — Write the name of every child/youth in the church on a separate link.

  — Write the names of neighbors on separate links.

  — Write the names of all the kids who came to Vacation Bible School on separate links.

  — Write the name of every volunteer in your church in connection with an appreciation service.

- It can be taken down and used in a special worship service, such as a Day of Prayer (see p. 341).

- It can provide information that may suggest the congregation would benefit from a certain sermon series, educational class, support group, and so on.

Prayer chains can also be used on a smaller scale:

- Make a chain with every child in nursery and place it across the childcare area.

- Make chains of those in Sunday school.

- Make a chain with every young person's name and string it through the youth room.

Prayer in Motion

Communication involves much more than speaking. In fact, body language often reflects the true meaning behind a person's words, and this is no less true when we are talking to God.

Body movements have been used in prayer for many years. They include bowing your head, closing your eyes, and folding your hands. They include standing, kneeling, lying prostrate, and holding hands around a circle.

Many prayers have been set to motions. Following are some examples you may want to try; also use them as a springboard for creating your own prayers in motion.

the Lord's prayer

Our Father	(Stand erect. Raise arms and hands, palms open. Raise face. Smile.)
in heaven,	(Look up, smiling. Raise arms over head. Hands with palms still open.)
holy be your name.	(Lower head and eyes. Lower hands to face. Fingers cover mouth, overlapping. Elbows wide.)
Your kingdom come,	(Spread arms wide. Hands with palms open and out.)
your will be done	(Lower head and eyes. Bring hands together, palms together. Fingertips at lips.)
on earth	(Keep last position, and kneel on one knee.)
as in heaven.	(Remain kneeling, but raise head and eyes and arms, hands up, palms out. Smile.)
Give us today	(Stand. Look up with confidence, arms in front, parallel to each other, bent at elbows, hands together, palms up and open. Fingers cupped.)
our daily bread.	(Swing elbows out. Keep palms up and open, overlap hands in front of stomach. Palms still up and open; fingers still cupped.)
Forgive us	(Bring right hand up as fist. Strike breast and keep fist there. Head and eyes are lowered.)
our sins	(Bring left hand up as fist. Strike breast and keep fist there.)

as we forgive those	(Head and eyes still lowered, extend right hand like a crucifixion.)
who sin against us.	(Extend left hand like right hand.)
Do not bring us to the test,	(Kneel on one knee. Bring left hand in front of face, palm open, fingers spread, thumb down, palm out. Bring right hand out in front, hand up, palm out, fingers spread.)
but deliver us from evil.	(Remain kneeling; hunch over. Lower head; bring hands over face and head in a protective position.)
For the kingdom,	(Remain kneeling. Straighten back. Look up confidently. Open arms by side with hands wide.)
the power,	(Stand up erect. As you rise, bring fists up to head height. Elbows bent.)
and the glory are yours	(Extend arms full length, face and head raised, smile. Wiggle hands and fingers.)
now and forever.	(Return to "the power" position.)
Amen.	(Slowly bow head.)

—Paul F. Bosch and Helen Eickmann. *Worship in Motion,* © 1975, The Lutheran Church— Missouri Synod. Used by permission.

prayer for illumination

God be in my head	[touch forehead]
And in my mouth	[touch mouth]
And in my heart.	[touch heart]
Be on my right hand	[touch right hand with left hand]
And on my left hand.	[touch left hand with right hand]
May the words of his/her (the pastor's) mouth	[reach forward with an outstretched hand]
And the meditation of my heart	[touch heart]
Be acceptable in your sight	[reach up with outstretched hand]
Through Jesus Christ our Lord.	[point up still higher with one finger]
Amen!	

[Hands down]

—Keith Tanis

Prayer Litanies

The litany, a prayer read by the worship leader with spoken or sung congregational responses, is a more formal, but very effective method of corporate prayer. It also requires considerable bulletin space, although an increasing number of churches are able to project litanies on a screen. See the example on page 350.

Come, Holy Spirit

Text: Norman B. Steen, 1989
Tune: Norman B. Steen, 1989; arr. Emily R. Brink, 1989
© 1990, CRC Publications

Come, Holy Spirit, from heaven shine forth with your glorious light! *(sung first time by leader)*
Refrain (sung by all): Come, Holy Spirit, from heaven shine forth with your glorious light!
Come Father of the poor, come generous Spirit, come light of our hearts!
Refrain

Perfect Comforter! Refreshing, renewing breath of God! You make peace to dwell in our soul.
Refrain

In our labor, you offer rest; in temptation, strength; and in our sadness, consolation.
Refrain

Most kindly, warming Light! Enter the inmost depth of our hearts.
Refrain

Without your presence, we have nothing worthy, nothing pure.
Refrain

Wash away our sin, send rain upon our dry ground, heal our wounded souls, make us holy as you are holy, so we may come with joy to the table of the Lord.
Refrain

With warmth bend our rigidity, inflame our apathy, and direct our wandering feet. Overcome our timidity and hesitancy. Empower us to be bold witnesses for Jesus Christ.
Refrain

On all who put their trust in you, and receive you in faith, shower all your gifts. Grant that they may grow in you, and persevere to the end; give them lasting joy! Alleluia!
Refrain

(spoken by all) Come Holy Spirit. O come, Holy Spirit. O Come Holy Spirit, from heaven shine forth with your glorious light! Amen.

—Norman B. Steen, "Let Us Pray," *Reformed Worship* 15, p. 26.
© 1990 by CRC Publications. Used by permission.

Prayer Refrains

One way to involve people more actively in intercessory prayer is to use a sung prayer refrain. A refrain can be used before, during, or following a spoken prayer, or in place of a spoken prayer. Choruses, refrains, Scripture songs, even single lines of well-known hymns are very appropriate.

Consider the following suggestions:

General
"Alleluia" (PsH 640)
"Be Still and Know" (SFL 225)
"Lord, Be Glorified" (SFL 71)
"Lord, Listen to Your Children Praying" (PsH 625)
"O Lord Hear My Prayer" (*Renew!* 173, *Sing!*)

Advent and Christmas
"Come, Lord Jesus" (SFL 138)
"Come, Thou Long-Expected Jesus" (PsH 329)
"O Come Let Us Adore Him" (refrain from "O Come, All Ye Faithful") (PsH 340)

Lent
"O Christ, the Lamb of God" (PsH 257)
"Worthy is Christ/Digno Es Jesus" (PsH 629)

Easter
"Alleluia! Alleluia! Give Thanks" (refrain only) (PsH 402)
"The Strife is O'er, the Battle Done" ("Alleluia" refrain only) (PsH 391)

Pentecost
"Breathe on Me, Breath of God" (PsH 420)
"Spirit of the Living God" (PsH 424)

The songs listed above can be found in the following sources:

- *Psalter Hymnal* (PsH), © 1987, CRC Publications (1-800-333-8300)

- *Songs for LiFE* (SFL), © 1994, CRC Publications (1-800-333-8300)

- *Renew!* (*Renew!*), © 1995, Hope Publishing Company

—Adapted from Emily Brink, "Sung Prayer Refrains," *Reformed Worship* 52, p. 23. © 1999 by CRC Publications.

Prayer Requests

Perhaps the most common prayer ministry is to receive prayer requests from worshipers and then to remember their needs in prayer. People share their needs, concerns, petitions, testimonies, and thanksgivings for answered prayers, and often in the process generate a warm sense of intimacy with others in the church.

Some worship leaders walk down the aisles with a microphone, so people can directly share their request with the congregation. Others listen to the requests and then repeat them to the whole congregation.

A third option is to have people submit their requests on index cards prior to the service or at a special time during the service (for example, during the offering). After they are received, the pastor or pray-er should be given a few minutes to look through them. (This is done by singing an appropriate song or hymn as preparation to prayer.) This option has a number of benefits: it allows the worship leaders the most control and protection; it ensures that more time is spent in prayer and less time in simply sharing needs and requests; and it provides the opportunity to pass along the cards to the prayer warriors or prayer team for use during their weekly meeting.

There are also a number of other ways prayer requests can be received from the congregation. Consider the following ideas:

- Place an insert in the bulletin the Sunday before Thanksgiving requesting people to list the things they are thankful for. These expressions can be compiled, printed, and handed out on Thanksgiving Day and become the focus of a prayer of thanksgiving.

- Keep prayer request cards in the pews or brochure rack, and invite people to submit their requests (see Prayer Request Box, p. 206).

- Encourage worshipers to fill out prayer cards on the first Sunday of each month. These cards can be used throughout the month at Sunday services, at the weekly prayer meetings, and by the church's prayer warriors.

- Begin a prayer chain (see p. 345) in your sanctuary.

Prayer Slides

For a unique approach to a typical prayer service, project pictures of the prayer concerns on a screen. (For example, if you will be praying for your church's ministries, take pictures of the various ministries in action and convert them to slides. Or at Thanksgiving, project pictures of the things your congregation has expressed thanks for.) Slides tend to make prayer needs visual, concrete, and specific and thus can also make prayer more meaningful.

Slides can also be used as a guide to prayer. For example, if the prayer will consist of several parts, the new section could be quietly introduced by simply changing the slide. The slides might look like this:

- prayers for the church (a picture of the building or people at worship)

- prayers for families (a picture of a household or two in the church)

- prayers for the community (a picture of a street near your church)

- prayers for the government (a picture of a local government building or an easily recognized federal building)

- prayers for the harvest (a picture of a crowd of people)

Slides can also be used to put together a sight-sound program that teaches and promotes the practice of prayer. For example, a short program could be designed to illustrate the Lord's Prayer or to underscore the importance of praying in a small group.

With various technologies being more readily available, some churches may prefer to use video technology or a presentation program such as Microsoft Powerpoint. These opportunities are an excellent way to involve members of your congregation who are gifted in technology.

Prayers for Worship Leaders

In many congregations, one or more elders meet with the pastor before the worship service to pray for him or her, seek God's blessing on his or her leadership, and ask that God may provide open, receptive hearts. When the pastor is the sole worship leader, this is most appropriate.

In an increasing number of worship settings, more and more people are becoming involved: worship leaders, musicians, technicians, and so on. As a result, many of these churches are encouraging all worship leaders to join in prayer together before the service.

While most churches hold these prayer sessions in a quiet room close to the worship center, some churches hold them in the front of auditorium as a reminder to worshipers that the entire worship experience is being bathed in prayer.

Responsive Readings About Prayer

Responsive readings of Scripture provide an opportunity for people to be involved in the worship service. Instead of having the pastor simply read the Scripture passage before the message, set up the biblical passage as a responsive reading, as in the following example from Luke 11:1-10.

Leader: One day Jesus was praying in a certain place. When he finished, one of his disciples said to him,

People: "Lord, teach us to pray, just as John taught his disciples."

Leader: He said to them, "When you pray, say: 'Father, hallowed be your name, your kingdom come. Give us each day our daily bread. Forgive us our sins, for we also forgive everyone who sins against us. And lead us not into temptation.'"

Then he said to them, "Suppose one of you has a friend, and he goes to him and says, 'Friend, lend me three loaves of bread, because a friend of mine on a journey has come to me, and I have nothing to set before him.'

People: "Then the one inside answers, 'Don't bother me. The door is already locked, and my children are with me in bed. I can't get up and give you anything.'"

Leader: "I tell you, though he will not get up and give him the bread because he is his friend, yet because of the man's boldness he will get up and give him as much as he needs."

People: "So I say to you: Ask and it will be given to you; seek and you will find; knock and the door will be opened to you."

Leader: "For everyone who asks receives; he who seeks finds; and to him who knocks, the door will be opened."

Responsive Prayers

The book of Psalms is the worship and prayer book of the Bible. Many of the psalms are, or can easily be made into, prayers that can meaningfully be prayed responsively. Psalms 1, 2, 16, 19, 22, 23, 24, 27, 32, 33, 34, 40, 42, 46, 51, 65, 84, 90, 91, 95, 100, 103, 104, 110, 118, 121, 136, 139, and 145 work well.

Psalm 51 (A Prayer of Confession)

Leader: Have mercy on me, O God, according to your unfailing love;

People: according to your great compassion blot out my transgressions.

Leader: Wash away all my iniquity and cleanse me from my sin.

People: For I know my transgressions, and my sin is always before me.

Leader: Against you, you only, have I sinned and done what is evil in your sight,

People: so that you are proved right when you speak and justified when you judge.

Leader: Surely I was sinful at birth, sinful from the time my mother conceived me.

People: Surely you desire truth in the inner parts; you teach me wisdom in the inmost place.

Leader: Cleanse me with hyssop, and I will be clean; wash me, and I will be whiter than snow.

People: Let me hear joy and gladness; let the bones you have crushed rejoice. Hide your face from my sins and blot out all my iniquity.

Leader: Create in me a pure heart, O God, and renew a steadfast spirit within me.

People: Do not cast me from your presence or take your Holy Spirit from me.

Leader: Restore to me the joy of your salvation and grant me a willing spirit, to sustain me.

Soft Ending

The conclusion of most worship services is easy to identify. We sing a doxology, the pastor offers the benediction, and we are dismissed.

There is another way to end the worship service, called a soft ending. With a soft ending, the pastor invites worshipers to remain in the sanctuary if they so desire, departing when they feel that their worship or prayer is complete.

For those who remain in the sanctuary, a number of things may happen:

- Additional singing or played music continues, quietly and reflectively. After about fifteen to twenty minutes, the music concludes.

- Worshipers may be invited to come forward for prayer and meet with trained prayer teams.

- People may be invited to remain in their seats and continue to reflect and pray.

- An invitation may be given to come forward to talk about salvation and to commit one's life to Jesus Christ.

Solemn Assemblies

A solemn or sacred assembly is a gathering of God's people for the specific purpose of confessing personal, corporate, and national sins in order to seek God's forgiveness and to be restored to God (see sample service on pp. 383-384). This time of repentance and calling out to the Lord is based on several Old Testament passages, including 2 Chronicles 7:14; Joel 1:14; and Joel 2:15.

Throughout history, a movement of prayer and repentance has preceded every major spiritual revival. Israel repented from withholding offerings and tithes (Lev. 23:27; Joel 1:13; 2:14) as well as from the sin of promise-making without promise-keeping (Eccles. 5:4; Nahum 1:15).

A solemn assembly is a time of recommitment to the Word of God as the final authority (see Neh. 8:18); a time of refraining from daily work in order to pray (Lev. 23:28; Num. 29:35); and a time of fasting (Lev. 23:27). Solemn assemblies are often preceded by a time of preparation, personal confession, and prayer—especially by the leadership.

Resources

World Intercession Network
Bane and Barbara James
P.O. Box 12609
Oklahoma City, OK 73157
405-787-7110
fax: 405-789-3957

Ron Gaynor
3571 Castlehill Court
Atlanta, GA 30084-3202
770-934-4773

Teaching Through Music

An increasing amount of music, especially in the Christian contemporary music (CCM) arena, deals with prayer. Such songs can be useful for teaching about prayer, as well as for reminding us to spend daily time in prayer. This music can be used—with discernment—in worship for adoration and praise, reflection and meditation, and to teach about prayer. While much of this music is designed for solo and ensemble performance, some songs can also be sung by the congregation.

The following list of songs, their writers, and their producers is far from exhaustive, but is a good starting point:

"Amen" (Glad, Lifesong)

"Breathe on Us Again" (Steve Fry, Maranatha)

"Deep Is Our Hunger" (Michael James, Reunion)

"Down on My Knees" (Susan Ashton, Sparrow)

"Enter In" (Chuck Girard, Word)

"Heal Our Land" (Michael Card, Birdwing)

"Heavenly Father" (Cheri Keaggy, Sparrow)

"Heavy on My Heart" (Aaron Jeoffrey, River Oaks Music)

"Help Me Now" (Kathy Tricoli, Reunion)

"In the Wilderness" (Michael James, Reunion)

"I Will Call on You" (Steve Green, Birdwing)

"I Will Listen" (Twila Paris, Ariose Music)

"Journey" (Eric Champion, Brentwood)

"Let Us Pray" (Steven Curtis Chapman, Sparrow)

"Like a Child" (Jars of Clay, Brentwood Music Inc.)

"Listen to Our Hearts" (Geoff Moore and the Distance, Forefront Communications)

"Midnight Oil" (Phillips, Craig, and Dean, Starsong)

"On My Knees" (Willow Creek, Word)

"Shelter" (Jaci Velasquez, Myrrh)

"Slip Away" (Kim Hill, Dwelling Place)

"Stretch Out Your Hand" (Malcolm du Plessis/Scott Smith, Maranatha)

"That's When I Find You" (Sierra, Shepherd's Fold)

"The Father Hath Provided Again" (Larnelle Harris, Lifesong)

"Yours Alone" (Laury Browning, Benson)

eas

worship

WORSHIP SERVICES

Note: The songs in these worship services can be found in the following sources:

Psalter Hymnal (PsH), © 1987, CRC Publications (1-800-333-8300)

Songs for LiFE (SFL), © 1994, CRC Publications

Sing! A New Creation (Sing!), © 2001, CRC Publications

Renew! (Renew!), © 1995, Hope Publishing Company

The Presbyterian Hymnal (PH), © 1990, Westminster/John Knox Press

Trinity Hymnal (TH), © 1990, Great Commission Publications, Inc.

The Worshiping Church (TWC), © 1990, Hope Publishing Company

A.C.T.S. Prayer Service

Greetings and Welcome

Adoration

Scripture: Psalm 145:1-7 (read responsively)

Hymns

"Come Thou Fount of Every Blessing" (PsH 486, PH 356, TH 400, TWC 45)

"Beautiful Savior" (PsH 461)

Prayers of Adoration concluded by singing "Father, I Adore You" (PsH 284, SFL 28, TWC 4)

Confession

Scripture: Psalm 51:1-17

Prayers of Confession followed by a time of silent prayer and ending with singing "Jesu, Jesu, Fill Us with Your Love" (PsH 601, SFL 251, PH 367, TWC 436)

Thanksgiving

Scripture: Psalm 100

Hymns

"All Creatures of Our God and King" (PsH 431, SFL 86, PH 455, TWC 356)

"Let All Things Now Living" (PsH 453)

Prayers of Thanksgiving concluded by singing "We Praise You, O God" (PsH 237, TH 83)

Supplication

Scripture: John 14:12-14; Matthew 6:33; 7:7-8; 11:28-30; 1 John 5:14

Prayers of Supplication concluded by singing "Lord, Listen to Your Children Praying" (PsH 625, SFL 54, TWC 629)

Parting Blessing: Jude 24-25

—Sandy Boersma, "Building Community Through Prayer," *Reformed Worship* 52, p. 27. © 1999 by CRC Publications. Used by permission.

Celebration of God's Creation

(*Note:* This service uses prepared slides.)

The Beginning
Prelude
Welcome and Introduction

[*Lights are dimmed; a teenage girl reads the poem "The Earth Reflects God's Greatness" (see next page); seven or eight slides illustrate the theme.*]

Hymn: "All the Earth, Proclaim the Lord" (PsH 176, SFL 21)
    solo/choir on stanzas, all on refrain
The Greetings

God's Good Creation
Scripture: Psalm 24:1-6
Prayer of Adoration
Hymn: "Sing Praise to God Who Reigns Above" (PsH 465, PH 483)

Contamination by Sin
Confession

[*Two members read from the contemporary testimony* Our World Belongs to God *(see next page); five or six slides illustrate waste, pollution, death.*]

Hymn: "O Christ, the Lamb of God" (PsH 257, SFL 44)

Redeemed by Christ
Scripture: Ephesians 2:1-10
Hymn: "If You But Trust in God to Guide You" (PsH 446, SFL 210, PH 282, TH 670)
Prayer for Illumination
Scripture: Colossians 1:15-17

Message: "If He Made It for His Son . . ."
Hymn of Response: "Praise the Lord! O Heavens, Adore Him" (PsH 148, TH 17)
Prayers of the People

[*Spoken prayers are interspersed between the stanzas of "For the Beauty of the Earth" (PsH 432, SFL 89, TH 473, TH 116)*]

    Prayer to Our Awesome God
    [*sing stanza 1*]

    Prayer for Blessings on the Earth
    [*sing stanza 2*]

    Prayer for Blessing on Humanity
    [*sing stanza 3*]

    Prayer of Thanksgiving to God
    [*sing stanza 4*]

The New Heavens and the New Earth
[*Reading of Isaiah 65:17-25 accompanied by slides of sunset and sunrise.*]

The Closing
Benediction
Hymn: "Let All Things Now Living" (PsH 453, PH 554, TH 125)
Postlude

    —Jack Westerhof, "A Service for Prayer Day," *Reformed Worship* 43, pp. 34-35.
    © 1997 by CRC Publications.
    Used by permission.

The Earth Reflects God's Greatness

The earth reflects God's greatness;
his art is everywhere—
from tiny snowflake patterns
to flowers wondrous fair.
The mountains tell his power,
the streams his gentle ways,
he made the changing seasons
and thought of nights and days.

The earth reflects God's caring;
his creatures large and small
can find their food and shelter—
there is a place for all.
The people God created
received his special skill;
he made them in his image
with spirit, mind, and will.

The earth reflects God's mercy;
the marks of greed and gain
have hurt the world of beauty,
made many a barren plain.
And so he calls his people
to help him heal the earth,
to ease the pain and suffering
till love can bring rebirth.

Praise God for all earth's blessings;
praise him for time to live,
to think and be creative,
to care and share and give.
Praise to our friend and Savior,
the Christ, whose feet have trod
this earth—he knows our weakness,
forgives, and shows us God.

—Marion Settle, 1988.
Published in *Rural Gleanings.*
Used by permission.

When humans no longer show God's image,
all creation suffers.
We abuse the creation or idolize it.
We are estranged from our Creator,
from our neighbor, and from all that God has
     made.

All spheres of life—
marriage and family, work and worship, school
     and state, our play and art—
bear the wounds of our rebellion.
Sin is present everywhere—
in pride of race,
in arrogance of nations,
in abuse of the weak and helpless.
in disregard for water, air and soil,
in destruction of living creatures,
in slavery, deceit, terror, and war,
in worship of false gods,
and frantic escape from reality.
We have become victims of our own sin.

—*Our World Belongs to God: A Contemporary
Testimony*, stanzas 16-17

Concert of Prayer

(*Note:* Taking seven to eight minutes for each section will extend this service to a full hour. The worshipers should be placed into groups of six to eight in order to facilitate more praying and participation.)

Welcome
Explanation of the Service

Part One: Adoration
Scripture: Psalm 47:2, 7-8; Leviticus 10:3
A short spoken prayer of adoration by the leader
Instruction: "Take time in your small group to offer your thoughts of praise and worship to God."
Response: "Father, I Adore You" (PsH 284, SFL 28, TWC 4)

Part Two: Confession
Scripture: Habakkuk 3:2
A short spoken prayer of confession by the leader
Instruction: "Ask the Spirit to search your heart and reveal any areas of unconfessed sin. Silently acknowledge these to the Lord and thank him for his forgiveness."
Response: "Create in Me a Clean Heart" (SFL 41, *Renew!* 181)

Part Three: Renewal
Scripture: 1 Thessalonians 5:16-18; Philippians 3:10-11
A short spoken prayer for renewal by the leader
Instruction: "Pause to add your own prayers for personal renewal."
Response: "Be Thou My Vision" (*Renew!* 151, PH 339, TH 642, TWC 532)

Part Four: Petition
Scripture: Psalm 61:1-4
A short spoken prayer of petition by the leader
Instruction: "Pause here to petition God for growth in your desire to know and please Jesus Christ. Pray for great love and commitment to him, for the grace to practice his presence and for the grace to glorify him in your life. Offer prayers regarding your activities for this day and any special concerns you may have."
Response: "In My Life, Lord, Be Glorified" (SFL 71, TWC 537, *Sing!*)

Part Five: Intercession
Scripture: Ephesians 4:4-6
A short spoken prayer of intercession by the leader
Instruction: "Take a few moments to intercede on behalf of your local church, other churches, educational ministries, your unchurched neighbors, leaders in government, and any other special concerns you may have."
Response: "Seek Ye First" (PsH 209, SFL 155, TWC 447)

Part Six: Affirmation
Scripture: 1 Samuel 15:29; Psalm 3:3; 2 Peter 3:9
A short spoken prayer of affirmation by the leader
Instruction: "Pause to reflect on these biblical affirmations."
Response: "Tell Out, My Soul" (PsH 478, *Renew!* 130, TWC 350)

Part Seven: Thanksgiving

Scripture: Psalm 118:28-29

A short spoken prayer of thanksgiving by the leader

Instruction: "Pause to offer your own expressions of thanksgiving."

Response: "Give Thanks" (*Renew!* 266, TWC 496, *Sing!*)

Part Eight: Closing

Scripture: Psalm 95:1-2; Psalm 96:1-3

A short spoken prayer of closing by the leader

Response: "Hallelujah, Praise the Lord" (PsH 189, SFL 24, *Renew!* 119)

—Adapted from the outline and
Scripture texts provided
by Cal Compagner.

Lectio Divina Service

Prelude
Welcome and Explanation

Gathering Songs
  "We Praise You, O God" (PsH 237, TH 97, TWC 377)
  "Father, We Love You" (PsH 634, SFL 77, TWC 10)

Reading (Lectio)
Scripture: John 17:9
Prayer for Illumination
Message: "Pray for Me"
Prayer of Application

Meditation (Meditatio)
Silent Prayer/Breathing Prayer

Inhale	*Exhale*
Lord Jesus Christ	Have mercy on me
Jesus increase	Self decrease
Spirit of God	Spirit of self
Mind of the Spirit	Lust of the flesh
Glory of God	Pride of life
Triune God	[your name]

Readings from Scripture of Christ Praying
Song: "As the Deer" (Renew! 9, Sing!)
Silent Praying
Song: "Be Still and Know" (SFL 225, Renew! 10, TWC 516)

Prayer (Oratio)
Reading: John 17:18
Prayers of the People

Contemplation (Contemplatio)
Quiet Music

Offering
Song: "Step by Step" (Sing!)
Blessing

—Clifford Bajema's book *At One With Jesus: Rediscovering the Secret of Lectio Divina* (CRC Publications, 1988) was helpful with the formation of this service.

Lord's Prayer Service

A Hymn Festival Using the Heidelberg Catechism to Reflect on the Lord's Prayer

(*Note:* To introduce each section of the service, the worship leader should say, "Together we pray . . ." and the congregation respond in unison with the next line of the prayer.)

Prelude: Variations on *Vater Unser* (Our Father)

Call to Worship: "Built on the Rock" (TWC 705)
    (stanzas 1-2, choir)
    (stanza 3, all)

Opening Prayer

Greetings

Our Father in Heaven
Choir: "Our Father, Clothed with Majesty" (stanza 1) (PsH 562)

Leader: Why did Christ command us to call God "our Father?"
People: At the very beginning of our prayer
      Christ wants to kindle in us
      what is basic to our prayer—
          the childlike awe and trust
          that God through Christ has become
      our Father.

      Our fathers do not refuse us
          the things of this life;
      God our Father will even less refuse to give us
          what we ask in faith.

                       (Heidelberg Catechism, Q&A 120)

Leader: Why the words "in heaven"?
People: These words teach us
      not to think of God's heavenly majesty
          as something earthly,
      and to expect everything
          for body and soul
          from his almighty power.

                       (Heidelberg Catechism, Q&A 121)

Hymn: "Children of the Heavenly Father" (PsH 440, TH 131, TWC 84)

Hallowed Be Your Name
Choir: "Our Father, Clothed with Majesty" (stanza 2)

Leader: What does the first request mean?
People: *Hallowed be your name means,*

Help us to really know you,
to bless, worship, and praise you
   for all your works
   and for all that shines forth from them:
     your almighty power, wisdom, kindness,
     justice, mercy, and truth.

And it means,

Help us to direct all our living—
   what we think, say, and do—
so that your name will never be blasphemed because of us
but always honored and praised.

(Heidelberg Catechism, Q&A 122)

Hymn: "Holy God, We Praise Your Name" (PsH 504, PH 460, TH 103, TWC 3)
   (stanzas 1-2, choir)
   (stanza 3, choir, with all joining on "And from morn to set of sun . . .")
   (stanza 4, all)

Your Kingdom Come
Choir: "Our Father, Clothed with Majesty" (stanza 3)

Leader: What does the second request mean?
People: *Your kingdom come means,*

Rule us by your Word and Spirit in such a way
   that more and more we submit to you.

Keep your church strong, and add to it.

Destroy the devil's work;
destroy every force which revolts against you
and every conspiracy against your Word.

Do this until your kingdom is so complete and perfect
   that in it you are
all in all.

(Heidelberg Catechism, Q&A 123)

Hymn: "Lead On, O King Eternal" (PsH 555, PH 447, TH 580, TWC 747)

Your Will Be Done on Earth as It Is in Heaven
Choir: "Our Father, Clothed with Majesty" (stanza 4)

Leader: What does the third request mean?
People: *Your will be done on earth as it is in heaven means,*

Help us and all people
    to reject our own wills
    and to obey your will without any back talk.
Your will alone is good.

Help us one and all to carry out the work we are called to,
    as willingly and faithfully as the angels in heaven.
(Heidelberg Catechism, Q&A 124)

Hymn: "Breathe on Me, Breath of God" (PsH 420, PH 316, TH 334, TWC 295)

Scripture

Message

Give Us Today Our Daily Bread
Choir: "Our Father, Clothed with Majesty" (stanza 5)

Leader: What does the fourth request mean?
People: *Give us today our daily bread* means,

Do take care of all our physical needs
so that we come to know
    that you are the only source of everything good,
    and that neither our work and worry
    nor your gifts
    can do us any good without your blessing.

And so help us to give up our trust in creatures
And to put trust in you alone.
(Heidelberg Catechism, Q&A 125)

Solo: "Give Us This Day Our Daily Bread" (PsH 290)

Offering

Offertory: Variation on *Vater Unser* (Our Father)

Forgive Us Our Debts, as We Also Have Forgiven Our Debtors
Choir: "Our Father, Clothed with Majesty" (stanza 6)

Leader: What does the fifth request mean?
People: *Forgive us our debts,*
      as we have forgiven our debtors means,

Because of Christ's blood,
do not hold against us, poor sinners that we are,
    any of the sins we do
    or the evil that constantly clings to us.

Forgive us just as we are fully determined,
    as evidence of your grace in us,
to forgive our neighbors.
(Heidelberg Catechism, Q&A 126)

Hymn: "Forgive Our Sins As We Forgive" (PsH 266, PH 347, TH 494)

And Lead Us Not into Temptation, but Deliver Us from the Evil One
Choir: "Our Father, Clothed with Majesty" (stanza 7)

Leader: What does the sixth request mean?
People: *And lead us not into temptation,*
but deliver us from the evil one means,

By ourselves we are too weak
to hold our own even for a moment.

And our sworn enemies—
the devil, the world, and our own flesh—
never stop attacking us.

And so, Lord,
uphold us and make us strong
with the strength of your Holy Spirit,
so that we may not go down to defeat
in this spiritual struggle,
but may firmly resist our enemies
until we finally win the complete victory.

(Heidelberg Catechism, Q&A 127)

Hymn: "Lead Me, Guide Me" (PsH 544, *Renew!* 176)

For Yours Is the Kingdom, and the Power, and the Glory Forever
Choir: "Our Father, Clothed with Majesty" (stanza 8)

Leader: What does your conclusion to this prayer mean?
People: *For yours is the kingdom*
and the power
and the glory forever means,

We have made all these requests of you
because, as our all-powerful king,
you not only want to,
but are able to give us all that is good;
and because your holy name,
and not we ourselves,
should receive all the praise, forever.

(Heidelberg Catechism Q&A 128)

Doxology: "To God Be the Glory" (PsH 632, TWC 46)

Benediction

Postlude: Variations on *Vater Unser* (Our Father)

—"The Lord's Prayer," *Reformed Worship* 20, pp. 42-43.
© 1991 by CRC Publications. Used by permission.

Prayers for Crops and Industry

We Gather for Worship
Prelude

Welcome

Opening Sentences (2 Cor. 4:5-7, 16-18)

Leader: We do not preach ourselves, but Jesus Christ as Lord, and ourselves as your servants for Jesus' sake.
People: For God, who said, "Let light shine out of darkness," made his light shine in our hearts to give us the light of the knowledge of the glory of God in the face of Christ.
Leader: But we have this treasure in jars of clay to show that this all-surpassing power is from God and not from us.
People: Therefore we do not lose heart. Though outwardly we are wasting away, yet inwardly we are being renewed day by day. For our light and momentary troubles are achieving for us an eternal glory that far outweighs them all.
Leader: So we fix our eyes not on what is seen, but on what is unseen. For what is seen is temporary, but what is unseen is eternal.

Hymn: "Amid the Thronging Worshipers" (PsH 239, TWC 340)

Opening Prayer

We Bow in Penitence
Call to Confession (Joel 2:12-14, 17)

Leader: God calls us to confess as he called his people through his prophet Joel:
"'Even now,' declares the Lord,
    'return to me with all your heart,
    with fasting and weeping and mourning.'
Rend your heart
    and not your garments.
Return to the LORD your God
    for he is gracious and compassionate,
slow to anger and abounding in love,
    and he relents from sending calamity.'
People: Who knows? He may turn and have pity
    and leave behind a blessing . . ."

Leader: People of God, do you weep for your sin?

People: Before God and his people, we declare that we have sinned.

Leader: "'Spare your people, O LORD.
> Do not make your inheritance an object of scorn,
> > a byword among the nations.
> Why should they say among the peoples,
> > "Where is their God?"'"

Declaration of Pardon (Joel 2:18-21, 23, 26-27)

Leader: "The LORD will be jealous for his land
> > and take pity on his people, [saying],
> 'I am sending you grain, new wine and oil,
> > enough to satisfy you fully;
> never again will I make you
> > an object of scorn to the nations.'"

People: "Surely he has done great things.
> Be not afraid, O land;
> > be glad and rejoice.
> Surely the Lord has done great things.

Leader: Be glad, O people of Zion,
> > rejoice in the LORD your God,
> for he has given you
> > the autumn rains in righteousness.
> He sends you abundant showers,
> > both autumn and spring rains, as before.

People: 'You will have plenty to eat, until you are full,
> > and you will praise the name of the LORD your God,
> > who has worked wonders for you;
> never again will my people be ashamed.'"

Leader: Then you will know that I am in Israel,
> > that I am the LORD your God,
> > and that there is no other;
> never again will my people be shamed.

Hymn: "Lord, You Have Lavished on Your Land" (PsH 85)

We Hear the Word

Prayer for Illumination (Joel 2:28-29)

Leader: Lord, you spoke through your prophet Joel:
> "I will pour out my Spirit on all people.
> Your sons and daughters will prophesy,
> > your old men will dream dreams,
> > your young men will see visions.
> Even on my servants, both men and women,
> > I will pour out my Spirit in those days."

People: You have called us to be your servants, Lord—young and old, men and women. Pour out your spirit on us so that we may hear your word and do your will.

Hymn: "Spirit of the Living God" (PsH 424, SFL 184, *Renew!* 90, PH 322, TH 726, TWC 297)

The Word of God for Children: Children's Message

The Word of God for Crops

Old Testament Readings: Genesis 1:11-12; Amos 4:7-9; Isaiah 35:1-2; 41:17-20
New Testament Readings: 1 Corinthians 15:37-38; Hebrews 6:7-8; Romans 11:33-36

Meditation on Crops

Prayer for Crops

Lord, you make a pink flower from a gray seed, an ear from a kernel, a carrot from a seed the size of a pinhead, an oak tree from an acorn. You have programmed your soil to provide food for your plants, wooden trees to make apples, feathered hens to lay eggs, grass-eating cows to give milk. And you, grand Creator, you have us take care of your grand creation.

In mercy, Lord, send rain to water our crops and gardens. Let your sun shine on our fields so that seeds will produce abundantly, so that vines and stalks and trees will hang heavy with fruit and grain. And Lord, let your grace be rich to our cattle as it is to us; let it keep our hogs free of disease, our hens laying eggs, and our cows giving milk. May our animals be fertile; may our lambs and calves and pigs frolic in your green pastures so that even in their play we may see your grace.

Help us to live on your good earth even as Adam and Eve in Eden—preserving and caring for the life and soil you bless, ever thankful that for our good, you gave your laws of nature and your law of love. Help us for our good and your glory to see those laws as you see them and as the psalmist saw them—as good and perfect, pleasant to think about.

And Lord, teach us to share the abundance you have given us, never gloating in our excess, but always giving our first bushels to feed the hungry in your name. Enlighten our hearts, Lord, so that our thank yous ever rise in a crescendo to your throne. See and hear us through the blood of your Son, Jesus. Amen.

Hymn: "We Plow the Fields and Scatter" (PsH 456)

The Word of God for Industry

Old Testament Readings: Genesis 11:1-8; 14:21-24; Exodus 1:6-14; 5:1-6:1; Proverbs 6:6-11; 26:13-16; Ecclesiastes 3:9-14
New Testament Readings: Matthew 4:1-11; Acts 19:23-41

Meditation on Industry

Prayer for Industry

Lord, you saw the wheel in your mind before we saw it roll on your good earth. You put iron in the bowels of your earth and imagined the great girders that would hold up bridges over land and sea. You heard the motor in your mind before we revved it up on our roads. You saw the computer chip before we harnessed it in our offices and the laser before we discovered how to use it for blasting mines or for performing delicate surgery.

Now bless our hands as we manipulate the machines we have made. Teach us how to use them wisely so that we will not be used by them. Bless our grinding and polishing, our honing and our hammering. Let our demands for precise and careful work be as rigorous as yours so that we may rest as safely in our cars and places as in your arms.

Help us in all this, Lord, with joy and thanks, to see your upholding hand, great Creator of metal and mountain, master artist of the sunset and rainbow. May we not sit on foam rubber without feeling your grace or read by a light bulb without feeling a current of thankfulness for your marvelous creation running through our veins.

Hear our prayer for your Son's sake. Amen.

Hymn: "Earth and All Stars" (PsH 433)

The Word of God for Life
   Old Testament Readings: Ecclesiastes 5:10-12, 18-20
   New Testament Readings: John 4:7-38; 12:23-26; Luke 12:22-34 or Matthew 6:25-34; Hebrews 11:26-27

   Prayer (Pray that we may live and work to serve God and obey him in everything.)

   Hymn: "Seek Ye First the Kingdom" (PsH 209, SFL 155, TWC 447)

Offering

Benediction

Parting Hymn: "This Is My Father's World" (PsH 436, SFL 95, PH 293, TH 111, TWC 384)

Postlude

> —Mike VandenBosch, "We Live and Work in God's World," *Reformed Worship* 14, pp. 38-39. © 1989 by CRC Publications. Used by permission.

Prayers for Healing

(During evening prayers, four prayer teams are stationed in the four corners of the worship center, each team consisting of two persons. In most cases one of the members of the team is an elder. They simply listen to the prayer need, offer a prayer, and provide a word of encouragement. With the person's permission, they also hold hands during prayer and offer a parting embrace. Ideally, prayer team members have the gift of intercession, compassion, discernment, or faith.)

Prelude

Song: "It Is Good to Sing Your Praises" (PsH 171, TWC 325)

Opening Prayer

Song: "Precious, Lord, Take My Hand"

Welcome and Mutual Greeting

Scripture: 1 Peter 4

Message: "The Walking Wounded"

Song: "My Jesus, I Love Thee" (PsH 557, *Renew!* 275, TH 648, TWC 101)
   (During this song the offering is received.)

Evening Prayers
   Announcement of procedure
      "You are welcome to walk up to a prayer team, share your need, and receive prayer. Throughout the prayer time, those of you who remain seated are encouraged to pray."

(*Note:* Piano, organ, violin, flute, and/or harp may provide quiet reflective background music while people are praying. You may also invite worshipers to sing prayerfully and reflectively. Select sufficient music for 20-30 minutes of prayer.)

Concluding Song: "Lord, Listen to Your Children Praying" (PsH 625, SFL 54, TWC 629)

Words of Blessing

Postlude

Prayers for the Nation

(*Note:* This service is most appropriate prior to a national election.)

Prelude

Worship

Songs

"Holy, Holy, Holy/Santo, Santo, Santo" (SFL 66, *Renew!* 208)

"Holy, Holy, Holy Is the Lord of Hosts" (*Renew!* 205)

"Come Let Us Worship God" (*Sing!*)

Opening Prayer

Mutual Greeting

Confession

Song: "In an Age of Twisted Values" (*Sing!*)

Offering

Word

Scripture: 2 Chronicles 6:12-13; 7:14

Message: "Can You Imagine . . ."

Response: "Heal Our Land" (solo)

Prayers

National

Prayer (offered by a member of the congregation)

Silence (two to three minutes for personal praying)

Response: "Hear Our Prayer, O Lord" (PsH 624)

State/Province

Prayer

Silence

Response: "Hear Our Prayer, O Lord"

Local

Prayer

Silence

Response: "Hear Our Prayer, O Lord"

Issues (abortion, crime, economy, education, family, harvest, the lost, peace, and so on)
Prayer
Silence
Response: "Hear Our Prayer, O Lord"

Conclusion: "Lord, Listen to Your Children Praying" (PsH 625, SFL 54, TWC 629)
Words of Blessing
Postlude

Prayers of the People

Prelude

Scripture Reading: Isaiah 56:7

Prayer

Song: "Come All You People" (*Sing!*)

Opening Sentences

Leader: Praise the Lord. How good it is to sing praises to our God, how pleasant and fitting to praise him! (Ps. 147:1)

People: I rejoiced with those who said to me, "Let us go to the house of the Lord." Our feet are standing in your gates, O Jerusalem. (Ps. 122:2)

Leader: The Lord builds up Jerusalem; he gathers the exiles of Israel. He heals the broken-hearted and binds up their wounds. (Ps. 147:2-3)

People: Great is our Lord and mighty in power; his understanding has no limit. (Ps. 147:5)

Song: "Sing a New Song to the Lord" (*Renew!* 113)

Prayers
(Note: Each of the following prayers may be led by a member of the congregation/community. Or, provide an open microphone and encourage worshipers to pray short prayers after the topic is announced.)

Prayer for World and Nation
Prayer for Economy (business) and Harvest (agriculture)
Prayer for Schools and Civic Organizations

Song: "I Lift My Eyes Up" (*Sing!*)

Prayer for Community and the Lost
Prayer for Home and Family
Prayer for Christ's Church and Ministry

Thanksgiving and Praise
Song: "Listen to My Cry, Lord" (PsH 61)

Offering

Closing Song: "Praise God, from Whom All Blessings Flow" (PsH 637, *Renew!* 83, PH 592, TH 731, TWC 809)

Blessing

Leader: We have been in communion with the Lord. Go forth in the strength and assurance that the Lord Jesus Christ goes with you. And all God's people said:

People: Amen.

Postlude

Service of Prayer After Fasting

Preparation

Time for Meditation: Ask yourself, "Why am I here? What does God want of me? How can I be part of building his kingdom?"

Moments of Welcome and Explanation

Prayer

Dear God, silence all voices within my mind but your own. Help me to seek and be able to follow your will. May my prayers be joined with those of my sisters and brothers in the faith, that together we may glorify your name and enjoy your fellowship forever. In Jesus' name, Amen.

Adoration

Scripture: Psalm 95:1-7

Song: "You Are Worthy" (PsH 232)

Unison Prayer

"Holy, holy, holy is the Lord God Almighty! All honor and praise and glory and majesty and wisdom and power are due your name, O Lord, now and forevermore. Amen."

Silent Prayers of Praise

Prayers of the People

Confession

Scripture: 1 John 1:8-9

Song: "O Christ, the Lamb of God" (PsH 257)

Unison Prayer

O God of mercy, you sent your only Son to save us from the pain of guilt and sting of death. We carry the burden of our wrongs; the things we should not have done, and the things we have failed to do. Take this burden from us, O Lord. Cleanse our hearts from sin and restore to us the joy of salvation; through Jesus who suffered for us. Amen.

Silent Prayers of Confession

Pastoral Assurance of Pardon

Thanksgiving

Scripture: Philippians 1:3-11

Song: "Lord, I Want to Be a Christian" (PsH 264, PH 372)

Litany

Leader: Gracious God, for causing light to come from darkness, for creating all things through your Word, for giving us a home on earth, and for the joy of living,

People: We give you thanks, O Lord.

Leader: For speaking through the Law and the Prophets and for revealing yourself through your Son Jesus Christ,

People: We give you thanks, O Lord.

Leader: For Christ's loving sacrifice, the forgiveness of sins and the promise of eternal life,

People: We give you thanks, O Lord.

Leader: For the apostles and their teachings and for the church universal,

People: We give you thanks, O Lord.

Leader: For Luther and Zwingli, Calvin and Knox, and all others who in every age seek to rekindle the faith,

People: We give you thanks, O Lord.

Leader: For [Edwin Crawford] and the charter members of [Cleveland Drive Presbyterian Church], for their vision and commitment,

People: We give you thanks, O Lord.

Leader: For [Lloyd Ellis] and the continued ministry of the church, for officers and staff of the past and present,

People: We give you thanks, O Lord.

Leader: For your steadfast love and faithfulness and our sure hope for the future,

People: We give you thanks, O Lord.
May our lives, our wills, and our deeds be a continual thank offering to you, O Lord, through Jesus Christ. Amen.

Silent Prayers of Thanksgiving

Pastoral Prayer

Supplication

Scripture: 1 Peter 5:6-11

Song: "Seek Ye First" (PsH 209, PH 333)

Unison Prayer

Almighty God, in this world we are under great pressure. We are weak and weary. Strengthen our faith so that by the power of your Holy Spirit we may overcome temptation and persevere through trials; through Jesus Christ our Lord and Savior. Amen.

Silent Prayers of Supplication

Pastoral Prayer

Intercession

Scripture: Matthew 18:18-20

Song: "Lord, Listen to Your Children Praying" (PsH 625, SFL 54)

Unison Prayer

Heavenly Father, we seek your Spirit to help us in our weakness and to enable us to pray as we ought. May we be instruments of your will and channels of your love. We pray for our church and its ministry, that we may be faithful to Christ now and in the future. We seek a vision of what you would have us be and do. Hear our prayers, for we pray with confidence in Jesus' name. Amen.

Extemporaneous Prayers of Intercession

Pastoral Prayer

Magnification

Scripture: Psalm 34:1-3

Song: "Bless His Holy Name" (PsH 627)

Benediction

—Jeffrey Carlson, "Fasting to Focus," *Reformed Worship* 19, pp. 30-31.
© 1991 by CRC Publications. Used by permission.

Solemn Assembly

Prelude

Silence

Trumpet Fanfare (see Ex. 19:16)

Reading of the Law (Ex. 20:1-17)

Response: "Remember Not, O God" (PsH 254, TH 488)

Opening Prayer

Welcome and Explanation

Praise and Worship
  "Come, O Come" (*Sing!*)
  "As the Deer" (*Renew!* 9, *Sing!*)
  "You Are My Hiding Place" (*Renew!* 107, *Sing!*)

Corporate Confession
Leader: "Surely the arm of the Lord is not too short to save, nor his ear to dull to hear.
People: But your iniquities have separated you from your God; your sins have hidden his face from you." (Isa. 59:1-2)
Leader: "When I shut up the heavens so there is no rain, or command locusts to devour the land, or send a plague among my people,
People: if my people, who are called by my name, will humble themselves and pray and seek my face and turn from their wicked ways, then I will hear from heaven and will forgive their sin and will heal their land." (2 Chron. 7:13-14)
Leader: "Seek the Lord while he may be found; call on him while he is near. Let the wicked forsake his way and the evil man his thoughts. Let him turn to the Lord, and he will have mercy on him, and to our God, for he will freely pardon." (Isa. 55:6-7)
People: (singing) "Seek Ye First" (first stanza only; may be repeated several times) (PsH 209, PH 333)
Leader: "For this is what the high and lofty One says—he who lives forever, whose name is holy: 'I live in a high and holy place, but also with him who is contrite and lowly in spirit, to revive the spirit of the lowly and to revive the heart of the contrite.'" (Isa. 57:15)
People: (singing) "Create in Me a Clean Heart" (SFL 41, *Renew!* 181)
Leader: "Restore to me the joy of your salvation and grant me a willing spirit, to sustain me. Then I will teach transgressors your ways, and sinners will turn back to you. O, Lord, open my lips, and my mouth will declare your praise." (Ps. 51:12-13, 15)

People: (singing) "Open Our Eyes, Lord" (*Renew!* 91, TWC 536, *Sing!*)

Leader: "The sacrifices of God are a broken spirit; a broken and a contrite heart, O God, you will not despise." (Ps. 51:17)

Offering
(Other forms of offering may be substituted in place of a monetary offering.)

Scripture: Nehemiah 8:1-6; 9:1-3; Psalm 139

Message: "A Solemn Soul Search"

Personal Prayers of Confession and Recommitment
Forgive us for any of the ways that we have harmed or hindered your church. We repent of the sins that have damaged . . .

. . . *the Unity of the Church*
   —pride, bitterness, anger, gossip
   —mistrust of the leadership
   —a critical spirit

. . . *the Mission of the Church*
   —not trusting God to provide
   —failure to be fully influenced by the grace of God
   —failure to share the grace of God with others

. . . *our Service to your Church*
   —our lack of servant leadership
   —the withholding of our resources: time, talents, treasures
   —our unwillingness to be fully obedient

. . . *the Worship of your Church*
   —a self-reliant spirit
   —a controlling spirit
   —a critical spirit

. . . *the Faith and Fellowship of Your Church*
   —failure to follow God's call in home, work, and church
   —failure to pray caused by an independent spirit
   —avoiding responsibility as members of Christ's body to be mutually accountable for our moral and spiritual lives
   —depending more on pragmatic rather than biblical principles
   —following patterns of sexual immorality
   —relying on ourselves instead of God
   —failing to love the world as God "so loved the world"
   —allowing busyness for God to be a substitute for intimacy with God

Silence

Assurance of Pardon: 1 John 1:8-9

Song: "Sanctuary" (*Renew!* 185)

Blessing

Postlude

DRAMAS AND READINGS
The Benefits of Nagging

(Based on Luke 18:1-8.)

Theme: Persistence is a benefit in prayer.

Cast: Two women and one man

Setting: Gertie sits on a single chair center stage and speaks with the audience. She drinks coffee, knits, and fidgets as she talks.

Gertie: So . . . nice of you to drop by. Really appreciate this chance to talk. I'm a real talker, you know. Love to talk. I remember my boss down at work once gave me a present he said fit me just right. I opened the box and there was one of those phony sets of teeth chatterin' away. A real kidder, Mr. Slocum. (*chuckles*) Anyway, how are things? Don't ask me how things are. I'll tell you a story that'll keep you here all day. Take the other day, for instance. I was out driving to the store at my usual slow rate. After all, what's the hurry? You know what I mean? Behind me is this young upstart of a driver using my classic Chevrolet as his ornament. I looked in my rearview mirror and, sure enough, it looked like the guy was in my back seat. Well, anyway . . . (*Lucy enters*) Well, Lucy, you could have knocked.

Lucy: Gertie McCarty, you have a big mouth.

Gertie: (*to audience*) What did I tell ya?

Lucy: Listen here. Gertie. I've had it with you. I worked long and hard for that auxiliary presidency. None worked harder than I did. And we all agreed that we wouldn't campaign. We'd just let people decide for themselves. I go away for a two-week vacation, come back, and everybody's talking about you, Gertie McCarty, as just right for the job.

Gertie: All I did was make a few phone calls.

Lucy: A *few* phone calls? Fess up, Gertie. How many auxiliary members did you call to sell yourself, to campaign your way into auxiliary hierarchy?

Gertie: I didn't keep a tally, Lucy.

Lucy: Come on, Gertie. How many?

Gertie: Maybe thirty.

Lucy: (*steaming*) Maybe thirty! That's the whole membership! Gertie, I know you through and through. You probably talked to those gals till you were blue in the face and they were so sick of your voice that they promised you their vote just to get you off the phone.

Gertie: Well, I never!

Lucy: Don't give me that, you, you politician, you! You jawboner! (*begins to exit in a huff*) You wheeler-dealer, you! (*exits*)

Gertie: (*gathers her composure*) Lucy is highly excitable, you know. So what if I did make a few calls? It worked, didn't it? Anyway, where was I? So . . . I'm riding in my Chevrolet with this hot-rodder on my tail. I'm feeling so pressured that when I come to this intersection, the light is turning red, and I'm too flustered to stop. So I drive on through to save my Chevrolet. You follow, don't you? The guy would have been wearing me for decorations if I hadn't. Well, sure enough, right there was a cop. And right away I saw his lights flashing. About a mile up Main I finally decide to pull over for him. Well, how was I to know he wanted me? I'll tell you, I taught that young officer something about the driver's side of things. I . . . (*knock is heard*) Sorry about this. (*goes to door*) Yes? Well, Mr. Brewster, it's about time you show up. Come on in. (*Brewster enters*)

Bob: I can't stay, Mrs. McCarty. I just came to let you know we surrender.

Gertie: Well, what do you know! What brought the change of mind, Bob?

Bob: Mrs. McCarty, in all my years in the grocery business, I've never seen a more persistent woman. The potato chips were of poor quality by your standards so you demanded your money back. Then you called every day when we refused, until we really couldn't bother with you any more. Worse yet were those letters to the Consumer's Service, the Better Business Bureau, and the district manager. (*takes out white handkerchief*) Mrs. McCarty, we surrender. Here's your eighty-nine cents. Now will you kindly leave us alone?

Gertie: Well, I'm just glad you came to your senses. My next tactic was a letter to the editor of the Gazette.

Bob: Let's lay it to rest, ma'am, OK?

Gerte: Sure.

Bob: Good-bye, Mrs. McCarty. (*begins to exit*)

Gertie: So long, Bob. See you down at the store.

Bob: If you'd like to shop somewhere else, it's certainly OK with us. (*exits*)

Gertie: Anyway . . . the young officer has me pulled over. He stands at my window and demands my license and my registration as if I were some kind of criminal. He has an angry look on his face as if running a red light were a felony or something. So I put the old choppers into action. In no time I had that fella swimming in a pool of talk-talk-talk. I explained about my Chevrolet, how dear it was to me. I explained about the tailgater. I explained in detail my fine driving record. I ignored every move he made to get my license. I told him about cousin Jim on the force, how the mayor and Mr. McCarty are such good friends. I mean, I pulled every stop! And you know what? The guy finally started smiling at me. Imagine that! He even laughed when I mentioned that Elliot Ness was a distant relative. Well, to make a long story short, I was insulted enough just to be pulled off the road with those lights flashing. Anyway, the officer just smiled and said, "Lady, just get in your car, and the next time you decide to run a light, do it when I'm not around, OK?!" And that was it.

I'll tell you, it pays to be persistent. Makes you wonder sometimes, doesn't it? It's a shame you have to be that way in a world like this, but what's a soul to do when people leave you no other choice? You just gotta work for what you get. There's no gettin' around it. Right? Well, isn't that right?! *(no answer)* You're all too busy thinkin' about what happens next, aren't you? *(gathers belongings)* Well, I'll tell you this, you ain't gonna get ahead sittin' there sayin' nothin'. And that's the truth! *(exits)*

—*Resources for Youth Ministry: Gifting,* © 1980, Board of Youth Ministry of the Missouri Synod Lutheran Church. Used by permission.

God and the IRS

Theme: God answers prayer.
Cast: Four teenage males
Setting: Teenager's bedroom or family recreation room

Scene 1

Jim: Hi, Mike. What's the matter? You look a little down.

Mike: Oh, hi, Jim. Yeah, I'm down all right. Tomorrow's the deadline for paying my tuition and I'm just not gonna be able to come up with the cash. So . . . school's out for me, I guess. It's back to the salt mines . . .

Jim: That's a shame. What about your folks? Can they help?

Mike: No not really. My dad's been out of work the last couple of months, and they're gonna need whatever cash they have just to live on.

Jim: Can you get a loan somewhere?

Mike: I've already tried. No luck. My credit's not good, my dad's credit is no good, and I still haven't paid off the last loan I managed to con the bank out of.

Jim: How much do you need?

Mike: $750. Cash, check, or money order.

Jim: Wow. That's a lot of dough.

(enter Bob)

Bob: Hi guys. What's new?

Mike: 750 bucks. That's what new.

Bob: Huh?

Jim: He means if he doesn't come up with 750 bucks by tomorrow, it's back to washing dishes at Mabel's.

Bob: Sorry to hear about it, Mike. Lucky for me, my old man has plenty of money. He just writes the school a check every year—no sweat.

Jim: Yeah, me too. Thank God for dads.

Mike: Well, that's great for you, but what about me? What am I gonna do?

Bob: Have you had much experience robbing banks?

Mike: Yeah, right. This is serious. (enter Pete) Hey Pete, you got 750 bucks you want to get rid of?

Pete: Hi Mike, hi guys. 750 bucks? What are you talking about? I couldn't afford a ticket to a free lunch.

Bob: Mike needs money for school by tomorrow or his education comes to a screeching halt.

Pete: A classic case of mal-tuition.

Mike: (sarcastically) Very funny. Ha. Ha.

Pete: I suppose you've already discussed trying to get a loan and so on . . .

Jim: No good.

Pete: Have you prayed about it?

Mike: What? Get serious.

Pete: I am serious. Have you prayed about it?

Bob: Come on, man. What is God gonna do? Drop 750 dollars out of the sky by tomorrow?

Pete: How should I know what God will do? But we are Christians, aren't we? We are supposed to have faith, you know.

Mike: I think robbing a bank is easier.

Jim: Look, Mike—it's worth a try. Jesus did say, "Ask and you will receive," didn't he?

Mike: But I'm not very good at praying. Especially when I'm depressed.

Bob: Pete, why don't you pray. It was your idea.

Pete: Okay by me. Let's pray right here.

(All four bow their heads, and Pete leads them in a prayer—which he can make up—asking God to help them solve Mike's money problems.)

Mike: Thanks, Pete. Well, look . . . I'd better get going and see if I can find a money tree somewhere.

All: See you later . . . Good luck, Mike . . . Hope you find that tree . . .

Scene 2
The Next Day (have someone hold up a card to that effect)

(Jim, Bob, and Mike meet again)

Jim: Hey, Mike. You're looking a little better than you did yesterday. You must have found that money tree.

Mike: Hey, you're not going to believe what happened.

Bob: Good news, I hope.

Mike: After I left you guys yesterday, I went over to my folks' house, and there was an envelope addressed to me from the Internal Revenue Service. Inside was a check for

$774.13. I made a mistake on my taxes last year and they discovered it and refunded my money. What a stroke of luck! I just couldn't believe it!

Jim: Wow . . . God sure answered that prayer in a hurry.

Mike: God nothing, man. It was the IRS. That check was in the mail before Pete ever prayed. Thank you, Uncle Sam!

—Reprinted from *Dramas, Skits & Sketches*,
© 1997 by Youth Specialties, Inc.,
300 S. Pierce St., El Cajon, CA 92020.
www.YouthSpecialties.com.
Used by permission.

Hailing the Chief

Theme: The real purpose of prayer
Cast: Nine individuals plus a narrator
Setting: President sitting behind a desk

Narrator: He sat at his desk in the Oval Office, waiting. He waited, even though there was a stack of letters to sign, a cable to read, a press conference to prepare for, a briefing with the cabinet to attend, a tea for an ambassador in the Rose Garden.

Looking up from his schedule, he smiled. Yes, there was a lot to do. But first, some people were coming—some very important people. At least he thought they were very important. That is why he kept inviting them to come to the Oval Office and talk with him. He longed to hear what was in their hearts and minds, to talk about how they felt, what they needed, how they could help him accomplish his goals.

Intercom: Mr. President, they're here, sir.

President: Ah, send the first one in, please. (*He leans forward on the edge of his chair, waiting.*)

(*The door opens and a housewife ushers herself into the room. Without acknowledging the president's smile or outstretched hand, she plops down in a chair. Then she shuts her eyes tight.*)

Housewife: (*in a nasal, singsong voice*) Dear Mr. President. Thank you for the world so sweet, thank you for the food we eat, thank you for the birds that sing, thank you, sir, for everything. Goodbye.

(*Before the president can say a word in response, the woman opens her eyes, gets up and walks out the door.*)

Narrator: The president sighed. Why did it always seem to go like this?

(*The president pushes the intercom button.*)

President: Next, please.

(*The door opens and in comes a man wearing a tuxedo. Again the president's hand is ignored.*)

Tuxedo Man: (*clasping his hands and looking at the ceiling*) O thou chief executive who art in the White House. O thou in whom so much doth constitutionally dwell, upon whose desk hath been placed a most effective blotter, incline thine ear toward thy most humble citizen; and grant that thy many entities may be manifoldly endowed upon the fruitful plain.

(The president winces and rubs his temples.)

Tuxedo Man: *(continuing in loud monotone)* And may thy thou dost harkeneth whatly didst shalt evermore in twain asunder.

President: Excuse me, but what . . .

Tuxedo Man: *(seemingly not hearing)* Goodbye. *(He walks out.)*

President: *(sighing and then speaking into the intercom)* Next, please.

(The door opens with no one seeming to be there. The president stands up and looks over his desk and sees a man crawling through the doorway on his hands and knees.)

Crawling Man: *(blubbering, but not looking up from the carpet)* Oh, Mr. g-g-reat and awful p-p-president. I am but a disgusting piece of filth in your presence. No, I am less than that! How dare I enter here? How dare I think that you would grant me anything but grind me into the floor?

President: Please get up. You don't have to do that. I want to talk with you.

Crawling Man: *(still groveling)* I deserve only to be squashed under the weight of your mighty desk. I could never have gotten an invitation to talk with you. It must have been a mistake. How can you ever forgive me for breaking in like this? Oh, I am so sorry, so sorry, so sorry . . .

(Still on his hands and knees, he crawls out. His groaning slowly fades into the distance).

President: *(Shaking his head, he slowly pushes the intercom button. Sounding tired.)* Next.

(In moments a young man enters wearing headphones and bobbing up and down to the music of his pocket stereo.)

Young Man: *(ignoring the offered hand)* Hey, Prez, what's happening? *(looking out the window)* Nice place you got here. I'm like, so glad we could have this little chat, you know? You're not bad for an old dude, I guess. You don't bother me, I won't bother you, okay? Well, I've got to go. Hang in there. *(He walks out.)*

President: *(drumming his fingers on the desk)* *(wearily)* Next, please.

(An elderly man marches in staring at a piece of paper in his hand. He too ignores the president's greeting.)

Elderly Man: Mr. President, *(keeping his eyes on the list)* I want there to be a parking space waiting for me when I go downtown this afternoon. Not a parallel parking space, either, one I can drive right into. Not one with a parking meter. You can see to it that none of those meter maids gives me a ticket. Now, this is important!

President: *(clearing his throat politely)* Speaking of important, how do you feel about my program to feed the hungry? Would you like to have a part in . . .

Elderly Man: And another thing! I lost my best golf club. A putter. Can't remember where I put it. Now, you find it for me, will you? Got to have that club before Saturday. I know you can do it. Goodbye. *(gets up and shuffles out the door)*

President:	*(slumping in his chair)* Next.

(There is a pause. At last a young woman enters slowly. She looks like she is sleepwalking—eyes nearly shut, jaw slack, her feet dragging. She yawns as she slides into a chair.)

Young Woman:	*(head dropping)* I know I should talk to you when I am more awake . . . but I've got so many things to do . . . so . . . sleepy . . . there was something I was going to say . . . what . . . is . . . .? I was going to say . . . uh . . . *(starts to snore)*
President:	*(buzzing his secretary, who steps in)* Could you help this young lady out? *(He sighs.)*
Secretary:	Certainly, Mr. President. *(helps the dozing girl to her feet)*
President:	*(gazing sadly out the window)* How many do we have left?
Secretary:	I'm sorry, sir. But as usual, most of the people you sent invitations to said they were too busy to talk. They had to watch TV, wax the car, do the dishes . . .
President:	*(dejectedly)* Isn't there anyone out there?
Secretary:	There is one, sir, but you wouldn't want to talk to him.
President:	Why not?
Secretary:	Because he's—just a child, Mr. President.
President:	*(shrugging)* May as well show him in.

(Moments later a little boy enters the room shyly. He looks around the room, his eyes wide.)

Boy:	Are . . . are you really the President?
President:	*(smiling)* I really am.

(The president offers his hand. The little boy reaches up and shakes it. Then he sits down, folds his hands in his lap and waits. The president watches, amazed, as the boy sits politely for nearly a minute.)

President:	Isn't there something you want to tell me? Something you have to recite, or ask for, or say?

(Little boy looks down for a moment, thinking. Then he looks up.)

Boy:	Yes, I guess there is.
President:	Well, what is it?
Boy:	Thank you for inviting me. That's all.
Narrator:	When the president heard that, he couldn't seem to say anything for a while. All he could do was smile. But then they talked and talked and talked for the longest, most wonderful time.

—Used by permission from *High Impact Worship Dramas*, © 1999 by John Duckworth, published by Group Publishing, Inc., P.O. Box 481, Loveland, CO 80539. www.grouppublishing.com.

If God Should Speak

Theme: The meaning of the Lord's Prayer
Cast: Two individuals; the second person should be heard, but not seen.
Setting: Person kneeling in prayer

"Our Father, which art in heaven . . ."

Yes.

Don't interrupt me. I'm praying.

But you called me.

Called you? I didn't call you. I'm praying. "Our Father, which art in heaven . . ."

There, you did it again.

Did what?

Called me. You said, "Our Father, which art in heaven." Here I am. What's on your mind?

But I didn't mean anything by it. I was, you know, just saying my prayers for the day. I always say the Lord's Prayer. It makes me feel good; kind of like getting a duty done.

Alright, go on.

"Hallowed be Thy name . . ."

Hold it. What do you mean by that?

By what?

By "Hallowed be Thy name."

It means . . . It means . . . Good grief, I don't know what it means. How should I know? It's just part of the prayer. By the way, what does it mean?

It means honored, holy, wonderful.

Yeah, that makes sense. I never thought what "hallowed" meant before. "Thy kingdom come, Thy will be done, on earth as it is in heaven."

Do you really mean that?

Sure, why not?

What are you doing about it?

Doing? Nothing, I guess. I just think it would be kind of neat if you got control of everything down here like you have up there.

Have I got control of you?

Well, I go to church.

That isn't what I asked you. What about that habit of lust you have? And your bad temper? You've really got a problem there, the way you spend your money . . . all on yourself. And what about the kind of movies you watch?

Stop picking on me. I'm just as good as some of the rest of those phonies at church.

Excuse me, but I thought you were praying for my will to be done. If that is to happen it will have to start with the ones who are praying for it. Like you, for example.

Oh, alright. I guess I do have some hang-ups. Now that you mention it, I could probably name some others.

So could I.

I haven't thought about it very much until now. But I really would like to cut out some of those things. I would like to, you know, be really free.

Good. Now we're getting somewhere. We'll work together, you and I. Some victories can truly be won. I'm proud of you.

Look, Lord, I need to finish up here. This is taking a lot longer than it usually does. "Give us this day our daily bread."

You need to cut out the bread. You're overweight as it is.

What a minute! What is this, Criticize Me Day? Here I was simply doing my religious duty and all of a sudden you break in and remind me of all my hang-ups.

Praying is a dangerous thing. You could wind up changed, you know. That's what I'm trying to get across to you. You called me, and here I am. It's too late to stop now. Keep praying, I'm interested in the next part of your prayer. . . (pause) Well, go on.

I'm scared to.

Scared? Of what?

I know what you'll say.

Try me and see.

"Forgive us our debts, as we forgive our debtors."

What about Linda?

See? I knew it! I knew you would bring her up. Why, Lord? She told lies about me, cheated me out of some money. She never paid back that debt she owes me. I've sworn to get even with her.

But what about your prayer?

I didn't mean it.

Well, at least you're honest. But it's not much fun carrying that load of bitterness around inside, is it?

No, I'll feel better as soon as I get even. Boy, have I got some plans for old Linda. She'll wish she never did me any harm.

You won't feel any better. You'll feel worse. Revenge isn't sweet. Think of how unhappy you already are. But I can change all that.

You can? How?

Forgive Linda as I have forgiven you. Then the hate and sin will be Linda's problem and not yours. You may lose the money, but you will have settled your heart.

But Lord, I can't forgive Linda.

Then I can't forgive you.

Oh, you're right. You always are. And more than I want revenge on Linda, I want to be right with you. *(pause) (sigh)* Alright. Alright. I forgive her. Help her find the right road in life. She's bound to be awfully miserable now that I think about it. Anybody who goes around doing the things that she does to others has to be out of it. Someway, somehow, show her the right way. And Lord, help me to forget it too.

There now! Wonderful! How do you feel?

Hmmm, well, not bad. Not bad at all. In fact, I feel pretty great! You know, I don't think I'll have to go to bed uptight tonight for the first time since I can remember. Maybe I won't be so tired from now on because I'm not getting enough rest.

You're not through with your prayer; go on.

Oh, right. "And lead us not into temptation, but deliver us from evil."

Good! Good! I'll do that. Just don't put yourself in a place where you can be tempted.

What do you mean by that?

Quit hanging around with that one group which always seems to be getting into trouble. Change some of your friendships. Some of your so-called friends are beginning to get to you. They'll have you completely involved in wrong things before long. Don't be fooled. They advertise they're having fun, but for you it would be ruin. Don't use me for an escape hatch.

I don't understand.

Sure you do. You've done it a lot of times. You get in bad situations, you get into trouble, and then you come running to me. "Lord, help me out of this mess, and I promise you I'll never do it again." You remember some of those bargains you tried to make with me?

Yes, and I'm ashamed, Lord. I really am.

Which bargain are you remembering?

Well, the time I almost got caught cheating on a test. I remember telling you, "Oh, Lord, don't let her tell the teacher. If she doesn't, I promise I'll be in church every Sunday and do anything you want me to do."

She didn't tell, but you didn't keep your promise, did you?

I'm sorry, Lord. I really am. Up until now I thought that if I just prayed the Lord's Prayer every day, then I could do what I liked. I didn't expect anything to happen like this . . . that you really listen.

Go ahead and finish your prayer.

"For thine is the kingdom and the power, and the glory, forever. Amen."

Do you know what would bring me glory? What would really make me happy?

No. But I'd like to know. I want to please you. I can see what a mess I've made of my life. And I can see how neat it would be to really be one of your followers.

You just answered the question.

I did?

Yes. The thing that would bring me glory is to have people like you truly love me. And I see that happening between us. Now that some of these old sins are exposed and out of the way, well, there's no telling what we can do together.

Lord, let's see we can make of me, OK?

Yes, let's see.

—*Talking with God* by Eunice and Bob McKinney and
Nelene and Jim Fox, © 1977, Board of Youth Ministry
of the Missouri Synod Lutheran Church. Used by permission.

The Lord's Prayer: A Drama in Candles

Theme: Explaining the Lord's Prayer
Cast: Nine individuals plus narrator
Setting: None

Candle 1:   (*carrying a white candle*) The Bible says: "Your Word is a lamp unto my feet and a light upon my path." We will turn on the light of the Lord's Prayer, and let it shine in our hearts, so that we may see God's truth.

Narrator: The white candle is the Christ Candle. It represents our Lord and Savior and the one who taught us to pray. (*This white candle may be used to light the other candles as they are presented*).

All: Let us pray the Lord's Prayer:

Candle 2:   (*carries blue candle*) The Address—"Our Father who is in heaven." What does that mean? Here God encourages us to believe that he is our Father and we are his children. So we are to pray to him with complete confidence just as children speak to loving earthly fathers.

Narrator: The blue candle reminds us of the blue heavens above. God is beyond the blue, but his light is everywhere, and from his throne in heaven, he is ever watching over us.

Candle 3:   (*carries green candle*) The first petition—"Hallowed be your name." What does that mean? God's name is holy; our request is that we may keep it holy and honor it in all our thoughts and activities.

Narrator: Green is the most enduring of colors. The cedar and pine are green all year. Throughout the winter and summer, they remain green. Green is the everlasting color. The name of God is "everlasting."

Candle 4:   (*carries purple candle*) The second petition—"Your kingdom come." What does that mean? God's kingdom comes into our world when we ask that it may come into our hearts and lives.

Narrator: Purple is the royal color. The robes of a king are purple, and the throne decorations are all in this majestic color. May God hasten the coming of the royal day, the day when Jesus Christ, his Son, shall reign in glory in his kingdom. Our prayer comes to fulfillment, when on our part we help others come into the kingdom of grace, and when we heed the call for laborers in his fields, to bring in the harvest.

Candle 5: *(carries brown candle)* The third petition—"Your will be done on earth as it is in heaven." What does that mean? While the good and gracious will of God is sovereign, God chooses to work through the prayers of his people.

Narrator: Brown represents the color of the earth, the brown of the ground of the world. We cannot pray, "Your will be done" if we are questioning, resentful, or disobedient to his will.

Candle 6: *(carries yellow candle)* The fourth petition—"Give us today our daily bread." What does that mean? While God gives daily bread to all people, we ask that he will continually remind us that he is the source of our daily needs and to receive our "daily bread" with thanksgiving.

Narrator: Yellow stands for the golden grain from which our bread is made. This is a prayer for physical needs. The Greek word for "bread" means "food," so this is a petition for all our temporal needs, whatever is needed to sustain our bodies—the present home for our soul and his spirit.

Candle 7: *(carries silver candle)* The fifth petition—"And forgive us our debts, as we also have forgiven our debtors." What does that mean? We ask in this petition that our heavenly Father will not hold our sins against us; we ask that his grace will continue to be sufficient; we ask that God will withhold the punishment we deserve. In the same spirit of God's grace, we commit to forgiving those who have wronged us.

Narrator: Silver is the color of the coin by which we pay our debts. This is a hard prayer for some of us to say when we remember how some people may have hurt us. This prayer tells us to forgive as God has forgiven us—even after we have offended him.

Candle 8: *(carries red candle)* The sixth petition—"And lead us not into temptation, but deliver us from evil." What does this mean? We ask God to protect us from the influence of Satan, the world, and our sinful nature and to keep us from every evil influence that might distract us from being faithful to God.

Narrator: Red stands for sin that comes from yielding to temptation. Red also stands for the blood which Jesus was willing to shed to cover our sins and pay the debt in full.

Candle 9: *(carries orange candle)* The doxology—"For yours is the kingdom and the power and the glory forever. Amen." What does that mean? After a celebration of the greatness of God, the "amen" is the exclamation point that "Yes, it will happen!" When prayer is offered in the will of God, God promises to hear us and answer our prayer.

Narrator: The orange color stands for the glory of God. It is frequently the dominant color in the setting of the sun. These final words are like the exclamation point on a sentence: It is your kingdom we serve—not ours. It is your glory we seek—not ours. It is your power that strengthens—not ours. After recognizing the cost, we bow our hearts in prayer. Amen.

(This litany may be followed by singing the Lord's Prayer.)

—Adapted from an idea used at the First Christian
Reformed Church of Oskaloosa, Iowa

The Warrior

Theme: Being a prayer warrior
Cast: One person
Setting: Living room/dining room. A person is vacuuming when the phone rings. The phone rings, and he/she answers and takes a message, continuing to clean throughout.

Oneida residence. [Name] speaking. . . . Oh, she isn't, she's working today. Would you like to leave a message? . . . Okay. Barb Bailey. . . . Your mom? Oh, sorry to hear that. What hospital is she in? . . . St. Joseph's. (*writes this down*) Okay, Barb, I'll give her the message. And tell your mom I'll be praying for her. . . . Okay. Bye. (*finishes note*)

Let see . . . hmmm . . . what can I use for Barb's mom? (*looks around*) Oh . . . how about this. Yeah, that looks pretty "hip." That should work. "Lord, please be with Barb's mom today and grant her a speedy recovery and guide the doctors' hands as they perform the surgery tomorrow. Amen."

(*to audience*) Bet you thought I'd forget, huh? Or worse, that I was just saying something to be nice, but wasn't really gonna do it. Not me. Not anymore. When I say I'm gonna pray for somebody, I do it. See, I've got this system. That "hip" looking thing over there will remind me to pray for Barb's mom because she's having a hip replacement tomorrow. So when I dust it next week, like I did today, I'll think of Barb's mom and pray for her. Like that candy dish over there. I wipe this down and I think of Karen Ann. She's a cute little girl in my Sunday school class. But she's got a bad temper. Nasty. Cute little thing but nasty! So she's the candy dish, because I pray for her, "God please make her sweeter." Catchin' on, aren't you! (*takes a piece of candy and eats it*)

I got this friend JoEllen. She's going through hard times right now. Divorce, money problems. She asked me to keep her in my prayers. So you know what I use for JoEllen? You're going to like this. The wall outlet. Yeah, I plug in the vacuum and say, "Lord, please give JoEllen the energy she needs to get through this day." I unplug the vacuum and pray, "Give her rest and peace at night. Amen." God hears, he really does. JoEllen says, "Marlene, I can tell you've been praying for me. No matter what kind of day I've had, every night when I go home to bed, I sleep just like a baby." I call it spiritual vacuuming. It can actually be kinda fun.

I windex that mirror in the front hall and offer up a prayer for Burton Gilmore. Know what I pray for him? Clarity. See, he's getting up there . . . but his mind is lagging behind. The other day he said, "Hey, Brenda [Bob], that's a nice new car you've got there! Brenda [Bob]! My goodness! I've been the man's neighbor for twenty-five years and now he's calling me Brenda [Bob]! I don't know who Brenda [Bob] is, but she [he] must have a real beater for a car if he thinks mine looks new. *(laughs)* Anyway, I think it's a pretty good system. 'Course it's not perfect. There have been problems now and then.

Like, redecorating. Mrs. Oneida does like to redecorate. Throws my whole prayer life into a loop.

And then there was the time I decided to pray for Diane Denneman's daughter Lucy. For her purity. Not that Diane asked me to . . . I just thought I should. See, Lucy's got this boyfriend. This very hormonal boyfriend. So, I picked this real curvy, pretty little vase over there on the table. Perfect for Lucy. Anyway, one day one of those yellow Nerf ball things came flying through the living room, lands right on the table, followed shortly thereafter by Champ, the Oneidas' dog, who pounced on it and knocked the vase to the floor. Shattered all over the place. Mrs. Oneida felt bad about the vase, but not nearly as bad as I felt for poor Lucy. What was that supposed to mean? Well, I'll tell you what it means. It means I'm gonna find another pretty vase or something and keep right on praying for Lucy. Because God's not givin' up on her . . . and neither am I.

People think all I do is clean houses. They're wrong. I'm on the front line of battle, praying for people every day. And I never give up. I won't. I learned my lesson with my own husband, Roy [wife, Rhonda]. *(shows ring finger)* Right there. See that ring? Seventeen years. For seventeen years I prayed for Roy [Rhonda] to give up his [her] addiction to alcohol. I bought this ring to remind me to pray for him [her], and when I was waiting tables or washing dishes or driving in my car and I would see this ring on my finger. I'd pray, "Lord please help him [her] end the circle of destruction his [her] life is becoming." It wasn't easy. And a lot of times I felt like giving up. But I didn't. One day Roy [Rhonda] got help. He [She] said to me, "[name], I think everyone else gave up on me . . . and God was just about to. And then he heard your prayer. All by itself. No one else cared. And God heard your prayer." Roy [Rhonda] has been sober about three years now. But I still wear the ring as a reminder. God hears our prayers. He really does. *(sound of dryer timer buzzing)* Oh . . . there's the dryer. You know what that means, don't ya? *(slight pause)* The clothes are done. *(exits)*

—Donna Lagerquist, taken from Sunday Morning Live Drama Book,
Volume 8, © 1998 by the Willow Creek Association.
Used by permission of Zondervan Publishing House.

Will She Call?

Theme: God misses his children when they neglect to pray.
Cast: One female
Setting: Chair beside table with telephone. Individual sitting by phone, talking aloud.

I hope my friend calls today. It's been a long time. She used to call all the time. We'd sit and talk for almost an hour every day. When she had problems, she'd call me first. She'd cry, we'd cry together, and I'd try to talk her through it. And eventually she'd be okay again. But, don't get me wrong. She would call to tell me about the good things that happened to her, too. The time she and her husband found out they were going to have a baby, after they had tried for so many years. I just about couldn't get a word in edgewise that time.

We used to be really good friends. Well, we'd have to be after talking that much to each other. She would open up to me . . . tell me things that she didn't think she could tell her pastor, or even her husband. Some things were just between us, and I think her husband understood that. I think it strengthened their marriage—him knowing that she had a friend she could tell anything to.

It was great for me, too. I had so much to tell her every time she called. She'd ask me about places she planned to go and things she planned to do. I'd tell her what to expect and what had happened to me in those same situations. Sometimes she didn't like what she heard or what my suggestions were, but that was fine. She'd get angry and yell or pout. I'd just stay on the line . . . that's what friends are for, right?

You don't think something has happened to her, do you? Maybe she's in trouble . . . maybe she's hurt. What if she's in some kind of trouble? If she would just call, maybe I could do something . . . I could come help her.

Maybe she's angry with me. She did get really upset when her husband lost his job and they couldn't make payments on their house. But she didn't even let me try to help . . . didn't even ask. I mean, I know people who know people. I could have done something.

What if she's just forgotten? She used to know my number by heart, but you can forget these things if you don't use them every day. What if she's just too busy? But she was busy before— in college, when she got married, even in her first job—and she always found time to call, at least for a little while.

Sometimes I hear the phone ring at mealtimes. I think it's probably her, but she has gone before I can even pick up.

Well, look at the time. She's probably in bed by now. Hmmm. We used to talk at bedtime, too . . . tell me about the day she'd had . . . talk about tomorrow.

If you see my friend, tell her I miss her. I still love her, and I want us to talk more.

I just want to talk to her.

—Taken from *The Time Has Come to Pray Worship and Drama Resources*, © 1997, The Wesleyan Church, Indianapolis, Indiana. Used by permission.

More Dramas on Prayer

From Willow Creek Community Church

Can We Talk? (ISBN 675510) by Mark Demel and Ted Thomas

Great Expectations (ISBN 672929) by Sharon Sherbondy

I Don't Want to Fight You Anymore (ISBN 673003) by Debra Poling

Just Ask (ISBN 676983) by James C. Tillman

No Interruptions (ISBN 673453) by Sharon Sherbondy

Plane Talk (ISBN 673666) by Judson Poling

Prayer Despair (ISBN 673666) by Judson Poling

Prayer Group Therapy (ISBN 673674) by Donna Lagerquist

Prayer Perplexity (ISBN 673682) by Judson Poling

Prayer Static (ISBN 673690) by Judson Poling

Quiet Time (ISBN 673739) by Sharon Sherbondy

Snow Job (ISBN 673895) by Donna Lagerquist

Sweet Hour of Prayer (ISBN 674018) by Sharon Sherbondy

The Waiting Room (ISBN 675634) by Donna Lagerquist

From Mainstay Church Resources

The Rehearsal by Doug and Melissa Timberlake

Dear Bobby by Doug and Melissa Timberlake

Hard Choices: Three Prayers by Doug and Melissa Timberlake, John Yarbough

Heroes of Faith by Robert Lackie

From Word Publishing

Honest to God by Deborah Craig Claar

From Creative Resource Group

It's a Lie by Kelly Wick

PRAYER RETREATS

RETREATS

A retreat is a short time for personal reflection and spiritual enrichment, a time set apart to reflect on one's personal walk with God, an opportunity for refreshment and renewal through silence and prayer. A retreat emphasizes time away from the fast-paced routines of daily life; it leaves behind the distractions of hectic schedules, phone calls, all-you-can eat buffets, and television. A retreat encourages Christian growth and involves fellowship, worship, and quiet time with the Lord.

Unfortunately, spiritual retreats have all but disappeared from the Christian life. In fact, most believers today have never been on a retreat. We frequently attend conferences, believing that from them we will gain spiritual insight, but conferences are not retreats.

A conference is an event with an emphasis on dispensing information and inspiration about a particular theme or issue. As the resident expert, the speaker's input is the key factor in the success or failure of the conference; the participants' role and involvement is primarily passive. The typical conference offers well-known speakers in well-equipped venues, requiring planning months in advance and packing as much into the time as possible to "get our money's worth." And so, after a conference leaders and participants typically arrive home mentally and physically exhausted.

The biggest difference between a conference and a retreat, however, is the goal. A conference is designed to convey infor-mation and to build knowledge, while a retreat is an experience that changes lives.

Retreats can play a significant role in building a person's relationship with God.

- *A retreat is personal.* It is fundamentally a one-on-one experience with the Lord.

- *A retreat is spiritual.* It provides the framework for participants to spend time with Jesus Christ. That is why a retreat emphasizes the practice of spiritual disciplines: silence, reflection, Bible study, prayer, journaling, and worship.

- *A retreat emphasizes dialogue*—primarily one-on-one with the Lord, but also with other participants. A retreat schedule incorporates significant blocks of time for meditation and prayer.

- *A retreat requires minimum input from leaders.* The retreat leader serves as a spiritual director and resource person, not a speaker. The leader simply guides the participants from one activity to the next.

- *A retreat requires full participation.* A retreat requires the full commitment and involvement of each participant at every step. For a short period of time, the participants will live, work, talk, pray, study, and share together as they build community. The interaction may be intense; but if someone is missing, the group suffers. Everyone is responsible for fully participating in the retreat.

- *A retreat is designed for transformation, renewal, and growth.* A retreat encourages re-creation: gaining new perspectives on God's Word, on life, on living out one's faith more constructively. On a retreat, participants come face to face not only with God, but also with themselves. By seeing God more clearly, participants see themselves, their gifts, and their calling more clearly.

Scripture tells us that Jesus retreated regularly. Luke writes that after Jesus celebrated the Passover with his disciples for the last time, he "went out *as usual* (emphasis added) to the Mount of Olives. . . . He withdrew . . . knelt down and prayed" (22:39, 41). Retreating—spending an extended period of time alone with his Father—was a vital part of Jesus' life and ministry. The same is true for Christ's disciples today.

Most believers, however, get caught up in the busy pace of life. They juggle their time at home, work, or school. They must find time for exercise, recreation, rest, and relationships. And as life becomes increasingly busy, the need for regular retreats—for times of silence and reflection—increases. People do not need more information; they need time to comprehend, evaluate, and assimilate what they already know. Retreats provide the opportunity for believers to slow down and think through their relationship to God (Ps. 27:14; Isa. 40:31).

In addition to providing the time for reflection, a retreat offers the setting for reflection. Believers need a place in which they can freely reflect on the issues they confront daily, discuss their spiritual doubts and questions, and share their frustrations. They need an atmosphere of caring, acceptance, and encouragement. They need an opportunity to hear God's voice, the quiet time to listen, and the absence of pressure to make decisions.

Retreats have benefits for small groups and congregations as well as for individuals. A spiritual retreat can breathe new enthusiasm into a listless group. Time together builds community, time in God's presence challenges the apathetic, and time in God's Word equips members for service.

Retreating is foreign to most people. It seems to defy many of the principles we are taught: always be industrious and productive; silence is boring and a waste of time; the most effective way to learn is listening to an expert. Overcoming these ingrained false notions will take some time, but the benefits and growth are worth the effort. John Westerhoff, a Christian educator and author, says, "If you would sponsor two weekend retreats a year you would have more and better Christian education than a whole year's worth of one-hour Sunday school classes."

holding a retreat

The following elements are important for planning a retreat:

Promotion

- Introduce the concept slowly.

- Begin small. Large numbers are not necessary for an effective retreat.

- Understand that, at least initially, there will be setbacks.

- Clarify who the retreat is for: senior citizens, middle schoolers, high schoolers, singles, parents, families, men, women, church leaders, prayer leaders, the entire congregation.

Planning

- Set specific goals. What do you hope to accomplish? Why are you going?

- Set your strategy. How will you meet the goal? Will you study a certain book of Scripture? Will you spend hours in prayer? Do you want to develop a certain discipline?

- Set aside time for recreation. Don't over-schedule. Leave room for rest, relaxation, and reflection.

- Rest includes more than sleeping. Plan time for a walk along the beach, a vigorous game of volleyball, an evening by a campfire. Recreation should be simple. Try to avoid highly competitive games that result in "winners" and "losers."

- Avoid the temptation to dispense too much information. While knowledge is important, the purpose of a retreat is to spend time with God.

- When scheduling, keep in mind that weekends often work into schedules the easiest.

- Twenty-four– to thirty-six–hour retreats work well. Start with shorter retreats. Extend them as people express an interest.

Logistics
- Keep the meals simple and easy to prepare. Make meal preparation a time of fellowship.

- The place should be comfortable, modest, and secluded. Select a place away from home or church. A quiet place in the country, woods, mountains, or shore is great. Some bed-and-breakfast inns also work well. A monastery with a worshiping community is ideal. During the winter months, many summer conference centers are available.

- Keep the sleeping quarters free of distractions—no television, radio, telephones, pagers.

Leadership
- The retreat leader serves as the spiritual guide for the retreat. The leader sets the tone, models the experiences, explains what is going to happen, facilitates the process, and makes him- or herself available to assist participants on an individual basis. While the task appears great, a number of mature Christians can provide this leadership very effectively.

- The retreat leader must be a mature Christian, a person of prayer, and well acquainted with silence.

- A typical high-powered "conference" speaker can be counterproductive at a retreat.

Format
- The goals, schedule, and format should be explained carefully before people register for the retreat, and again the first night.

- Begin the retreat by having people introduce themselves. Have each participant answer a thoughtful question like "How has the Lord graced your life in the last month?" or "How has the Lord used you to touch the life of another?"

- The typical retreat involves short periods of instruction, study, and discussion followed by extended periods of personal or communal prayer, silence, meditation, and journaling.

- Worship is also important at retreats. Encourage group members to participate in leading. Keep worship simple.

- Use a variety of spiritual disciplines and prayer formats.

- If your group is larger than six, break into small groups.

- Explain each discipline thoroughly before asking people to participate. Some will accept it willingly; some will have questions; some may have reservations; a few may even refuse to participate.

- Keep the schedule flexible and relaxed.

AFFINITY RETREAT

Participants: Any affinity group: men's or women's group, parents, youth, church staff, and so on

Goals:
- To explore different prayer formats.
- To build the community of the group.
- To give individuals a "rest" from ministry and provide time with God.

Morning

7:00-7:30	Arrival
7:30-8:00	Morning Worship
8:00-9:00	Morning Prayers
	—fifteen minutes for praise and thanksgiving
	—fifteen minutes for personal and communal confession
	—fifteen minutes of receptive silence
	—fifteen minutes of petition and intercession
9:00-9:30	Break
9:30-10:30	Group Bible Study
10:45-11:45	Personal solitude and meditation on the passage studied in the small group
	—Is there a promise for me to claim?
	—Is there a command for me to obey?
	—Is there a sin for me to confess?
	—Is there a sin for me to avoid?
	—Is there an example for me to follow?
	—Is there a new thought or idea?

Afternoon

12:00-12:45	Lunch
1:00-2:00	Personal solitude and meditation
	—How can I apply what I have learned today?
	—Make a specific and realistic goal.
	—Record (journal) your feelings and resolutions from the morning.
2:00-3:30	Recreation
	—Take a walk together
	—Lie down like spokes of a wheel with your heads as the hub. Close your eyes and listen to nature's symphony.
	—Have a nature scavenger hunt.

3:30-4:30	Evening Prayers
	—fifteen minutes for praise and thanksgiving
	—fifteen minutes for personal and communal confession
	—fifteen minutes of receptive silence
	—fifteen minutes of petition and intercession
4:30	Head for home
5:30-6:30	Dinner at church (If it is a women's retreat have the men of the church prepare dinner; if a men's retreat, have the women prepare dinner; a youth retreat, have parents cook; a staff retreat, have the board fix dinner, and so on.)
6:30-7:30	Worship and Celebration
	Worship
	Testimonies
	Prayer
7:30-8:00	Dessert Fellowship

—From *Experiential Education: X-Ed* (Abingdon, 1975, pp. 72-77)
by John and Lela Hendrix.

CONGREGATIONAL RETREAT

Participants: Speaker and fifteen or more retreaters

Goals:
- To learn about how prayer fits into the daily Christian life.
- To enhance the unity and fellowship of the congregation.
- To give individual believers quiet time with God.

Friday evening

6:00-7:00	Dinner
7:00-8:00	"Prayer and the Past" (Dismiss for 45-60 minutes of silent prayer with an emphasis on personal confession.)
8:00-10:00	General Session
	Praise and Worship
	Introductions
	Speaker: "Prayer and the Present"
	Communion—served to each other
10:00-11:00	Small group prayer (men upstairs, women downstairs)
11:00	Retire

Saturday

7:30-8:30	Breakfast
8:30-9:15	Small group prayer (same small groups)
9:15-10:15	General Session
	Praise and Worship
	Speaker: "Prayer for the Future"
10:15-10:30	Break
10:30-12:00	Foot-washing and Discussion
12:00-12:30	Prayer Walk—personal time to listen to God
12:30-1:00	Lunch
1:00	Head for home

notes

- Throughout the night keep a prayer chapel open. Participants can sign up for prayer in thirty-minute time frames.
- Have breakfast in silence.
- Use placemats at meals to explain the next session and offer structure for personal prayer times.

MINISTRY LEADERS' RETREAT

Participants: Fifteen or more ministry leaders

Goals:

- To experience different formats of prayer to enhance individual prayer lives.
- To provide an opportunity for leaders to encourage each other.
- To give individuals a "rest" from ministry and provide time with God.

Friday evening

3:00-5:30	Registration
5:30-7:00	Dinner (prayer format: spontaneous prayer, see p. 104)
7:00-9:30	Time Together 1
	Welcome
	Introduction of Leaders
	Introduction of Participants
	Overview of Retreat
	Prayer Time: Summit Style (see p. 95)
	Communion (Participants serve themselves.)
9:30	*Selah* time
	Fellowship
	Personal Quiet Time (Encourage participants to use the Hour of Prayer format; see pp. 65-66.)

Saturday

7:00-8:00	Personal Quiet Time
8:00-9:00	Breakfast (prayer format: praying a psalm)
9:00-9:30	Time Together 2
	Worship
	Explanation of "How to Spend a Day in Prayer" (Encourage participants to fast for lunch; make juices and fruit available at a central location.)
9:30-5:30	A Day in Prayer (Suggest the following schedule.)
	—Thirty Minutes of Silent Listening
	—Scripture Reading
	—Readings for reflection
	—Reflection
	—Prayer
	—Journal Writing
	—Recreation
	—Rest

	—Repeat the cycle
	—Thirty Minutes of Silent Reflection
5:45-7:15	Dinner at a Local Restaurant
7:30-9:30	Time Together 3
	Worship
	Prayer Time
	Communion (Participants serve each other.)
9:30	*Selah* time
	Fellowship
	Personal Quiet Time (Encourage participants to use A.W.C.I.P.A. prayer format; see pp. 45-46.)

Sunday

7:00-8:00	Personal Quiet Time
8:00-9:00	Breakfast (prayer format: silence)
9:00-12:00	Time Together 4
	Worship
	Prayer Time: Celebrate God's attributes using Alphabet Prayer (see pp. 41-42)
	Anointing and Commissioning Time (a time of laying hands on and praying for each participant and their calling/ministry)
	Communion (Retreat coordinators serve the participants. This time could also include a foot-washing.)
12:00-1:00	Lunch
1:00	Head for home

PERSONAL RETREAT

Goals:
- To spend some time alone with God.
- To pause for a "Sabbath rest."
- To be personally refreshed, renewed, and re-created.

schedule

Arrive and get settled

Opening prayer
> Our God, who always calls us to prayer, teach me in these hours to pray as I should and for what I should. In Jesus name. Amen.

Thirty minutes of silent listening

Scripture reading (begin with a different passage with each new cycle)
> Matthew 4:1-11
> Psalm 63
> Mathew 6:1-17
> Romans 8:18-39

Response
> Journaling
> Prayer
> Action

Readings (see selections on pp. 415-416)

Reflection and response

Recreation/Rest

(Repeat the cycle above beginning with Scripture reading.)

Thirty minutes of silent reflection

Covenant (closing) prayer

My Lord, how good it is, how blessed, to be with you in this place in prayer. Send me from this place in the power of your ever-present Spirit. Amen.

—Rueben P. Job and Norman Shawchuck, *A Guide to Prayer for All God's People: Prayer and My Life* (Nashville: Upper Room, 1990), pp. 345-348. This guide contains twelve personal one-day retreats in addition to devotional material for the entire year.

readings for reflection

If our thirst for cosmic confirmation and caring is secretly longing to be quenched, and if God's transforming love yearns to quench that thirst, what are the conditions under which this double search of human beings for God, and God for human beings, can best be carried out? Prayer is obviously a proven channel. But prayer that transforms seems to require certain optimum conditions that tilt us towards its authentic practice and that clear the way in spite of the dispersion and the web upon web of preoccupations which tend to usurp our earthly life. When I go to have my chest x-rayed each year, I am required to strip off my ordinary bodily coverings and to expose my chest to the piercing rays of this light. Solitude, solitariness, seems to express a similar preparatory readying function in its stripping me and preparing me for exposure to the radiant beams of love that the x-ray focus of prayer accomplishes.

—Douglas Van Steere, *Together in Solitude*

"I would like to pray again." What a beautiful grace to want to pray. Prayer is a gift, yet it is the work of a lifetime. Why do people stop praying? Why do they begin again? Prayer is always a lost and found phenomenon. Prayer, like each human life, has many stages of growth and development, decline and loss.

Prayer, like love, is not something one achieves once and for all. It is a special kind of consciousness, awareness, attention, and presence.

—Edward Farrell, *Gathering the Fragments*

Christian prayer is always a response to a presence already felt. The awareness of a desire to pray again is already prayer. As the desert fathers so often said, "If you want to pray, you are already praying."

—Edward Farrell, *Gathering the Fragments*

God knows how to make sense of these bits and pieces of revelation. Prayer turns them over and over and lets them go, returning to a few well-worn images, phrases, feelings, or corners of dark peace like the tongue to a sore tooth. Some days prayer is absolutely minimal: a resentful body taking its chair, a mind dry and rebellious. Other days prayer is easy and obvious: How is it going, my love? But in maturity all days are prayerful. For better or for worse, richer or poorer, in sickness and health, God has us until death parts the last barrier and we consummate our long longing. Mature prayer thinks of itself as paying with an old and battered blank check. Even though each payment increases its debt, it keeps pushing its dog-eared mite forward. For it knows dimly, but adequately, that progress is deeper indebtedness. If everything is grace, any better perception means more laud of God, greater abasement of self. It is the Baptist's formula: He must increase, I must decrease. So the constant liturgical refrain: Praise God!

—John Carmody, *Maturing a Christian Conscience*

We tend to turn to prayer in extreme moments—Great joy, "O, how good God is!" When all human sources have failed, "O God, help me." Anguish, guilt, fear send us to God when no aid is near or, if near, would not understand. But prayer may be so much more: a way of life, a resource, a comfort, a continuing communion.

This continuing communion does not come about without effort. It is an exercise of the spirit that has a discipline of its own. I like to send myself to a dictionary for the actual definition of a word which I have been using rather freely. Webster enlarges my concept of the word *discipline:* "training which corrects, molds, strengthens, or perfects." There is nothing harsh about that, rather something encouraging. Through training a desired end can be achieved.

—Elizabeth Yates, *A Book of Hours*

More things are wrought by prayer
than this world dreams of.
Wherefore, let thy voice
rise like a fountain for me night and day.
For what are men better than sheep and goats
that nourish a blind life within the brain,
if, knowing God, they lift not hands of prayer
both for themselves and those who call them friend?
For so the whole round earth is every way
bound by gold chains about the feet of God.

—Alfred Lord Tennyson

Most people think of prayer as an audible activity which calls for the cessation of all other activities. There can also be an inwardness of prayer which does not interfere with other activities and produces no outward, visible indications that it is taking place. There can be a continual prayer of the heart and mind which does not interrupt our daily routine. There can be such a profound prayerfulness at the center of our beings that our entire lives are saturated with prayer. We need to rediscover the inwardness of prayer and the miraculous potential for having a continual inner communion with our Lord.

—Robert V. Dodd, *Praying the Name of Jesus*

Prayer is something more than that which we do with our minds. It also involves our hearts and spirits—the deeper part of our personalities to which only the Spirit of Jesus has access. Prayer in its highest form requires more than conscious effort. It also requires the surrender of our innermost selves to Jesus, giving him permission to make our lives a continually flowing fountain of unceasing prayer. When we have learned how to do that, we will have discovered the secret of the prayer of the heart.

—Robert V. Dodd, *Praying the Name of Jesus*

PRAYER AND FASTING RETREAT

Participants: A dozen or more retreaters

Goals:
- To experience the practice of prayer and fasting.
- To build the community of the small group.
- To give individuals a "rest" from ministry and provide time with God.

Note: This is a 24-hour prayer and fasting retreat. It can also be used in connection with the 30-Hour Famine sponsored by World Vision (P.O. 70094, Tacoma, WA 98481-0094; 1-800-7-FAMINE or www.30hourfamine.org).

Evening

5:00-6:00	A light dinner (avoid high-fat and sugary foods)
	(For a 30-hour fast, the noon lunch becomes the last food intake.)
6:00-6:30	Personal time
	—Why are you fasting?
	—Personal commitment to fast for twenty-four hours.
6:30-8:00	First Session
	Worship
	Prayer (use the A.C.T.S. prayer form)
	Explain the purpose and variations/types of fasting
	Testimonies (invite one or two people who have been fasting and praying for some time to share their experiences)
8:30-9:00	Refreshment break (juice and liquids)
9:00-10:00	Small group (study Matthew 6:16-18 and pray together)
	—What do you expect to happen when you fast?
	—How do you think fasting would help prayer?
10:00-11:00	Recreation (free time or group recreation)
11:00	Lights out

Morning

7:30	Rise and shine (juices available)
8:00-9:00	Personal time
9:15-10:30	Worship and group prayers
10:30-11:00	Break (refreshments)
11:00-12:00	Small group (study Luke 10:38-42 or another passage about prayer)

Afternoon

12:00-4:00   A service project in the neighborhood/community (keep the work light; avoid working outside if the day is too warm; have plenty of liquids available)

4:00-5:00   Hour of personal prayer and reflection

    —Was this fasting/retreat a helpful experience?

    —One important thing I have learned about prayer is . . .

    —One important thing I have learned about fasting is . . .

    —One thing about this retreat I am thankful for is . . .

    —I am willing to make the following commitments to continued prayer and/or fasting . . .

5:00-6:00   Small group (share responses formed during your personal time; build in continuing accountability)

6:00   A light dinner (a full meal is not advised immediately following a 24-hour fast)

notes

- Have fruit juices and liquids available. Watermelon, lemon, grape, apple, and carrot juices are best. Acidic juices (orange, grapefruit, tomato) should be mixed with water. Avoid carbonated and caffeine drinks.

- Some foods such as crackers, rice, and soup should also be available for those may require it because of health concerns.

- If hunger pains increase, increase your liquid intake.

- For fasts exceeding twenty-four to thirty hours, consult a physician. Anyone taking prescription drugs should consult their physician before participating in a fast of any length.

SMALL GROUP RETREAT

Participants: Seven to twelve small group members

Goals:
* To explore some of the different prayer formats.
* To build the community of the small group.
* To give individuals a "rest" from ministry and provide time with God.

Friday evening

6:00-7:00	Arrive and get settled
7:00-8:00	Dinner
8:30-10:00	"Sharing Your Spiritual Journeys" (Question: "What has the Lord been doing in your life to bring you to where you are today?")
10:00-10:15	Break
10:15-11:30	Around the fire(place) (Question: "What is the source of your spiritual struggles?")
	—Conclude by listing your struggles on a piece of paper; throw them in the fire.
11:30	Solitude and rest

Saturday

8:00-9:00	Breakfast
9:00-10:00	An hour in personal prayer
10:00-11:30	"Sharing Your Resources" (Question: "What people, resources, events have been most helpful in your spiritual life?")
12:00-1:00	Lunch
1:00-4:00	A time of solitude for rest, recreation, reading, and reflection
4:00-5:30	"Essentials to a Healthy Walk with God" (Question: "What are the four or five essential elements in a healthy prayer life? How are you doing in meeting those essentials?")
5:30-6:30	Dinner
7:00-8:00	A walk of reflection (Question: "What is the Lord calling me to do?")
8:00-10:00	"Into the Word" (Question: "What Scripture is the Lord laying on your heart?")
	—Spend some time in Listening Prayer (see pp. 75-77). Ask God to bring you a Scripture for each member in the group. Ask God to give you one for yourself. After thirty to forty-five minutes of listening, come back together. Have members share the Scriptures they "received" for each person—one by one. Discuss how the passages resonate.

10:00-10:15	Break
10:15-11:30	Around the fire(place) (Question: "Has this time away been helpful spiritually?")
	—Share what God has revealed to you and what you believe he is calling you to do. Test God's leading against what other members of the group are hearing/sensing. At the conclusion, have everyone write on an index card what they are committing to do. Give these to the group leader for future reference and accountability.
11:30	Solitude and rest

Sunday

8:00-9:00	Breakfast
9:00-10:00	An hour in prayer—study, reflection, and prayer
10:00-11:30	Worship and Prayer (Summit Style, see p. 95)
11:30-12:30	Communion and Commissioning (Following communion, one by one, each person kneels and receives the "laying on of hands" by other group members who lift them up in prayer.)
12:30-1:30	Lunch
1:30	Head for home

Section 8

RESOURCES

ANNUAL PRAYER EVENTS

Fasting and Prayer Gatherings (second weekend in November)

This international prayer conference is sponsored by Campus Crusade for Christ. Christian leaders offer short reflections followed by a call to pray. While several thousand people gather in the host city, the conference is available worldwide over satellite hookups.

100 Lake Hart Drive, Dept. 2800
Orlando, FL 32832-0100
1-800-888-fast
www.fastingprayer.com

March for Jesus

This worldwide initiative calls people to come together, walk the streets of their community, and sing praises to Jesus.

P.O. Box 3216
Austin, TX 78764
512-416-0066
fax: 512-445-5393
e-mail: 104203.262@compuserve.com
www.mfj.org

Nationally Broadcast Concert of Prayer (first Thursday evening in May in the U.S.)

On each National Day of Prayer, a three-hour (8-11 P.M. EDT) national prayer service is held in one U.S. city and telecast worldwide over cable (Sky Angel) and the Internet.

901 E. 78th St.
Minneapolis, MN 55420-1300
612-853-1758
fax: 612-853-8488
e-mail: efca@compuserve.com
www.concertofprayer.org

National Day of Prayer (first Thursday in May in the U.S.)

Shirley Dobson has made this one of the best-known prayer initiatives. Materials (including worship helps, posters, bumper stickers) are available to assist churches and communities in holding special prayer services at city halls and places of worship.

P.O. Box 15616
Colorado Springs, CO 80935-5616
719-531-3379
fax: 719-548-4520
e-mail: ndptf@aol.com

International Day of Prayer for the Persecuted Church (November)

This prayer initiative has developed in response to the thousands of Christians who are being intensely persecuted for their faith.

P.O. Box WEF
Wheaton, IL 60189-8003
630-688-1754 (1-888-Lets-Pray for material)
e-mail: idop@xc.org
www.persecutedchurch.org

(For more information on the persecuted church, visit Voice of the Martyrs at www.vom.org.)

Praying Through the Window

This is a focused prayer event for people, cities, and nations in the 10/40 and/or 40/70 window (see explanation on p. 277) occurring every October. A calendar and other material are available. Christian Information Network has a manual to assist in organizing this prayer effort.

11005 State Highway 83, Suite 159
Colorado Springs, CO 80921-3623
719-522-1040
fax: 719-277-7148
e-mail: cin@cin1040.net
www.Christian-info.com

PrayUSA

Although the focus of prayers is the United States, this is a worldwide prayer initiative. A prayer guide (available in several different languages and age levels) is available.

c/o U.S. Prayer Track
7710-T Cherry Park Dr. PMB 224
Houston, TX 77095
713-466-4009
1-888-PrayUSA
fax: 713-466-5633
www.prayusa.com
www.usprayertrack.org

See You at the Pole (third Wednesday in September)

Since prayer was outlawed in U.S. public schools, students have gathered annually for a prayer service around the school's flagpole. This is a student-initiated and student-led movement. (See p. 239 for a description of this ministry.)

12335 World Trade Dr., Ste. 16
San Diego, CA 92128
e-mail: pray@syatp.com
www.syatp.com

SERVANT PRAYER MINISTRIES

Adopt-a-People Clearing House
This organization keeps track of those praying for people groups around the world and provides information to intercessors so they can pray effectively.

P.O. 17490
Colorado Springs, CO 80935

Aglow International
Aglow International is a women's prayer group ministry.

P.O. Box 1749
Edmonds, WA 90820-1749
425-755-7282
fax: 425-778-9615
e-mail: aglow@aglow.org
www.aglow.org

Canadian Prayer Alert
This initiative seeks to mobilize Canadians to pray for revival and spiritual awakening by organizing a network of prayer groups.

P.O. Box 300
Vancouver, BC V6C 2X3
604-514-2112
fax: 604-514-2002
e-mail: prayer@ccc-van.crusade.org
www.crusade.org

Canadian United Prayer Track
The Canadian United Prayer Track publishes a quarterly prayer newsletter (Global Prayer Advance) to help mobilize churches and believers to pray for the lost throughout the world.

2146 Robinson St.
Regina, SK S4T 2P7
306-569-8999
fax: 306-569-1536
www.efc-canada.com/taskforc/visi.htm

Children's Global Prayer Movement
(see Esther Network International)

Christian Information Center
This ministry initiated by Ted Haggard and the New Life Church of Colorado Springs monitors prayer around the world and is integrally involved in the Adopt-a-People prayer movement.

P.O. Box 63060
11005 Highway 83 North
Colorado Springs, CO 80962-3060
719-536-9100
e-mail: info@wpccs.org
www.wpccs.org

CitiReach International
(See Prayer for Cities, p. 273)

College of Prayer
This is an intensive three-year program open to pastors and church leaders for discussion of issues related to prayer. Each session includes prior reading and a well-known keynote instructor.

Woerner World Ministries
Rev. Paul Radford, registrar
505 South Flager Drive, Suite 606
West Palm Beach, FL 33401

Concerts of Prayer International

Encourages citywide interdenominational prayer gatherings. David Byrant explains this prayer approach in his book Concerts of Prayer.

P.O. Box 770
New Providence, NJ 07974
908-771-0146
fax: 908-665-4199
e-mail: copinj@aol.com
www.copi.org

DAWN Ministries

(See Prayer for Cities, p. 273)

Denominational Prayer Leaders Network

(contact through Harvest Prayer Ministries, see p. 426)

This is a network of denominational prayer leaders who meet annually to share what is happening in their respective denominations, to provide mutual encouragement, and to pray for one another.

Esther Network International (see Children's Prayer Ministry, p. 150)

As part of the AD2000 movement, this ministry is mobilizing one million children to intercede for their generation.

Evelyn Christenson Ministries

4265 Brigadoon Drive
St. Paul, MN 55126
612-566-5390
fax: 612-566-5390

Every Home for Christ

This prayer ministry works with over one hundred denominations in 120 countries to help train local churches to pray for and share the gospel with every home in the world.

P.O. Box 35930
Colorado Springs, CO 80935-3593
719-260-8888
1-800-423-5054
fax: 719-260-7505
e-mail: info@ehc.org
www.sni.net/ehc

First Friday Prayer Focus

First Friday encourages believers to set aside the first Friday of each month to fast and pray for revival, the church, the nation, and elected leaders. A free newsletter outlines the prayer focus for the coming months.

1-800-USAPray
www.ifa-usapray.org
www.nationalprayer.org

Frontline Ministries

Frontline is the prayer ministry of Tom White, a consultant in strategic spiritual warfare, intercession, and prayer evangelism.

P.O. 786
Corvallis, Oregon 97339-0786
541-754-1345
fax: 541-754-4140
e-mail: 103112.3123@compuserve.com

Generals of Intercession

This prayer ministry focuses on identifying specific strongholds in people's lives, in communities, in organizations, and in nations. Generals of Intercession assists in identifying, training, supporting, and keeping intercessors accountable.

P.O. Box 49788
Colorado Springs, CO 80949
719-535-0977
fax: 719-535-0884
e-mail: genint@aol.com

Global Harvest Ministry: AD2000/United Prayer Track

This ministry mobilizes intercessors, local churches and denominations, and prayer networks to pray for the evangelization of all people groups in the world. The primary focus is on the 10/40 (40/70) window (see explanation on p. 277). They publish the Global Prayer News.

P.O. Box 63060
Colorado Springs, CO 80962-3060
719-262-9922
1-800-689-5961
fax: 719-262-9920
e-mail: info@globalharvest.org
www.wpccs.org

Great Commission Prayer Movement

This is the prayer ministry of Campus Crusade for Christ International. They provide resources, materials, conferences, and prayer expeditions.

100 Lake Hart Drive, Dept. 2800
Orlando, FL 32832-0100
407-826-2800

Harvest Evangelism

Prayer Evangelism, the ministry of Ed Silvoso, involves small home prayer groups called Lighthouses.

P.O. Box 20310
San Jose, CA 95160-0310
408-927-9052
1-800-835-7979
fax: 408-927-9830
e-mail: harvean@aol.com
www.harvestevan.org

Harvest Prayer Ministries

This prayer ministry provides a retreat center, consultation, and resources (for example, prayer-a-grams) to build your prayer ministry. It has also recently joined with Houses of Prayer Everywhere (HOPE), which helps to make households and churches Lighthouses of prayer.

11991 E. Davis Road
Brazil, IN 47834
812-443-5800
fax: 812-443-5505
e-mail: harvestprayer@email.com
info@hopeministries.org
www.harvestprayer.com
www.hopeministries.org

Houses of Prayer Everywhere (HOPE)

(See Harvest Prayer Ministries, above.)

Intercessors for Canada

Intercessors for Canada assists the local church by encouraging prayer and fasting for government and church leaders.

P.O. Box 125
Niagara Falls, ON L2E 6S8
905-357-5143
fax: 905-357-3314
e-mail: niagaracc@aol.com

Intercessors for America

Intercessors for America assists the local church by encouraging prayer and fasting for government and church leaders.

17 Royal St. SW
P.O. Box 4477
Leesburg, VA 20177
703-777-0003
1-800-872-7729
fax: 703-777-2324
e-mail: usapray@aol.com
www.ifa-usapray.org

International Reconciliation Coalition for Indigenous People

P.O. Box 1417
Castle Rock, CO 80104
303-660-9258
fax: 303-660-0621
e-mail: ircoal@aol.com

International Renewal Ministries

(See Prayer-Summit Style, p. 95, and Pastors' Prayer Summits, p. 127.)

Lydia Fellowship

1474 Valcartier Drive
Sunnyvale, CA 94087
408-732-2947
fax: 408-732-2972
e-mail: tryna@bahl.com

Mapping Center for Evangelism

The Mapping Center assists local churches in strategic spiritual mapping for prayerwalks, praying for the community, establishing Lighthouses, and connecting with first-time visitors.

8615 Rosehill Road, Suite 101
Lenexa, KS 66215
913-438-7301
fax: 913-438-7303
e-mail: support@map4jesus.org
www.map4Jesus.org

Mission America

Mission America, organized following Lausanne II, is a prayer evangelism ministry whose membership includes more than 350 religious leaders and 180,000 churches in 67 denominations. Their major collaboration is Celebrate Jesus 2000 and focuses on a four-year sequence of prayer, personal witness, proclamation, and preservation.

5666 Lincoln Dr., Suite 100
Edina, MN 55436
612-912-0001
fax: 612-912-0002
e-mail: nfrizzell@compuserve.com
www.missionamerica.org

(Mission America also maintains the www.lighthousemovement.com website.)

Moms in Touch International
(See Moms in Touch, p. 162.)

National Association of Local Church Prayer Leaders
(See Prayer Coordinator, p. 182.)

National Children's Prayer Network
(See Children's Prayer Ministry, p. 150.)

National Pastors' Prayer Network

This network supports pastors in prayer and provides resources on its website.

1130 Rondville Dr. 1D
Paletine, IL 60074
847-991-0153
e-mail: phil@nppn.org
www.missionamerica.org/prayernetwork.html
www.nppn.org

National Prayer Advance

Promotes prayer as the foundation for revival.

901 E. 78th St.
Minneapolis, MN 55420-1300
612-853-1758
fax: 612-853-8488
e-mail: 74114.230@compuserve.com
www.globalhavest.org

National Prayer Committee

This ministry is a network of servant prayer ministries headed by David Bryant that meets annually to coordinate initiatives and encourage one another.

P.O. Box 770
New Providence, NJ 07974
908-771-0146
fax: 908-665-4199
e-mail: copinj@aol.com
www.copi.org

Operation Mobilization
P.O. Box 444
Tyrone, GA 30290-0444
770-631-0432

Prayer Explosion

This ministry helps form women's prayer groups.

304 Carriage House Lane
Riverton, NJ 08077
609-786-7233
fax: 609-786-1269
e-mail: oni-prayexplosion@juno.com

Prayer Room Network
(See Prayer Room, p. 212.)

Prayer Watch International
(See Prayer Coordinator, p. 182.)
This ministry, started by Bjorn Pedersen, provides training and support around the world for prayer leaders in the local church.

Praying for You

Focuses on relational prayer witnessing.

P.O. 35834
Phoenix, AZ 85069
602-863-3400
www.prayingforyou.org

Presbyterian Renewal Ministries International

PRMI sponsors prayer training seminars throughout North America. These "Dunamis" retreats are week-long, intensive trainings in prayer, prayer healing, prayer warfare, and prayer evangelism.

115 Richardson Blvd.
P.O. Box 429
Black Mountain, NC 28711-0429
828-669-7373
fax: 828-669-4880
e-mail: prmi@prmi.org
www.prmi.org

Reach Out Ministries

3961 Holcomb Bridge Rd. Suite 201
Norcross, GA 30092-2207
770-441-2247
e-mail: 72002.1704@compuserve.com
www.reach-out.org

Renewal Ministries

This ministry, under the leadership of Terry Teykl, provides seminars, consultation, and written resources on prayer. This is also the parent ministry of Prayer Point Press.

2100 N. Carrolton Dr.
Muncie, IN 47304
765-759-5165
fax: 765-759-5857
e-mail: jangof@renewalministries.com
www.renewalministries.com
www.prayerpointpress.com

See You at the Pole

(See See You At the Pole, p. 239.)

Sentinel Group

This ministry is involved in spiritual mapping.

P.O. Box 6334
Lynnwood, WA 98036
425-672-2989
fax: 425-672-3028
e-mail: SentinelGp@aol.com
www.sentinelgroup.org

U.S. Prayer Track

The U.S. Prayer Track sponsors the annual PrayUSA initiative from Ash Wednesday through Palm Sunday.

7710-T Cherry Park Drive, PMB 224
Houston, TX 77095
1-888-PRAYUSA
www.prayusa.com
www.usprayertrack.org

Waymakers

Waymakers focuses their ministry on prayerwalking and neighborhood houses of prayer to promote evangelism in local communities.

P.O. Box 203131
Austin, TX 78720-3131
512-419-7729
fax: 512-219-1999
e-mail: 72650.2666@compuserve.com
www.waymakers.org

Word Ministries

This ministry promotes mentoring others in prayer and offers seminars, materials (including the "Prayers that Avail Much" series), and speakers.

www.prayers.org

World Prayer Center

This center serves as home to a number of national and international prayer ministries. Prayer conferences are held throughout the year.

P.O. Box 63060
11005 Highway 83 North
Colorado Springs, CO 80962-3060
719-536-9100
e-mail: info@wpccs.org
www.wpccs.org

Youth with a Mission Renewal Ministries (YWAM)

Prayer Ministry
P.O. Box 1634
Port Orchard, WA 98366
360-876-3432
fax: 360-876-3432
e-mail: ywamportorchard@narrows.com
www.ywamportorchard.com

RESOURCES

Prayer (bulletin insert)

This bimonthly bulletin insert is a prayer encourager for members of your congregation. Includes stories about answered prayer, ideas for prayer ministries, brief teaching articles on prayer, and helpful prayer resources. Issues are available in bulk by subscription. Free samples are available. (See pp. 201-202.)

Faith Alive Christian Resources
2850 Kalamazoo Ave. SE
Grand Rapids, MI 49560
1-800-333-8300
www.FaithAliveResources.org

Global Prayer News

The free newsletter from Global Harvest Ministries.

Global Harvest Ministries
P.O. Box 63060
Colorado Springs, CO, 80962-3060
719-262-9922
fax: 719-262-9920
e-mail: info@wpccs.org
www.wpccs.org

The Harvest (video)

This video underscores the importance of prayer in bringing in the harvest. A seventeen-minute true story that will challenge and inspire you to pray.

1-800-729-4351
in Canada, 1-800-667-0558
www.theharvest.com

How to Have a Prayer Ministry (audio and video)

This is a course in building a prayer ministry by C. Peter Wagner.

Charles E. Fuller Institute
P.O. Box 90910
Pasadena, CA 91109
1-800-999-9578

Light Your World

A newsletter designed to teach worshipers about prayer—can be photocopied and inserted in your church bulletin.

11991 E. Davis Road
Brazil, IN 47834
812-443-5800
fax: 812-443-5505
e-mail: info@hopeministries.org
www.hopeministries.org

Morning Star Journal

This periodical will keep you abreast of prayer needs around the world.

16000 Lancaster Hwy.
Charlotte, NC 28277-2061
704-542-0278
fax: 704-542-0280
www.eaglestar.org

The Observatory

The Observatory is a research facility and spiritual mapping repository at the World Prayer Center designed to assist spiritual mappers.

The Observatory
11005 State Highway 83, Suite 119
Colorado Springs, CO 80921
e-mail: observatory@wpccs.org
www.wpccs.org/observatory

The Power of Prayer (video)

Illustrates the role of prayer in American history.

Group Publishing
P.O. 485
Loveland, CO 80539
1-800-447-1070
fax: 970-669-4372
www.grouppublishing.com

PrayerNet Weekly E-Mail Newsletter
e-mail: 104224.3107@compuserve.com.

Pray! Magazine

With six issues each year, Pray! focuses on themes by major prayer leaders. Each magazine also includes news, reviews, and prayer ideas.

P.O. Box 35004
Colorado Springs, CO 80935
719-531-3548
fax: 719-598-7128
www.praymag.com

Target the Nations

Target the Nations is a CD that provides specific information about each of the 11,886 people groups that live in the 233 countries of the world to help intercessors pray.

e-mail: Galcomusa@aol.com

Transformations (video)

This video, narrated by George Otis Jr., examines the transformation of four communities around the world through the power of prayer. Produced by the Sentinel Group (1999).

1-800-668-5657

UpLink

This is the monthly newsletter of the U.S. Prayer Track.

7710-T Cherry Park Dr. PMB 224
Houston, TX 77095
1-888-PRAYUSA
www.prayusa.com
www.usprayertrack.org

Youth Ministry and Spirituality Project

This project, under the direction of Mark Yaconelli, is currently working with classic and contemplative prayer forms to encourage spiritual growth among young people.

San Francisco Theological Seminary
2 Kensington Road
San Anselmo, CA 94960-2905
1-800-447-8820
www.sfts.edu (click on Programs and Resources)